THE THEOLOGY OF THE UNITED CHURCH OF CANADA

THE THEOLOGY OF
THE UNITED CHURCH OF CANADA

Don Schweitzer,
Robert C. Fennell,
and Michael Bourgeois,
Editors

WILFRID LAURIER
UNIVERSITY PRESS

Inspiring Lives.

Wilfrid Laurier University Press acknowledges the support of the Canada Council for the Arts for our publishing program. We acknowledge the financial support of the Government of Canada through the Canada Book Fund for our publishing activities. This work was supported by the Research Support Fund.

Library and Archives Canada Cataloguing in Publication

The theology of the United Church of Canada / Don Schweitzer, Robert C. Fennell, and Michael Bourgeois, editors.

Includes bibliographical references and index.
Issued in print and electronic formats.
ISBN 978-1-77112-395-2 (hardcover).—ISBN 978-1-77112-397-6 (EPUB).—ISBN 978-1-77112-398-3 (PDF)

1. United Church of Canada—Doctrines. I. Schweitzer, Don, editor II. Bourgeois, Michael, 1956–, editor III. Fennell, Rob, editor

BX9881.T44 2019   287.9'2   C2018-902781-9
                                          C2018-902782-7

Front-cover image: *A Song of Faith* (stained glass fused with hand-painted text), by Sarah Hall, RCA. Image used with the permission of the artist. Cover design by Angela Booth Malleau, design .booth.ca. Interior design and composition by James Leahy.

© 2019 Wilfrid Laurier University Press
Waterloo, Ontario, Canada
www.wlupress.wlu.ca

This book is printed on FSC® certified paper. It contains recycled materials, and other controlled sources, is processed chlorine free, and is manufactured using biogas energy.

Printed in Canada

CONTENTS

Acknowledgements

The editors wish to thank all who have provided their support and encouragement in bringing this volume to fruition, including the contributors, our families and colleagues; Atlantic School of Theology, Emmanuel College, and St. Andrew's College for financial and other support for this project; the staff at Wilfrid Laurier University Press; Emma CushmanWood Ceruti for preparing the bibliography; and Sarah Hall for granting permission to use her *A Song of Faith* for the book cover.

Don would like to thank in particular Melanie Schwanbeck for her help with computing issues, Katelyn Haskell, library technician, for her help in tracking down materials, Luke Warman of XL Print and Design for creating a high-resolution version of the image *Jesus Christ, Liberator*, and the University of Saskatchewan for providing a publishing subvention from its Research Services Publications Fund.

Abbreviations

AIS	*The Authority and Interpretation of Scripture*
BCO	Book of Common Order
BEM	*Baptism, Eucharist and Ministry*
BESS	Board of Evangelism and Social Service
BFM	Board of Foreign Mission
BHM	Board of Home Missions
BOM	Board of Overseas Mission
BOU	*Basis of Union* (1925)
BWM	Board of World Mission
CGP	*Celebrate God's Presence*
DMC	Division of Mission in Canada
DWO	Division of World Outreach
EARP	Ecumenical Agenda Research Project
EMC	Ethnic Ministry Council
FCSO	Fellowship for a Christian Social Order
Forms	*Forms of Service*
GC1	The First General Council of The United Church of Canada
ICIF	Inter-Church and Inter-Faith Committee
IMC	International Missionary Council (Jerusalem 1928)
Manual	*The Manual*, The United Church of Canada
MMF	Missionary and Maintenance Fund
MV	*More Voices: Supplement to Voices United: The Hymn and Worship Book of the United Church of Canada* (2007)
PLURA	The Presbyterian, Lutheran, United, Roman Catholic, and Anglican Churches in Canada
PROK	Presbyterian Church in the Republic of Korea
ROP	*Record of Proceedings* of General Councils of The United Church of Canada

Statement	*A Statement of Faith* (1940)
Song	*A Song of Faith* (2006)
TRC	Truth and Reconciliation Commission of Canada
TRUE	*Toward a Renewed Understanding of Ecumenism*
UCA	United Church of Canada Archives
UCC	The United Church of Canada
UCPH	United Church Publishing House
UCA	United Church Archives
UCW	United Church Women
VU	*Voices United: The Hymn and Worship Book of The United Church of Canada* (1996)
WA	Woman's Association
WMS	Woman's Missionary Society
WCC	World Council of Churches
Year Book	The United Church of Canada *Year Book*

INTRODUCTION

John H. Young

"Does the United Church have a theology?" That question has been posed from time to time, often acerbically by the denomination's critics, though sometimes anxiously by some of its members. The viewpoint exists that The United Church of Canada, as a "non-creedal church," has little interest in theology and, as a result, attaches little importance to it. This viewpoint continues despite developments that would challenge it. For example, in his chapter in *The United Church of Canada: A History*, Michael Bourgeois presents compelling evidence to support his contention that the United Church has a rich history of theological discussion. One could also argue that the 2012 addition of three "faith statements" to the existing Doctrine section of the United Church's *Basis of Union*, and especially the remit process leading up to their inclusion, witnesses specifically to the importance of theology in the United Church. Unquestionably the process increased awareness within the denomination of its theology and theological traditions.

One hope of those who developed the concept of this book is that the resulting product might finally lay this old canard to rest. The book recounts how UCC perspectives on certain doctrines have developed over the years. In that recounting, one discovers a plethora of theological affirmations, sometimes accompanied by lively discussion, all aimed at helping the church to live faithfully in its context and to be thoughtful about the pastoral implications of the faith tradition its professes.

This introductory chapter provides some general background on theology in The United Church of Canada. It will begin by looking at the place of theology in the denomination's life. It will then examine how UCC theology has developed from the time formal consideration of church union began in the early twentieth century down to the present. In doing so, it will seek to place the UCC's theological trajectory in the broader context of North American Protestant thought. Then it will examine why and how each of the UCC's four formal statements of doctrine came to be. Finally, it will recount the process by which three statements developed subsequent to church union were added to the Doctrine section of the *Basis of Union*, along with some reflections about the significance of that action.

The Place and Importance of Theology in the United Church

During its history, the UCC has signalled the importance of theology in several ways. It has not had a formal creed to which members must subscribe in a literal way. However, it has required members both to offer a profession of their faith in response to particular questions and to state their intention to live as followers of Jesus as conditions for formal membership in the church. In that aspect of its being and understanding, it has been quintessentially Reformed.[1]

The central place of a profession of faith in the life of the UCC appears most obviously in that requirement for membership. But it is not found there alone. Some invitations to the table in the Communion liturgies in service books previous to the current *Celebrate God's Presence* stressed that one was welcomed to the table on the basis of professing Jesus as one's Saviour and Lord and intending to follow his way. While the World Council of Churches' (WCC's) *Baptism, Eucharist, and Ministry* document, ecumenical conversations, and the Liturgical Renewal Movement have led in the last several decades to a greater emphasis on baptism as the entry point to receiving communion, that older tradition continues to have influence.

In a practice much less common to both the Methodist and Reformed traditions, Ministry Personnel in the UCC are not obligated to offer a literal subscription to the denomination's doctrinal statements. Rather they are required to say that they are in "essential agreement" with them and that they see the UCC's statement of doctrine "as being in substance agreeable to the teaching of the Holy Scriptures."[2] The requirement of "essential agreement," which came to the UCC courtesy of the Congregationalists at the time of the church union negotiations, reveals several key UCC understandings regarding theology and theological development.

The requirement for candidates to state that they are in "essential agreement" with the UCC's statement of doctrine is not, as has sometimes been suggested, an indication that the UCC regards theology as of relatively little importance because its Ministry Personnel have to be only in "essential agreement" with its doctrinal statements. In fact, the opposite is the case. The term is an indication of the importance the denomination places upon theology, and it captures two key aspects of the UCC's theological tradition.

First, those who developed the *Twenty Articles of Doctrine* for the *Basis of Union* believed, according to T.B. Kilpatrick, a member of the Doctrine sub-committee, that while there were eternal verities in church doctrine, the language in which such truths were expressed was always contextual. Further, they judged that theological statements needed to be reworked from time to time to take account of changing circumstances and contexts. So doctrinal statements, while certainly not fluid, were not fixed either. They thought that the UCC, if it were being faithful, would need to restate its faith from time to time in the context and circumstances of new generations or eras.[3]

Second, the term "essential agreement" reflected a Congregationalist understanding that the UCC adopted, namely, that a candidate for ministry could have new theological insights or understandings, insights or understandings that got "lost" when one required literal adherence or subscription to a statement of faith or specific answers to questions for which only one "right" answer was acceptable. At the same time, the concept of "essential agreement" included the notion that an examining committee would indeed "examine" a candidate vigorously in order to determine whether said candidate stood sufficiently within the denominational tradition to be able to preach and to teach the faith in the context of the denomination's tradition. In fact, contrary to popular opinion in some quarters, the Congregationalist understanding that the UCC adopted, far from being a casual approach to doctrine, was one of greater, rather than less, rigour when it came to the theological examination of candidates for ministry.[4] These historical underpinnings of the UCC's approach to theology or doctrine reveal two features built into the denominational tradition from its very beginning: an importance attached to theology and a certain fluidity in relation to things theological.

In using the term "United Church Theology," it is important to recognize a distinction between the UCC's four theological statements from different periods in its life, statements that comprise the Doctrine section of the *BOU*, and a number of other expressions of theology. These other expressions have a less "formal" status, but they have contributed to the ethos (of which theology is a part) of the UCC in the sense of a lived theology.

By "other expressions of theology," things such as the following come to mind: the writing, statements, and actions of key figures in the life of the ucc; the reports and actions of key denominational committees; the hymns, sermons, and liturgies that inform theological understanding at a local level; educational materials produced by the denomination or recommended by the denomination, whether aimed at children, youth, or adults; and cultural artifacts that provoked significant discussion within the ucc (e.g., the statue of the Crucified Woman, or Pierre Berton's book *The Comfortable Pew*). This introductory chapter will not address these "other expressions of theology," but such expressions will, rightly, figure prominently in the discussion of the various topics addressed in subsequent chapters of this book.

The ucc's approach to making formal theological statements, be it a formal statement of faith or an official denominational statement on a particular topic (e.g., *The Authority and Interpretation of Scripture*), has been conciliar and consultative. While a committee does the drafting and writing work, the resulting statement or document has to receive the approval of General Council, the ucc's national governing body. When there is a desire, as was the case at the 40th General Council in 2009, to consider adding to the Doctrine section of the *BOU* some subsequent statements of doctrine adopted by meetings of the General Council since 1925, the "remit" process requires that an absolute majority not only of the ucc's Presbyteries but also of the key governing Board of each of its Pastoral Charges vote in the affirmative before any such addition could be made. In the ucc, while individual members contribute to the development of such statements, neither an individual nor a committee can speak authoritatively to declare that something will be the formal theological position of the ucc. Only members meeting as a court of the church, or in a collective body with governance authority in particular areas of the life of the church, can make such decisions.

On a related point, the generally consultative nature of the conciliar system has been supplemented by a pattern of consultation by the committee or committees charged with the task of developing such statements or positions. In an earlier period of the ucc's life, such consultation took the form of the committee assigned with the task seeking the viewpoint of those it judged had particular expertise to offer. As time passed, the circles of consultation grew wider so that, for example, when the Committee on Theology and Faith worked on a statement on *The Authority and Interpretation of Scripture* (1986–1992), it sent a study document to every United Church Pastoral Charge and to some ecumenical partners inviting their feedback on the subject. When preparing the statement of faith, *A Song of Faith*, the

Committee on Theology and Faith again consulted widely, in addition to holding a symposium to test a draft, as part of the process for bringing the statement to a meeting of the General Council.

Any United Church committee or task group charged with the preparation of resources—whether a Sunday School curriculum, or new worship resources, or a statement on Israel and Palestine—is expected to think through and express the theological underpinnings of the particular enterprise. However, since the decision of the 7th General Council (1936) to have the UCC develop a new statement of faith, the UCC has always had a standing committee responsible for studying key theological questions or issues, for developing resources, and for preparing statements for the consideration of the entire church. Initially known as the Commission on the Statement of Faith (since the committee was struck to prepare what is now known as the 1940 *Statement of Faith*), the name was subsequently changed to the Committee on Christian Faith. This committee has undergone two other subsequent name changes, first to the Committee on Theology and Faith and then to the Theology and Inter-Church Inter-Faith Committee. This last name change resulted from the decision to combine the Committee on Theology and Faith with the United Church's Inter-Church Inter-Faith Committee.

Setting United Church Theology in a Broader Context

In mainline Protestantism, Liberal Theology, with its optimism about what the human being could accomplish, was entering its heyday in the late nineteenth and early twentieth centuries. This time period coincides with (and not accidently so) the growing conviction that some form of church union was necessary in Canada. Ecclesiastical bodies on both sides of the Atlantic began to take a more active role in society in the sense of commenting on social events and engaging in social activity. This greater liberalism and increased activism was not restricted to English-speaking Protestants in Great Britain, the United States, and Canada. The rise of Liberal Theology had begun in Germany in the early nineteenth century, and it continued to have an effect there. Liberal Theology's inherent optimism, its belief that the kingdom of God was just around the corner if only everyone in society had the necessary education to perceive right from wrong and the capacity to seize the opportunities available in "modern society," provided a powerful impetus to remove what its supporters saw as artificial barriers standing in the way of the advancement of God's kingdom. One of those barriers was the divided nature of the Christian Church or, at least, the divisions plaguing its Protestant section.

During this same era, the rise of a historical-critical approach to the study of the Bible began to have a substantial impact on mainline Protestant churches in Canada, the United States, and Western Europe. This approach demonstrated that the Bible was composed of many books, written by many persons over a lengthy period of time, and included different types of literature. This approach undercut the effects of appeals to certain denominational positions that had been based (to at least some degree) on a reading of the Bible as God's dictated word. This new way of approaching the Bible carried over into other aspects of church life. It led an increasing number of church members, not to mention church leaders, to think again about the merits, or lack thereof, of the denominational barriers that separated them. Hence the rise of historical criticism and the influence of Liberal Theology combined to undermine the support systems for traditional denominational lines.

Those in the Presbyterian, Methodist, and Congregational Churches in Canada who were most attracted to the idea of church union would have self-described as liberal evangelicals. They represented a movement in all three denominations that reworked an inherited tradition of revivalism and of personal regeneration in light of Liberal Theology. The resulting liberal evangelical tradition combined an emphasis from Liberal Theology on the use of one's gifts and resources for the common good, including a campaign for various social reform causes, with a continued stress on the importance of theology and the sharing of the faith tradition. It is no exaggeration to say that this rising liberal evangelicalism played a major role in bringing about church union.

In Protestant Christianity in the West, the 1920s saw a gradual move from Liberal Theology to Neo-Orthodox theology. Karl Barth's 1919 commentary on Romans is often seen as the beginning of this transition. By the end of the Second World World, Neo-Orthodoxy dominated Protestant theology in the West. To note a few key aspects of this movement only in the broadest of terms, Neo-Orthodoxy emphasized God's transcendence (in contrast to a stress on God's immanence in Liberal Theology), the reality and inevitability of sin, the Bible as either the primary or the only source of divine revelation, and God's gracious action to save us as we human beings had no possibility of doing so for ourselves. Its origins lay in the loss of the idealism and optimism of the late-nineteenth-century Western view that human progress toward goodness and a better world was almost inevitable.

The First World War fatally undercut that late-nineteenth- and early-twentieth-century idealism and optimism, with its accompanying idea of what the human being could accomplish. The Great Depression finished off the remaining vestiges of that theological trajectory.

Proponents of Neo-Orthodoxy saw themselves as realists in terms of the human condition, but they had great faith in the transcendent God known to them in Jesus the Christ. Many of its key leaders, including Reinhold Niebuhr of the United States, were either openly socialist in their political views or had socialist leanings. This theological school of thought was not a politically conservative one. Karl Barth was its most famous figure. Paul Tillich and New Testament scholar Rudolph Bultmann were other key figures.

Neo-Orthodoxy was the dominant theological force in Western Protestant thought until the mid- to late 1960s. Theological students in any Protestant theological school in Canada or the United States from the late 1940s through to the early 1960s would generally have read the same theologians, and they would have been Neo-Orthodox theologians. Toward the end of the 1960s, Neo-Orthodoxy's hegemonic position began to break down.

Various factors led to the diminishment of what had been this dominant school of thought among mainline Protestant clergy, seminary teachers, and students. One factor was a greater exposure to Roman Catholic thought as a result of Vatican II. The Roman Catholic tradition had had some particularly creative minds coming to the fore during and after the Second World War. Protestant seminary professors and students now began to read these theologians much more and to integrate into their own thinking some of the concepts they found there.

The development of theologies that sought to deal with the particular context in which various oppressed or disadvantaged groups did their theology was a second factor. For example, the struggle of African Americans for equality led to the rise of Black theology, with James Cone its primary figure. Feminist theology had its rise in this era. Liberation theology, too, began in the late 1960s; centred in Latin America, it had a profound effect on other similar theologies that endeavoured to speak to and for those located in the underside of society. Asian theologians became more visible in North America as many wrote in terms of their context. The increased and more recent attention to Indigenous spiritualities seems yet another manifestation of this same trend. An early 1970s criticism of Neo-Orthodoxy was that almost all its key theologians were white, male, middle- and upper-middle-class, and either Western European or North American.

Some commentators observed that while Neo-Orthodoxy could speak well to the context of its key thinkers, it did not speak well to the very different contexts of the Third World, African-Americans, women, and others. In a broader sense, the breakdown (beginning in the late 1960s) of what had been a general societal consensus and a conformist way of life in the 1950s and early 1960s in Western Europe, the United States, and Canada came to be reflected in theology. It was an era of liberation movements and of growing awareness of disparities and differences in the wider world, and theology became much more contextual.

Other currents of thought within the dominant culture in the United States also challenged Neo-Orthodoxy. The Death of God theologians of the late 1960s and early 1970s had initially been influenced by Neo-Ortho-doxy but, for a variety of reasons, lost the capacity to believe in God or, at the very least, God as they had come to know the deity through Neo-Orthodox thought. Human suffering, especially its extent and seemingly capricious nature, appears to have been a particular stumbling block that led many of the Death of God theologians to their position.

Process Theology, a theological school that made particular use of some of the insights of the philosopher Alfred North Whitehead, challenged the notion of divine omnipotence in the literal sense of that term. Its proponents argued that while God was the most powerful entity one could imagine, the fact that every creature had freedom and therefore power made the idea of a literally "all-powerful" God a conceptual impossibility. One key figure in this movement, Charles Hartshorne, in his argument for the existence of God as most powerful but not all-powerful, made use of the proof for the existence of God developed by the late-eleventh-century thinker Anselm of Canterbury. In doing so, Hartshorne gave renewed attention to the work of this medieval theologian.

One could sum up these developments by saying that whereas earlier eras tended to have one dominant theological perspective (though those particular perspectives came and went as one moved from one era to another), the latter part of the twentieth century and the early part of the twenty-first century have not had one dominant theological movement or perspective.

The United Church of Canada reflected what was happening elsewhere in Western Protestantism. Neo-Orthodoxy was the dominant theological perspective in the UCC for many years. If its influence began slightly later in the UCC, in contrast to the Presbyterian Church in Canada, Neo-Orthodoxy was certainly the pre-eminent theological perspective for the two decades after the Second World War. However, by the 1970s, that dominant position was also changing. The UCC, like other denominations in the United States and Canada, would see a plethora of theological perspectives emerge. A consensus in the UCC that one particular theological perspective was preferred no longer existed. As was also true elsewhere, context—geography, time, gender, wealth, status, ethnicity, and so forth—played a major role in how one approached the task of doing theology.

The Doctrine Section of the *Basis of Union*

The formal theology of the UCC is expressed in the Doctrine section of the *Basis of Union*, which contains three statements of faith and a creed. These four documents collectively form that Doctrine section, and the specific statements come from different periods in the denomination's life. Each statement is considered a "subordinate standard," for all statements of faith or statements of doctrine are subordinate to Scripture.

Twenty Articles of Doctrine

The first of these four statements, *Twenty Articles of Doctrine* was part of the BOU upon which the founding denominations agreed to come together. At the 1902 Methodist General Conference meeting in Winnipeg, Principal William Patrick, a Presbyterian "ecumenical guest" (to use a contemporary term) invited the Methodists in Canada to consider coming together with the Presbyterians in Canada. The Congregationalist observer at this same gathering asked that his denomination be invited to the party. Patrick's initiative, and the enthusiastic response of both the Methodists and the Congregationalists, led to the establishment of a Joint Committee to explore the possibility of such a union. The Joint Committee, having determined that such a union was both feasible and desirable, proceeded in a series of annual gatherings between 1904 and 1908 to put together the BOU. The Joint Committee divided itself into five subcommittees, one of which was the Doctrine subcommittee. That subcommittee's forty members—sixteen Methodists, sixteen Presbyterians, and eight Congregationalists, under the leadership of Nathaniel Burwash, the leading Methodist theologian of the day and the Chancellor of Victoria University—found creating a statement of doctrine for the proposed denomination to be easier than subsequent commentators would have imagined possible. Indeed, they confessed that they had had few difficulties in the task, though the relationship of candidates for ministry to the Doctrine statement, a topic assigned to another subcommittee, almost proved a deal breaker.

Two factors contributed principally to the relative ease with which the Doctrine subcommittee did its work. First, practical considerations strongly drove the desire for church union. Neither the Methodists nor the Presbyterians, not to mention the Congregationalists, had the resources to meet both the needs of eastern Canadians moving west in the late nineteenth and early twentieth centuries, and the perceived need to "Canadianize and Christianize" immigrants, especially those from central and eastern Europe, who were flooding into the prairies in the decade or so prior to the onset of the First World War.

Second, and perhaps more germane to this chapter, during at least the last quarter of the nineteenth century, the three founding denominations (Presbyterian, Methodist, and Congregational) had been moving toward a generally common understanding of some key theological concepts that traditionally had been points of division among them. One was the Calvinist understanding of predestination. By the late nineteenth century, an increasing number of Canadian Presbyterians had become uncomfortable with some aspects of the traditional understanding of predestination, including, in particular, the notion of Limited Atonement. Samuel Dwight Chown, the Methodist General Superintendent, may have exaggerated only a little when he observed: "Calvinism is a creed outworn in many respects and many of our Presbyterian friends were glad to drop its more uncouth aspects and place their present views in the genial garb of Methodist phraseology."[5]

The committee used two existing statements—a "Brief Statement of the Reformed Faith" (Presbyterian Church, United States, 1905) and "The Articles of the Faith of the Presbyterian Church of England" (1890)—as the primary bases for their work. Claris E. Silcox, in his encyclopedic study of the church union process, reported that Article 12, "Of Sanctification," was taken almost directly from an 1886 Canada Congregationalist document.[6] Methodist theological motifs appear in various places in the statement.

That said, the committee did struggle at points. Article 2, "Of Revelation," appears from the minutes to have been the subject of the greatest debate. There were eight changes during the course of the sessions, most minor but one substantive. The substantive one, adopted in 1907, changed a reference to the Holy Scriptures as "the only infallible rule of faith and life" to describing them "as containing the only infallible rule of faith and life."

The Doctrine section, as completed in 1908, saw only a few minor changes and the addition of one article during the period in which the

BOU as a whole was a matter of debate in the denominations contemplating the union. Subsequent to the union, there have been only two changes to the *Twenty Articles of Doctrine*. Both are in Article 17, "Of Ministry." One change was to take account of the decision to ordain women, which meant adding that God called men *and women* to ministry. The other, through a remit ratified by the 32nd General Council (1988), added to this article the recognition that ordered ministry consisted of both ordained and diaconal ministers. Previously the article had spoken only of ordained ministers.

While the Doctrine subcommittee appeared well pleased with its work, the response in the three denominations varied. The Congregationalists, while expressing their support, had lost their appeal to have a simpler statement. Among some supporters and some opponents of the church union enterprise, there was a sense that the Doctrine section was unadventurous and insufficient for a modern church and for the challenges of the day. Those supporting union and holding such positions chose to overlook their objections in the interest of seeing church union proceed, for they judged that to be the more important goal.

Interestingly, while a number of Presbyterians chose to remain in the continuing Presbyterian Church on the grounds that the proposed *Twenty Articles of Doctrine* had left out Presbyterian distinctives or essentials found in the *Westminster Confession* (and for some it was a sufficient ground for opposition that the proposed statement of doctrine was not the *Westminster Confession*), other Presbyterians chose to stay as continuing Presbyterians because they judged the *Twenty Articles of Doctrine* not sufficiently modern and therefore inadequate for a twentieth-century church.[7] Thus, those in the Presbyterian Church who chose to enter the union represented, on the whole, the theological middle ground of Canadian Presbyterianism, persons who would probably have been most comfortable describing themselves as liberal evangelicals.

Statement of Faith (1940)

As noted above, at least some UCC leaders at the time of church union believed that the *Twenty Articles of Doctrine* in the BOU had not addressed the needs of a "modern church." This concern did not diminish following the events of 1925 and was one motivator for the development of a "contemporary" statement of faith as the new UCC moved through the 1930s. A second and related factor was world events since 1908, the year in which most of the work on what would become the *Twenty Articles of Doctrine* was completed. The devastation of life and the discrediting of Liberal Theology's heady optimism about human progress during the First World War, the Roaring Twenties, and the Great Depression had all changed the context since the *Twenty Articles of Doctrine* had been written.[8] Theologically, Neo-Orthodoxy exerted increasing influence on theological thinking. The sense that church members needed a more usable faith statement—the *Twenty Articles of Doctrine* being judged wanting in that regard—also contributed to the desire for a new expression of the church's faith. Finally, UCC leaders at the time were well aware of the Reformed tradition's practice of seeing faith statements or statements of doctrine as "subordinate standards," a deposit to which subsequent generations could choose to add. Provision for such later additions had been explicitly made in The United Church of Canada Act, the federal legislation that created the UCC, and in its provincial counterparts.[9] While the concept of "subordinate standards" was later to become almost lost in the UCC's collective memory, no such amnesia existed in the 1930s.

A "memorial" or request from London Conference to the 7th General Council (1936) initiated the project to develop a new faith statement. The wording of the initial General Council motion concerning the matter reflected at least part of the motivation: "We believe that the time is opportune for the preparation of a Statement of Faith that shall embody in concise and intelligible form what we in the United Church conceive to be the substance of Christian belief."[10] As a recent UCC document pointed out, the framing of the motion suggested "that some in the United Church regarded the Doctrine section of the *Basis of Union* as neither concise nor intelligible."[11]

A commission of fourteen academics and key denominational leaders prepared the initial draft of the 1940 Statement. Regional groups, based in centres where a UCC theological school existed, then reviewed the draft, making suggestions for revision. This work happened between 1936 and 1938. During the next two years, the Commission on the Statement of Faith studied the responses from the regional groups, sent out a revised draft to the regional groups, received responses from the regional groups to the revised draft, and prepared the final statement for the 9th General Council (1940).[12] That General Council assembly adopted a motion, without any amendments even being proposed, to "give general approval to this Statement of Faith and commend it to the church for the instruction of the young and for the guidance of believers."[13]

It is also noteworthy that, partway through the process of drafting the Statement, the commission had to resolve two aspects of the task it judged the 7th General Council (1936) had not made clear. One was the "character of the statement"[14] and the second was the intended constituency. The commission determined

> that the document as finally issued should be one of affirmations rather than of apologetic defence of the Christian faith and in terms which are expressly those of religion. As to the constituency, it was thought that it may be wise in the end to prepare two documents, one of which shall be more amplified than the other in stating the primary beliefs held by the Church.[15]

The Preface to John Dow's book, *This Is Our Faith*, suggests that the "more amplified" statement took shape in his book, for he noted that his work "was prepared to give fuller exposition to a short Statement of Faith presented to the Ninth General Council of The United Church of Canada in 1940.... I have endeavoured to reflect the views of the Commission which drew up the Statement; but, as I was left with complete freedom of interpretation, I must accept responsibility for what is here written."[16] While members of the commission wrote *Highways of the Heart*, a book of meditations on the 1940 SOF published in 1941, it seems likely that the intention to provide the "more amplified" statement was fulfilled by Dow's book rather than by *Highways of the Heart*.

Contemporaries judged, and historians have concurred, that the *Twenty Articles of Doctrine* did not reflect generally the theological currents of the mid-1920s when church union was finally consummated. Some have wondered how adequately the *Twenty Articles of Doctrine* reflected even the theological currents and concerns of the early twentieth century. No such charge of ignoring the contemporary theological scene could be levelled against the 1940 SOF. It picked up the trends in Biblical and theological scholarship of its day, in particular Neo-Orthodoxy. The document was *au courant*, and it had significant influence in the UCC from its approval in 1940 well into the 1960s. It formed the basis of many UCC educational resources (e.g., curricula designed for church membership classes) during that era.

One place where the influence of Neo-Orthodoxy is most evident is found in the explanation of how divine revelation takes place. In the *Twenty Articles of Doctrine*, while Scripture is the primary source of revelation, God was also revealed "in nature, in history, and in the heart of man [*sic*]."[17] In the 1940 SOF, God is revealed only in and through Scripture. As Michael Bourgeois has pointed out, the broader theological perspectives of the denomination come through particularly when one reads Dow's book.[18]

The United Church Creed (or A New Creed)

In 1968, the Executive of the General Council adopted what is now the UCC's third subordinate standard, A New Creed. The initiative to write a creed specifically for the denomination arose as part of the work on a new baptismal service, this particular service itself being part of a larger project to produce a new liturgical service book for ministers.[19] Until this time, a creed was not regularly used in Sunday morning services in many UCC congregations. It was customary, however, to use the Apostles' Creed on Sundays when Holy Communion or the Lord's Supper was celebrated. The Nicene Creed was rarely used.

The matter of a creedal statement that could be used as part of the baptismal liturgy was referred to the Committee on Christian Faith in 1965. The Committee had not had a chance to work on this referral when, following the 22nd General Council (1966), the Sub-Executive of the General Council added to their agenda the task of trying to write a "modern credal [sic] statement."[20] The Committee on Christian Faith worked on such a statement and brought a draft to the 23rd General Council (1968).

When one looks at the committee's description of its work in its report to the 23rd General Council, the emphasis on the need for a creed that could speak to the "modern" or "contemporary" world stands out. Those two words appeared with some frequency, and they reflected a key concern that lay behind the desire for such a creed. It is also noteworthy that the argument that carried the day when the General Council rejected the draft the committee brought forward, and sent that document back to the committee for further work, was the concern that the draft did not speak sufficiently to the contemporary world. The minutes indicate the proposed Creed was to "be re-drafted in a manner that will give more adequate expression of the Christian Gospel for our time."[21]

The committee incorporated some noteworthy changes after the rejection of its initial effort by the 23rd General Council. "Who works within us and among us by his Spirit" was changed to "Who works in us and others by the Spirit." "We proclaim his Kingdom" in the initial draft became "to proclaim Jesus, crucified and risen, our judge and our hope." The emphasis on proclaiming Jesus rather than "God's Kingdom" certainly fit better with the emphasis of the age. The late 1960s and the 1970s had a strong emphasis on Jesus, both in the church and in popular culture (as in the musicals *Jesus Christ Superstar* and *Godspell*).[22]

The Executive of the General Council approved the revised draft in the fall of 1968. Further revisions to make the language inclusive and to add the line, "to live with respect in Creation," happened in 1980 and 1995 respectively. This creed quickly gained popularity both in Canada and abroad.[23] When the new UCC faith statement, *A Song of Faith*, was presented at the 39th General Council (2006), the chairperson of the Committee on Theology and Faith had to reassure commissioners on several occasions that *Song* was not intended to replace *A New Creed* in the denomination's life. The notion that *Song* might be mandated for use in worship as a substitute for this now-beloved creed was a point of significant anxiety for many.

A Song of Faith

The UCC's fourth subordinate standard is *A Song of Faith*. The 39th General Council when it met in 2006 adopted this statement of faith, though it was only after the actions of the 40th (2009) and 41st (2012) General Councils that it became a subordinate standard and therefore a part of the Doctrine section in the BOU.

When the Committee on Theology and Faith was working on *The Authority and Interpretation of Scripture* in the late 1980s and early 1990s, both the General Council and some of its various Divisions sent other requests to the committee. One such request was that the committee develop a contemporary statement of faith as a replacement for the 1940 SOF and as an expression of what the UCC believed, given the rapid changes of the late twentieth century and an increasingly secularized Canada. Since the committee had already committed to do major studies on a "Theology of Call" and on Christology, the committee turned to this request only after completing work on those two projects.

In doing its work on a new statement of faith between 2000 and 2006, the Committee on Theology and Faith examined various statements that the UCC had made during its history. However, it gave particular attention to statements various committees and task groups had made since the mid-1960s. The Committee on Theology and Faith also placed great importance on context, maintaining a pattern and an emphasis found in other denominational documents of the period, not to mention many of the broader theological movements of the era. In addition, the committee committed itself to addressing what is sometimes called "religious pluralism," or the relationship of Christianity to other faiths, something not explicitly included in earlier statements of faith. It tested preliminary ideas with a constituency beyond the members of the committee itself.

In writing the document, the committee opted to use a poetic style rather than the propositional style prevalent not only in earlier UCC documents but also in statements of faith produced by other denominations, particularly those in the Reformed tradition. When it had completed a draft, it held a major symposium in Toronto in the fall of 2005. It invited various individuals, representing different constituencies and perspectives in the UCC, to comment on that draft document. The document then underwent further revision in light of the comments made at that gathering.

When the committee presented *Song* to the 39th General Council (2006), the General Council approved it unanimously. Indeed, the members of the Committee on Theology and Faith present at the meeting received a standing ovation from commissioners after the Council had voted its approval.

The statement has been used to a significant degree in worship services in some congregations, sections of it forming or informing elements such as the Call to Worship or short prayers. It has also drawn praise in some quarters in the denomination for the unambiguous way it has claimed certain particularities of the Christian tradition even while addressing "new" issues such as the relationship of Christianity to other faiths. This affirmation suggests, on the part of those making it, a view that the denomination had been unwilling to claim as forthrightly as it ought to have done certain Christian distinctives.

Adoption of the 1940 *Statement of Faith*, *A New Creed*, and *A Song of Faith* as Subordinate Standards

The concept of a "subordinate standard," so much a part of the thinking of the Joint Committee that produced the BOU, appears generally to have been lost in the UCC's institutional memory until its rediscovery in 2009. The reasons for its loss are a mystery. However, the concept has been recovered.

In 2009, a proposal from Saskatchewan Conference sought to remove the *Twenty Articles of Doctrine* from the BOU, even though the *Twenty Articles of Doctrine* were the only subordinate standard the UCC had at that time. The proposal asserted that various General Councils over the years had adopted other key faith statements such as these three. Those subsequent statements had been approved by the denomination's national governing body, and they had been widely used in the life of the church. However, they had no formal or official status apart from having been adopted at some point in time by a General Council. Some persons from the Saskatch-ewan Conference who spoke in debate also asserted that the *Twenty Articles of Doctrine* were dated. Therefore the proposal's objective to remove the *Twenty Articles of Doctrine* from the BOU and to treat it as a historic expres-sion of faith would mean viewing it in the same way the other three state-ments had been seen until then, namely as statements adopted by General Councils of the UCC at a particular point in time. Rather than removing the *Twenty Articles of Doctrine* from the BOU, a highly problematic step for several reasons, the General Council adopted unanimously an alternative proposal. That proposal asked the UCC, via its remit process, to add these three subsequent faith statements to the Doctrine section of the BOU as sub-ordinate standards.

Given the importance of the subject matter, namely affecting the "arti-cles of faith," these remits needed to be voted upon not only by Presbyteries (the usual requirement) but also by the Session or its equivalent in each Pastoral Charge. In advance of such voting, study material to aid Presbyter-ies and Pastoral Charges in considering the matter was circulated. It should also be noted that, to be adopted, a remit must achieve an absolute major-ity, in this case, an absolute majority both of Presbyteries and of Pastoral Charges; in other words, a non-vote is, in reality, a negative vote. The remit for each statement was passed by both Presbyteries and Pastoral Charges, and by solid margins. The 41st General Council (2012) then ratified these remits, making these three statements part of the Doctrine section of the BOU, together with the *Twenty Articles of Doctrine*.

One important consequence of the consideration and adoption of these additional subordinate standards is that the UCC was doing what those who drafted the original BOU had assumed the church would do, even if the memory of the concept had been largely lost for a time. The UCC had certainly continued in the spirit of its founders by developing subsequent statements of faith to express the faith tradition in the context of later gen-erations. What it had apparently forgotten was the possibility of taking the additional step of seeing whether it wished to make such statements subordinate standards, once sufficient time had passed to see if they fit the criteria of being seen by the church to be valuable in its life and to be beloved by it.

These remits on doctrine have had three significant impacts on theol-ogy in the UCC, impacts that will continue as the denomination moves into the future. First, the remit process has led a greater engagement with and interest in theology at the congregational level. In this regard, members of some pastoral charges reported that, contrary to their initial expectations, as they reflected on the remit process they had genuinely enjoyed having discussion about theology in their governing boards. They had found such discussions neither dry nor dull. Second, the denomination recovered an important concept of the Reformed tradition, namely, that it was possible to add new subordinate standards if the church was of a mind to do it. The willingness to do so has also reinforced a sense that is part of the Reformed tradition and that certainly was part of the UCC's founding ethos, namely, the way the denomination expresses core aspects of the faith tradition is not timeless, even if it judges those core aspects themselves to be. Third, (and here I am more speculative about the reason, though not the phenomenon) I have noted that recent Theology graduates from Queen's Theological College and Queen's University (where I taught until 2016) experienced a greater rigour in the examination of their theology subsequent to these remits than had generally been the case before. This phenomenon occurred both in their annual interviews and in their final ordination interview with the respective church committees. This more rigorous examination suggests an increased awareness of the importance of theology as something central to the life of the church and the practice of ministry. It may also represent an effort to move again to the kind of theological examination of candidates our denominational forebears had in mind when they developed the concept of essential agreement.

A Concluding Word

In this second decade of the twenty-first century, The United Church of Canada carries out its witness and its work in a Canada that is increasingly secularized and pluralistic. To make such an observation about the current context is neither to critique nor to rue this development—it is to state the obvious. In such an environment, the denomination needs to give greater attention to theology—its importance in the lives of Christians and the church—and to reflection upon it. The current context requires us to recognize a reality that has always existed: any denomination, not to mention any faith tradition, is, by definition, particular. Knowing that reminds us that certain distinctives—theological concepts, particular understandings about church governance, and some developed habits or patterns as to how to interact with the wider society—are all part of the denomination's ethos. They make the UCC what it is. A key idea behind the development of this volume is to shed light on some of those key theological concepts and how they have been lived out in The United Church of Canada.

NOTES

1   By "quintessentially Reformed," I have three things in mind. First, and spe-
    cific to this point about membership in the UCC, church membership in its
    fullest sense, and certainly in terms of governance both within and beyond
    the congregation, requires an individual to make a profession of faith as a
    condition for achieving such membership. Second, the UCC's primary author-
    ity and ultimate standard is Scripture; all statements of faith or statements
    of doctrine are "subordinate standards," that is, subordinate to Scripture.
    Third, the church, including its statements of doctrine, is always being
    reformed. These three characteristics would be common to what is called the
    "Reformed tradition," a group or family of denominations who locate their
    theological roots in the work of Ulrich Zwingli and John Calvin.

2   *The Manual* (Toronto: UCPH, 2016), 40.

3   See T.B. Kilpatrick, *Our Common Faith* (Toronto: UCPH, 1928), 62–66.

4   Phyllis Airhart made this point explicitly during her two theme addresses to
    the 91st Annual Meeting of the Bay of Quinte Conference, May 29–30, 2015.

5   Samuel Dwight Chown, "That They May Be One," January 1912. UCA, Samuel
    Dwight Chown Papers, box 3, file 67, p. 7.

6   Claris E. Silcox, *Church Union in Canada* (New York: Institute of Social and
    Religious Research, 1933), 137.

7   Allan L. Farris, "The Fathers of 1925," in *The Tide of Time: Historical Essays by
    the Late Allan L. Farris* (Toronto: Knox College, 1978), 118–120.

8   See *Our Words of Faith: Cherished, Honoured, and Living* (Toronto: UCC,
    2010), 15.

9   Ibid., 5–6.

10 UCC *Proceedings*, GC7 [1936], (Toronto: UCC, 1936), 49.

11 *Our Words of Faith*, 15.

12 UCC *Proceedings*, GC9, 1940, 167.

13 Ibid., 40.

14 UCC *Proceedings*, GC8, 1938, 209.

15 Ibid.

16 John Dow, *This Is Our Faith* (Toronto: BESS, UCC, 1943), vii.

17 See article 2.3.2, "Of Revelation," *The Manual*, 12.

18   Michael Bourgeois, "Awash in Theology: Issues in Theology in The United Church of Canada," in Don Schweitzer, ed., *The United Church of Canada: A History* (Waterloo, ON: Wilfrid Laurier University Press, 2012), 266–67.

19   That project would result in two liturgical service books, one for ministers and one intended for use in the pews. The hope and the desire for greater participation by the laity in regular worship services and in the liturgies for the sacraments lay behind the development of the latter volume.

20   UCC *Proceedings*, GC23, 1968, 311.

21   Ibid., 56.

22   An earlier version of these two paragraphs appeared in *Gathering* (Lent-Easter 2018). Reprinted by permission.

23   By way of a personal anecdote, the United Methodist congregation I attended in Dallas in the late 1970s and early 1980s while working on my PhD used this creed from the UCC every Sunday in their worship service.

CHAPTER ONE

THE TRIUNE GOD

Catherine Faith MacLean

I stepped into the pulpit and spread my arms to speak the invocation. The organ sounded a gathering note, and they were off: *Holy, holy, holy, Lord God Almighty …* I stopped. A phrase later I began again, joining the congregation in the hymn. I didn't know that morning in Tide Head, New Brunswick, that a sung invocation of the Triune God was the way they began worship. It was a habit, a practice, an expectation, an unwritten rule, a quiet Presence.

The doctrine of the Trinity is that quiet Presence across The United Church of Canada. It is deeply embedded in liturgical understandings and theological activities. Often it is habitual practice, experience of God bidden and anticipated, taken for granted. There are expectations that Trinitarian faith is what makes us Christian. There are benedictions, baptisms, and prayers at bedside where triune vocabulary comes by rote. There are political rallies, ecological debates, and ethical dilemmas in which God as one Person or another is expected to show up. There are theological conversations that question and redefine the Mystery. There are dear hearts who cling to the shamrock of faith as the sun sets on the dying day.

In this chapter, I will refer to statements, hymnals, service books, study materials, and theological commentary to explore the UCC's expressions of the doctrine of the Trinity. I will reflect on how the development of understandings and the choice of language gave expression to the triune mystery over ninety-five years of Trinitarian church life.

The Olden Days

Trinity Sunday pops up in the liturgical calendar every year, straightaway on the heels of Pentecost. Some preachers and liturgists are thrilled; others yearn for biblical sources and sigh about leftovers from the olden days.

A. McKibbin Watts, the former longtime editor of *Touchstone*, suggested the following adaptation of the Trinitarian formula from the Athanasian Creed as an option for Trinity Sunday.[1]

> Now this is Christian faith.
> We worship one God in Trinity,
> and the Trinity in unity.
> For the Father is one person,
> the Son is another,
> and the Holy Spirit is another.
> But the Godhead of the Father, of the Son,
> and of the Holy Spirit is all one,
> The glory equal, the majesty co-eternal.

Dating from the fifth century, the Athanasian Creed is the earliest creed to state the equality of the three persons of the Trinity. It is long, and it unequivocally presents an eternal fire for those of us who do a poor accounting of our deeds. With regard to the Trinity, though, it sealed the deal by articulating Christ as essential to the timeless holiness of God. It is named for Athanasius of Egypt, the bishop who energized the argument against Arius, whose popular heterodoxy claimed that the Father was superior in the Trinity.

The Nicene Creed is the most widely used of all creeds, according to the World Council of Churches.[2] It dates from the fourth century. In 589, a phrase was added asserting that the Spirit proceeds from the Son as well as the Father. The Nicene Creed affirms one God in three distinct persons. It is found in the joint Anglican–UCC *Hymn Book* (1971), and in the UCC's own *Voices United* (1996). "God in three Persons, blessed Trinity" is the final line in "Holy, Holy, Holy," and it is sung to a tune called *Nicaea*. The Apostles' Creed is even earlier, dating from the late second century. Concise, it is found in all of the UCC's hymnals and on the inside cover of many of its service books, conveniently at hand for liturgical use. Its Trinitarian confessions have deep resonance throughout the Christian world: "I believe in God the Father Almighty, creator of heaven and earth. I believe in Jesus Christ, God's only Son our Lord.... I believe in the Holy Spirit." Douglas Hall reflects:

> Both the Apostles' and the Nicene Creeds confess belief in God, Jesus Christ, the Holy Spirit—not belief that such affirmations as are made in the creeds

concerning the divine Being are true. Faith, like all of the major subjects of biblical religion, is a relational term, and it means simply trust—*fiducia.* "I believe in God the Father Almighty," and so on, does *not* mean that one believes in the existence of God, that God must be regarded as Father, that he created everything, and so forth. All of this means, rather, I trust God the Father, Mother, Parent, Source of Life, and so on: God, in all God's knownness and unknowability, is the Presence in whom I place my faith, my hope, my life and future.[3]

In *trust* and in the name of the Trinity, the church baptizes the faithful, buries the dead, reflects on changing seasons and understandings, and shows up prepared for love, justice, hope, and relationship. In *trust* and faithful action patterned on the Trinity, the church experiences and celebrates the wholeness and unity of God. This takes us back to the point Mac Watts was making: there is confidence and clarity about faith in the Trinity. That confidence took generations to achieve. Those who yearn for biblical sources and sigh about leftovers from the olden days would say any clarity has vanished like fog under the morning sun. Difference of opinion is the quandary, the pleasure, and the pastoral challenge of theological inquiry.

The Trinity is an unending flow of giving and receiving among the Three Persons. This *perichoresis* is cyclical, each Person resting within the others yet flowing. It conjures the interweaving movements of dance.[4] In a dance, partners are united but we see each dancer uniquely. God dances, and calls us into the dance. This triune movement is the faithful, Christian pattern of reality: the pattern of living, the pattern of ethics, the pattern of love. It is so exquisitely simple that children can understand it.[5] Children know circle dancing. It is so beautiful, musicians and poets and prayer-writers invoke it: they know awe. It is so complex, theologians and preachers pause before it: they know the danger of mystery. Comprehending the Trinity does not rest on blind faith. It is life; it is beauty; it is historical theology. God is a mystery that cannot be understood so much as experienced. Of course, dance is a metaphor. There are other familiar metaphors. Northrop Frye wrote, "We think of God as the author of our being and hence use the metaphor of 'Father' for him."[6] The threeness of the dancing God reflects the basic communal unit. One is solitary; two is intimate; three makes a community. The model for human living, the Triune God, is a community, not a binary intimacy nor a solitary being.[7]

Scripture

The doctrine of the Holy Trinity arose through deliberations of church councils guided by the Holy Spirit. The word Trinity does not appear in Scripture, but "triadic" references appear at several points in the New Testament, including the baptism of Jesus; the command to baptize the nations in Matthew 28; John's prologue; the promise of the Advocate; and Paul's comment about the Spirit who intercedes with sighs too deep for words. In Genesis 18, three angels visit Abraham. This passage has been called a prefiguration of the Holy Trinity, but this can be regarded only as mystery, not as critical biblical scholarship. The Trinitarian formula most commonly cited in worship is 2 Corinthians 13:13: "The grace of the Lord Jesus Christ, the love of God, and the communion of the Holy Spirit be with all of you." This verse appears time and again in UCC liturgical and commissioning materials. The denomination has claimed it in practice in deep and resonant ways.

God's relationships within God's self are referred to as the immanent Trinity: the dancers. In the mystery of the Triune God who is love, each Person has the others to love and from whom to receive love. The Trinity is an unending flow of giving and receiving. God's relationship with the rest of creation and creatures is the economic Trinity: the dance we share. How God works, the indivisible Trinity and the modelling of love in relationship, is the fundamental basis for pastoral care, congregational life, outreach, social justice, ecumenical commitments, church unity, the church's teachings on family life, and ethics. The UCC is often seen as a church in action, a spiritual home for social justice, and this outward expression of love is an echo of Trinitarian relationship. We are dancers in community, called to love others as God loves us.

Three Churches Dance into Union

The theological heritage brought to the union that formed The United Church of Canada in 1925 drew from the Presbyterian, Congregationalist, and Methodist traditions. Each of them was grounded in presuppositions about the Trinitarian reality of God. The Presbyterian *Westminster Confession* claimed:

> In the unity of the Godhead there be three persons, of one substance, power, and eternity; God the Father, God the Son, and God the Holy Ghost. The

Father is of none, neither begotten nor proceeding; the Son is eternally begotten of the Father; the Holy Ghost eternally proceeding from the Father and
the Son.[8]

The Congregationalists' *Commission Creed* confessed:

We believe in one God, the Father Almighty, Maker of heaven and earth, and
of all things visible and invisible; And in Jesus Christ, his only son, our Lord,
who is of one substance with the Father; by whom all things were made; And
in the Holy Spirit, the Lord and Giver of Life, who is sent from the Father and
Son, and who together with the Father and Son is worshipped and glorified.[9]

The Methodists' *Articles of Religion* likewise stated:

There is but one living and true God, everlasting, without body or parts, of
infinite power, wisdom and goodness; the Maker and Preserver of all things,
visible and invisible. And in unity of this Godhead there are three persons, of
one substance, power and eternity, the Father, the Son, and the Holy Ghost.[10]

Little wonder, then, that the processional hymn at the Inaugural Service
of the UCC finished with this line: "Yet she on earth hath union with God
the Three in One." The service included the "Hallowing of Church Union,"
which began:

To the glory of God the Father, who has called us by His grace;
And of His Son Jesus Christ, who loved us and gave Himself for us;
And of the Holy Spirit, who illumines and sanctifies us:
All: This Church of Christ is consecrate.[11]

So also the prayer constituting the General Council called upon the Three
Persons:

God Almighty, Father of our Lord and Saviour Jesus Christ, who loved the
Church and gave Himself for it; Thou who on the day of Pentecost didst shed
the Holy Spirit upon the Church waiting for the promise of the Father: we wait
before Thee with one heart, that the same Lord Jesus may be made known in
the midst of us, our only King and Head; and the same Holy Spirit, breathing
among us, may dispense among us His manifold gifts of grace and truth.[12]

The new denomination was off and running: guided, blessed, and modelled by the Triune God, dancing into the future.

The Twenty Articles of Doctrine (1925)

In the UCC's first creedal formulation, God comes first. As R.C. Chalmers wrote, "God comes before the Bible or any other manifestation of Himself."[13] This order is consonant with Methodist and Congregationalist approaches to statements of faith. Thus the article 2.3.1, "Of God," in the Doctrine section of the *Basis of Union* sets the reality and nature of God above all other considerations:

> We believe in the one only living and true God, a Spirit, infinite, eternal, and unchangeable, in His being and perfections; the Lord Almighty, who is love, most just in all His ways, most glorious in holiness, unsearchable in wisdom, plenteous in mercy, full of compassion, and abundant in goodness and truth. We worship Him in the unity of the Godhead and the mystery of the Holy Trinity, the Father, the Son, and the Holy Spirit, three persons of the same substance, equal in power and glory.

Reflecting on this and other elements of the *Twenty Articles of Faith*, T.B. Kilpatrick affirmed, "The Christian doctrine of God leads us into mystery, but not a blank mystery."[14] He wrote of "a personal God" yet distinguished personality from individuality: God is a living person, the ultimate reality. God "lives within Himself a full life, a life of relationships, a life of fellowship."[15] "Person" and "substance" are unhelpful terms, he said, borrowed from Greek and Latin philosophy, and they lead us to think of three independent individuals. Yet if there were no distinctions within the Trinity, and God seemed only one, how would Jesus fit? Kilpatrick clarified:

> Distinctions are *within* the Godhead, and each possesses the eternity of the Divine essence. One is the Father, the ground and source of all being and all good. One is the Son, who is the eternal manifestation of the Father's glory and the eternal object of the Father's love. One is the Spirit, who is the living bond between the Father and the Son, and is the eternal energy of God in His creative and redemptive work.[16]

Kilpatrick spoke of experience preceding doctrine: the early church knew the indwelling Spirit, the living Lord, and the heavenly Father, and later prepared doctrine that stores "the blessed experience" for generations to come.[17] He discarded Deism, Unitarianism, and Tritheism and credited early Christian Jewish monotheism as the beginning of Trinitarian experience.[18] The Trinity, he claimed, was based in Scripture and experience, and nothing less.

The Holy Trinity appeared straightaway in a liturgical service book. One year after Union, the General Council Committee on Church Worship and Ritual published *Forms of Service for the Offices of the Church* (1926). It is an elegant, slim, brown leather book, easily slipped into a pocket for ministers travelling in multi-point charges. Trinitarian blessings abound in this collection of services from the three major uniting churches. The three orders for baptism of children and adults are in the name of the Trinity. Orders for Ordination of Ministers, the Setting Apart of Deaconesses, and the Commissioning of Missionaries invoke the Triune God. An Order for the Installation of Officers and Teachers of the Church School requires a hymn calling on the Holy Spirit and gives directions about following Christ and building up the kingdom of God—Trinitarian in effect. The first of two Orders for Reception of Baptized Persons into Full Communion ascertains trust in and service to Jesus, but not a Trinitarian question, and intriguingly asks, "Are you in heart and conscience in essential agreement with the faith and order of The United Church of Canada as set forth in the *Basis of Union*?"[19]

The Hymnary of The United Church of Canada was published soon after, in 1930, and its first section is "The Holy Trinity." There are five Trinity hymns and four more noted; three are recommended for children. The church nurtured an understanding of God through these hymns. The Committee on Church Worship and Ritual prepared a discrete section titled, "For Little Children," conscious of the impact of singing on faith formation. Along with baptismal hymns, "more than any other hymns in the collection, these hymns were to shape the future of the church by shaping the theology of its children."[20] Susan Lukey examined these hymns and found they are witness to the faith the church wanted children to absorb for the leadership that Canada, the church, and the world would need. As Lukey notes,

> The image of God taught by the committee is kind, good and loving, not frightening. Children sang about being obedient and good, rather than needing forgiveness. The God of judgment has given way to the God of love, the distant God to the immanent One.... The immanence of God is most evident

in a hymn that was new in *The Hymnary* but which quickly became a favourite in the United Church: "This Is My Father's World" (#589). Here, God can be heard passing by "in the rustling grass." This anthropomorphism places God clearly within the realm of the world rather than within the realm of heaven.[21]

God was the loving Father who could be counted on to care for and help children. Although terms such as Almighty and Most High appear, the most frequent appellation for God is Father. He is loving and close to children. At times "he" may be the rugged, masculine father who defends the child: "Fully in His sight His children stand / by his strong arm defended" (#593). Just as often, "he" is a father who shows many traditional maternal qualities in gently nurturing, guarding, and caring for children, having made the world in which they play, safely and securely. Jesus in these hymns was the loving Saviour, Master, and Shepherd who tenderly gathers and cares for the children. There were few hymns addressing the Holy Spirit, so the committee included "Holy Spirit, Hear Us" (#616) in the "For Little Children" section. The verses explain how the Holy Spirit helps them as they sing, pray, read Scripture, become more like Jesus, and make ethical decisions.[22]

The Book of Common Order (1932) values both innovation and tradition. Worshipping congregations were called to be innovative, "free to follow the leading of the Spirit of Christ in their midst" and still respect tradition: "the experience of many ages of devotion shall not be lost, but preserved— experience that has caused certain forms of prayer to glow with light and power."[23] Trinitarian formulas abound in prayers, as seen in the Table of Lessons for the season after Christmas:

> O God, who makest us glad with the yearly remembrance of the birth of thy only Son Jesus Christ: Grant that as we joyfully receive him for our Redeemer, so we may with sure confidence behold him when he shall come to be our Judge; who liveth and reigneth with thee and the Holy Spirit, one God, world without end. *Amen.*[24]

Wedding rings as well as the couple were blessed in the name of the Trinity.[25] Psalms finished: "Glory be to the Father, and to the Son: and to the Holy Ghost; as it was in the beginning, is now, and ever shall be: world without end. Amen."[26] The Lord's Supper concluded with a Trinitarian benediction. Reception to Full Communion included a vow referencing the Trinitarian formula of the Apostles' Creed.[27] The services continue into all parts of church life, installing church school teachers and stewards, ordaining ministers, and setting apart deaconesses. One knows ministers whose copies of the BCO are weather-beaten from cemetery committals, pencil-marked from baptisms, and purple-stained from communion. Trinitarian phrases touched those who wept, who prayed, who worshipped, generation after generation.

A Statement of Faith (1940)

In the *Twenty Articles of Doctrine*, the Trinity is subsumed within the article on God, while Jesus and the Holy Spirit are addressed in subsequent articles. The 1940 *Statement of Faith* instead outlines God, Jesus Christ, and The Holy Spirit, before moving a separate, fourth article, The Holy Trinity.

> Knowing God thus, as Creator and Father, as Redeemer in Christ, and as Holy Spirit working in us, we confess our faith in the Holy Trinity. So we acknowledge and worship one God, Father, Son, and Holy Spirit.

Political and spiritual urgency was in the air when the 9th General Council authorized *A Statement of Faith* in 1940. R.C. Chalmers wrote, "the totalitarian tendencies of our time are the perverted expression of that deep hunger in the heart of man for some ruling principle."[28] Careful, thoughtful theological work was needed for that troubled time.

In 1943 John Dow published *This Is Our Faith: An Exposition of the Statement of Faith of the United Church of Canada*. It is lyrical, doxological writing. God is spirit, he says, "mysterious invisible reality all around, entering every corner and cranny of life, always penetrating, always alive, invigorating; sometimes jostling, imperious, compelling, like a tempest blast, sometimes gentle, wooing, caressing, like a summer breeze."[29] Dow outlines the essential nature of God in which we cannot think of the divine reality without the mighty act of the unique incarnation of Jesus, nor sustain a redeemed life without the activity of the Spirit:

> But how was it possible for me in the Word preached to see Jesus and in him to recognize God Himself appropriating me? Why did my soul tremble in that joy and not another's? Because there is a third participant in that vitalizing contact. A power took hold of me and gently but irresistibly made me confront Jesus: I enjoyed a sharing of, or partnership in, the Spirit of God.[30]

Here we see an essential understanding that God is present and personal, that life and our lives have purpose, and that God will never let us go. Dow clarifies the denomination's understanding of the Three-Personed God by looking to Greek and Latin terminology. Greek Christians spoke of one Being (*ousia*) of God within which were three underlying realities (*hypostasis*). The Latin Christians translated *hypostasis* to *persona*. They meant persons in the sense that you and I can have a relationship with each of them. In English, however, the word can mean *persona* as in an actor's role, rather than a personality. Hence it is wrong, for instance, to think of Jesus as merely "a phase or attribute of the divine." The word "person," Dow goes on to say, is additionally problematic because it sounds like three separate individuals. He wants us to understand the Godhead as *less definite* than "person" but *more definite* than "aspect" or "attribute."[31] In addition to what Dow calls the analogy of a society, he calls on Augustine, who spoke of God in the analogy of love: the lover, the beloved, and the love that binds. This language appears again in *A Song of Faith*, sixty years after the time of Dow's writing. He is clear that there are not "three Gods nor even three manifestations of God." Indeed, "our assertion is that we always deal with God in His wholeness."[32]

If *This Is Our Faith* was meant for adult readers, young people were not left out. My cousin once took me to her Sunday school class. The teacher gave me a turn to answer a *Catechism* question: "Who is God?" Surprised at the plain question, I stammered something about Abraham, Jesus, and St. Paul. I was wrong, apparently. "God is the Almighty Father," the teacher corrected, "who made and controls all things according to His holy, wise, and good purpose."[33] In 1944 the Committee on Christian Faith published this *Catechism*, a series of eighty-six questions as a summary of a "great body of Christian truth, essentially unchanged throughout the ages."[34] The tenth question is *What do we mean when we speak of the Trinity?* The answer is: "We mean that God has revealed Himself as the Father in heaven, as the Lord Jesus Christ who suffered and died for us, and as the Holy Spirit who works within us renewing our minds and hearts." The brevity is noteworthy, concealing centuries of complications. But it was a good start.

A Companion to the Catechism, published a year later and expressly intended for congregational teaching, "reclothed the skeleton" of the sparsely articulated answers.[35] "The Trinity is not just an abstract theory," wrote Arthur Lochead, its author. "It is a spiritual experience that God has given to His people." Christians "believe as firmly as Jews or Mohammedans or Unitarians that there is but one God," but this one God is like a stage actor with three roles, the "one God appearing in different circumstances as Father, Son and Holy Spirit." He explains that God was known as one almighty Creator until after the resurrection when believers began to worship Jesus as God, and a third form of God's activity was revealed at Pentecost when they recognized this Spirit as the Spirit that rested on Jesus at his baptism. [36] The *Companion* went into a twelfth printing in 1966, around the time I attended my cousin's Sunday school.

Ecumenical Councils

Another core expression of the UCC's Trinitarian faith and life is the denomination's active participation in several ecumenical bodies, some of which it was instrumental in founding. "We must address the crisis of faith and articulate why we do what we do," Lois Wilson says. If we are interested in a robust faith, a faith that makes change, "we must be ecumenical; we must be in the public square."[37] The UCC is a founding member of the WCC, in which Trinitarian faith is considered essential: "The World Council of Churches is a fellowship of churches which confess the Lord Jesus Christ as God and Saviour according to the Scriptures, and therefore seek to fulfill together their common calling to the glory of the one God, Father, Son and Holy Spirit."[38] The global, political, worshipping, patient, risk-taking, ecumenical network brings a worldwide public voice to the activity of churches in the name of the Holy Trinity. Trinitarian identity empowers this community. Similarly, the World Communion of Reformed Churches affirms as its basis "the Word of the triune God, incarnate in Jesus Christ and revealed in the holy Scriptures of the Old and New Testaments through the power of the Holy Spirit. It is to this triune God that the church bears witness."[39] The World Methodist Council churches "stand within the continuity of the one universal Church, confessing Jesus Christ as Lord and Savior, worshipping the one God, Father, Son and Holy Spirit, preaching the one gospel, and accepting the authority of the holy Scriptures, and the creeds of the early church."[40] Finally, the Canadian Council of Churches professes that it is "a community of churches which confess the Lord Jesus Christ as God and Saviour according to the Scriptures and therefore seek to fulfill together their common calling to the glory of one God, Father, Son and Holy Spirit."[41] Membership and work within these ecumenical associations have been significant in the UCC's sense of identity, especially as vehicles for the pursuit of social justice and human rights. At the same time, their Trinitarian foundations have always been on display.

There is nothing straightforward about those foundations, however. It is the "poverty of language," John Mackintosh Shaw wrote in 1953, that presents imprecision and confusion when discussing the Trinity. "'One God in

Three Persons' was simply an attempt to conserve and express in intellectual terms, in the language of the day, the richness or fulness [sic] of the Christian experience of God."[42] Analogies drawn from human life are helpful but inadequate, even Augustine's "memory, understanding and will" and "love, the object loved, and the love which unites the two." Mathematical analogies help: a unit is one and a unity is made up of parts. Shaw is adamant that the Triune God is the essence of experience, not speculation or the development of comparative religion.

"No one has thought of a better way of expressing what has really happened," observed Norman Langford, writing for teachers of young teens in a Canadian Bible Lesson Series in 1954. Belief in God is reasonable, intelligent, and *true* (his italics), and he claims that there is mystery about it. Langford calls the doctrine of the Trinity "one of the most important achievements of theology." For a teaching tool he offered the Medieval Shield of the Trinity, a compact triangular drawing with geometric symmetry indicating equivalence and distinctiveness. The teacher would conclude the lesson with these words: "We know God, then, in three ways: as the Father in heaven revealed by Jesus; as Jesus Christ who reveals the Father; as God, the Holy Spirit, working in us to make us Christian in thought and deed." He acknowledges that "it is a hard doctrine to grasp."[43]

In the clear and helpful *The Word and the Way*, the first published teaching text in the 1960s Sunday School series called *The New Curriculum*, Donald Mathers did not offer lengthy teaching on the doctrine of the Trinity, but wrote succinctly: "The authority of God, of Christ, and of the Spirit may be distinguished, but they are not different, and this is what the doctrine of the Trinity means when it affirms the unity of the three persons in the Godhead."[44] This *New Curriculum* taught about Jesus through Bible stories, interpretation, and ethical living. God was taught as a loving Father to nursery, kindergarten, and grade one children in books such as *God Is Always with Us* and *Fairest Lord Jesus*. The older children's curriculum is heavily Christological, with little commentary on the Spirit. In *Power to Become*, high school seniors were taught docetism, monarchianism, Arianism, and the incarnation.[45] The focus on Jesus reflects a priority of Christology over Trinitarian theology. The longest commentary on the Trinity is the mere two and a half pages in *Project:World*, intended for teenagers. It presents the Trinity as the three major ways of God's communication and disciples' experience. The Shema, the compelling presence of Jesus, plus the power of the Spirit at Pentecost and "a thousand experiences since" are mystery not philosophy. It offers the analogy of eye, hand, and foot: different work, one body.[46] Phyllis Airhart observed that the release of *The New Curriculum* "coincided with the stir over John A.T. Robinson's *Honest to God*, so it was widely but wrongly assumed to be an expression of the theological trends of the 1960s—as if the United Church had rushed publication to be 'relevant' to the debate."[47] Bishop Robinson called on the church – his Church of England and the wider Western church – to discard ideas of a God "out there." "In traditional Christian theology," Robinson wrote, "the doctrine of the Trinity witnesses to the self-subsistence of this divine Being outside us and apart from us."[48] But that perspective did not always sit well. Was God really outside and apart from us? Was the Trinity an irrelevant theological construct? Would the church change vocabulary or look for new meaning?

A New Creed (1968)

The meaning and liturgical expression of baptism led in large part to the creation of both *A Statement of Faith* and *A New Creed*.[49] That discussion is found in the chapter on sacraments in this volume. *A New Creed* began with the affirmation, "Man is not alone." The opening phrase, the Committee on Christian Faith wrote, "should not be mistaken as a displacement of God from the centre of this expression of faith." It rather makes "contact with contemporary persons beset by questions about man, lostness and loneliness on the one hand and man's self-sufficiency in world affairs on the other."[50] A witness to the Triune God immediately follows: God is acknowledged first as "who has created and is creating"; second as Jesus, "the true Man who reconciles and makes new"; third as the Spirit "who works in us and others."[51] Note that it defines what the three Persons *do*. The Committee drew "attention to the fact that almost every creed which has established itself in the life of the Church has followed a Trinitarian pattern, with affirmations about God the Father, God the Son and God the Holy Spirit, and concluding with statements about the church and human destiny."[52] The Committee respectfully acknowledged contemporary problems with the classical creeds. One problem is meaning: issues of "substance" and "persons" found in the Nicene Creed have historically subtle meanings, all of which may not be "a very useful instrument for the instruction of the young or the praise of the congregation."[53] Another problem is emphasis: the classical creeds may be seen to present the faith with an intellectual or doctrinal emphasis rather than emphasizing moral and social implications.[54] The ancient heresies were old news, and clarity was the issue. As was emphasized by others in years gone by, religious *experience* of the Triune God inspires one to seek increasingly connected, moral, and socially just relationships. The Committee decided to stress the church's response to God through action: "to love and serve others, to seek justice and resist evil."[55] The faith expressions of congregants are the heart of any theological proposition. *A New Creed* affirmed faith in the Triune God, yet embraced modern life.

The Committee on Christian Faith subsequently recommended that "in the service books soon to be published there be included at least the Apostles' Creed, the Nicene Creed, the Statement of Faith by the United Church of Christ in the USA and the new creed prepared by this Committee."[56] Indeed, the contemporary faith statements were placed conveniently inside the front cover of the 1969 *Service Book for the Use of Ministers Conducting Public Worship*, and the historic creeds inside the back cover. In the *Service Book for the Use of the People*, all four are found near the end of the book.

In the same era, *The Hymn Book of the Anglican Church of Canada and the United Church of Canada* lists sixteen hymns under Holy Trinity in the subject index. In the Festivals section, Trinity Sunday has four hymns. *The Hymn Book* was published in 1971 as Canadian church culture began to shake with liturgical renewal after Vatican II. Roman Catholic folk masses featured new songs with guitars; they had gone straight from Latin to contemporary language. Protestants were still singing heritage hymns with traditional wording like "was, wert, and ever shall be." Pressed for fresh music, the Joint Committee went looking for new material. Yet Trinitarian expressions in this collection are few, left in the dust behind popular hymns such as "Lord of the Dance" (#106) and "Sing We of the Modern City" (#125).

Feminist Critique and Inclusive Language

Questions and critiques raised by the feminist movement found their way into matters of faith, theology, and liturgy soon thereafter. "The work of fostering religious consciousness which is explicitly incompatible with sexism will require an extraordinary degree of creative rage, love, and hope," Mary Daly wrote in 1971.[57] She went on:

> It is important to realize that, even when very abstract conceptualizations of God are formulated in the mind, images have a way of surviving in the imagination in such a way that a person can function on two different and apparently contradictory levels at the same time. Thus one can speak of God as spirit and at the same time imagine "him" as belonging to the male sex.[58]

Daly was among the first to sound a warning about the male-bound language of Trinitarianism and its impact on human self-perception and the injustice it fosters in human relating. Daly argued that as the credibility of a masculine divinity decays, so does the understanding that the incarnation necessarily must be reflected in the male sex. The power of the awareness that all human beings are made in the image of God will take hold.[59] As the impact of feminist theology did take hold and inclusive language became standard within the UCC, vocabulary changed understanding. Feminine articulations expanded understandings not only of the Third Person, but the First Person and the Second Person as well, the latter visually in the bronze statue "The Crucified Woman," as discussed in the chapter on Christology in this volume. Elaine Pagels's studies of the Gnostic Gospels offered feminine alternatives.[60] For example, the Spirit, traditionally translated from the Greek neuter term *pneuma*, is also *ruah*, a feminine word in Hebrew. The Greek feminine term for wisdom, *sophia*, posits a feminine power of wisdom in whom God created the world. Feminist theologians critiqued patriarchal overlays and overturned traditional language, metaphors, and concepts of God. As a result, the UCC's expressions of faith and theology began to change.

Meanwhile the WCC presented *Baptism, Eucharist and Ministry (BEM)* in 1982. As Peter Wyatt says, baptism is our passport in the ecumenical church.[61] BEM built on work of the Canadian Council of Churches in 1975 when the five PLURA churches (Presbyterian, Lutheran, United, Roman Catholic, and Anglican) reached an understanding for recognition of baptism. Key to both agreements is baptism in the name of the Father, the Son, and the Holy Spirit.[62] PLURA is well known for social justice initiatives. Embedded within that desire for and pursuit of justice is the mutual recognition of baptism, social activism, and the Trinity. This is faith in action. Still, conversation about Trinitarian formulas remained lively. The debate in the UCC was one of conflicting values: ecumenical relationships versus contemporary contextual expression. Even as the denomination built on ecumenical relationships with "promising convergences in their convictions and perspectives,"[63] it asked: can the traditional baptismal formula be replaced outright with metaphors or expressions that are contemporary and contextual, that are more descriptive of Trinitarian functions, that employ inclusive language, or that are feminist? Creator, Redeemer, and Sustainer, for instance, or Source, Creator, Breath of Life? The answer—in order to remain in communion with ecumenical partners—was no.

In the 1980s, a series of five soft-covered booklets to supplement the *Service Book* provided "the church with a 'new generation' of services that are faithful to theological and liturgical developments."[64] The Trinity was embedded in liturgical understandings and theological activities, in old and new expression. A suggested Sunday morning greeting is the traditional verse from 2 Corinthians. A subsequently popular communion prayer invokes: "We thank you God, Father and Mother of us all."[65] This blessing is offered after services of penitence and healing:

> Now may the Holy Trinity keep you strong in faith and love;
> God defend you on every side, and guide you in truth and peace.[66]

Fresh Trinitarian blessings appeared, such as this one, for a wedding:

> May the blessing of the God of Abraham and Sarah and of the Son, born of our sister, Mary, and of the Holy Spirit who broods over the world as a mother over her children, be upon you and remain with you always.[67]

Liturgical language was starting to respond to the challenges presented by feminist theology.

Ralph Milton's lighthearted *This United Church of Ours* sold 35,000 copies in eleven printings through the 1980s and 1990s. It "became the standard text for UCC membership classes across Canada.... No other book or publication has been used as extensively for this purpose."[68] Although it is not an official publication of the denomination, it expressed theological perspectives that were readily received by UCC members. Milton writes:

> Christians have three ways of describing God. We call that the Holy Trinity. The word Trinity isn't mentioned in the Bible but the three ways of understanding God certainly are. The concept of the Trinity evolved later as a way of describing what people found in the New Testament.
>
> We think of Yahweh, the God of our ancestors, as all-powerful, everlasting, all-holy, all-loving. Eventually we simply run out of superlatives because there's nothing we can ever say about God that would do justice to the reality. That's why it's helpful to think of God as a parent, a strong, just and loving mother or father. Of course, if we have not had a happy family life, that may not be very helpful at all. We may then need to think of God as the very best aunt, or uncle, or friend or social worker we can imagine.

When we think of God who knows what it's like to be us, we think of Jesus: God the Son. One of the names for Jesus was "Emmanuel," which means, "God with us." So, if we want a flesh and blood example of what God is like, we think of Jesus the Christ.

And sometimes we're aware that God is right around us and inside us. That's when we speak of God as the Holy Spirit.

There aren't three Gods, just three different ways of knowing one God. Our joyful, lifelong journey is getting to know the love of that God.[69]

Charlotte Caron has identified that many see Trinitarian theology as an obstacle to women's co-equal humanity. She wrote about the variety of theologies across the denomination, observing: "For many with orthodox views, hierarchy composes part of God's order: God reigns above all. From the most conservative perspective the order flows downward—God (in the Trinity), angels, rulers, religious leaders, men, wives, children, others."[70] Hierarchy, grounded in God, presses down women, children, all of us. There must be other ways to understand and express God, if God is love.

The UCC experienced a flowering of affinity for Celtic theology beginning in the mid-1980s. It was as though the veneer of Augustinian theological expression had been peeled back[71] and legendary, poetic, symbolic Gaelic sensibilities shone through. Trinitarian concepts became popular as Celtic images and language were introduced in worship and retreats. In Celtic theological dispositions, the three-personed nature of the Trinity is straightforward. The mathematical analogy holds: the Trinity is singular, as a clan or a team is singular. Ivan Gregan writes of signs of the Triune God in the natural world, one thing in different states such as a tree, which is root, trunk, branches; or an egg, which is shell, yoke, albumen. He recalls an Irish rhyme:

Three joints of the finger, but still only one finger fair,
Three leaves of the shamrock, yet no more than one shamrock to wear,
Frost, snow-flakes and ice, all water their origin share,
Three Persons in God; to one God alone we make prayer.[72]

Gregan says, "The Trinity leads to and reflects concepts of community and relationship. It's not that everything is God, but that in everything you can see God."[73] Significantly different from classical theism, Celtic theology sees God as part of creation and beyond it, a form of panentheism. Augustine's

Mediterranean basin church used gendered terms decisively, but in Celtic theology the Person who is the Source is not the Father in the sense of gender identification but rather in parental form.

By the 1990s, the church was singing its faith with fresh vocabulary. *Voices United: The Hymn and Worship Book of the United Church of Canada* (*VU*) (1996) lists theological categories including "The Nature of God" and "The Triune God." There are twelve hymns about the Trinity in the table of contents, three others referred to, and thirty-two more in the topical index. The third verse of Sylvia Dunstan's "Bless Now, O God, the Journey" begins: "Divine, Eternal Lover, you meet us on the road." "She Comes Sailing on the Wind," by Gordon Light, was a huge hit among United Church members. Here the Spirit is seen before, during, and after the earthly life of Jesus. "Dear Mother God, your wings are warm around us" is the first line of a hymn by Janet Wooton. Carolyn McDade's "Long before the Night" offers a feminine sense of God: "Long before she wrapped her scarlet arms around the hills there was a love, this ancient love was born." In "Spirit of Gentleness," Jim Strathdee uses descriptions such as "restlessness" and "free." "Praise with Joy the World's Creator," from the Iona community, gives a verse to each person of the Trinity, and finishes with gender-neutral phrasing:

> Praise the Maker, Christ, and Spirit, one God in community,
> Calling Christians to embody oneness and diversity.
> This the world shall see reflected: God is One and One and Three.

Bruce Harding observed several changes between *The Hymnary* and *Voices United*. The role of the Spirit shifted from helping Jesus to being a wild and restless wind. Jesus became less a master to be obeyed and more a friend. The Father became the Creator but lost the sense of parent-as-Provider.[74]

Brian Wren wrote "Bring Many Names," another favourite in *Voices United*. He spoke of it as a parade of images for God; if you don't like one float, there's another one coming.[75] Here is the beginning line of each of the six verses:

> Bring Many Names, beautiful and good
> Strong mother God, working night and day
> Warm father God, hugging every child
> Old, aching God, grey with endless care
> Young, growing God, eager, on the move
> Great, Living God, never fully known

Ron Klusmeier speaks of Brian Wren as a bridge between what was and what can be.[76] Wren takes us from "Holy, Holy, Holy, merciful and mighty" to "God the All-Holy, Maker and Mother / Spirit All-Seeing, knitting and blending / Christ all-Completing, Nature enfolding."

The Roman Catholic/United Church Dialogue of Canada prepared *In Whose Name? The Baptismal Formula in Contemporary Culture* in 2001, just a few years after *VU* appeared. The report acknowledged that Grace is a more prominent doctrine in the everyday faith of UCC people than Trinity. "Trinity Talk" is second-order theological reflection focusing on our "relationship to Jesus as the fundamental origin of Trinitarian faith." Called to an "active and world-oriented love, United Church people tend to be drawn toward 'economic' conceptions of the Trinity; in fact, to speak of the 'immanent' Trinity may come only with struggle."[77] The report speaks of the "genuine pastoral concern" in the feminist critique of Father/Son language, which "suggests that God is more like a man than a woman and, conversely, that men are more God-like 'more in the image of God' than women are."[78] Consequently, the report considered both gender-neutral and feminine terms for the Triune God. New phrases came into the common lexicon not only for baptism but also for Sunday morning benedictions, hospital prayers, and small-group reflection: "Father, Son, and Holy Spirit; One God, Mother of us all";[79] "Source of Life, Living Word and Bond of Love"; "Father, loving source of all that is; Son, who came into our midst in Jesus born of Mary; Holy Spirit, who breathes renewal and strength in the journey of faith"; "God, the Source of love, Jesus Christ, the love incarnate, and the Holy Spirit, love's power." These expressions frequently describe the *functions* of the Persons, such as Creator, Sustainer, Redeemer, Sanctifier, Fulfiller. On the one hand, these functions teach about the expansive loving actions of the Triune God; on the other hand, taken individually, they may appear to narrow God's actions or inaccurately assign certain functions or tasks to specific Persons of the Trinity. This last move is a form of modalism, which has long been considered a distortion, if not a heretical view, of the Trinity.

A variety of recent theologians have struggled with these issues, including Sallie McFague, Harold Wells, and Douglas Hall. McFague, while not a UCC member, has influenced the denomination's thinking for several years. She has sought a paradigm for God and God-language to replace a distant, often-absent monarchical model, and moved toward a panentheism in which God is both radically transcendent to the world and radically immanent in the world. "This God cares so much about the *oikos*, the inhabited world," McFague writes, "that we are allowed to think of it as God's *body*. It is an outrageous thought, but both the Hebrew and Christian traditions suggest it is a better way to think than of God as a heavenly spirit who is indifferent to the world."[80] This is a radically present image of God. It is an understanding of God that leads us to engage vital ecological concerns:

> The God whose glory is in every creature fully alive cannot be a solitary, distant being. The "trinity" is a *model*, a way of speaking of God, that tries to express God's profound involvement in, with, and for the world.... The trinity is certainly about God, but just as important, it is about God and the world; it is a way of talking about God's transcendence and immanence in relation to the world.[81]

Harold Wells also reminds us about the immanent Trinity:

> What we are confronted with in the Gospel story is not a singular monadic Person relating to us in three ways, but something—Someone—much more profound and mysterious: God in relation to God! To dismiss the immanent Trinity, or God's own eternal triunity, misses the relationship of God in God-self, which is part of the Gospel narrative.[82]

The mutual indwelling of this profoundly communal three-personed God is awe-inspiring and consoling. When my loved one experiences pain, I do too. Look for awe and consolation in Douglas John Hall's writing:

> What I am doing here involves an intentional application of the principle of divine unity in trinitarian thought or at any rate an insistence upon the unity of God's *work*, as in the dogma of coinherence or *perichoresis*. That is, what we posit of the second person of the Trinity cannot be reserved for the Son only but applies in some quite definitive sense to the Father and the Spirit as well— *no matter how radical the consequence.*... If Jesus Christ is the Revealer of God and not merely a subordinate who, finally, submits to the will of his superior (the Father Almighty), then the cross must be understood to apply to God's own being and acting and not only to that of the Christ.[83]

Hall in these words repudiates the modalism of assigning specific functions or tasks to certain Persons of the Trinity. God in Christ knows the cross; indeed *all of God* knows the cross. God suffers.[84] This is real being, not simply activity. "What could replace God?" Douglas Hall asks, "social concern, or community? But these can't be long term for faith. They are consequences of faith."[85]

The first stated theological principle in compiling liturgical resources for *Celebrate God's Presence: A Book of Services for The United Church of Canada* (2001) was a Trinitarian commitment: "celebrate the presence of God, who is revealed in the biblical story and uniquely in Jesus, the Word made flesh, and who by the Spirit is at work in the church and in the world."[86] In this resource published in 2001, worship leaders were given fresh, imaginative Trinitarian language for hospital visits, small-group functions, and numerous other occasions. The editors refer to the 1975 PLURA agreement for mutual recognition of baptism by water and in the traditional form, Father, Son and Holy Spirit.[87] The editorial work for this collection was thorough, far-reaching, and imaginative. Note the expansive language presented in a communion prayer:

> You, Holy God, Holy One, Holy Three,
> Our Life, our Mercy, our Might,
> Our Table, our Food, our Server,
> Our Rainbow, our Ark, our Dove,
> Our Sovereign, our Water, our Wine,
> Our Light, our Treasure, our Tree,
> Our Way, our Truth, our Life.[88]

Further expanding of the imagination is found within the blessings for the conclusion of worship:

> May the God who dances in creation,
> Who embraces us with human love,
> Who shakes our lives like thunder,
> Bless us and drive us out with power,
> To fill the world with her justice.[89]

This benediction calls on *perichoresis*, vividly describes God's Triune activity, and inspires the blessed ones to similar action.

Just three years later, in 2004, *That We May Know Each Other: United Church–Muslim Relations Today* introduced a respectful, constructive way through Trinitarian theology into interfaith relations. This approach differs qualitatively from the concerns of Kilpatrick and the *Catechism* writers who saw Islam and Unitarianism as opponents to Christianity. Rather than a test for salvation, the Trinity is described as a lens: "Contemporary, historically informed thinking is finding that the doctrine of the Trinity, rather than being a dogmatic block to interreligious dialogue, is a basis and stimulus to it for Christians. The emphasis on Jesus Christ as a saving experience of and encounter with God is increasingly seen in a non-exclusivistic way."[90] Now the doctrine of the Trinity is seen as an invitation to interfaith relationship, rather than triumphalism or syncretism. The writers wrote of their trust that

> At the heart of Trinitarian thinking was not only the issue of God's presence in Jesus Christ but also of how and in what sense God is present in the world after the conclusion of Jesus' earthly life and how God was present to human beings before Jesus.... Can we not also expand these insights to see the Spirit as emerging and guiding the entire evolutionary processes of nature as well as throughout the world of human history?[91]

These are welcome words. Understandings of faith deepen as we engage with neighbours: "Jesus is God's self-expression 'once and for all' but not 'once and that's all.'"[92]

A Song of Faith (2006)

In 1945, Arthur Lochead noted: "Those who met together in patient and careful preparation of the Catechism will never forget the deep devotion to Christ and the fervent love of the Gospel that enlightened many of the discussions."[93] Sixty years later, too, preparing a "timely and contextual"[94] statement of faith was a joy. It would become the fourth of the United Church's subordinate doctrinal standards. The Theology and Faith Committee (of which I was then a part) that studied, discussed, and composed this statement of faith worked hard to define the Trinity. Popular terms at the time were "Creator, Redeemer, and Sustainer," but they are functional, modalist terms. They speak of God's relationship to us as the economic Trinity, but they are not names. They do not identify the Persons. *A Song of Faith*'s Trinitarian statement is found on the first page:

> With the Church through the ages, we speak of God as one and triune: Father, Son, and Holy Spirit.

We also speak of God as
    Creator, Redeemer, and Sustainer
    God, Christ, and Spirit
    Mother, Friend, and Comforter
    Source of Life, Living Word, and Bond of Love,
and in other ways that speak faithfully of the One on whom our hearts rely,
the fully shared life at the heart of the universe.
We witness to Holy Mystery that is Wholly Love.

These several metaphors invite reflection about the reality of the Trinity within human experience, and they invite conversation about how we describe God. In the Appendices, the committee remarked that

> the statement of faith recognizes the adequacy of *all* images or metaphors that speak faithfully of "the One on whom our hearts rely." However, the first designation of God in the statement of faith, that of Holy Mystery, serves as a reminder that all subsequent attempts to name the divine are simply that—*attempts* to describe a reality that is always greater than human language can encompass.[95]

The Holy Spirit receives more attention in *Song* than in the earlier three statements of faith. Human "hunger for relationship" is acknowledged in the Appendices, where the committee went on to say:

> The theme of "relationship" runs throughout the statement of faith. God's desire for relationship is cited as the source of Creation and the nature of the Holy Trinity. The statement of faith holds up Jesus' challenging ethic of love as central to Christian faith. And it uses words such as "partnership," "solidarity," "community," and the quest for "right relationship" to talk about the gifts of the Spirit and tasks of the church. [96]

The claim that "God seeks relationship" is a fundamentally Trinitarian affirmation of God and God's action among us. *Song* begins with that acknowledgement of mystery and the action of God, *seeking relationship.*

God is Holy Mystery,
beyond complete knowledge
above perfect description.
Yet,

in love,
the one eternal God seeks relationship.
So God creates the universe
    and with it the possibility of being and relating.

Gordon MacDermid cautioned other members of the Theology and Faith Committee: "In the United Church, we describe ourselves as Trinitarian, but talk ourselves into being Unitarian."[97] In his carefulness with vocabulary he pointed out that the current term "creating spirit" sounded like a convergence of first and third Persons, erasing distinctions, and that popular narratives of Jesus merely as friend sounded like buddy stories, totally human. Such liabilities remain in the day-to-day expressions of theology and faith among United Church members.

The following year, 2007, *More Voices: Supplement to Voices United: The Hymn and Worship Book of the United Church of Canada* was published, listing sixteen hymns in the Trinity index. Bruce Harding notes that the Provider sense of the parenthood of God is restored in hymns such as "May God's Sheltering Wings."[98] A fresh Trinitarian hymn is "The Play of the Godhead," which sings of the dance. Another is "When We Seek Language," which is set to a tune called *Perichoresis* and speaks of the challenge of Trinitarian doctrine and doxology:

When we seek language to praise you, O God,
All we can utter seems stale, tame or odd.
Tongue-tied and word-lost, we struggle to find
Phrases that slight neither heart, soul, nor mind:
Infinite intimate unbounded friend,
cosmic companion who loves without end,
Nearer than heartbeat, more subtle than breath,
keener than insight, and stronger than death.

Expressing the unutterable magnificence of God, it is a teaching hymn that praises God's triune actions, without naming the three Persons. There are also songs in *More Voices* that come from First Nations writers and composers. I am cautious about appropriating those lyrics as Trinitarian, though: there is a loosely hinged gate along the fence between appreciation and syncretism. Teresa Burnett-Cole reminds me that "Creator" is a personal First Nations term; my Christian Trinitarian reference to God as the Creator and Provider is something quite different.[99]

In recent years, Don Schweitzer has offered a *joyful* understanding of the Triune God. He characterizes the Trinitarian life of God as "a dialogue, the communication and celebration of the divine goodness and beauty among the three 'Persons' of the Trinity." He speaks of the love and joy they share. "As people's lives become a prayer in response to God's Word," writes Schweitzer, "they become a part of this ongoing dialogue of love and joy that makes up the divine life." We are agents, too; we matter: expressing in our lives the ongoing beauty and goodness of God, we are able to confront the challenges of contemporary circumstances.[100] Love, joy, and change: the Triune God is indeed not a defunct esoteric theological construct, but a perichoretic invitation to all the changing scenes of life, in God and in community.

In a Nutshell: Holy, Holy, Holy

"Trinity" is the second most common name for congregations in The United Church of Canada.[101] In such naming, there is deep resonance for this term and for the truth it expresses: the Relationship behind relationships, the pattern of giving and receiving love that is the pattern of reality, pattern of living, pattern of ethics. The doctrine of the Trinity reveals human attempts to understand the mystery of the wholeness and unity of God within God's self and for us. This pattern, the elegant simplicity, the ragged complexity, the fresh gendered and non-gendered names, and the ongoing dance: these are attempts over generations to understand our experience of God in Three Persons, Blessed Trinity.

NOTES

1 Mac Watts, "A Suggestion for Trinity Sunday," *Touchstone: Heritage and Theology in a New Age, Inc.* 25, no. 2 (May 2007): 5–6.
2 Steven Chambers, ed., *This Is Your Church: A Guide to the Beliefs, Policies and Positions of The United Church of Canada* (Toronto: The United Church Observer, 1982), 7.
3 Douglas John Hall, *What Christianity Is Not: An Exercise in "Negative" Theology* (Eugene, OR: Cascade, 2013), 75.
4 Edmund Hill in Elizabeth A. Johnson, *She Who Is: The Mystery of God in Feminist Theological Discourse* (New York: Crossroad Publishing, 2015), 220.
5 Interview with Susan Chisholm, Halifax, NS, August 2016.
6 Northrop Frye, *The Double Vision: Language and Meaning in Religion* (Toronto: UCPH, 1991), 64.

7   Interview with Earl Reaburn, Edmonton, AB, summer 2016.

8   Cited in Randolph Carleton Chalmers, *See the Christ Stand!* (Toronto: Ryerson Press, 1945), 281.

9   Cited in ibid., 294.

10 Cited in ibid., 296.

11 Cited in William S. Kervin, *Ordered Liberty: Readings in the History of United Church Worship* (Toronto: UCPH, 2011), 17.

12 Cited in ibid., 19.

13 Chalmers, *See the Christ Stand!*, 124.

14 Thomas Buchanan Kilpatrick, *Our Common Faith* (Toronto: Ryerson Press, 1928), 91.

15 Ibid., 86.

16 Ibid., 89–90.

17 Ibid., 88

18 Ibid., 86–87.

19 The Committee on Church Worship and Ritual, *Forms of Service for the Offices of the Church* (Toronto: UCPH, 1926), 22, 27, 30, 94, 103, 110, 132, 137–38, 143, 35, 126.

20 Susan Ann Lukey, "Precious Jewels: A Study of the Baptismal and 'For Little Children' Hymns of *The Hymnary* (1930) of the United Church of Canada," Master of Theology thesis, Vancouver School of Theology (March 1995), 191.

21 Ibid., 165, 161.

22 Ibid., 175.

23 *The Book of Common Order of the United Church of Canada*, 2nd ed. (Toronto: UCPH, 1950), iii.

24 Ibid., 77.

25 Ibid., 166–67.

26 Ibid., 1, 10, 19.

27 Ibid., 151.

28 Chalmers, *See the Christ Stand!*, 254.

29 John Dow, *This Is Our Faith: An Exposition of the Statement of Faith of the United Church of Canada* (Toronto: BESS, UCC, 1943), 3.

30 Ibid., 75.

31 Ibid., 82–83.

32 Ibid., 84.

33 The Committee on Christian Faith, The United Church of Canada, *Catechism* (Toronto: BESS, UCC, 1944), 3.

34 Arthur W. Lochead, *A Companion to the Catechism* (Toronto: UCPH, 1945), iii.

35 Ibid.

36 Ibid., 11–12.

37 Interview with Lois Wilson, Toronto, ON, April 15, 2016.

38 oikoumene.org.

39 wcrc.ch.

40 worldmethodistcouncil.org.

41 councilofchurches.ca.

42 John Mackintosh Shaw, *Christian Doctrine: A One-Volume Outline of Christian Belief* (Toronto: Ryerson Press, 1953), 96.

43 Norman Langford, *Discovering Our Church:* Canadian Bible Lesson Series, October-November-December 1954 for the Intermediate Teacher Unit 2: "The Church's Faith" (Toronto: UCPH, 1954), 39–41.

44 Donald M. Mathers, *The Word and the Way* (Toronto: UCPH, 1962), 186.

45 Eveleigh Smith, *Power to Become* (Toronto: UCPH, 1965), 183.

46 R.C. Chalmers, *Project: World* (Toronto: UCPH, 1966), 124–25.

47 Phyllis D. Airhart, *A Church with the Soul of a Nation: Making and Remaking the United Church of Canada* (Montreal and Kingston: McGill-Queen's University Press, 2014), 266.

48 John A. T. Robinson, *Honest to God* (London: SCM Press, 1963), 14.

49 Kervin, *Ordered Liberty*, 45, 56.

50 *Creeds: A Report of the Committee on Christian Faith* (Toronto: DMC, UCC, 1969), 17.

51 *The Manual*, 20.

52 Ibid., 9.

53 Ibid., 11.

54 Ibid., 13–14.

55 Ibid., 9.

56 Ibid., 21.

57 Mary Daly, "After the Death of God the Father: Women's Liberation and the Transformation of Christian Consciousness," in *Womanspirit Rising: A Feminist Reader in Religion,* ed. Carol P. Christ and Judith Plaskow (San Francisco: Harper and Row, 1979), 62.

58 Ibid., 56.

59 Ibid., 59.

60 Elaine Pagels, "What Became of God the Mother?," in Christ and Plaskow, 110–11.

61 Interview with Peter Wyatt, Ottawa, ON, June 2015.

62 World Council of Churches, *Baptism, Eucharist and Ministry* (Geneva: WCC, 1982), 2; Canadian Council of Churches Commission on Faith and Witness, *Initiation into Christ* (Winfield, BC, and Ottawa: Wood Lake Books and Novalis, 1992), 4.

63 BEM, vii.

64 The Working Unit on Worship and Liturgy, Division of Mission in Canada, *The Celebration of Marriage for Optional Use in The United Church of Canada* (Toronto: UCC, 1985), 3.

65 Working Unit on Worship and Liturgy, Division of Mission in Canada, *A Sunday Liturgy for Optional Use in The United Church of Canada* (Toronto: UCC, 1984), 35.

66 Working Unit on Worship and Liturgy, Division of Mission in Canada, *Pastoral Liturgies and Prayers for Special Occasions for Optional Use in The United Church of Canada* (Toronto: UCC, 1990), 20, 23, 29.

67 *The Celebration of Marriage*, 17.

68 Ralph Milton, *This United Church of Ours*, 2nd ed. (Winfield, BC: Wood Lake Books, 1991), 4.

69 Ibid., 121–22.

70 Charlotte Caron, *Eager for Worship: Theologies, Practices, and Perspectives on Worship in The United Church of Canada*, The McGeachy Papers, vol. 7 (Toronto: Division of Ministry Personnel and Education of The United Church of Canada, 2001), 186.

71 PhD student seminar, "Methodology," Toronto School of Theology, Spring 1983.

72 Ivan Gregan, "Hearing the Call of God" in *Three Ways of Grace: Drawing Closer to the Trinity*, ed. Rob Fennell and Ross Lockhart (Toronto: UCPH, 2010), 28.

73 Interview with Ivan Gregan, Dartmouth, NS, May 2016.

74 Interview with Bruce Harding, Victoria, BC, January 22, 2016.

75 Remarks by Brian Wren, Naramata Centre summer program, early 1990s.

76 Interview with Ron Klusmeier, Victoria, BC, January 23, 2016.

77 The United Church of Canada's Committee on Inter-Church and Inter-Faith Relations, *In Whose Name? The Baptismal Formula in Contemporary Culture* (Toronto: UCC, 2001), 5–6.

78 Ruth Duck, cited in *In Whose Name?*

79 The Riverside Church in New York City is given as the source of this phrase. *In Whose Name?*, 25.

80 Sallie McFague, *Life Abundant: Rethinking Theology and Economy for a Planet in Peril* (Minneapolis: Fortress Press, 2001), 142.

81 Ibid., 143.

82 Harold Wells, *The Christic Center: Life-Giving and Liberating* (Maryknoll, NY: Orbis Books, 2004), 175.

83 Douglas John Hall, "The Trinitarian Presupposition of the Theology of the Cross," in *Douglas John Hall: Collected Readings*, ed. David B. Lott (Minneapolis: Fortress Press, 2013), 146.

84 Douglas John Hall, *Imaging God: Dominion as Stewardship* (Grand Rapids, MI: Eerdmans, 1986), 113, 119.

85 Interview with Douglas Hall, Montreal, QC, October 2015.

86 The United Church of Canada, *Celebrate God's Presence: A Book of Services for The United Church of Canada* (Toronto: UCPH, 2000), xiii.

87 Ibid., 322.

88 Gail Ramshaw in ibid., 258.

89 Janet Morley, cited in *Celebrate God's Presence*, 71.

90 The Committee on Inter-Church and Inter-Faith Relations, UCC, *That We May Know Each Other: United Church–Muslim Relations Today* (Toronto: UCC, 2004), 66.

91 Ibid., 67.

92 Ibid.

93 Lochead, *A Companion to the Catechism*, iii.

94 These words were offered by Peter Wyatt at General Council when a new statement of faith was commissioned, and became the catchphrase for the project.

95 www.united-church.ca/sites/default/files/resources/song-of-faith.docx, 12.

96 Ibid., 14.

97 Catherine Faith MacLean, Theology and Faith Committee meeting notes.

98 Interview with Bruce Harding, Victoria, BC, January 22, 2016.

99 Interview with Teresa Burnett-Cole, Ottawa, ON, June 2, 2015.

100 Don Schweitzer, *Jesus Christ for Contemporary Life: His Person, Work, and Relationships* (Eugene, OR: Cascade, 2012), 283–84.

101 Trinity (127 preaching points) is second only to St. Andrew's (171). UCC, *Yearbook* (2014).

CHAPTER TWO

SCRIPTURE AND REVELATION IN THE UNITED CHURCH OF CANADA

Robert C. Fennell

Spending time with more than one United Church congregation or group will quickly reveal that approaches to Scripture vary widely within the denomination. Without a firm requirement that all persons adhere to a single interpretive approach or even to a common doctrinal standard, there is a great deal of freedom in how UCC members may treat the Bible. Individuals may revere or reject it; they may honour it as the inspired Word of God; regard it as merely one piece of literature among millions of others; find in it a treasure trove of wisdom; see it as containing the actual words of God; or hold any number of other perspectives. Nonetheless, the denomination itself, in its conciliar decisions and publications, does not express such a broad range of options. Rather, there is consistent regard for the Bible's unique power to transform human lives and to communicate about the reality and purposes of God. The centuries-old struggle to interpret the sacred text is alive and well in the UCC, but the denomination has always held it in high regard and has privileged its witness to each generation. A recent major theological development in the UCC (a decision of the General Council in 2012)[1] in fact identified the Bible as the authority to which all doctrinal statements and claims are defined as "subordinate."

This chapter considers the Bible within the theological category of revelation. Revelation, here, means the ways in which God self-discloses, or the ways humans come to know or experience God. I will divide the topic, then, into two parts. The first concerns revelation proper and the way the UCC has expressed its understanding of the doctrine of revelation. The second part is focused on one particular aspect of revelation (Christian Scripture) and, within that focus, the denomination's practices of interpretation. I will give special attention to the four subordinate standards of the denomination (the 1925 *Twenty Articles of Doctrine*; the 1940 *Statement of Faith*; *A New Creed* from 1968; and *A Song of Faith*, published in 2006). I will also review a number of other denominational documents to see how they can inform this discussion. Finally, I will reflect briefly on some aspects of revelation and Scripture that are unresolved within the UCC's denominational documents.

Revelation as a Theological Category, 1925–1940

Revelation is that area of Christian doctrine that seeks to understand and describe how God self-discloses to human beings. It begins with the premises that God does choose to reveal God's self ("What God communicates is never less than Himself [*sic*]"),[2] and that what is revealed can be discerned. There are a few ways to examine these premises. For example, one might speak of inward revelation, whereby God addresses or moves human hearts, minds, or imaginations; and outward revelation, those means God uses that are external to human beings, such as nature, history, or the Bible. Classically, *general* revelation (such as nature or history) has been distinguished from *specific* revelation (God's self-disclosure in the Bible and in Jesus Christ). The UCC's *Twenty Articles of Doctrine*, set out in the 1925 *Basis of Union*, included an article that combines these concerns:

> 2.3.2 Of Revelation—*We believe that God has revealed Himself in nature, in history, and in the heart of man*; that He has been graciously pleased to make clearer revelation of Himself to men of God who spoke as they were moved by the Holy Spirit; and that in the fullness of time He has *perfectly revealed Himself in Jesus Christ*, the Word made flesh, who is the brightness of the Father's glory and the express image of His person. We receive the Holy Scriptures of the Old and New Testaments, as containing the only infallible rule of faith and life, *a faithful record of God's gracious revelations*, and as the sure witness of Christ.[3]

In the *Twenty Articles of Doctrine*, there is no separate article on Scripture, but five sources of revelation are noted here in article 2.3.2: nature, history, the human heart, Jesus Christ, and Scripture. Additional sources of revelation that are sometimes named by other Christian denominations are not mentioned here, such as non-Christian religious traditions, the sacraments, or the church itself. The emphasis regarding revelation in most UCC materials after 1925 has been on Jesus Christ, Scripture, nature, and the inward discernment of the heart. Scripture has had a prominent role as a mode of revelation that helps one to understand other modes. In this sense, the UCC holds to a doctrine of Scripture as specific revelation without naming it as such.

Thomas Kilpatrick, writing *Our Common Faith* in 1928 to explore and explain the doctrine of the new UCC to its members, unpacks article 2.3.2 by noting that "'revelation' … does not mean the announcement of propositions regarding the Divine nature."[4] From very early in the denomination's history, emphasis was placed on being attuned to the reality of God in relational terms, not on assenting to specific tenets or convictions. Revelation was a doctrine about a person, as it were, not principally about ideas or arguments. But some sources of revelation are better than others, according to Kilpatrick. History and nature are variable, inadequate sources for discerning revelation. John Calvin, one of the UCC's theological ancestors, had argued the same thing in the sixteenth century.[5] As Kilpatrick put it, in reference to the phrase in the *Twenty Articles* about "the heart of man" [*sic*]: "More intimately and more definitely God reveals Himself in the heart of man. In the secret place of personality, where man knows himself, there is audible to his inward ear a still small voice, which speaks to him with Divine authority."[6] Even better, in Kilpatrick's estimation, is God's self-disclosure in and through Jesus Christ, who in turn makes use of Scripture to self-reveal. This latter pattern is the one most commonly seen throughout the denomination's theological work in the following century: namely, an emphasis on Jesus Christ as the normative self-disclosure of God, in and through Scripture in particular. In the 1950s, for example, A.G. Reynolds suggested that "the Bible is like a telescope, which is intended to be looked *through* and not *at*. We should look through and beyond the Bible to Christ, at whom the Bible is, so to speak, 'aimed.'"[7] The theme was taken up again in 1966 when the report of the Committee on Christian Faith expressed its "full agreement" that "for Christians, the revelation of God which has been given to us in the life, death, and resurrection of Jesus Christ is central, essential and ultimate" and that "our knowledge of this revelation in Jesus Christ comes through the Bible in the ongoing life of the Church as it is guided by the Spirit."[8]

In 1940, the UCC published *A Statement of Faith*, another creed-like document designed "to state [the church's faith] afresh in terms of the thought of [our] own age and with the emphasis [our] age needs" while "seeking always to be faithful to Scripture and to the testimony of the Universal Church, and always aware that no statement of ours can express the whole truth of God."[9] There is a sense of provisionality here, as the denomination expressed a measure of humility about its ability to speak only to its own context and era. There is also, however, a sense of stability within the doctrine that underlies *Statement of Faith*. The Preamble speaks of "the unchanging Gospel of God's holy, redeeming love revealed in Jesus Christ."[10] Once again, there is a framing presupposition that—pre-eminently in Jesus Christ—God is self-disclosing. Even though the words, idioms, and metaphors may change from generation to generation, the person and work of Jesus are a stable source of human beings' awareness and experience of the divine reality. This is echoed in article II of *Statement*, which claims that the cross of Jesus Christ "reveals at once God's abhorrence of sin and His saving love in its height and depth and power." Note again this language of revelation: God *reveals* Godself to us on the cross. The UCC is claiming here that the execution of Jesus of Nazareth was not just one more act of capital punishment against a political prisoner. In Jesus—and in his death—God reveals something of God's own self.

As a correlate, article III of *Statement* speaks of the work of the Holy Spirit, who actively self-discloses via the inner life of the human creature. By speaking of the Holy Spirit as the One "inspiring every right desire and every effort after truth and beauty," *Statement* expresses in greater detail the denomination's view of universal revelation. That is, revelation is not regarded as the exclusive domain merely of the Christian Church. Every longing and action that is Godward, as it were, reveals something of God at work in the world, active in human life and activity. This falls within the category of "general" revelation, mentioned above. In article IX, however, there is a much more developed view of Scripture as the laser focus of God's self-revealing: "We believe that the great moments of God's revelation and communication of Himself to [human beings] are recorded and interpreted in the Scriptures of the Old and New Testament.… We believe that, while God uttered His Word to [us] in many portions progressively, the whole is sufficient to declare His mind and will for our salvation." Care is taken in article IX not to overstate what Scripture can do. It is not the source of all knowledge and data. It is not a book of magical power. But it does reveal God's "mind and will," especially with respect to salvation. In a thematic emphasis that grew in importance during the ensuing decades of the UCC's life, the Bible is said in this article to *point* to revelation, rather than to function as revelation itself: "we acknowledge in Holy Scripture the true witness to God's Word and the sure guide to Christian faith and conduct." This understanding of the Bible falls within the category of "specific" revelation.

In other words, Scripture does something unique that other sources of knowledge about God cannot provide.

Finally, *Statement* alludes briefly to the sacraments as a locus of revelation in article X: "We believe that the Sacraments of Baptism and the Lord's Supper are effectual means through which, by common things and simple acts, the saving love of God is exhibited and communicated." The ordinary things of life—wine, bread, water—have the capacity to disclose God's love. When Christians gather around the sacraments, and share them in times of worship, they help to reveal what God is like. They are, in a sense, physical Scriptures. They help to tell about God and to create an experience of God's presence.

In summary, then, during the first decades of the UCC's existence, revelation was understood broadly in both general and specific terms. Nature, history, the human heart, and the sacraments were all seen as sites of God's self-disclosure, as described in the *Twenty Articles of Doctrine* and *Statement*. Revelation is also possible outside the Christian tradition. The more specific modes of revelation, however, were understood to be the person and work of Jesus Christ and the Holy Spirit, especially construed in relational terms. Finally, the Bible is regarded as the pre-eminent location in which to discern God, though the distinction is made that the Bible points toward revelation without being identical with it.

1940s–1960s: *This Is Our Faith, A Companion to the Catechism, and The New Curriculum*

Shortly after the UCC's General Council adopted the *Statement of Faith* in 1940, a new devotional/study book was published. *This Is Our Faith*, by John Dow, was written to help UCC members explore and understand their faith in light of how the *Statement* had expressed it.[11] In this study commissioned by the denomination, Dow took up the common theme of progressive revelation through Scripture, traversing the Old Testament[12] and culminating in the advent of Jesus Christ, who reveals God par excellence. Dow reiterates a litany of forms of revelation that are familiar from the *Twenty Articles of Doctrine* and the *Statement*: Scripture; Jesus Christ; nature and the physical world; and history. Dow also states explicitly that other faith traditions are means by which God self-reveals. Dow is quick to say, however, that these non-Christian expressions are "imperfect forms of the living and true God," and unfortunately he slides in a pejorative caveat: "these ethnic faiths have often been the futile speculations of darkened minds."[13] The sensibilities and theological understandings of the UCC today would certainly not cast such aspersions upon other faith traditions. .

A *Companion to the Catechism* (1945), written to provide more substantial instruction than the sparely written *Catechism* (1944), placed particular emphasis on revelation as specifically God's activity. It is "God who draws aside the veil,"[14] and thus revelation is not a human-driven project of finding God. This resource added to the list of sites in which to see God's self-disclosure with an impressive variety of sources: now science, poetry, art, music, legislation, social reform, and justice for all persons were ways to discover God. History, "the lives of great and saintly men and women," and the Hebrew Scriptures were also named as revelatory.[15] But, like previous UCC teaching, the *Companion* reasserted that "the supreme revelation of God is made in the life and teaching and death of Christ."[16]

By the 1960s, the UCC began to reflect greater openness and regard for the self-disclosure of God in other religious traditions and cultures, without the pejorative language of inadequacy or "futility" that John Dow had used two decades earlier. In that sense, the denomination reverted to its earlier, less hostile perspective with regard to non-Christian traditions. There was greater appreciation of God's self-revelation to non-Christians before or apart from encounters with Christianity. This is not a shift that can be attributed to a single factor or a decisive doctrinal pronouncement. The denomination's historical pattern of revising its perspectives in light of surrounding cultural norms had an impact. For example, greater exposure to other religious traditions occurred within Canada following a change in federal immigration policy and the resulting shifts in immigration from regions that had been less commonly represented in Canadian society, such as Asia, Africa, and the Middle East.[17] The changing understanding of God's activity among non-Christian majority cultures with which overseas mission personnel interacted also impacted UCC theological reflection significantly.[18]

Donald M. Mathers's influential contribution to the adult study materials within *The New Curriculum* Sunday school program was entitled *The Word and the Way: Personal Christian Faith for Today* (1962).[19] Mathers consistently returned to the theme of a God who desires to self-reveal, especially through the person and work of Jesus Christ. The heart of the Christian way (for individuals) and the Christian church (as a collective) is, to Mathers, intimately and inextricably bound up with a relationship with the Word—that is, with the reality of God: "When Jeremiah says, 'the Word of the Lord came to me,' he is not talking about being given some words of wisdom to pass on, but about coming face to face with holiness.... He is talking about encountering God himself [*sic*]. When the Gospel of John calls Jesus Christ the Word of God it means that in Jesus Christ [people] were brought face to face with God."[20] In self-disclosure, especially in Jesus Christ, God reveals God's purpose, nature, will, and so on. But the key issue is not the transmission of facts, arguments, or details, but rather the self-giving of God in a relational way. The vital and unsubstitutable value of Scripture, then, is its capacity to point to Jesus Christ, God's pre-eminent self-disclosure. In itself, the Bible is not revelatory. Here we see the impact of Karl Barth's perspective on the Word and the word, articulated in his *Church Dogmatics* nearly half a century earlier. The Bible *points* to revelation; the books of the Bible "testify and bear witness" not to the text itself, but to God's being and acts.[21] It shows us the one who is the Revealer and invites us into relationship with that One. Mathers restates Reynolds's idiomatic expression from a decade earlier: "The Bible is like a telescope: it is for looking through, not looking at."[22]

The Late 1960s and Beyond

In the 1960s, there was both an expansion and retraction in the conversation about revelation. A range of sources of God's self-disclosure was discussed, but there was disagreement about their status and also about the status of sources such as history and the natural order. *A New Creed,* introduced in 1968, assisted in clarifying the issues. This confessional statement offered new, contemporary language for the communal faith expression of UCC members, in contrast to the historic Apostles' Creed and Nicene Creed. *A New Creed* met with broad acceptance and was quickly incorporated into liturgical practices as well as local faith-formation activities such as confirmation classes. This creed spoke of revelation in concise statements, indicating, for example, that God "has come in Jesus, the Word made flesh, to reconcile and make new" and "works in us and others by the Spirit."[23] The clear Christological emphases of *A New Creed* point to the denomination's confidence that the self-disclosure of God is seen most completely in and through the person and work of Jesus Christ. This is a view that is consistently upheld in all four of the UCC's subordinate standards. Likewise, the work of the Holy Spirit is understood as a site of revelation. The self-revealing of God "who has come in Jesus, the Word made flesh" is not a neutral event, however. That is, in the incarnation, God is at work to "reconcile and make new." The incarnation—the ultimate self-disclosure or revelation of God—is an event with salvific, transformative consequences. In the Holy Spirit, according to *A New Creed*, God "works in us and others." This language is a nod toward an understanding of God's work and revelation through both Christian and non-Christian traditions. As noted earlier, this emphasis arose in part through deepening encounters with persons of faith in non-Western cultures.

Although the language of *A New Creed* is intentionally spare, since it was intended for liturgical use, the terms in which it is couched were carefully chosen and doctrinally allusive. They point toward an active God whose presence in history, time, creation, and human society has a specific purpose—namely redemption and reconciliation. In partial response to the Death of God theological trend in the 1960s, and the individualism of late modernity that emphasizes self-sufficiency, *A New Creed* indicated that it is indeed God who saves. The saving work of the triune God is also, then, revealed in and through Jesus Christ and the Holy Spirit. In response, the church is called "to celebrate God's presence" and "to proclaim Jesus, crucified and risen, our judge and our hope." In an echo of John Wesley's legendary deathbed utterance,[24] the creed concludes with the phrase, "God is with us. We are not alone." God has made known God's self and God's purposes, and the church responds with joy and thanksgiving: "Thanks be to God."

The denomination returned to the question of revelation in the *Report of the Commission on Ethics and Genetics* in 1977:

> But we recognize also that God is experienced as intimately involved with all the processes of nature, as well as with the history of [hu]mankind. [God] is not merely the one who occasionally moves from some other world to the earthly realm by means of intercession and intervention. Rather, [God] is involved in the process of creation, and the ongoing unfolding of the purposes and fulfilments [God] continues to reveal to his world and to his creatures. God accomplishes continuing creation, not by acting outside of the processes of nature, but through them.[25]

Here we find a denominational document on genetic manipulation appealing to premises ensconced in the 1925 *Twenty Articles of Doctrine*. That is, God's presence can be discerned in and through history and the natural order. The continuity is noteworthy. God's self-revealing activity is ongoing, present, and even embodied in creation. There is no room here to suppose (in Deistic terms) that God is radically separate and dissociated from creation. The life of God does not occur on a distant, celestial plane, but—in a way that this *Report* does not clarify—human and earthly life is taken up into God's life.

By the 1980s, the categories of *reason* and *experience* were explicitly added to the litany of means by which God self-discloses. Given the extent to which the UCC was embedded within modernity and its Enlightenment norms since its inauguration in the early twentieth century, it is somewhat surprising not to see the inclusion of reason in denominational documents before this late date. But reason and experience did become central to the task of describing how God is at work. The application of the "Wesleyan Quadrilateral" to theological discernment—a relatively recently developed tool that correlated Scripture, tradition, reason, and experience—was a key reason for these inclusions (see below for a fuller discussion of this development). *Future Directions for Christian Education in the United Church of Canada* (1987) reassured its readers that "'reason' enables us to explore creation through all the human and natural sciences.... It is through these gifts of mind and spirit that we receive the truths God reveals to us."[26] The denomination's theological disposition in the 1980s undoubtedly made ample room for the role of reason as a locus of God's self-disclosure. Reason was understood broadly to include elements such as the data gleaned from the empirical and social sciences, as well as the scholarly study of the Bible. These elements were central in the vigorous debates about sexuality at that time.[27] So personal experience also began to be held up in the 1980s, at least provisionally, as a kind of revelatory source. Critics regarded the inclusion of personal experience as simply the adoption of unfiltered ideology as a source of revelation, or even—at its worst—as the primary source. A more recent expression of the emphasis on experience is found in the perspective that the gathered community (usually understood as the ecclesial community) is itself a site of God's self-revelation. For example, in *Water: Life before Profit* (2006), we find the claim that "it is in community that we most poignantly find God and it is in community that God seeks to find us."[28] At the same time, the specific revelation found in Jesus Christ through Scripture is needed in order to verify that which is discerned within the category of "community."

The hymn tradition is another important source for seeing how the UCC expresses its faith about God's self-disclosure. The hymn "In the Darkness Shines the Splendour" echoes the Christological claim that the "Word made flesh reveals [God's] glory."[29] A newer hymn like "Creating God, Your Fingers Trace" and old favourites like "How Great Thou Art," "Great Is Thy Faithfulness," and the musical settings of Psalm 8 speak of God's presence and power in and through the natural order of creation: "Summer and winter and springtime and harvest, sun, moon, and stars … join with all nature in manifold witness to thy great faithfulness, mercy, and love."[30] Certainly these themes are iterated in many prayer and liturgical resources as well.

A Song of Faith, the most recently adopted subordinate standard or faith statement of the UCC, represents another phase of the denomination's understanding of God's self-revelation. Published in 2006, *Song* begins by acknowledging the finitude of human understanding with respect to God: "God is Holy Mystery, beyond complete knowledge, above perfect description."[31] God's creative power and presence are affirmed, as well as the loving and redemptive purposes of God in creation and in human lives. Creation itself reveals God: "Each part of creation reveals unique aspects of God the Creator, who is both in creation and beyond it." The Holy Spirit is likewise "creatively and redemptively active in the world" to heal and transform. A variety of experiences and locations—"word, music, art … sacrament … community and … solitude"—are understood to be disclosive of God's presence. Like previous faith statements of the UCC, *Song* affirms the uniquely revelatory status of Jesus Christ: "We find God made known in Jesus of Nazareth, and so we sing of God the Christ, the Holy One embodied." In Jesus, God is revealed in an unparalleled way. As noted above in my discussion of *A New Creed*, the incarnation is understood in *Song* as part of the salvific work of the triune God:

> By becoming flesh in Jesus,
> God makes all things new.
> In Jesus' life, teaching, and self-offering,
>> God empowers us to live in love.
> In Jesus' crucifixion,
>> God bears the sin, grief, and suffering of the world.
> In Jesus' resurrection,
>> God overcomes death.

God's redemptive work is expressed in Jesus's making new, empowering, bearing sin, and overcoming death. *Song* continues the theme of revelation to affirm that the continuing presence and self-disclosure of the Spirit in the world guides the church toward renewal, transformation, mission, and service to others. Ministry, worship, and the sacraments play their part in this dynamic.

In sum, the UCC engages a wide scope of sources when seeking God's self-revelation. Scripture, the sacraments, church life, human experience, nature, history, and reason bear witness to God. They point to the One who is revealed. They are the media for that transmission of experience and knowledge. There is an important distinction, however: none of these is the revelation itself. Each one is more like John the Baptist pointing to Jesus Christ, who points to God. Consistently, we find that the publications and statements of the UCC give attention and due regard to the means by which revelation takes place *without confusing the means of communication with that which is communicated.* We turn now to the matter of the Bible, and its particular place within this discussion of the doctrine of revelation.

Specific Revelation: The Bible

Among the many sources of revelation the UCC has identified over the years, the Bible remains central because of its unique capacity to disclose the person and work of Jesus Christ, who is God's primary self-revelation. As David MacLachlan notes, "The Bible has authority for us primarily because it speaks about Jesus Christ, the one the Christian community throughout its history has confessed as Lord and professed to follow in discipleship.... We cannot determine what our faith and work as Christians should be without listening to and studying the Bible."[32] In and through Jesus, the denomination has repeatedly declared, God is most fully revealed. In and through Scripture, God and God-in-the-flesh (Jesus Christ) are most fully attested. One place this conviction is crystallized is the *Catechism*. This resource, published in 1944, was designed especially to teach younger persons the Christian faith in light of the *Statement* (1940). The *Catechism* echoed the axiom of progressive revelation through time across the biblical witness as a whole. Climactically, "it is Christ that gives meaning to the whole revelation."

This thematic of Jesus Christ as the "key" to interpretation is well attested by many decades of UCC resources. However, this was not at all novel. This is an interpretive move found across virtually all of Christian history. Luther, Calvin, and Wesley—three important Protestant forebears of the UCC—as well as the Roman Catholic tradition, all make this assumption when it comes to biblical interpretation. Thus the UCC held to an understanding of Christ and Scripture, the living Word and the written Word, as being in a symbiotic relationship in terms of God's self-revelation. At the same time, the Word is not identical to Scripture. As the Committee on Christian Faith noted in the 1970s, "we cannot simply equate the Word which the Church hears with Scripture. Scripture can never replace Jesus as the Word of God."[33] While Scripture contains or points toward the Word, its boundaries cannot enclose the fullness of God's Word ("The Word of God, in every case, [is] larger than the text of the Bible.")[34] Even so, the Word cannot be heard in its fullness apart from Scripture. As the sixteenth-century Reformers argued, any claim "to have a word from the Lord" must be "tested against Scripture."[35] In other words, God does not self-reveal in a way that contradicts Scripture, when read *in toto*. Without the test of Scripture, readers are prone to become captive to ideologies, private imagination, and idols.

The UCC could never be accused of being biblicist or literalistic. There has always been a robust sense of the Bible as a human document, even though it is God-inspired. As an important study remarked in the early 1990s, "Christians do not believe in the Bible; we believe in the God who is witnessed to in it.... [As a result] not everything found in the Bible is to be taken as a direct word of God to us."[36] This conviction expressed a view that emerged most clearly after the Second World War: the Bible ought no longer to be understood as infallible. When in 1925 the *Twenty Articles of Doctrine* referred to the Bible as "containing the only infallible rule of faith and life,"[37] this reflected a then-popular view of Scripture as flawless and perfect. In time, with the growing prevalence of modernist modes of thought, this perspective faded. In particular, there was a gradual clarification in the UCC that while Scripture might "contain" an infallible rule, the Bible itself is not the infallible rule. By the time *The New Curriculum* appeared in the 1960s, the language of "infallibility" no longer held sway. As Mathers argued in one of *The New Curriculum* books, "If it is [biblical] infallibility you want, you need an infallible church, too."[38] The implication was clear enough: there is no infallible church. Accordingly, interpretive work will never be infallible, and so the church must no longer look to Scripture as if it were infallible. The 1966 report of the Committee on Christian Faith emphasized the point: "the scriptures ... must not be regarded as infallible objects of faith. As human words of witness to God (as self-revealed) they are subject to the fallibility that belongs to human limitations and sin. Infallibility belongs alone to God."[39] From that point on, the term was abandoned. But the problem of interpretation became only more fraught.

Theological Method: "Wesley's Quadrilateral"

It wasn't until the 1980s that a mediating rubric emerged to balance the denomination's interests in a variety of sources of revelation. The 1986 General Council introduced "Wesley's (or Wesleyan) Quadrilateral," engaging

Scripture, tradition or heritage, reason, and experience "in order to get as balanced a perspective as possible."[40] There was immediate enthusiasm for this approach. It appealed to an authoritative past within the UCC's Methodist roots (the connection to the Wesleys). It made use of a number of factors that were then in current use. It also reduced the centrality of the Bible, which, I would argue, was a priority of some in the late-twentieth-century UCC. That is to say, the Bible was increasingly considered as *one of* the sources, though still an important one, of God's self-disclosure on the basis of which to undertake theological reflection—but not the only one. Greater appreciation for other sources of knowledge, such as the natural sciences, found its way into UCC theological work. At the same time, some theological affirmations (such as the full human dignity of gay and lesbian persons, and the desire to include them fully in the life and ministry of the church) were problematic when a strictly literal interpretation of the Bible was applied. Other factors came to be seen as important, and sometimes as modifiers of a "Scripture-only" theological method. Note the language used by the Division of Mission in Canada the following year, 1987: "Each [experience, Scripture, tradition, and reason] can disclose God's relationship to us as a people of faith, and each can be a source for discerning God's intentions for our societal as well as our personal lives."[41] In short, each source has the capacity to be revelatory, and the Bible does not stand alone in the pursuit of wisdom. The quadrilateral was applied in a way that encouraged the introduction of sources and factors beyond the Bible into the denomination's theological work. This method was widely embraced. "Wesley's Quadrilateral" has had surprising durability, even though the person who coined the term (the late Albert Outler, a Methodist from the United States) later wrote that he regrets doing so, because in Wesley's method, "Holy Scripture is clearly unique."[42] The result, as Outler notes, is a temptation to regard all four elements (Scripture, tradition, reason, and experience) as co-equal correlates, something that John Wesley himself would never do. To begin with, "experience" to Wesley always meant experience of the Holy Spirit, not life experience in general. Nor would Wesley ever have accepted the ranking of experience, reason, and tradition as equals of Scripture. Wesley considered the Bible as the pre-eminent source of God's self-disclosure, and therefore an overriding or governing norm for all other factors in theological discernment. Just the same, the UCC's most comprehensive and authoritative study of the Bible told readers that "God calls us to engage the Bible ... in dynamic interaction with human experience, understanding, and heritage."[43] The four correlating factors are not only worthwhile, but— in this rubric—divinely mandated: "*God* calls us...."

Notwithstanding the popularity of the quadrilateral, the emphasis on Jesus Christ as the doctrinal keystone in the UCC's interpretation of Scripture has persisted. This emphasis wanes and waxes over the years but does not disappear. By 1992, for example, the denomination could still say, "God's historic self-revelation in Jesus Christ is crucial in establishing what has legitimate authority in Christian community."[44] Or, again, the same document stipulates that for Christians, "God's gracious self-revelation in the historic reality of Jesus Christ is the lens through which we must see and the scale by which we must weigh anything that claims authority in relation to us."[45] The Christological norm, as it is expressed here, is the chord most often struck in the UCC's treatment of the Bible over the years. At times it has been stated in strongly exclusivist terms, as in Dow's work: "If in Christ God did something for men [sic] that was utterly unique, there cannot be many ways to salvation, but only one."[46] In more recent years, such exclusivist claims have been softened, relativized, or indeed rejected by the denomination.

At the same time, the extended description of Jesus's life, ministry, death, and resurrection in *Song* (2006) points toward the confidence of the denomination in the reliability of the gospels' accounts of him. There are no intimations of doubt about the authenticity of the New Testament's witness in this respect. The Bible is considered trustworthy and true, a source to which the denomination looks for authentic guidance:

> Scripture is our song for the journey, the living word
> passed on from generation to generation
> to guide and inspire,
> that we might wrestle a holy revelation for our time and place
> from the human experiences
> and cultural assumptions of another era.

Note here the phrase, "living word," suggesting ongoing revelation in and through the text of the Bible. Even so, it is not a flat, static repository of data. Revelation must be "wrestled" from the text and understood contextually in light of experience and cultures both ancient and contemporary. This wrestling is aided by the Holy Spirit, who wills that the Bible take a norming role within the church: "The Spirit breathes revelatory power into scripture, bestowing upon it a unique and normative place in the life of the community." To this gift of the Spirit, human reason must add its efforts in the work of critical investigation and in interpretation that seeks to enact God's purposes—that is, to interpret with liberation in mind: "The Spirit judges us critically when we abuse scripture by interpreting it narrow-mindedly, using it as a tool of oppression, exclusion, or hatred." Without attempting to say everything that might be said about the Bible, *Song* names clearly that the Bible is trustworthy, is an instrument of God's self-revelation, and requires thoughtful and faithful communal practices of interpretation. This subordinate standard touches once again on the centrality of Jesus Christ not only to revelation understood broadly, but also to the meaningfulness and interpretation of the Bible.

Approaches to Interpretation

Like any contemporary Christian community, the ucc has a spectrum of knowledge about the Bible within its membership. Some are profoundly aware of its contents, its theological themes, its various tensions and teachings. Many more have a passing familiarity, recognizing a few key stories, topics, and figures. Still others have virtually no knowledge at all of Scripture. With such a range of capacity and previous learning, it is no surprise that the denomination has offered a wide range of approaches to interpretation.

For beginners who are children, various Sunday school curricula have emphasized Biblical knowledge and sometimes the memorization of verses. Hearing or retelling stories, creating drama, and making craft projects are broadly used pedagogies for instructing young people in the content of Scripture. As critical capacities enlarge into adolescence, pedagogies typically shift toward personal engagement and reflection on social phenomena such as poverty or war in light of the Bible. Adult study materials tend to blend subjective reception of biblical materials with scholarly resources. A good example of the latter is found in *Asking Questions, Exploring Faith* (1996). In this resource, participants are encouraged to respond to questions about their personal thoughts and impressions of biblical materials without directive input from a group leader or teacher. For instance, the following format is recommended:

> To explore each story, use the following process:
> Read the story.
> Pursue the following questions:
> – What engages me?
> – Whom do I identify with? Why?

- What puzzles me?
- What contradicts or challenges me? How?
- What do I need explained?
- At the end of the process, finish the Bible study by posing these two questions:
    What images, words, and experiences in this passage connect with my life?
    What is the meaning of the story for my life?[47]

In conjunction with this highly subjective and personal mode of engagement, participants in this study process are given excerpts from scholars to read, and are offered reading lists for further scholarly exploration. This approach—a blend of subjective sharing within a group context, paired with personal reading of more advanced materials—is a commonplace method of Bible study in UCC congregations. *Asking Questions, Exploring Faith* is explicitly geared to adults who are new to UCC congregations, but it is representative of a method in widespread use. Despite the proliferation of this form of Bible study, the denomination has not shied away from developing its own perspectives on biblical interpretation that go beyond the personal responses of individuals. There have been serious efforts to articulate common interpretive norms and techniques for the range of UCC readers— young and old, laypeople, ministry personnel, and scholars. The emphasis on developing interpretive practices is a reflection of the denomination's collective conviction that all persons will benefit from reading Scripture. It is not only the preserve of an elite scholarly or priestly class.

Six Principles for Interpretation

We have seen already that "Wesley's Quadrilateral" has been invoked in the UCC in recent decades, and that there has been a shift away from a notion of infallibility toward a broader sense of the "Word" as exceeding the bounds of "the book." But how is one to engage the text itself, when it comes time to understand and interpret what is read? Among the many reports, studies, books, essays, and statements issued by the UCC and authors affiliated with the denomination, six themes can be discerned that characterize the UCC's approach to interpreting the Bible: Christocentrism; arcing toward justice; Scripture interprets Scripture; pneumatic reading; experiential and contextual interpretation; and communal testing.

The first interpretive principle that appears consistently throughout UCC materials is *Christocentrism*. That is, the person and work of Jesus Christ are seen as a crucial lens through which the text must be assessed. As the

1940s *Catechism* put it, "it is Christ that gives meaning to the whole revelation [to which the Bible attests]."[48] Jesus Christ is the unifying theme and hermeneutical key for understanding the Bible. There is a reductiveness to this, of course, in that (for example) the name of Jesus is not evoked in the Old Testament. The way this is handled is by means of a theological perspective dating from the earliest Christian writers who saw Jesus Christ as the *scopos* (main theme, point of view, unifying perspective) of the Bible as a whole—Old and New Testaments taken together. This rests upon the theological presupposition that God does indeed self-disclose in and through Jesus Christ:

> The Christian reader approaches the Bible in the confidence that what the Bible as whole is talking about is God's promising and yet judging self-disclosure to humankind in Christ. As Jesus Christ is the point at which God's invitation to human wholeness and mutuality was most clearly spoken, so Jesus is for us the central norm by which scripture is to be judged.[49]

Or, as Reynolds wrote several years earlier, "It is Christ who gives meaning and unity to the Bible. He is the centre of it.... When we read the Bible, then, we must look for Christ in it. He is the key to our interpretation of it and our attitude towards it."[50]

In relation to general revelation (through history, nature, or "the human heart," for example), specific revelation via the person of Jesus Christ intensifies and focuses God's self-disclosure. With the Christocentric lens, then, the denomination has identified and chosen a specific interpretive approach that is well attested across all eras of the Christian movement. However, this is not merely a matter of "finding Jesus in every passage." There is no intent to contort the text so that it will speak about Jesus, and only about Jesus. Rather, *it is in light of* Jesus Christ, his life, ministry, death, and resurrection, that the UCC tries to make sense of the Bible. Thus *The Authority and Interpretation of Scripture* claimed that "Jesus Christ is the foundational authority for testing even our engagement with Scripture."[51] The work and person of Jesus are at the heart of this criterion: does interpretation (as did Jesus) bear witness to the One God, promote healing and reconciliation, denounce injustice, and herald God's Kingdom or Shalom Community? If interpretation succeeds in these things, it is legitimate, for it will correspond to Jesus Christ in an authentic way.

Adapting the phrasing of Martin Luther King Jr., I suggest that the second interpretive principle of the UCC is *arcing toward justice*.[52] Since its origins, and certainly with greater vigour in the last decades of the twentieth and the beginning of the twenty-first centuries, the UCC has emphasized the need for social justice. This is itself grounded in the Bible, such as the prophets' protests and the ministry of Jesus. Consequently, the denomination places a high value on interpretation that advances the cause of justice. In particular, faithful and legitimate interpretation must tend in the direction of liberative praxis—that is, actions that enable empowerment and justice, especially for those who are disenfranchised. The biblical text does not have monolithic or unidirectional power, however: it does not cause justice to spontaneously erupt in human societies. Rather, the dynamic interchange between readers and Scripture is, ideally, the site of transformation—in contrast to the capacity of that interchange to be a site of oppression, as when it is erroneously interpreted. Because "engaging the Bible is ... authoritative when it is experienced as liberating,"[53] it is crucial to attend to matters of privilege, power, oppression, exclusion, and systemic injustice. The Bible, and readers' encounters with it, is understood as a tool for liberation when used authentically and faithfully: "As members of the United Church continue to struggle to live out the Christian faith today, we need to recognize and confess those times when we have participated in structures of oppression and when we need to be transformed by the liberating word of God."[54] Negatively stated, this interpretative principle indicates that "the Bible is not the word of God when it is used to justify structures and dynamics of unjust relationships."[55] Accordingly, biblical interpretation requires, calls forth, and informs the human community's task of being and becoming liberative agents of God's grace.

Scripture interprets Scripture is a third interpretive principle, though it is not often expressed in this exact phrase. The UCC, true to its sixteenth-century Reformation roots, has always advocated the practice of reading the Bible as a whole work, rather than as independent units of data that bear little relation to each other. As a result, there is a process of dialogue that occurs in interpretation, whereby each portion of Scripture is understood in light of the whole of Scripture. So, for example, one studies the parables of Jesus in relation to the prophetic Hebrew tradition, or one reflects on the Exodus in view of what God has done in the resurrection of Jesus. Each word and sentence matters, but the UCC does not practise prooftexting. Instead, the broad themes of the Bible—covenant, forgiveness, reconciliation, care for creation, love, and so on—are in continuous theological dialogue with each other, and with each individual portion of the text. As Reynolds puts it, "To understand a passage of Scripture, we should ask ourselves: What light does this passage throw on the Gospel? Any? Or what light does the

Gospel throw on it? In what way is this passage related to the redemptive purpose of God revealed in Christ?"[56] Like Martin Luther, an indirect forerunner of the UCC, and like Augustine of Hippo, who lived in the fourth and fifth centuries, Reynolds claimed that "the Bible is its own interpreter. One passage will help us to understand another passage."[57] Several decades after Reynolds's claim, a widely used adult education resource produced by the UCC restated the principle: "We cannot give to every passage in the Bible an equal amount of authority.... A major concern, therefore, is to ask what relationship a given passage in the Bible ... has to the gospel of Christ. Does the text help us to understand and be obedient to that gospel[?]"[58]

Like the Christocentric principle above, this perspective adopts and assumes a very ancient principle of Christian interpretation: there is a unity to the biblical text as a whole, particularly in terms of its theological integrity. The text is trustworthy, in other words, in that the themes it addresses again and again are attested with enough consistency that a passage that is difficult to understand can and should be seen in the light of the whole testimony of the canon.

A fourth interpretive principle advocated by the UCC is *pneumatic reading*, that is, interpretation under the guidance of the Holy Spirit. Like other principles identified here, this approach is ancient and broadly attested across the Christian tradition. Related to the conviction that the biblical text is inspired by God (but not God's verbatim words), pneumatic reading anticipates the involvement of the Holy Spirit in the work of interpreting that very text. Consider the following claims:

[The Bible] must be read with eyes and ears sensitive to the leadings of the Holy Spirit[.][59]

We can only understand the Bible when it is interpreted in the light of the Holy Spirit.[60]

The UCC's 1940 *Statement* is especially committed to the importance of this dynamic: "The full persuasion of the truth and authority of the Word of God contained in the Scripture is the work of the Holy Spirit in our hearts; ... using Holy Scripture, the Spirit takes of the things of Christ and shows them unto us for our spiritual nourishment and growth in grace."[61] Indeed, without the Holy Spirit, interpretation is inauthentic or even false. The words of the Bible alone cannot accomplish anything in anyone but, with the Holy Spirit's help, can guide, sustain, teach, and transform.

Fifth, the UCC advocates for biblical interpretation that is *experiential and contextual*. The dynamic interaction between texts and readers, in light of their contexts, is the site of revelation, especially insofar as it brings about a more just world. Rather than supposing it is possible to interpret in a wholly bias-free manner, or with a "view from nowhere," the denomination holds the view that "God calls us to engage the Bible with an awareness of our theological, social, and cultural assumptions.... Every interpretation is driven by interests shaped by our personal and social contexts."[62] Contextual considerations came to the fore in Biblical interpretation particularly in the late twentieth century. The study process leading to the watershed document AIS highlighted that "context is crucially important for people as they seek to engage the Bible in a faithful manner."[63] Unless and until interpretation takes into account both the ancient context of the Bible and the contemporary context of readers, there is a sense of unreality or dislocation to the reading. Indeed, such a context-free approach tends toward inauthentic readings, whether through hyperspiritualization or the imposition of personal agendas (eisegesis). Awareness of and accounting for the world around us—the realities of society, church, and world communities—are essential. Political, social, and economic factors, and others, all play a role, and interpreters need to know where they stand in relation to them: "We all bring our assumptions and situation in life to the Bible, and this has an effect in what we hear it saying to us. Our assumptions about life and about ourselves and God may even muffle the Word we need to hear."[64]

Careful attention must also be given to the time, place, and values of those who first composed the text. These writers and their communities did not envision today's circumstances. There is plainly a distance between the contexts of the ancient writers and those of contemporary readers, and that distance needs to be acknowledged and understood. At the same time, the UCC maintains that there is significant, life-shaping meaning to be engaged through reading, interpreting, and applying Scripture in every time and place. Indeed, as noted above, access to God's self-disclosure would be limited or even blocked without access to the Bible.

The sixth and final interpretive principle of the UCC, as I have summarized it here, is that understandings of Scripture ought to be *tested communally*. The practices of communal discernment have long been valued within the denomination, and not least with respect to understanding Scripture. Reading together, discussing, praying, employing the intellect and the heart, and reflecting on the text in light of other sources of knowledge and various contexts are all important practices. Wherever possible—and especially when making decisions—such communal work is to be done. On the one hand, this is a clear judgment against private interpretation that one might seek to impose upon others: "As we hear the Gospel as Good News for ourselves, we need to be careful to test our hearing with others whose life circumstances, and consequent hearing of the Good News, may be quite different from our own."[65]

On the other hand, the ucc has never favoured a high view of the denomination itself having a magisterial function. That is, the ucc does not ask its members to accept unquestioningly the interpretation of the Bible as promulgated by an official church court or body. Reynolds advises that the Bible is best understood when read "by believers in the fellowship of the Church and under the guidance of the Holy Spirit."[66] Local practices vary, of course. In some gatherings, the community is elevated above the status of the text. In some Indigenous traditions, the teachings of the elders are more important than the imported Hebrew and Greek texts of another culture, even as the Bible takes its honoured place within the sacred bundle at the centre of the circle.[67] Thus in the ucc, communal reading is profoundly valued, as the community's own wisdom is brought into a dynamic relationship with the biblical text.

Outstanding Issues

In *Song*, the ucc restated the perspective that understanding Scripture is essential for perceiving and experiencing God. The sacred text is the matrix through which Christians can "wrestle a holy revelation for our time and place from the human experiences and cultural assumptions of another era." Despite the historical, geographic, linguistic, and cultural differences between its human authors and contemporary readers, the Bible provides an irreplaceable source of wisdom to those who seek God's self-disclosure. In a similar refrain, *Song* claims that "the Spirit breathes revelatory power into scripture." By the power of the Holy Spirit, in other words, God's purposes and presence are made known via the Bible. At the same time, it is evident that the role of the Holy Spirit, with respect to revelation and the interpretation of Scripture, has been understated in the ucc. This is unexpected, in that the Holy Spirit is so vital to expressions of personal spirituality as well as in various denominational exhortations and publications. It is also unexpected given that, in particular, the ucc's theological ancestor John Calvin repeatedly argued for the centrality of the Spirit in the right understanding of the sacred text. This is an area in which I would recommend that supplemental research be done.

Another curiously unresolved issue is crystallized in Karl Barth's work, in which he makes the distinction between the Bible *as* the Word of God and the Bible *becoming* the Word of God.[68] This tension is expressed in the UCC in that several important distinctions have not been thoroughly worked out. That is, from time to time, Scripture is anointed as revelatory in itself; at other times it is relegated to the status of indicating where revelation may be found (extratextually); and still elsewhere, the Bible is sidelined or minimized in favour of the revelation provided by experience, reason, or creation. This is another area that warrants further investigation.

Conclusion

The status of the Bible, and the best ways in which to interpret it, remain contentious in the UCC today. It would be naive to suppose that there is a clear consensus among all UCC members and adherents. All I have been able to do in this chapter is to outline areas of agreement articulated by the denomination. Still, Scripture is predominantly regarded within the UCC as a reliable source of God's self-disclosure and as a guide not only for theological work, but also for personal conduct and ecclesial common life. Scripture has a "unique and normative place in the life of the community."[69] Indeed, the General Council, on the strength of a historic process of voting across the denomination, declared that the four key faith statements of the UCC are "subordinate" to Scripture. Because it has distinctive revelatory power to disclose God, the Bible continues to inform Christian practices (prayer, worship, discipleship, service, preaching, pastoral care, ethical living, decision making, and so on) profoundly. Finally, the Bible functions normatively in the UCC, especially because of its capacity to relate important dimensions of Jesus Christ's life and significance. The UCC has not relegated the Bible to the status of "mere myth," one more curious document in the vast smorgasbord of spirituality. Indeed, it remains central for the denomination, its life, and its work.[70]

NOTES

1   UCC, *Proceeedings*, GC41, 2012, notes on page 151 that three remits were approved, confirming the status of four subordinate standards as the basis of United Church of Canada doctrine. The minutes record this as a "historic

moment ... the first time a Category 3 Remit has been passed both by pastoral charges and presbyteries."

2   John Dow, *This Is Our Faith* (Toronto: UCC, 1943), 169.

3   *Twenty Articles of Doctrine*, article 2.3.2; emphasis added.

4   Thomas Kilpatrick, *Our Common Faith* (Toronto: Ryerson Press, 1928), 92.

5   Calvin held that creation plainly discloses God to all persons; however, like "grubs crawling upon the earth," we cannot see God's beneficence in creation, having become "dull ... ungrateful ... blind ... [and] all our sense ... perverted." Although in nature God "renders himself near and familiar to us, and in some manner communicates himself [*sic*]" we do not benefit from this self-disclosure. We need "another and better help"—namely Scripture. See John Calvin, *Institutes of the Christian Religion*, edited by John Baillie, translated by Ford Lewis Battles, *Library of Christian Classics*, vol. 20 (Philadelphia: Westminster, 1960), 1.5.1, 1.6.1, 2.6.1.

6   Kilpatrick, *Our Common Faith*, 94.

7   A.G. Reynolds, *The Means of Grace* (Toronto: UCC, 1952), 13.

8   "Report of the Committee on Christian Faith," UCC, *Proceeedings*, GC22, 1966, 509.

9   "Preamble," *A Statement of Faith*.

10   Ibid.

11   Dow, *This Is Our Faith*. This book was so popular and so well received, it was reprinted at least seventeen times! Dow is also noteworthy for popularizing in the UCC the notion of the Bible as a "library"—a collection of documents assembled with care toward a particular end.

12   Editor's note: Dr. William Morrow has noted in an email to Don Schweitzer that at present there is no standard terminology for designating the body of scriptures jointly esteemed by Jews and Christians and that Jewish scholarship generally prefers the term Tanakh, although there are several ways of spelling this. The United Church's most recent statement on United Church–Jewish relations, *Bearing Faithful Witness* (Etobicoke, ON: Committee on Inter-Church and Inter-Faith Relations, 1997), noted that today "Christians who want to move away from all appearance or suggestion of supersessionism, and who want to respect the sensitivities of people who see pejorative valuation in words like 'old' and 'new,' are trying to find another way of referring to what we have traditionally called the 'Old Testament.'" *Bearing Faithful Witness*, 10. However, no consensus has emerged regarding what term or terms should be used in this regard, and some in the United Church question whether the term "Old Testament" is inherently supersessionist. Accordingly the editors have decided not to standardize the term used for these writings

in this book, and instead have let the terms chosen by the author of each chapter remain as they are. Thanks to Dr. Christine Mitchell of St. Andrew's College and Dr. William Morrow of Queen's School of Religion for information on this matter.

13   Dow, *This Is Our Faith*, 171.

14   Arthur W. Lochead, *A Companion to the Catechism* (Toronto: UCPH, 1945), 12.

15   Ibid., 13.

16   Ibid.

17   Of the Immigration Act of 19 January 1962, Tobi McIntyre writes: "This new act stated that any unsponsored immigrant that had the required education skill or other quality was able to enter Canada if suitable, irrespective of colour, race, or national origin." Tobi McIntyre, "Visible Majorities: History of Canadian Immigration Policy," *Canadian Geographic*, Jan./Feb. 2001, http://www.canadiangeographic.ca/magazine/jf01/culture_acts.asp.

18   See the "Report on World Mission" in UCC, *Proceedings*, GC22, 1966, 301–493, and especially 341–44ff., in which the activity of the Holy Spirit is affirmed among people who have not experienced Christian witness.

19   Donald M. Mathers, *The Word and the Way: Personal Christian Faith for Today* (Toronto: UCPH, 1962).

20   Ibid., 92.

21   Ibid., 101.

22   Ibid., 95.

23   *A New Creed*.

24   John Wesley is reputed to have said, "The best of all is that God is with us" immediately before he died.

25   UCC, *Proceedings*, GC27, 1977, 53–57.

26   Division of Mission in Canada (United Church of Canada), *Future Directions for Christian Education in the United Church of Canada* (Toronto: UCC, 1987), 5–6.

27   See, for example, the following reports issued by The United Church of Canada: *In God's Image … Male and Female: A Study on Human Sexuality* (1980); *Gift, Dilemma, and Promise: A Report and Affirmations on Human Sexuality* (1984); and *Toward a Christian Understanding of Sexual Orientation, Lifestyles, and Ministry* (1988).

28   United Church of Canada, *Water: Life before Profit* (2006), 5, http://www.united-church.ca/files/beliefs/policies/2006/pdf/w143.pdf.

29   *Voices United*, 92.

30   Ibid., 265, 238, 288, 730–32.

31   *A Song of Faith*.

32 David MacLachlan, "Come to the Bible for Challenge Too," in Mary Anne MacFarlane, ed., *Asking Questions, Exploring Faith: Sessions on Life Issues, Baptism, and Church Membership for Newcomers in the Congregation* (Toronto: UCC, 1996), 33.

33 David Lochhead, ed., *The Lordship of Jesus: Report of the Committee on Christian Faith* (Toronto: UCC, 1978), 12.

34 UCC, *The Authority and Interpretation of Scripture* (Toronto: UCPH, 1992), 67. Cf. Dow, *This Is Our Faith*, 179: "The Word of God is not just the sum of words that make up the Bible."

35 Lochhead, *Lordship of Jesus*, 13.

36 *Authority and Interpretation*, 67.

37 *Twenty Articles of Doctrine*, article 2.3.2.

38 Mathers, *The Word and the Way*, 98.

39 "Report of the Committee on Christian Faith," in UCC, *Proceedings*, GC22, 1966, 509.

40 UCC, *Proceedings*, GC31, 1986, 163.

41 The Division of Mission in Canada [UCC], "The Theological Base for Our Educational Ministry," in *Theological and Educational Convictions for the Learning of a Pilgrim People: Future Directions for Christian Education in The United Church of Canada* (Toronto: UCC, 1987), O-5.

42 Albert Outler, "The Wesleyan Quadrilateral—in John Wesley," *Wesleyan Theological Journal* 20, no. 1 (1985): 7–18.

43 *Authority and Interpretation*, 10.

44 Ibid., 22.

45 Ibid., 23.

46 Dow, *This Is Our Faith*, 171.

47 MacFarlane, *Asking Questions*, 13.

48 Lochead, *Companion to the Catechism*, 32.

49 The Division of Mission in Canada [UCC], *In God's Image ... Male and Female: A Study on Human Sexuality* (Toronto: UCC, 1980), 14.

50 Reynolds, *Means of Grace*, 13.

51 *Authority and Interpretation*, 71.

52 King famously said, "The arc of the moral universe is long, but it bends toward justice." Evidently he in turn was adapting an earlier author's remarks. See Garson O'Toole, "Quote Investigator" (November 15, 2012), http://quoteinvestigator.com/2012/11/15/arc-of-universe/.

53 *Authority and Interpretation*, 26.

54 Ibid., 31.

55 Ibid., 68.

56   Reynolds, *Means of Grace*, 15.

57   Ibid., 15.

58   MacLachlan, "Come to the Bible for Challenge Too," 34.

59   Philip Cline, "God Still Speaks through the Bible," in MacFarlane, ed., *Asking Questions*, 32.

60   Reynolds, *Means of Grace*, 14.

61   *A Stament of Faith*, article IX.

62   *Authority and Interpretation*, 72.

63   Ibid., 6.

64   MacLachlan, "Come to the Bible for Challenge Too," 34.

65   Division of Mission in Canada, "The Theological Base for Our Educational Ministry," O-7.

66   Reynolds, *Means of Grace*, 14.

67   As related by Adrian Jacobs in conversation to the author.

68   See Karl Barth, *The Doctrine of the Word of God* (*Church Dogmatics* I/1), trans. G.T. Thomson (Edinburgh: T&T Clark, 1936): §4, 111–35.

69   *A Song of Faith*.

70   Portions of the conclusion are adapted from Robert C. Fennell, "How Does the United Church Interpret the Bible? Part III: A Song of Faith," *Touchstone* 29, no. 2 (May 2011), 21–29. Used with permission. I also wish to express my thanks to Matthew Heesing for his research assistance.

CHAPTER THREE

THE GOOD CREATION: FROM CLASSICAL THEISM TO ECOTHEOLOGY

Harold Wells

It is by no means obvious to everyone that creation is good, or even that the world is "a creation" at all. This is especially so in our time of frequent natural disasters and climate crisis. Yet, in *A New Creed*, The United Church of Canada declares its faith that

> We are not alone,
> We live in God's world.
> We believe in God:
> Who has created is creating....[1]

Rich experiences of beauty, order, and love undergird our conviction that the world, and our lives within it, are not meaningless accidents, but derive from a purposeful, mindful Creator. The first thing the creed says about creation is that it is "God's world." Thus the theologies of creation and of God are closely intertwined; if the world is indeed a creation, it must be understood in relation to its Source in the Creator. Yet thought about God as Creator must also cohere with what we know of creation—from Scripture and from contemporary science and experience of the world.

The United Church of Canada, formed in 1925, is very young and exists within a vast ecumenical and historical context. Its theology, therefore, cannot be considered in isolation from our long Christian history prior to church union, or from theologies that have originated elsewhere. In this chapter we cannot do justice to all of these, nor say with certainty where every person in "the pews" sits theologically. Still, we need to recognize that besides official faith statements and documents, and the contributions of theologians and scholars, questions and insights arising from the pews also have their impact.

A Questioning Milieu

Questions about the world as God's creation are real for church people, as for everyone else. They arise especially out of the physical sciences. What we have learned from them since the sixteenth century may evoke awe and praise for the Creator but may also intimidate and give rise to doubt. Copernicus and Galileo, Bacon and Newton, transformed our sense of Earth's place in the solar system, taught us about the functioning of natural laws, and inculcated respect for scientific methods of inquiry. In the early twentieth century, Einstein deepened our awareness of the mysteries of time and space. Since the discovery that the galaxies are rushing away from each other, astronomers, mathematicians, and physicists have calculated that an expanding universe was initiated by an unimaginable explosion—a so-called "Big Bang" about 14 billion years ago.[2] It is astonishing that this mysterious event was pregnant with all the beauty and splendour of planet Earth, its teeming, myriad forms of life, and contained all the elements and laws necessary for the appearance of our amazing humanity. Consider the glory of music and architecture, poetry and philosophy, science and technology, all potentially *there* in that initiating moment. Yet telescopes reveal planet Earth as a speck of dust circulating in one tiny solar system within the Milky Way galaxy that contains "at least a hundred billion stars,"[3] which is in turn one of billions of galaxies! We know that this little planet (presumably one of billions) was formed naturally about 4.5 billion years ago as a result of "gravitational instability in a condensed galactic cloud of dust and gas."[4]

The greatest shock to human pride came with Charles Darwin's publication in 1859 of *The Origin of Species* concerning his discovery of the evolutionary development of all biological species, including that of intelligent humankind.[5] Recent anthropological research suggests that our most recent common ancestor with the chimpanzees lived about six million years ago. Numerous human species (of the genus *Homo*) existed on the earth for approximately two and a half million years before the appearance of humans like us, *Homo sapiens*, a mere 200,000 years ago.[6] New awareness of the *continuum* of all life forms, from the simplest bacteria to the wisest human being, was humiliating to many, since hitherto we had seen ourselves as direct creations of God.[7] Basic to Darwin's theory was that evolution proceeds by a random process of "natural selection," by which the fittest (those best adapted to their environments) survive while others go extinct. This raises the question whether humans are products of divine love, or of evolutionary brutality.

Although the basic reality of evolutionary development is almost universally accepted within the relevant sciences, Darwin's concepts have been modified, through subsequent scientific discoveries, especially in the field of genetics. It is now more accurate to speak of "neo-Darwinian" evolutionary theory.[8] Debate rages among some theologians and some scientists as to whether a purely blind, entirely mindless, process could have produced apparently purposeful forms of life. Some atheistic scientists point out the evident randomness and wasteful dead ends in what appear to be unplanned, often cruel evolutionary processes.[9] On the other hand, other scientists, while not rejecting evolution as such, defend a theory of "intelligent design," arguing that the neo-Darwinian theory of evolutionary development is not adequate in itself to account for the "irreducible complexity" of, for example, the most elementary biological cell. As we are awestruck by the immensity of the cosmos, so also are we fascinated by the microcosmic levels of physical reality. These scientists point out that the cell, the most basic building block of life, is an immensely complex phenomenon, involving an assemblage of carefully crafted molecules, dependent in turn on similarly complex proteins, which could not possibly have come together by random chance. They argue, therefore, for the existence of an intelligent Designer.[10] Believers are likely to find in such data indications of a Creator who is engaged with the evolutionary processes of creation, breathing novelty, as well as order, into a magnificent creation. However, some theologians (evolutionary theists) warn against confusing science with religion, insisting that for Christian faith, "God" cannot become one factor in a scientific argument. Nor should "God" be inserted into scientific theories to fill "gaps" in scientific knowledge.[11]

At any rate, a contemporary, scientific history of the planet and of the universe clearly does not point to an all-controlling deity who creates, orders, and rules over all things by divine fiat. I suggest that, since the late nineteenth century, we have seen a gradual collapse of what is called "classical theism."[12] By classical theism I mean a doctrine of an all-controlling, unchangeable, and invulnerable deity—an all-powerful "God" who unilaterally determines the destinies of individuals, nations, and planets. Most people are long past ascribing calamities of the weather and heinous diseases, let alone torture chambers, the abuse of children, and vast poverty, to the will of an inscrutable deity. Nor do we find it credible that vastly destructive volcanoes or the arrival of life-destroying asteroids occur at the command of a loving God. Creation, within such a theism, becomes essentially the passive recipient of mysterious divine decrees. While many theologies jostle together in the UCC today, I suggest that the distinctive theological perspective growing within the church may be called "ecotheology." Eco- is the prefix commonly used (as in *ecosystem*) to refer to the way all living organisms interact interdependently. Alternatively, we might speak of a theology of "mutual indwelling," or "being-with"—inclusive of, but broader than "ecological theology." *Ecotheology* implies a profound and dynamic interconnectedness among all creatures, but also between Creator and creation, a perspective evident in the UCC's most recent subordinate standard, *A Song of Faith*.[13]

I shall begin by reaching far back into UCC history to explore the doctrine of creation in its earliest theological roots.

Ancient Roots

The theology of creation in the UCC is rooted in the Bible. In the *Basis of Union* (1925), the *Twenty Articles of Doctrine* affirmed belief in "the scriptures of the Old and New Testaments," confessing that "we build upon the foundation laid by the prophets and apostles, Jesus Christ himself being the chief cornerstone."[14] Here we can glimpse briefly only a few creation texts.

Many biblical texts are not to be interpreted literally as fact or history, but as symbolic and poetic. The ancient biblical authors knew nothing, of course, about the evolution of life forms. We read the creation texts, then, as foundational expressions of faith, insight, and witness. In the opening verses of the Bible (Genesis 1) the poetry of this post-exilic text declares: "In the beginning, God created the heavens and the earth" (Genesis 1:1). Who is this "God?" It is the holy, compassionate One who led Israel out of Egypt and centuries later was still present with them in exile. The ancient Hebrews were inspired by the insight that God could not be tied down to any one place or nation. The term "created" implies that this holy One transcends all creatures and creation itself. The Creator is sovereign. Repeatedly in this later of the two Hebrew accounts, we hear several times: "God said ..." The Word of God calls creation into existence. Creatures do not ask to be created or co-operate in their creation. Further, God saw all of creation and declared that it was "very good" (Genesis 1:31). God is delighted with it. It is beautiful. Creation is good also in that the man and woman are created together to live in a mutually supportive relationship. As God orders the "formless void" (Genesis 1:2), the man and woman, created together in God's image, are given dominion (1:28)—the task of co-operating with the Creator in the ordering of the chaos. "Dominion" implies a certain power and authority on the earth. Such power has been exercised by *Homo sapiens* for many millennia and has perpetrated the extinction of countless species that shared the planet with us.[15] But God's call to dominion is exactly the opposite of any permission to abuse or destroy the earth's creatures. The first Genesis narrative must be read in light of the second.

In the second, more ancient, and quite different creation account, beginning at Genesis 2:4, humans are clearly not divine but created "from the dust of the ground" (Genesis 2:7). They are given an important task: to "till and keep [the garden]" (2:15). This is a gentle image of humanity cultivating and caring for the earth. Again, creation is good in that human creatures are created to live in relationship: "It is not good for the man to be alone" (2:18). Human creatures are essentially interdependent and need one another to be fully human. We are created for love and for joy. Further, in the next chapter it is clear that human freedom is not absolute: God defines the meaning and purpose of creatures, placing limits on human autonomy (Genesis 3:2–3). Dire destruction follows when humans seek to "be as God."

In many Hebrew texts God is glorified as Creator not only of planet Earth, but also of the heavens: "The heavens declare the glory of God, and the dome of the sky proclaims God's handiwork" (Psalm 19:1). Creation is good not only for humans, but for the vast host of animals and plants, forests, and seas. All have their own life, independent of human beings. "Sun, moon, and shining stars, wild animals and cattle, praise the name of the Lord!" (Psalm 148:3, 10). The Spirit (God's Wind or Breath) lives and acts within creation, and her creative activity is ongoing, as in the great creation Psalm 104: "When you send forth your Spirit, they are created, and you renew the face of the ground" (v. 30).[16] This joyful praise is foundational for all that followed in Judeo-Christian thought about creation.

The New Testament too declares that the creation speaks of the Creator. The apostle Paul claims that "ever since the creation of the world [God's] eternal power and divine nature, invisible though they are, have been understood and seen through the things which he has made" (Romans 1:20). John's gospel links creation to Jesus Christ: the Word of God, through which God created all things, was made flesh in Jesus (John 1:14). We also hear that "in him all things in heaven and earth were created" (Colossians 1:16). Creation, then, carries eternal meaning and destiny, made known in Christ. But it is not in itself divine. Rather, creation is vulnerable and stands in need of redemption. It is "groaning in labour pains," and "will be set free from its bondage to decay" (Romans 8:21–23). That our planet, and indeed the whole material universe, is in itself mortal and finite, is confirmed by contemporary science. One day it will be swallowed up by the sun, which, in turn, will finally burn away and become extinct.[17] The physicist-theologian John Polkinghorne comments: "If the universe is a creation it must make sense everlastingly, and so ultimately it must be redeemed from transience and decay."[18] Christians, then, are not nature worshippers. That is why Christian faith and worship are centred not in the mortal creation, but in the risen Christ and, through Christ, in the eternal God.[19]

The authors of the BOU insisted, in forming the UCC, that they were not inventing a new religion: they acknowledged "the teaching of the great creeds of the ancient church."[20] Accordingly, the Apostles' Creed and the Nicene Creed are found in *Voices United*, the second-most-recent official hymn book of the UCC.[21] For many years, the Apostles' Creed was often used in the worship life of the UCC, and it is still used today in some congregations. Originating in the church at Rome about the middle of the second century, it declares: "I believe in God, the Father Almighty, Creator of heaven and earth." To confess the goodness of creation was an objective of this creed. It plainly excluded the teaching of Marcion (also mid-second century), who rejected the Hebrew Bible and its God, who, he believed, was the violent creator of this evil world of matter and flesh. Marcion despised sexual reproduction as repulsive, denying that Jesus was born of a woman.[22] The goodness of creation was rejected also by various groups of gnostics who claimed to be "in the know." They too were dualists, considering "spirit" to be good, but matter and flesh to be evil. The physical world was thought to be the result of a pre-cosmic disaster, in which spirits were trapped in mortal bodies. The gnostic Valentinus taught that Jesus was pure spirit who only appeared to have a real body of flesh; his suffering and death were a mere appearance (*dokesis*).[23] The Apostles' Creed rejected this "docetism." Jesus was "born of the virgin Mary." That is, he was a real child of flesh. He "suffered under Pontius Pilate, died and was buried," implying that in Jesus the Creator was present and embodied within the physical world of space and time. The creed boldly insisted that God was the Creator of all things ("heaven and earth"). The claim that God was "Almighty" excluded any metaphysical dualism of good and evil, declaring that ultimately no power outside of God could limit or defeat God. The creed was formulated to defend this hopeful, life-affirming message.

The Council of Nicaea, about two centuries later (325 CE) declares: "We believe in one God, the Father, the Almighty, maker of heaven and earth, of all that is, seen and unseen."[24] Here the council affirmed invisible as well as visible dimensions of creation. "Heaven" may imply the skies above, but also a "heavenly" created realm.[25] The second article insists that Jesus is of "one Being" (*homoousios*) with the Father, opposing Arius, who denied that the infinite, holy God could be incarnate in a creature of mortal flesh. Even if the Greek "substance" language of Nicaea seems fitted for a context very different from today, its confession of the incarnation of God in Christ is important for the doctrine of creation: the deep engagement of the Creator in the flesh of Jesus, crucified and risen, testifies to the goodness and dignity of the whole material creation. The third article, amplified by the Council of Constantinople (381), asserts that the Spirit is "the Lord, the giver of life, who proceeds from the Father, who with the Father and Son is worshiped and glorified, who has spoken through the prophets." This trinitarian affirmation emphatically asserts that the Spirit, who breathes within the whole created order, is one with the Creator of all things. Thus Christians of the fourth century declared that the world is a good creation—the dwelling place of God, no cosmic accident, no meaningless absurdity. Thus human existence in the flesh, including sexuality, is God's good gift. The pleasures of good food and drink, the delights of eye and ear, the exuberance of sport and dance—all of these are to be embraced as God's good gifts. For the early Christians, and for us today, it is a defiant, life-giving doctrine.

The ancient creeds, however, did not yet reach "classical theism," though some fourth-century theologians, under the influence of Greek thought, had already moved in that direction. We find in them no assertion of God's immutability or impassibility, for example. They actually imply (but do not explicitly state) God's suffering with the world, in Christ.

Creation in Classical Theism

While we cannot give a full account here of the long history of classical theism that the UCC inherited, we can glimpse some of its main features concerning the doctrine of creation. The concept of God without passions was stated most starkly by Thomas Aquinas in the thirteenth century when he wrote: "*relatio in Deo ad creaturam non est realis.*" That is, "being related to creatures is not a reality in God."[26] Though elsewhere Aquinas wrote about God's omnipresence, and God's love for the world, he states here that what happens among creatures actually has no impact upon God. Rather, God is immutable (cannot change), since God, "embracing the whole fullness of perfection, cannot acquire anything." God's omnipotence is such that "God's will is the cause of all things."[27] Moreover, according to Aquinas, God is utterly impassible, since nothing can act upon God. Therefore, God, in Christ, does not suffer. He writes: "The Word of God, whose nature is divine, is impassible.... Christ's passion, therefore, did not pertain to his divinity."[28]

Regarding God's power over creation, John Calvin, the Reformed church father of the sixteenth century, affirmed the presence of God's Spirit in all creation,[29] but above all he emphasized divine sovereignty. For Calvin this meant total divine control over creation, for the heavenly Father "so embraces all things under his power—so governs them at will by his nod—so regulates them by his wisdom, that nothing takes place save according to his appointment."[30] God's power, then, becomes a kind of omnicausality or divine determinism, discounting any real autonomy in the created order.[31] Such a monarchical monotheism must be seen as insufficiently Trinitarian.[32] Moreover, an all-controlling divine monarch tends to legitimize domineering rulers and an imperialistic, oppressive Christianity.

Twenty Articles of Doctrine

Leaping another four centuries forward, we hear echoes of the ancient creeds, and also of classical theism, in the UCC's BOU (1925). Article IV asserts that God is the "Creator, Upholder and Governor of all things; that he is above all things and in them all; and that He made man in His own image, meet for fellowship with Him, free and able to choose between good and evil, and responsible to his Maker and Lord." Notably, in Article II, creation is accorded revelatory significance in that God is said to be "revealed in nature, in history, and in the heart of man." Article V speaks of "our first parents who, being tempted, fell under the power of sin, and because of whom all men are born with a sinful nature."[33] Historian John Webster Grant comments that this seems "surprisingly conservative, especially in relation to the period that produced it."[34] In the late nineteenth century, a number of theological teachers, both Methodist and Presbyterian, were open to the new biblical criticism and evolutionary science, and by the 1920s there was "widespread acceptance within the church of Darwinism."[35]

We should recognize that John Wesley stands behind this openness within the Methodist-UCC tradition. Wesley was the great English (Anglican) evangelist who lived and worked in the eighteenth century. As founding father of the Methodist movement, he opposed Calvin's doctrine that God is the cause of all things, particularly repudiating his doctrine of predestination and insisting on the freedom of men and women to accept or reject the gospel. Far preceding evolutionary science, Wesley was nevertheless open to the science and philosophy of his day.[36] In his theology, we see early cracks in the cement of classical theism.

An important Wesleyan Methodist in Canada was the evangelical liberal theologian and church leader Nathanael Burwash. A passionate advocate of Wesleyan evangelical faith, Burwash was also adamant in his affirmation of "the higher criticism" in biblical studies, and of reason and science.[37] In the publication in 1859 of Darwin's *On the Origin of Species*, Burwash recognized a challenge to any literal interpretation of the Genesis accounts of creation. By 1885 he had accepted evolutionary theory—"the most influential scientific doctrine of our time."[38] As professor of Systematic Theology at Victoria College in Toronto, Burwash successfully defended the biblical scholar George Jackson, who was attacked at the General Conference of 1910 for his critical lectures on the Genesis creation texts. This victory for the historical-critical method of interpretation set the tone for biblical studies in the Methodist Church, and later the ucc.[39] It is remarkable, then, that the 1925 *Twenty Articles of Doctrine* reflected nothing about evolutionary science. However, the acknowledgement of evolution by theologians in the late nineteenth century already marked a gradual crumbling of classical theism. To accept evolutionary thought was to recognize that God's relation to creation must be understood in a new way.

Little of this is reflected, however, by T.B. Kilpatrick in his official comment on the *Twenty Articles of Doctrine* in 1928. The former Presbyterian professor at Knox College writes in the tones of classical theism when he speaks of God as infinite, eternal, unchangeable, supreme, and omnipotent. Concerning creation, Kilpatrick writes of the "cooperative task of theology and science in their harmonious action." God's creative action is not over and done with, he says, for all is controlled by "one Master mind, one controlling and ordering will."[40]

A Statement of Faith

In 1940, following the First World War and the Great Depression, and faced with the crisis of the Second World War, the ucc stated its doctrine in terms slightly more traditional than in 1925. *A Statement of Faith* refers only to the authority of Scripture, saying nothing of "nature, history and the heart of man," and does not repeat the 1925 assertion that God indwells creation.[41] It has no article devoted to creation, but includes a doctrine of God as "the eternal, personal Spirit, Creator and Upholder of all things." It assures believers that God, as "Sovereign Lord, exalted above the world, orders and overrules all things in it, to the accomplishment of His holy, wise and good purposes."[42]

In 1943 John Dow wrote cautiously on the question of evolution: "Whether the process was long and gradual ... whether it happened by divine fiat or evolutionary development—these are marginal questions."[43] Scientific information, then, according to Dow, had no relevance to a theology of creation. Randolph Chalmers offered in 1945 a more positive affirmation of science and of historical-critical biblical studies. He refers to the Genesis accounts of creation as "not literal," but "mythical."[44] These UCC theologians did not, however, seriously integrate the new scientific vision into their theologies of creation. We shall see that efforts to do this would appear some decades later. But first we must acknowledge the influence of twentieth-century theologies from outside Canada upon theology in the UCC.

Major Movements from Outside of Canada

Since the earliest days of the UCC, various theologies from a wide international, ecumenical context have moved away from classical theism toward a vision of an intimate, mutual relation of God and creation. Canadian theologians have made their distinct contributions but have not arrived at their theologies *ex nihilo*. Here we mention briefly some genres or individuals whose thoughts have found their way into the creation theology of the UCC.

Neo-Orthodoxy is an important theological movement, as described by John Young in the Introduction to this volume. Neo-Orthodoxy had a major influence in the UCC in the last three quarters of the twentieth century and still inspires significant numbers of church members early in the twenty-first. Mainly affirmative of traditional Christian doctrine, Neo-Orthodox thinkers have nevertheless accepted modern science and biblical criticism.[45] An influential Neo-Orthodox figure for many in the UCC has been Reinhold Niebuhr, a social ethicist of Union Theological Seminary in New York City. He reasserted key doctrines of the Reformation, emphasizing especially the finitude and sinfulness of human beings and the absolute need for God's grace. He is also notable for his "Christian realism," especially his recognition of structural, or systemic, sin and the ambiguities implicit in all human morality and social relations.[46]

Karl Barth, the Swiss Reformed theologian, wrote voluminously of the good creation in his *Church Dogmatics*, vol. III. Barth was sharply critical of any "natural theology," which derived knowledge of God from creation as such. Christian doctrines of God and creation could not be developed independently of God's self-revelation in Christ. For Barth, the Creator is none other than the God of the covenant with Israel and Father of Jesus Christ. The Creator, therefore, must be understood in a trinitarian way, as Father, Son, and Holy Spirit.[47] Barth understood that this carried the implication that God could not be the immutable or impassible deity of classical theism. Rather, God passionately loves the world and, in Christ, suffers under the power of human sin, with and for the world. He disagreed vigorously with Calvin on the nature of God's power. Barth wrote: "God can be weak and impotent, as a man is weak and impotent." God's glory consists not in majestic coercive power, but "in the fact that because he is free in his love, he can be and actually is lowly as well as exalted."[48] In this, Barth broke decisively with classical theism. Barth and Niebuhr have been major mentors to many UCC theologians and ordained ministers for decades.[49]

Liberal theologies have been a major presence in the UCC from its beginning, with strong roots in the Social Gospel of the early twentieth century. Paul Tillich, a German-American philosophical theologian, is often described as Neo-Orthodox but is also appreciated by many liberal and progressive theologians. He also moved decisively beyond classical theism, speaking of the "God beyond God," God as "Being Itself" or "the Ground of Being." While maintaining a notion of God as transcendent, he drew God and creation very close together.[50] For Tillich, the God "beyond theism" is encountered in the depth of human experience. He was criticized by UCC theologian Kenneth Hamilton for pressing biblical concepts into a prior philosophical system of thought.[51] Others were inspired by his engagement with the context of modern culture, and his engagement with socialist politics. Some liberal theologians, and some progressives whose thought has been popular among significant numbers of UCC people, have been fundamentally informed by Tillich and have moved drastically away from classical theism. These include the English bishop J.A.T. Robinson in his famous book *Honest to God*.[52] The progressive theologian and US bishop John Spong speaks of Tillich first among his mentors.[53] Spong writes of the "death of theism," and seeks a theology "Beyond Theism but Not Beyond God."[54]

It is interesting to consider that many in the UCC considered Neo-Orthodoxy "liberal" in the 1960s. This was evident in the conflict over the *New Curriculum*. This educational program, for church folk of all ages, was a serious effort of the church to build a theologically literate laity, introducing church members to non-literal interpretations of the Bible, intending to help them reconcile their faith with modern science—all of this while steadfastly reaffirming the basics of trinitarian faith. The curriculum stimulated anger and division among many church people. Particularly influential with laypersons, however, was the adult study book *The Word and the Way* by Donald Mathers. In a Neo-Orthodox way, he implicitly assumed evolutionary science, declaring that "science describes how the world took shape" but the doctrine of creation affirms that "all things were made by God" and "that he is in control of his creation" and "it is good."[55] While the curriculum was unpopular with many members, it served to move the UCC decisively away from biblical literalism and fundamentalism.

Process Theology contrasts sharply with Neo-Orthodoxy, and also departs dramatically from classical theism (see the Introduction to this volume for more on Process Theology). This approach takes seriously the evolutionary and processive nature of the physical world. That is, it recognizes the dynamic atomic and molecular character of the physical world in which nothing is static but everything is in motion and in process. Whitehead argued that God too must be "in process." He developed a panentheistic doctrine of God (all things in God, God in all things). Hartshorne argued (contrary to Aquinas) that if God is "perfect," God cannot be static and must be capable of enhancement in some respects.[56] For Whitehead and Hartshorne, God and creation are mutually dependent. God is personal, and immanent in all things, developing in and with the world. God knows the failures and sorrows, the triumphs and joys, of all creatures.[57] Various process theologies have been developed and have informed the work of UCC authors, notably Pamela Dickey Young. She develops a theology of creation and of Christ in which evolution and process are thoroughly integrated.[58] Don Schweitzer does not endorse fully a Whiteheadian metaphysic, yet speaks of the Holy Spirit as the "growing edge of God." Drawing upon German theologian Jürgen Moltmann, Schweitzer shares process emphases on the immanence of God in creation, the suffering of God in the suffering of all creatures, and the impact of the experiences of creatures upon God.[59]

Dietrich Bonhoeffer, a theologian of the German "Confessing Church" who was executed by the Nazis in 1945 because of his political activity, wrote poignantly in his *Letters and Papers from Prison* of the God who is "the beyond in the midst of life." Bonhoeffer can be seen as Neo-Orthodox, but departs more sharply from classical theism. For him, God does not intervene as a kind of *deus ex machina* (the god of the Greek drama who is lowered by a machine onto the stage to set things right when everything seems hopeless).[60] From his prison cell, Bonhoeffer proposes a poignant "theology of the cross" that is rigorously Christ-centred: "The God who is with us is the God who forsakes us (Mark 15:34).... Before God and with God we live without God. God lets himself be pushed out of the world on to the cross. He is weak and powerless in the world, and that is precisely the way, the only way, in which he is with us and helps us."[61] In close proximity to the Nazi Holocaust of the Jews, Bonhoeffer was an inspirer of post-Auschwitz theology. It was surely impossible to love and worship a God who, safe and serene in heaven, had willed and caused the Holocaust! His move away from classical theism was influential in both liberal and Neo-Orthodox theologies in the ucc after the Second World War.

Ecological theologies, usually originating in the United States or Europe from the 1980s, have had considerable impact on theology and environmental ethics in the ucc. These place Scripture into relation with the data of ecological destruction arising out of modern industrial civilization, and rethink doctrines, especially of creation, in view of environmental crisis. Ecological theologians have generally espoused panentheistic doctrines of God and creation. Influential thinkers here have been Jürgen Moltmann, who developed an ecological trinitarian panentheism, and Thomas Berry, who finds in creation itself the primary revelation of God. In the ucc there are diverse ecological theologies in the work of Douglas John Hall and Bruce Sanguin, among others.[62]

Feminist and ecofeminist theologies, originating mainly in the US, have had a huge impact on ucc theology of God and creation, its language of worship, and its ethics. Since the 1960s, perhaps the most important feminist pioneer has been Rosemary Radford Ruether. She calls for "God language beyond patriarchy," denouncing the domineering male deity of classical Christian theism who legitimizes all the worst of male behaviour toward women and human domination of nature. As an ecofeminist, Ruether has vigorously opposed the dualism of body and spirit, critiquing "the correlation of dominated woman and dominated nature," seeking an ecological/feminist theology of nature.[63] Another theologian in this genre is Elizabeth Johnson, whose work is well known in the ucc. She offers a trinitarian eco-feminist panentheism.[64] A feminist theologian of the ucc is Marilyn Legge, who contributes a Canadian feminist theological ethic that emphasizes embodiment and materiality, and expounds economic, political, and cultural aspects of feminist thought.[65] Another is ucc minister Loraine MacKenzie Shepherd, who writes of "cross-marginal connections" that link feminist concerns to those of others who are marginalized: Aboriginal people, racial and religious minorities, the disabled, and non-human creatures.

She celebrates "the rainbow diversity" of sexual orientations as an aspect of God's good creation and the indwelling of the Spirit within "holy bodies" and the land.[66]

A New Creed

Amid the tumult of the 1960s, with the appearance of liberationist and feminist theologies, many members of the UCC had become uncomfortable with the Apostles' Creed. In 1966, the Committee on Christian Faith presented a new creed for liturgical use, and after wide consultation, a text was approved by General Council in 1968.[67] It was innovative in that it began with human experience: "Man is not alone / he lives in God's world." It was amended for inclusive language in 1980: "We are not alone / we live in God's world." Jesus as "true man" was replaced by Jesus "the Word made flesh." This rewording was part of a wider development in the 1970s and 1980s: the feminist criticism of the use of masculine nouns and pronouns meant that the use of "God the Father" was greatly diminished in UCC worship, "Father" often replaced by "Creator."[68]

Notably, this creed moves beyond what I have called classical theism in its statement that "We believe in God, who has created and is creating." One commentator explains: It is "the same God we have met in Jesus. It is the God who, by the processes of birth, growth, healing, by the life-giving energy which flows through all things, continues to sustain the universe through every moment of its existence."[69] Here is clear acknowledgement that God's work in an expanding and evolving universe is continuous. Some aspects of classical theism are absent from A New Creed, such as the notion of God as ruling and controlling all things. The term "Almighty" is also notably absent. But then "deism" is also set aside: "God" is not the eighteenth-century clockmaker deity who made the world with its natural laws but then remained absent and inactive. Rather, "God works in us and others by the Spirit." The call to "seek justice and resist evil" reflected an older Social Gospel stream in the UCC, as well as the new Indigenous, Black, and liberation theologies of the time.

By the early 1990s, a new awareness arose in society, and in the UCC, of a growing environmental crisis. Ecological and ecofeminist theologies had carried much influence in the church. It was now widely recognized that human beings had done great harm to the earth and that this needed to be recognized in confessional language. In 1994, the UCC's Toronto Conference sent a petition to General Council to include a line in A New Creed that would recognize the Christian calling to care for the earth. Council asked its Theology and Faith committee to prepare the wording. After wide consultation, the wording "to care for the earth" was felt to be too anthropocentric, failing to acknowledge the interrelationality of humankind and the earth. The words "to live with respect in creation" were proposed, to be inserted after "to celebrate God's presence," and before "to love and serve others." The executive of General Council agreed in March 1995, and the words were added to the creed and printed in *Voices United* (1996).[70] Thus, respect for creation was recognized as part of the Christian mission in the world. The revised wording of *A New Creed* moved the UCC further toward what I refer to here as "ecotheology."

"Ecotheologies" in the UCC

Among the many theological authors of the contemporary UCC, I can mention here only a few who make important contributions to the theology of creation, all of whom can be described as ecotheological.

Indigenous Theology in the UCC has roots in Aboriginal religion and spirituality, which far preceded ecotheology in mainstream Christianity. It contributes importantly to ecotheology in the UCC. A key person here has been Jessie Saulteaux, an Assiniboine elder of the Carry the Kettle First Nation in Saskatchewan. She envisioned an educational program for Aboriginal theological students, and such a school was founded and named in her honour in Manitoba. Similarly, Francis Sandy, from Christian Island in Ontario, a trained lay minister of the UCC, dreamed of a training school to prepare Aboriginal students for ordained and other ministries of the church. In 1987 a school was founded and named in his honour. Today the two institutions have come together in the Sandy-Saulteaux Spiritual Centre in Beausejour, Manitoba. Their goal is to honour both Christian and Traditional Aboriginal teachings and practices. Melody McKellar and Bernice Saulteaux, both UCC ministers, describe ways in which Aboriginal ritual practices, such as sweetgrass smudging ceremonies, Sun Dance and Rain Dance, and various symbols and natural medicines, are used to promote physical and spiritual wholeness. Their allegiance to traditional Indigenous ways goes hand in hand with reverence for Jesus, and a deep faith in God as Creator. They grieve the way in which Aboriginal spiritual traditions have been despised and rejected by Christians, and the struggle many have endured to hold together their tradition with their Christianity. They celebrate the healing power of this coalescence of Christianity and Traditional Aboriginal spirituality.[71]

Stan McKay, a former moderator of the UCC, writes of the "centrality of the earth in our experience of the truth about our creator. We seek to integrate life so that there will not be boundaries between the secular and religious. For us, the Great Spirit is in the daily earthly concerns about faithful living in relationship with the created order."[72] McKay is critical of the anthropocentric character of European theologies and calls for a holistic approach. Janet Silman contends that Christian theology can be transformed by traditional Indigenous understandings.[73] Before the missionaries came, she points out, the Indigenous peoples already knew Gitchee Manitou as their Creator. Their emphasis on the close relation of Creator and creation, and their emphasis on the Spirit and prophecy, are reminiscent, she believes, of Hebrew scriptures.[74]

David Hallman is a former staff person of the UCC and an outstanding environmentalist, from whom I have borrowed the term "ecotheology." He uses the term broadly to include ecological theologies, but also liberative theologies that emphasize economic and social justice that see God, Earth, and human beings in intimate relationality. Hallman is one of the first in the UCC to speak in ecumenical contexts of "One Earth Community," and his work is reflected in the General Council report by that name.[75] He offers a Christological basis for his theology: "First, we believe that the word became incarnate, and lived and lives among us. This world is important in God's sight."[76] Hallman carries this thought forward into detailed studies of acid rain, ozone depletion, nuclear power, and was one of the first to warn of greenhouse gases and climate change.

Douglas John Hall is internationally recognized for his articulation of contextual method in theology. Hall, a student of both Niebuhr and Tillich and a UCC minister and theologian, remains in some ways Neo-Orthodox, retaining many aspects of traditional doctrines of God and creation. However, he departs from notions of God as immutable and impassible. Building on Martin Luther's "theology of the cross," Hall points to the suffering God, Creator of a dynamic, "processive" world. The Bible, he argues, presents an ontology of communion, of "Being-with." All of "being" is "being with." Even God is not "God alone," but always God in covenant relation.[77] All of creaturely being is essentially a being-in-relation, and our humanity in God's image is a being-with—with God, with other humans, with nature. Hall writes critically of "a patriarchally conceived deity in the service of empire," for the God of the cross cannot be conceived as pure power.[78] Questioning "God the Father Almighty," Hall is critical of the Western Christian triumphalism that legitimizes human mastery over the natural world. Human "dominion" must be understood as stewardship, imaging

God's dominion over creation, which is servanthood, suffering, and self-emptying *(kenosis)* as revealed in the Cross: "It belongs to that divine suffering—that voluntary relinquishment of absolute power, that kenosis—that God will exercise God's own dominion indirectly, through a creature, one who shares with all creatures their ephemeral and vulnerable nature and destiny. God limits God's self in creation."[79]

Bruce Sanguin, a UCC minister in Vancouver, is widely appreciated among liberal and progressive church members. His several books are steeped in biblical texts, evolutionary science, and process philosophy. He writes: "The Bible affirms the dignity of natural and human history as an arena in which God is active, alluring all creation toward a promise of fulfilment."[80] He describes himself as a panentheist, espousing the belief that "the Being of God includes and penetrates the whole universe, so that every part of it exists in God, but (as against pantheism) that this Being is more than, and is not exhausted by the universe."[81] At times, Sanguin sounds pantheistic, as though creation itself is divine. He can speak of the earth as a "sacred revelation" and "embodiment of the divine."[82] He develops a middle position in the debate about "intelligent design,"[83] acknowledging randomness and dead ends in the evolutionary process, and denying that God "designed" from the beginning a full blueprint for the development of creation. Yet God as Creator is the Supreme Intelligence within creatures that accounts for the "exquisite coincidences," such as the Spirit's marvellous work with bacteria to establish ideal oxygen levels for future life, and the "stunning miracle" of consciousness in humans.[84] Sanguin speaks of the autonomy of creatures and of God as self-emptying presence within the process. Referring to Philippians 2:7, he extends the christological *kenosis* to creation: "God makes room for all levels of creation to unfold with dignity and in integrity … making room for genuine novelty and surprise."[85] He also asserts the eternal life of individuals. Building on faith in the resurrection of Jesus, he believes that the divine Wisdom "gathers up each and every being and centre of consciousness from the 14 billion year history of the universe and not only records them, like a cosmic hard drive, but *preserves* them as living entities, for eternity."[86]

A Song of Faith

A felt need of the UCC toward the end of the twentieth century was for a confessional statement that would reflect an updated scientific awareness, but also liberationist, feminist, ecological, and interfaith perspectives that were flourishing at the time. The Theology and Faith Committee, chaired by Michael Bourgeois, presented its work to General Council in 2006.

Contrasting dramatically with 1925 and 1940, it exemplifies in its doctrine of creation what I have called "ecotheology."[87] It begins in humility, reflecting an element of agnosticism in the UCC: "God is Holy Mystery, / beyond complete knowledge, / above perfect description." Yet it clearly affirms that God is personal: "in love, / the eternal God seeks relationship." It stands in continuity with the ancient creeds and earlier UCC official doctrine, reaffirming "the One and Triune God," Jesus the Christ as "the Holy One embodied" and "God incarnate," and "God the Spirit, who from the beginning has swept over the face of creation, animating all energy and matter and moving in the human heart." God is eternal and transcendent, as "Creator, the Maker and Source of all that is." Concerning creation, *Song* is cognizant of contemporary scientific visions of the earth and the universe, celebrating "a world of beauty and mystery, of living things, diverse and interdependent, of complex patterns of growth and evolution, of subatomic particles and cosmic swirls." In agreement with the *Twenty Articles of Doctrine* (1925), *Song* sees creation is revelatory: "Each part of creation reveals unique aspects of God the Creator, who is both in creation and beyond it." With Genesis, it affirms that "all creation is good." Its eschatological vision is that of "creation healed and restored"—a "new heaven and new earth." Aware of ecological crisis, *Song* speaks ethically of "our integral connection to the earth and one another," and of Christians' mission to "participate in God's work of healing and mending creation."

Conclusion: A Church Called to Action

At the beginning of this chapter, I referred to our time of frequent natural disasters and climate crisis.[88] Fossil fuels, with their emissions of carbon dioxide, are dramatically raising the average temperature of the globe, which results in the melting of the polar regions and the rise in sea levels, many extreme weather patterns, severe drought, and devastating forest fires. Shocking numbers of biological species are disappearing. We are beginning to see ominous food and freshwater shortages. With intensified human conflict over land, food, and water, the danger of war, even nuclear disaster, is heightened. One climate scientist cautions us of "the end of civilization as we know it."[89] Another warns of an uninhabitable planet if humanity continues with business as usual.[90]

A classical theistic notion of God and creation might well ascribe the climate crisis to the will of God and look to an all-controlling deity for the solution through supernatural divine intervention (as in the case of a governor of Texas, who, in the midst of devastating forest fires, publicly prayed for rain, but also called for the abolition of the Environmental Protection Agency).[91] But a *deus ex machina* (in Bonhoeffer's terms) will not intervene and fix everything. The laws that have enabled the evolution of life remain in force, and the Creator will not set aside the order of the universe to accommodate human folly. In the ecotheological perspective, there are no guarantees that life as we know it will be preserved on this planet.[92] The UCC understands itself, therefore, to be called to be a church in action.

Christian people, including UCC members, have often been in denial about this crisis—often indifferent and contributing to the problem. However the UCC General Council spoke out about the danger of climate change as early as 1992. The report to Council, "One Earth Community," enunciated ethical principles for sustainable development, including a criticism of high-consumption lifestyles, the priority of justice for the poor, and respect for biodiversity.[93] Again, in 2000, General Council's "Energy in the One Earth Community" specifically called for a reduction in the use of fossil fuels and for increased use of renewable sources of energy.[94] Both of these reports encouraged Church members to alter their own lifestyles, called for educational resources on these issues, and asked individuals and congregations to communicate with their governments on the urgency of dealing with climate change. In 2015 General Council voted to divest the church's treasury from fossil fuel companies and to invest instead in renewable energy sources. It was a courageous and potentially costly decision.[95] Some congregations and many church members (though only a few) have altered their lifestyles, installed solar panels, divested and diverted funds, engaged in public education, or participated in demonstrations, in pursuit of environmental sustainability.

A New Creed declares that "We trust in God," and that "in life, in death, in life beyond death, God is with us." The eternal God, mighty Creator and Source of all power, is at work within the marvellous healing and restorative powers of the good creation. *A New Creed* also declares that "[God] works in us and others by the Spirit." The imaginative use of human "dominion," through responsible investment and research, creative new technologies that respect natural ecosystems, and determined political action will be necessary if God's hope for this planet is to be fulfilled. Within that struggle, The United Church of Canada continues to confess that

> We are not alone,
> We live in God's world.
> We believe in God:
>> Who has created and is creating....

NOTES

1   *A New Creed, The Manual, 2013*, 36th rev. ed. (Toronto: UCPH, 2013), 20.

2   Robert John Russell, *Cosmology: From Alpha to Omega* (Minneapolis: Fortress Press, 2008), 11–24.

3   Ibid., 39.

4   Tim Flannery, *Here on Earth: A Natural History of the Planet* (Toronto: HarperCollins, 2011), 41.

5   Charles Darwin, *An Annotated Origin: A Facsimile of the First Edition of the Origin of Species* (Cambridge, MA: Harvard University Press, 2009).

6   Yuval Noah Harari, *Sapiens: A Brief History of Humankind* (Toronto: McClelland & Stewart, 2014), 3–5.

7   John F. Haught, *God after Darwin: A Theology of Evolution* (Boulder, CO: Westview Press, 2008), 26.

8   Ted Peters and Martinez Hewlett, *Theological and Scientific Commentary on Darwin's Origin of Species* (Nashville, TN: Abingdon, 2008), 26–32.

9   Richard Dawkins, *The Blind Watchmaker* (London: Penguin, 1991), 5.

10 Michael J. Behe, *Darwin's Black Box: The Biochemical Challenge to Evolution* (New York: Free Press, 1996), 10–12; also Denyse O'Leary, *By Design or by Chance?* (Kitchener, ON: Castle Quay Books, 2004).

11 Haught, *God after Darwin*, 195–200; Michael Bourgeois, "Science and Religion: Evolution and Design," *Touchstone* 25, no. 3 (September 2007): 18–32.

12 "Classical theism" is discussed by Don Schweitzer, *Jesus Christ for Contemporary Life* (Eugene, OR: Cascade/Wipf and Stock, 2012), 68–70; Jürgen Moltmann speaks similarly of "theism" and "general monotheism" in *The Crucified God*, trans. R.A. Wilson (London: SCM, 1974), 214–16, 236.

13 *The Manual*, 20–28.

14 Ibid., 11.

15 Harrari, *Sapiens*, 65–74.

16 See Arthur Walker-Jones, *The Green Psalter: Resources for an Ecological Spirituality* (Minneapolis, MN: Fortress, 2009), 139–42.

17 William R. Stoeger, "Scientific Accounts of Ultimate Catastrophes in Our Life-Bearing Universe," in *The End of the World and the Ends of God*, ed. John Polkinghorne and Michael Welker (Harrisburg, PA: Trinity Press International, 2000), 22–25.

18 John Polkinghorne, *The God of Hope and the End of the World* (New Haven, CT: Harvard University Press, 2002), 148.

19 Harold Wells, *The Christic Center: Life-Giving and Liberating* (Maryknoll, NY: Orbis, 2004), 126–31.

20 *The Manual*, 11.

21   *Voices United: The Hymn and Worship Book of The United Church of Canada* (Toronto: UCPH, 1996), 918, 920.

22   Justo L. Gonzalez, *The Story of Christianity*, vol. I: *The Early Church to the Dawn of the Reformation* (San Francisco: HarperSanFrancisco, 1984), 61–66.

23   Henry Chadwick, *The Early Church* (London: Penguin, 1993), 33–41.

24   *VU*, 920.

25   Karl Barth wrote that "heaven is the creation inconceivable to man, earth the creation conceivable to him. He himself is the creature on the boundary between heaven and earth." *Dogmatics in Outline*, trans. G.T. Thomson (London: SCM, 1966), 59.

26   St. Thomas Aquinas, *Summa Theologiae* (London: Blackfriars, 1964), 8:1a.45.3.

27   Ibid., 1a.19.6.

28   Ibid., 3a.45.12.

29   John Calvin, *Institutes of the Christian Religion*, trans. Henry Beveridge (London: James Clarke, 1962), I, xiii, 14, vol. I, 122.

30   Ibid., I, xvii, 11, vol. I, 93. See also ibid., III, xxiii, 8, vol. II, 232–33.

31   See the critique of Calvin by David Bentley Hart, "Providence and Causality: On Divine Innocence," in *The Providence of God*, ed. Fransesca Aran Murphy and Philip Ziegler (London: T. & T. Clark, 2009), 34–56.

32   See Elizabeth A. Johnson, *Ask the Beasts: Darwin and the God of Love* (London: Bloomsbury, 2014), 156.

33   *The Manual*, 12.

34   John Webster Grant, *The Canadian Experience of Church Union* (Richmond, VA: John Knox Press, 1967), 32.

35   Grant, *The Church in the Canadian Era* (Vancouver: Regent College Publishing House, 1972), 61.

36   John Wesley, *The Appeals to Men of Reason and Religion and Certain Related Open Letters*, in *The Works of John Wesley*, ed. Gerald R. Cragg, vol. 11 (Oxford: Clarendon Press, 1975).

37   Robert C. Fennell, "How Does the United Church Interpret the Bible? Part I: 1904–1940s: Tradition and Resistance," *Touchstone* 26, no. 2 (May 2008): 16–17.

38   Nathanael Burwash, *Manual of Christian Theology on the Inductive Method* (London: Horace Marshall and Son, 1900), 1:442.

39   Marguerite Van Die, *An Evangelical Mind: Nathanael Burwash and the Methodist Tradition in Canada, 1839–1918* (Montreal and Kingston: McGill-Queen's University Press, 1989), 6, 104.

40   Thomas Buchanan Kilpatrick, *Our Common Faith* (Toronto: Ryerson Press, 1928), 80, 107, 109.

41   Michael Bourgeois, "Awash in Theology: Issues in Theology in The United

Church of Canada," in *The United Church of Canada: A History*, ed. Don Schweitzer (Waterloo, ON: Wilfrid Laurier University Press, 2012), 261, 267.

42   *The Manual*, 15.

43   John Dow, *This Is Our Faith: An Exposition of the Statement of Faith of The United Church of Canada* (Toronto: BESS, UCC, 1943), 13.

44   Randolph Carleton Chalmers, *See the Christ Stand! A Study in the Doctrine of The United Church of Canada* (Toronto: Ryerson Press, 1945), 126, 134.

45   See Douglas John Hall, *Remembered Voices: Reclaiming the Legacy of "Neo-Orthodoxy"* (Louisville, KY: John Knox Press, 1998).

46   Reinhold Niebuhr, *The Nature and Destiny of Man*, 2 vols. (Louisville, KY: Westminster John Knox Press, 1996); *Moral Man and Immoral Society* (New York: Charles Scribner's Sons, 1932).

47   Karl Barth, *Church Dogmatics*, vol. III, pt. 1, trans. and ed. T.F. Torrance and G.W. Bromiley (Edinburgh: T. & T Clark, 1958), 11–14.

48   Ibid., vol. IV, pt. 2, 129–30.

49   An important Neo-Orthodox teacher in the United Church for over thirty years was William O. Fennell, who taught Systematic Theology and served as principal at Emmanuel College. Fennell deals with aspects of the doctrine of creation in *God's Intention for Man: Essays in Christian Anthropology* (Waterloo, ON: Wilfrid Laurier University Press, 1977). I refer here also to Kenneth Hamilton of Winnipeg, the author of many theological works of the Neo-Orthodox genre; also A. McKibbin Watts (for many years editor of the *Touchstone* journal), Gordon Harland in Winnipeg, David Demson at Toronto, Donald Mathers at Kingston, Martin Rumscheidt in Halifax, Douglas John Hall at Montreal, and others.

50   Paul Tillich, *Systematic Theology*, vol. II (Chicago: University of Chicago Press, 1957), 29–44.

51   Kenneth Hamilton, *The System and the Gospel: A Critique of Paul Tillich* (Grand Rapids, MI: William B. Eerdmans, 1967).

52   John A.T. Robinson, *Honest to God* (London: SCM, 1963).

53   John Shelby Spong, *A New Christianity for a New World* (San Francisco: HarperSanFrancisco, 2002), xvii.

54   Ibid., chapter 4. See discussion of Spong by Harold Wells, "The Resurrection of Jesus according to 'Progressive Christianity,'" *Touchstone* 30, no. 1 (January 2012): 35–43.

55   Donald M. Mathers, *The Word and the Way* (Toronto: UCPH, 1962), 17, 67. On the New Curriculum see Phyllis D. Airhart, *A Church with the Soul of a Nation: The Making and Re-Making of The United Church of Canada* (Montreal and Kingston: McGill-Queen's University Press, 2014), 264–67.

56 Charles Hartshorne, *The Divine Reality* (New Haven, CT: Yale University Press, 1948), 18–22.

57 A.N. Whitehead, *Process and Reality*, ed. David Ray Griffin and Donald Shelburne (New York: Free Press, 1978), 346.

58 Pamela Dickey Young, *Christ in a Post-Christian World* (Minneapolis, MN: Fortress, 1995), chapters 4–6.

59 Don Schweitzer, "What Do Acts of Liberation Mean for God?" *Toronto Journal of Theology*, Supplement 1 (May 2008): 165–77. Also "The Holy Spirit as Giver, Gift and Growing Edge of God," *Touchstone* 26, no. 2 (May 2008): 23–34.

60 Dietrich Bonhoeffer, *Letters and Papers from Prison*, ed. Eberhard Bethge, 3rd ed. (London: SCM, 1967), 282.

61 Ibid., 360.

62 Jürgen Moltmann, *God in Creation: An Ecological Doctrine of Creation*, trans. M. Kohl (London: Press, 1985); Brian Swimme and Thomas Berry, *The Universe Story from the Primordial Flaring Forth to the Ecozoic Era* (San Francisco: HarperSanFrancisco, 1992); Douglas John Hall, *The Stewardship of Life in the Kingdom of Death* (New York: Friendship Press, 1985); Bruce Sanguin, *Darwin, Divinity and the Dance of the Cosmos* (Kelowna, BC: Woodlake/Copperhouse, 2007); Harold Wells, "The Flesh of God: Christological Implications for an Ecological Vision of the World," *Toronto Journal of Theology* 15, no. 1 (Spring 1999): 51–68; Ross L. Smillie, *Practicing Reverence: An Ethic for Sustainable Earth Communities* (Kamloops, BC: Copperhouse/Woodlake, 2011).

63 Rosemary Radford Ruether, *Sexism and God-Talk: Toward a Feminist Theology* (Boston: Beacon Press, 1983).

64 Elizabeth A. Johnson, *She Who Is: The Mystery of God in Feminist Theological Discourse* (New York: Crossroad, 1993); *Quest for the Living God: Mapping Frontiers in the Theology of God* (New York: Continuum, 2007).

65 Marilyn J. Legge, *The Grace of Difference: A Canadian Feminist Theological Ethic* (Atlanta, GA: Scholars Press, 1992).

66 Loraine MacKenzie Shepherd, *Feminist Theologies for a Postmodern Church* (New York: Peter Lang, 2002); *Story after Story: Canadians Bend Bound Theology* (Winnipeg: On Edge Publishing, 2003), 125–26.

67 UCC, GC23, 1968, *Proceedings*, 322–23.

68 William Haughton, "A New Creed: Its Origins and Significance," *Touchstone* 29, no. 3 (September 2011): 20–29.

69 Patricia Wells, *Welcome to the United Church of Canada: A Newcomer's Introduction to A New Creed* (Toronto: UCC, 1986), 3.

70   UCC, GC35, 1994, *Proceedings,* 149–50; Minutes of General Council Executive, November 1994 and March 1995.

71   Melody McKellar, "Colonial Effects of Women's Leadership," in *Story after Story,* ed. Loraine MacKenzie Shepherd, 9–11; McKellar and Bernice Saulteaux, "Aboriginal Voices," in ibid., 3–9.

72   Stan McKay, "An Aboriginal Perspective on the Integrity of Creation," in *Ecotheology: Voices from the South and North,* ed. David G. Hallman (Maryknoll, NY: Orbis Press, 1994), 216.

73   Stan McKay and Janet Silman, *The First Nations: Canadian Experience of the Gospel-Culture Encounter* (Geneva: WCC, 1995), viii.

74   Silman, *The First Nations,* 42, 46.

75   See UCC *Earth Community,* GC34, *Proceedings,* 1992, 127–28.

76   David G. Hallman, *Ecotheology,* 264.

77   Douglas John Hall, *Imaging God: Dominion as Stewardship* (Grand Rapids, MI: Eerdmans, 1986), 113, 119.

78   Hall, *Professing the Faith: Christian Theology in a North American Context* (Minneapolis, MN: Fortress, 1993), 92, 97.

79   Ibid., 350.

80   Bruce Sanguin, *The Advance of Love: Reading the Bible with an Evolutionary Heart* (Vancouver: Evans and Sanguin, 2012), xiv–xv.

81   Sanguin, *Darwin, Divinity, and the Dance of the Cosmos,* 69.

82   Ibid., 36.

83   Ibid., 126–27.

84   Ibid., 26, 92.

85   Ibid., 122.

86   Ibid., 228.

87   *The Manual,* 20–28.

88   Tim Flannery, *Atmosphere of Hope* (Toronto: HarperCollins, 2015), 3–131.

89   Andrew Weaver, *Keeping Our Cool: Canada in a Warming World* (Toronto: Penguin, 2010), 85.

90   James Hansen, *Storms of My Grandchildren* (New York: Bloomsbury, 2009), chapter 11.

91   Tom Rand, *Waking the Frog: Solutions for Our Climate Change Paralysis* (Toronto: ECW, 2014), 18.

92   Harold Wells, "Climate Holocaust, Mortal Planet and *Eschaton," Touchstone* 30, no. 3 (Sept. 2012): 7–20.

93   UCC, GC34, *Proceedings,* 1992, 127–28.

94   UCC, GC37, *Proceedings,* 2000, 696–708.

95   UCC, GC42, *Proceedings,* 2015, 172–78.

CHAPTER FOUR

SIN AND REDEMPTION IN
THE UNITED CHURCH OF CANADA

Sandra Beardsall

In 1919, T. Albert Moore was the General Secretary of the Department of Evangelism and Social Service of the Methodist Church (Canada). On June 16 he wrote to Hugh Dobson, the church's Western Field Secretary, about "a peculiar condition with regard to evangelism." Moore noted that "a desperate effort is being made by some of the brethren, who, by the way, have never been outstandingly successful in Evangelism, to put over on the Church the old type of Evangelism and to insist upon the Department engaging one or two special men whom they think are wonderful on these lines.... We are not much afraid, however," Moore assured Dobson. "We will win out during this Conference."[1]

Eighty-seven years later, in 2006, Peter Foster, a business writer with the *National Post*, weighed in on the theology of The United Church of Canada. Foster had heard David Hallman, then the UCC's national Program Coordinator for Energy and the Environment, in an interview on CBC Radio's *The Current* with Anna Maria Tremonti. "The Church," noted Foster, "having abandoned dealing with most real thorny moral issues, such as abortion, has recently declared a crusade against bottled water. Dr. Hallman suggested that the aggressive marketing of bottled water might be part of a dastardly plot under which Canada's poor would eventually be deprived of tap water. Canada might be divided into a nation of water haves and have-nots. Greater nonsense," Foster spouted, "can hardly be imagined."[2]

Since even before its inception, then, the UCC has not lacked for opinions—from within and outside the church—about the appropriate attitude toward sin, if not redemption. The "old type" of evangelism against which T.A. Moore railed was that of the sin-drenched pleader, groaning on the mourner's bench for salvation, then leaping to her feet to testify to her conversion. Moore had imbibed Washington Gladden's late-nineteenth-century theology of "social salvation," and was busy engaging the church in the politics of temperance, the Lord's Day, and education and housing for the poor. The way forward, for Moore, as for many other Methodist leaders, linked sin and redemption less to an inner experience that would guide them to personal perfection than to the outer experience of the social good, the in-breaking the Kingdom, the redemption of the whole of creation. The Methodist General Conference of 1910 had explicitly worried that the "old type" of evangelism, particularly the focus on personal testimony at the class meeting, involved too much introspection. It is this focus on the social good—be it abortion or water justice—that Peter Foster, nine decades on, would term "nonsense."

In the words of an early interpreter of the UCC's doctrine, regarding sin, "endless debate has arisen regarding various aspects of this gloomy and mysterious subject."[3] Yet for all the disputes—and think of the homes and churches that could have been heated using the wind and fire of those disputes!—the UCC's official theology of sin and redemption has not substantially changed in ninety years. Human beings have surrendered to sin, the church has consistently stated, and only God can redeem them, which God does, graciously, in Jesus Christ. But what constitutes sin, and what redemption actually entails—for God and for humanity—has become doctrinally more complex, and in practice has often been divisive over the decades. In this chapter we will investigate the intersections of official theological positions on sin and redemption with the implicit and lived expressions of those theologies in the UCC's life and witness, insofar as we can observe them. The "lived expressions" are far-ranging and include many of the church's discussions of social and ethical issues. They will help us determine whether and how the theologies developed for the UCC's social and ethical stances have aligned with its doctrinal statements.

This chapter will examine sin and redemption in four chronological parts, clustered around the church's four official subordinate doctrinal statements: "Original Sin/Dynamic Redemption: Church Union to 1939" (the *Twenty Articles of Doctrine*);[4] "Realism or Resignation? 1940–1965" (*A Statement of Faith*);[5] "Liberation and Lament: 1966–1999" (*A New Creed*);[6] and "A New Song for an Older (but Wiser?) Church" (*A Song of Faith*).[7] Each part will examine first the church's key doctrinal positions, then tease out examples of the lived expression of these doctrines. This exploration through time will show that the UCC's view of sin has become increasingly sophisticated and complex. It has changed its "list" of sins over the decades but has rarely equivocated on what constituted "sin" in any particular era. However, the church has not attended as closely to its theology of redemption. "Redemption," and its sister concept, reconciliation, which were so easy to define in the "old evangelism," have become increasingly difficult to describe, and they are particularly challenging for the UCC today. Redemption, for example, means "rescue." Can one be rescued from more than one's sinfulness? In the process of this inquiry, we will meet a host of persons who, through the decades, have sought to bring a very public community of Christians to an examination of that most brutal and startling of human conundrums: the burden of sin and the gift of redemption.

Original Sin/Dynamic Redemption: Church Union to 1939

His sermon for tomorrow is spread out on the little table by the bed, the text that he always uses for his first Sunday. *As for Me and My House We Will Serve the Lord*. It's a stalwart, four-square Christian sermon. It nails his colours to the mast. It declares to the town his creed, lets them know what they may expect. The Word of God as revealed in Holy Writ—Christ Crucified—salvation through His Grace—these are the things that Philip stands for.[8]

Thus one of Canada's best-known fictional narrators, Mrs. Bentley, describes the "signature" sermon of a Depression-era prairie minister. "Christ Crucified—salvation through His grace" suggests careful observance of Articles 2.3.5 and 2.3.6, on sin and the grace of God,[9] of the founding doctrines of the UCC. The novel is steeped in irony, however. The reader is immediately set on edge: does the Rev. Bentley *really* stake his soul on this unambiguous declaration of classical Protestant theology? Or is this "stalwart" sermon simply a device that allows a doubting cleric to appear respectably orthodox?

This fictional vignette mirrors the debates that swirled around the production of the doctrinal section of the *Basis of Union*.[10] Those sympathetic to the doctrinal statement as adopted saw a sincere expression of a theological consensus, which was "a miracle in itself."[11] Critics argued that it was hastily and carelessly constructed by a committee that was seeking the path of least resistance to church union and thus failed both Presbyterian doctrinal purists and those who saw the classical Protestant doctrines as "hopelessly antiquated."[12] Generally, however, opponents complained about what had been left out of the articles, rather than what had been retained.[13]

Indeed, there is little evidence that there was contemporary opposition to the relentlessly Reformed view of original sin and substitutionary atonement presented in Articles 2.3.5 through 2.3.7 (on sin, grace, and "the Lord Jesus Christ"). Based largely on a 1905 American Presbyterian statement of faith,[14] these articles offer a classic description of original sin: "all men are born with a sinful nature" and "no man can be saved but by His [God's] grace." That grace is given by God in his "only begotten Son," who in turn "offered Himself a perfect sacrifice," which satisfied "Divine justice" and "made propitiation for the sins of the whole world."[15]

Since these articles on sin and atonement were rarely referenced by those writing in the early decades of the ucc's life, it is hard to know what ucc members understood humanity's "sinful nature" to be. T.B. Kilpatrick, a Presbyterian theologian and champion of church union, gives us the most reliable clue in his 1928 exegesis of the *Twenty Articles of Doctrine*. Sin's "root in human nature," he states, lies in a failure to trust God: "Man would not submit himself in trustful submission to God's revelation of what is good. Sin is essentially rejection of God. One writer calls it 'deicide'—the attempt to dethrone the Almighty." This separation from God makes it impossible for humans to extract themselves from their "bondage," which leads to "death." [16] Thus, although "our first parents ... fell,"[17] the "Fall" does not appear to have been contingent upon a literal reading of the story of Adam and Eve, and on the sexual transmission of a "sinful nature" to all humanity, but rather upon the confidence that human beings are somehow predisposed, in their freedom, to resist trusting God. Only God can save them from this alienation, by grace and the ultimate sacrifice of Christ on the cross. This script, it appears, was taken as given, and perhaps the fictional Rev. Bentley is enacting a common pulpit ritual when he "nails his colours to the mast."

Reformed theology, however, has a more fulsome view of redemption. As early as 1556, Calvinists were noting that "although His death did sufficiently reconcile us to God ... yet the Scriptures ordinarily attribute our regeneration to His resurrection.... For as by death sin was taken away, so our righteousness was restored by his resurrection."[18] While the *Twenty Articles of Doctrine* do not make the link to the resurrection, they do take redeemed souls on a journey from substitutionary atonement into several articles worth of redemption. Their life in Christ entails their "regeneration" by the Holy Spirit (2.3.9), who makes them "new creatures," to "enlighten and empower them" (2.3.8). Further, the faith that saves us brings us to "repentance," which is the confession of our sins and intention to be obedient (2.3.10), adoption as "sons" (2.3.11), and finally "sanctification" (2.3.12), by which the faithful "grow in grace" so that they might "attain that maturity and full assurance of faith whereby the love of God is made perfect in us" (2.3.12).[19]

This cluster of doctrinal assertions is interesting for two reasons. First, it details a complex of interactions between God and humanity that suggests that redemption is not simply a forensic transaction, but rather a deeply relational and dynamic process. As T.B. Kilpatrick puts it, to have given ourselves to Jesus is a "starting-point, the opening of a great career."[20] Second, the article entitled "Of Sanctification" represents a significant mending of fences between Methodist Arminianism and Calvinist orthodoxy. The complaint that the doctrine was "not distinctly Calvinistic or Arminian but both in an uncontroversial form"[21] is the sort of epithet that is often thrown at ecumenical convergence. In fact, in John Webster Grant's words, the article "tactfully" quotes "a statement of faith that had been adopted by Canadian Congregationalists in 1886."[22] It suggests, as the Wesleys did, the possibility of God's love being made "perfect in us," while emphasizing the journey of faith and hope, rather than the controversial notion of "entire sanctification." This relational, dynamic view of redemption seems entirely suited to a union church with an activist mission on behalf of the nation.

In the lived experience of the UCC, however, there is little evidence of attention to this cluster of theological statements about sin and redemption in the years bracketing church union. Increasing secularization threatened the heart of the church's message. The First World War shattered liberal Protestant visions of humanity's progress toward the peaceable kingdom. Presbyterian opposition tainted the notion that church union was a fore-ordained gift of God to the Canadian nation. After union, the economic and social devastation of the Great Depression plunged the young denomination into crisis mode, both materially and spiritually. When UCC leaders confronted sin and redemption, the focus was on neither "original" sin nor the processes of redemption, but on defining the sins of the age.

The framers of church union had cut their leadership teeth on the social issues that had come to define mainstream Protestantism in the late nineteenth century. Samuel Dwight Chown, for example, early in his ministry, participated in the temperance movement, leading to the torching of one of his churches and a bomb planted at his parsonage by anti-temperance factions. But it also led to wider church leadership, and eventually the General Superintendency of the Methodist Church.[23] T. Albert Moore, before his national Methodist and UCC roles, was the General Secretary of the politically powerful Lord's Day Alliance of Canada.[24] Battling sins against the social good—organized gambling, organized Sunday sports, and the "liquor interests"—had come to compete with personal sinfulness and conversion as hallmarks of evangelical Christianity. By the early twentieth century, the "social good" had come to represent a much-expanded vision of a "Christian social order," as envisioned by the social gospel movement. In 1907, an alliance of churches and labour groups came together to form the Moral and Social Reform Council of Canada (later the Social Service Council of Canada). This activist organization had the ear of the federal government as it sought to battle economic and social inequity in Canada.[25]

While the young UCC rallied noisily around a cluster of readily named sins against the social good, another, less explicitly articulated, sin entered the lexicon of the nascent union denomination: Christian disunity. "If three Christian communions in this twentieth century after the birth of our Lord cannot discuss a religious policy of vast import to the future of the Dominion calmly and self-restrainedly," declared historian Arthur Morton, "then the sooner they learn to do so the better."[26] Even the anti-unionists were forced to explain that they were not against Christian unity, but that organic union was the wrong way to attain it.[27] Bitterness at the Presbyterian anti-unionists lingered. T.A. Moore, as the UCC's General Secretary, refused to seek rapprochement with the continuing Presbyterians until they retracted their "malicious lies."[28] The notion that disunity was a sin would weave its way into and out of the UCC imaginary in the ensuing decades. As we shall see, it did not apply to pre–Vatican II Roman Catholics, but it surfaced when the Anglicans and the Christian Church (Disciples of Christ) eschewed union in the 1970s. In later decades it receded, as the church espoused a "whole world ecumenism" that downplayed ecumenical relations in favour of finding common ground with anyone seeking the healing of creation.[29]

It is difficult to know how sin and redemption played out in the lives of UCC members in the church's earliest decades. Worship in the founding denominations did not tend to feature congregationally spoken prayers, and the clergy had free reign when praying. Only the Presbyterians suggested that the minister's long opening prayer would include prayers of confession and supplication. The *Book of Common Order* of 1932 included congregational prayers of confession that drew heavily on the Anglican *Book of Common Prayer*. These focused on general disobedience, concluding with the bleak admission: "There is no health in us."[30] However, Sunday worship was more likely to include one of the two prayers of confession, similar in tone and content to those of the BCO, found at the back of the 1930 *Hymnary*.[31]

UCC worshippers also sang their faith, and we have more evidence of preferences in hymnody. The 1928 draft version of the denomination's new hymn book omitted most "gospel songs," evoking a hue and cry that filled the letters pages of the *New Outlook*.[32] The final 1930 version added a "Gospel Call" section of forty-five hymns, almost all of which feature sinners "poor and wretched," "weak and vile," and at the very least "wandering and weary."[33] Thus, Sunday worship in the first decades of the UCC's life might well have featured an opening extemporary prayer with a general confession of sinfulness, a "four-square" sermon featuring substitutionary atonement, and hymn singing liberally sprinkled with references to sin-sick souls and Jesus's "blood most precious."[34] Quarterly communicants would have been exhorted to examine their consciences before receiving the elements.[35] All this in a church founded in liberal Protestantism and committed to being a moral force in and voice for the nation.

The onset of the economic depression of the 1930s "led many in the UCC to believe that the Depression was the result of a spiritual malaise which had left the country bereft of an adequate set of religious values," argues Ian Manson.[36] In an attempt to tackle sin on both social and personal fronts, the UCC set up a commission on Christianizing the Social Order as well as two commissions to deal with evangelism. The national church also invited Frank Buchman from the US, and his Oxford Group, to bring small-group evangelism to the United Church, for the purpose of personal conversion. The Group held local "house parties" designed to entice people to conversion. Buchman was "obsessed with rooting out sin." However, he railed mainly against premarital sex and masturbation.[37] Theologian Richard Roberts called this approach to sin "singularly naïve and unanalyzed,"[38] and the editor of the *New Outlook* called the Group's discussion of sin at a Toronto meeting "the most unblushing piece of exhibitionism we had ever seen."[39] While the *New Outlook* received some letters defending the Oxford Group, and there was a small increase in new adult memberships at several churches where the group had evangelized, interest waned, and the Group left Canada by the mid-1930s.

Meanwhile, the two commissions on evangelism concluded that both the churches collectively and Christians individually needed to repent of past mistakes and deepen the life of prayer, while the report of the Committee on Evangelizing the Social Order articulated the social sins of rampant capitalism and called for radical economic reform. Richard Roberts drew these concerns together when he stated that repentance had "to spring from penitence for personal complicity in collective sin."[40] By the late 1930s, then, sin had taken on multiple meanings in the UCC, both personal and corporate. While there were calls for repentance, we do not see in print how this repentance would bring about redemption, and certainly not redemption as a gift won for humanity in Jesus Christ. A gloom was gathering: war clouds abroad and a rapidly secularizing society at home. It seemed the right time to "update" the church's official doctrine.

Realism or Resignation? 1940–1965

"I'm only a sinner, saved by grace," a faithful "old person" testified each Sunday night during the 1950s at the UCC after service in Nipper's Harbour, Newfoundland.[41] This old person's denomination, however, was not convinced that the complex nature of sin and redemption could be so simply expressed. In 1940, it had prepared a "concise and intelligible" statement of the "substance of Christian belief."[42] This *Statement of Faith*[43] reflected the influence of Karl Barth's theological turn away from liberal optimism to an overwhelming sense of humanity's abject inability to usher in the Kingdom. The article on sin ("Man and Man's Sin" 2.4.5) continues to present the paralysis of original sin, but in a tone that highlights human concupiscence. The first appearance of humanity in the articles, as an abstract "Man," moves quickly from God's sharing with human beings his "thought, purpose, and freedom," to humanity's disastrous use of that freedom. *Statement* describes, as the *Twenty Articles of Doctrine* do not, the turmoil that human selfishness has wrought: both to our "brother man" and to ourselves.[44] The statement goes on to collect the several aspects of redemption lodged in several of the *Twenty Articles of Doctrine* and summarizes them mostly in one article (2.4.6).[45] It begins with substitutionary atonement as the place of forgiveness, then describes Christ's "resurrection and exaltation" as filling believers with the sense that "they too are conquerors." A later article, "Christian Life and Duty" (2.4.11), describes more fully the work of the redeemed.

While this condensation of the theology of redemption indeed makes *Statement* more "concise and intelligible" than its predecessor, and brings resurrection into the equation, it also articulates a more restricted view of human possibility. While the "redemption of man is at once an awful mystery and a glorious fact," this article in many ways reduces—or at least restrains—what human beings may expect from their new relationship with God. Gone is the delight of the "new creation," the promise of "adoption," and the tantalizing hope of sanctification as "perfect love." The best one can do is to "grow up in all things into Christ"[46]—a biblical but abstract notion.

The abundance of male language for humankind helps to give the statement a more "muscular" tone.[47] Why human beings sin is never clearly defined—only that it happens and is disastrous. Redemption comes across as a momentary relief followed by a lot of work. It is telling that in his 1943 exposition of *Statement*, John Dow spends twenty-one pages of the chapter on "Redemption" continuing to describe sin (after beginning to do so in a twelve-page chapter on "Man and Man's Sin"), and only three pages on forgiveness, victory, and grace.[48] When he finally describes redemption, Dow notes that "the Cross is charged with a power that passes into human penitents with a renewing energy.... Under the impulse of the resurrected one men can face the ordeals before which they once quailed, and come out more than conquerors."[49] This language of "conquering," echoing Article 2.4.6, presents redemption as a Manichean victory: the "forces of darkness fade away before the legions of light."[50]

Phyllis Airhart describes the competing theologies, approaches, and personalities involved in producing *Statement* and suggests that in the ensuing compromises, *Statement* may have turned out more Barthian than intended.[51] The failure of Western Protestantism, despite its growing ecumenical unity, to prevent the evils unleashed in the Second World War no doubt helped to dampen the optimism of the founders' activist vision, compounding existing anxieties about a climate of spiritual malaise. The UCC was also catching a wave. Kevin Kee points to the cover of *Time* magazine of March 8, 1948. It features Reinhold Niebuhr, a sometime ally of Barth and an influential "Christian realist," with the caption: "Man's story is not a success story." "Some of the traditional doctrines," states Kee, "were back in vogue."[52] Indeed, the UCC stood by its 1940 statement for nearly three decades. By 1952, 100,000 copies had been printed, and Dow's companion book was in its eighth edition.[53]

At the same time, the church was growing at a record pace. This postwar boom is well documented.[54] However, the careful statisticians of the Board of Evangelism and Social Service detected an emerging threat: the number of new "adherents" was double that of new members. The church's own laity, they warned, needed to be better evangelized.[55] They employed a variety of tools, including a cluster of pamphlets and studies, intended to assist the pew sitter. These generally adhered to the views of *Statement*, focusing on sin and redemption as personal challenges. "Sin rests upon the whole human race," asserts *A Companion to The Catechism*.[56] "Why is it so difficult to love ... our fellow employers or employees?" asks an article in the mission booklet *Calling Canada to Christ*. The answer: "Primarily because of our own sinfulness and in particular our inordinate self-love."[57] The church's 1959 Lenten study booklet is titled *YOU and the Devil*. Each chapter reviews one of the "seven deadly sins," beginning with Pride, and an explanation of original sin. It ends with an assertion that "We Can Beat the Devil," because of the "battle" with the devil that Jesus fought on the cross "for all the sons of men."[58]

The UCC also worked with revivalist Charles Templeton to evangelize both its own members and the wider public. Templeton had left behind fundamentalism for "modern, respectable open-minded Christianity."[59] His message presented sin in classical Protestant terms ("We have all sinned. We cannot forgive ourselves"),[60] but he developed it to resonate with an increasingly affluent middle class. One of his most popular sermons, "Chrome-Plated Chaos," attacked the alienation of modern North American life: "We have knowledge but not wisdom, houses but not homes, speed but not direction, and medicines but not wealth.... We are lost!"[61] In terms of specific sins, Templeton drew on the North American fear of its growing teenage population—those rebels without a cause—to condemn "the 'barroom vices' that ostensibly lead to juvenile delinquency."[62] He invited his listeners to a personal conversion and "a Christ who seemed to speak to all facets of their lives."[63] Handsome and articulate, Templeton repeated these messages through a series of large and successful evangelistic campaigns across Canada and the US from 1948 to 1955.

The bestselling resource the UCC produced in this era, however, was *The New Curriculum*.[64] Its adult resources are somewhat ambiguous in their presentation of original sin and substitutionary atonement,[65] and where these are posited, it is generally in gentler tones than *Statement*. They carefully explain sin and redemption for the modern person who may not know she needs to be redeemed. *The Word and the Way* emphasizes salvation as "a fellowship and a reconciliation," which leads us to the "wish to be a reconciler."[66] The children's books approach the Christian life through experience and storytelling. The kindergarteners do not discuss "when things go wrong" until they have been immersed in "being loved" and encountered the "experience of the holy and mystery" and of "covenant belonging."[67] This catechetical method is rather the opposite of the heavy-handed a priori approach of *Statement* and the *Companion to the Catechism*. *God Is Always with Us*, the first Primary book, uses biblical stories and relatable modern vignettes to assure children that "God is always with us," "God never loses us," and "It's good to know that God doesn't hold things against us when we do wrong."[68] The children's books in *The New Curriculum* do not repudiate the doctrinal statements, but they invite children (and their teachers and parents) into a deeply relational theology that is almost absent from the 1940 statement. They also give voice to women's theological writing—a rarity in the mid-twentieth-century UCC apart from mission literature.

Meanwhile, the national UCC continued to combat the sins it had inherited at church union: alcohol consumption, Sunday sports and theatre, and gambling. These, however, were increasingly losing battles. When a municipal referendum permitting Sunday commercialized sports passed in Toronto in 1950, it was publicly "hailed as the people's victory."[69] BESS encouraged the Lord's Day Alliance to fight the legality of such legislation,[70] but a diverse Canadian population with time and money on its hands would not be joining the fray. Gambling, too (primarily horse racing and Bingo), continued to exercise the national church, but the main efforts were directed to church members themselves. A 1949 pamphlet encouraged its readers to "direct this human capacity for risk and adventure toward noble ends."[71]

The temperance fight had also largely exited the public sphere to become a crusade within the church, but even at General Council a motion for "mandatory total abstinence" among church members was soundly defeated in 1948. Nearly a decade later, General Council established a Commission on Temperance Policy and Program, which reported in 1960.[72] While still advocating "Total Abstinence," it called for church members "to be informed in their own opinions and tolerant toward their fellow church members who hold different views." The recommendation passed without amendment.[73] This significant change in church policy shifted the understanding of sin and redemption into the realm of human relationship: sin is alienation from one another; redemption is respectful tolerance.[74] In considering marriage breakdown in 1962, the church took a similarly conciliatory tone on the issue of divorce and remarriage, acknowledging that "human weakness and sin may thwart God's perfect will for this relationship," but that this sin need not prevent the "achievement of a new marriage by the help of his gracious and redemptive love." Those wishing to remarry need to repent their failures and have "sincere desire for the grace of God which will enable them to forgive and be forgiven."[75]

Such tolerance did not extend to Roman Catholicism. The weakening of young people's ties to the UCC gave rise to the greater possibility of inter-church or "mixed" marriages, even as the Protestant and Roman Catholic churches maintained their two solitudes. UCC leaders believed it was important to warn that the distinctions were serious and potentially dangerous. *What's the Difference? Protestant and Roman Catholic Beliefs*

Compared, first published by the church in 1954, had gone to nine printings and 210,000 copies in 1962.[76] The booklet, set out in Q & A format, primarily highlights the deficiencies of Roman Catholicism. "What is wrong with Roman Catholic teaching about salvation?"[77] it asks. The Roman Catholic Church "constantly links merit with grace," rather than tying *faith* to grace. The booklet goes on to describe the Protestant teaching on original sin, with Christ as the sole mediator.[78]

Communism also came to the fore as an evil force in this era. Airhart points out that even the UCC's radical theologians downplayed their socialist views in the chill of the Cold War.[79] Niebuhr maintained a suspicion of socialism and a deep antipathy toward Communism to which North American Protestant churches readily assented.[80] The American corporate and government elite worked closely with church leaders in the 1940s and 1950s to develop a spirit of conservative religious revival in order to "create a religious citizenry that grounded material power in sacred wisdom and immunized itself to the atheistic, immoral, and corporeal siren song of Communism."[81] Templeton readily co-operated in this program: he was "convinced that Communism was a worldwide threat that could only be defeated by a democracy made strong by a God-fearing population."[82]

To add fire to this fevered state, the national UCC was smarting from its loss of one of its key mission fields, China, to Mao's Communist revolution. In one of the most cowardly moves of its history, the General Council in 1952 formally distanced the UCC from James Endicott, a long-time China missionary, because he had informed External Affairs minister Lester Pearson that the US was using germ warfare in Korea.[83] With Endicott condemned as a "traitor" and a "Prince of Lies" in the Canadian secular press, the church was anxious to prove "it was not harbouring a subversive element."[84] James Endicott "does not speak for, or in any way officially represent, the United Church," declared General Council.[85]

Even in the midst of a limited view of human redemption, however, some in the UCC of the 1940s and 1950s continued to believe in the social mission of the redeemed to bring about the Kingdom of God. In 1941, the church formed the forty-five-member "Church, Nation and World Order Commission," intent on preparing a report that would describe a "Christian democratic order" for postwar Canadian society.[86] General Council in 1944 called for the ensuing report to be printed and distributed widely throughout the church.[87] In 1950 General Council received a one-hundred-page report prepared by the Commission on Culture, which had been tasked with describing the interface of faith and culture in contemporary society, including "the role of the Church in the redemption of culture."[88] This massive study still takes human alienation from God as fact, and individual redemption as necessary, but it returns to the church a more expansive and interactive role in society—shades of a more engaging social witness that would emerge in the decades to come.[89] Meanwhile, the ucc participated in many ways in this positive redemptive vision, even if it did so without naming the theology at work: for example, through hosting Alcoholics Anonymous and Al-Anon groups in countless church basements, and through its support of prison chaplaincies and "rescue" homes for unmarried mothers. As the Board of Home Missions report of 1950 concluded its section on institutional work: "It would be indeed revealing if the church only knew how many have been reclaimed and restored through the power of the Gospel and this Christian missionary service."[90]

In 1955, Templeton, the church's most high-profile preacher of the need for personal conversion and a God-fearing nation, declared he could no longer go on, and he quit his evangelist's career. "My convictions as to some aspects of Christian doctrine became diluted with doubt," he said.[91] Templeton's anxieties prefigured a new and changed world for Canada's Christian churches. Doubt and disinterest were on the horizon. Fewer and fewer ucc worshippers would be willing to testify: "I'm only a sinner, saved by grace." Change was in the air.

Liberation and Lament (1965–1999)

"The New Creed expresses our theology well." So states the classified advertisement of Grasslands Pastoral Charge, "in lovely South West Saskatchewan," seeking a full-time ministry person in April 2016.[92] This brief testimony speaks to the depth of the regard ucc members hold for their denomination's 1968 attempt to produce a "modern creedal statement suitable for use in the liturgy."[93] That a very wordy church could produce such a concise statement of faith is almost a miracle, and perhaps part of A New Creed's enduring mystique.

The move to create a new creedal statement was symbolic of an epic shift in Canadian Protestant life.[94] Membership was falling. The warnings of the mid-1950s had become the reality of the mid-1960s. Babies born in the early 1960s were not brought for baptism at the rates of previous years. Sunday school enrolments began to drop in 1962. Professions of faith peaked in 1958, when the rate of baptisms should have caused a peak in 1972, meaning that between their infant baptisms and the attainment of puberty, the children of the early 1960s had exited the church.[95] In 1965, membership fell for the first time in the history of the ucc.[96] Further, between 1960 and 1967 there was a 50 percent drop in new candidates for ordained ministry.[97] The ucc was slowly awakening to the fact of its recent and precipitous decline. Neither the hard edges of the 1940 *Statement*, nor the softer approach of *The New Curriculum*, it seemed, could cajole Canadians to come to church. Perhaps more relevant faith and worship materials would help.

A New Creed was not intended to be a full doctrinal statement, but rather one for optional use in worship at the time one would normally recite a creed, likely the Apostles' Creed. It was created to be short (nearly the same length as the Apostles' Creed), "memorable," and to express the gospel so as "to lead men to praise."[98] Thus, like the Apostles' Creed, it does not mention human sin directly. Its direct relationships to sin and redemption are confined to one of the lines about Jesus's mission: "to reconcile and make new," and two aspects of the church's purpose: "to seek justice and resist evil," and "to proclaim Jesus, crucified and risen, our judge and our hope."[99] This simple creedal language restores some of the vision of the 1925 *Twenty Articles of Doctrine*, by focusing on the "newness" of the redeemed, Jesus as reconciler, and the church's role in justice seeking. Believers "resist evil," but the mortal combat of the 1940 *Statement* is absent. While the framers did not intend to eliminate sin—including original sin—from the ucc doctrinal lexicon, the absence of humanity's "sinful nature" and the softening of the "judgment and wrath of God" to Jesus as "our judge and our hope" in *A New Creed* no doubt contributed to its warm acceptance. For the new cultural catchword was not "wrath." It was "liberation."

Liberation

For reasons too numerous to investigate here, "original sin" was on its way out of mainstream North American Protestantism by the late 1960s. Colonized nations were winning their independence. Civil rights groups and war resisters were on the march. The American Indian Movement was opening a new chapter in Indigenous communities. Middle-class women were rediscovering their feminist voices. Even the Roman Catholic Church was opening its windows to the world. Niebuhr was yesterday's news; now the cover of *Time* magazine famously asked: "Is God Dead?"[100] The spirit of the age was liberation, not "man's helplessness and need."[101] And many of these liberated souls, aware of the power dynamics at work in naming sins and sinners, were not interested in hearing "dead white men," their oppressors, pronounce them utterly sinful and incapable of doing good.

The new theologies that emerged eschewed classical Protestantism and Neo-Orthodoxy. Sin returned to the public square as "the will of a privileged minority who have made possible the construction and maintenance of an unjust society, the capitalist society."[102] As a report on global economic justice put it: "Our faith needs to be strengthened and informed by a Christian understanding of sin and evil so that we do not become lost in naïve sentimentality."[103] In the context of injustice, human redemption may not apply to personal sin, but may indeed be "rescued"—from tyranny not of one's making. A 1997 church study guide, *Reconciling and Making New,* expanded the notion of redemption in just this way, noting that for many who suffer, "salvation means compassion and justice, made known in Jesus as he binds up the broken-hearted, and promises good news to the poor and liberation to the oppressed."[104] Liberation, however, was not confined to political and economic contexts, but extended to the planet and even the cosmos. If there was alienation, it was humanity's alienation from its own "creaturely-ness," the clay out of which our "first parents" were fashioned. Popular movements like Creation Spirituality emphasized "original blessing" and the goodness of creation, and the UCC embraced a focus on "whole world ecumenism," partnering with any and all, of any—or no—religious faith, who would help "mend the world."[105]

This positive theological anthropology dovetailed with a rapidly changing Canadian social ethic, inviting church members to consider human identity and morality in new ways. The UCC officially tackled the thorny issues of abortion, human sexuality, and sexual orientation with a boldness that won it both admiration and scorn. In the process of considering these issues, theologies of human sin and redemption emerged to varying degrees, rarely explicitly linked to the UCC's official doctrines. In the 1970s, General Councils passed and then refined statements on abortion and contraception, and did the same with human sexuality and sexual orientation through most of the 1980s. In both cases, the earliest versions of the resolutions avoided the language of sin entirely. The first abortion resolution contains no explicit theology at all,[106] while there is a euphoric, almost libertarian view of human sexuality in the earliest sexuality report in 1980.[107]

However, the final statements of 1982 (*Contraception and Abortion*)[108] and of 1988 (*Membership, Ministry and Human Sexuality*)[109] include confessions of human sin. The "taking of human life is evil," and "all have sinned and fallen short of God's intention for us."[110] The 1988 resolution clarifies that sexual orientation is not a source of sin, but that fractiousness with one another, and "injustice and persecution against gay and lesbian persons" are. Neither of these landmark resolutions describes redemption theologically; however, both tacitly equate it with the appropriate use of human freedom and the restoration of human dignity and of right human relationships. This notion of "right relationships" would come to dominate the church's life from the mid-1980s on.

Lament

If the end of the twentieth century brought theologies of liberation, it also brought home the terrible reality that the UCC had participated in unspeakable sin and evil. Both as an institution and through the actions of its members, it had participated in "empire" by placing the colonial project at the heart of its mission, abroad and at home, and by benefiting from an unjust global economy.[111] It had assisted in the degradation of the earth. Its trusted leaders had committed sexual violence against children and others. And not only had it denigrated Indigenous spiritualities and replaced them with its doctrines of original sin, it had enthusiastically contributed its resources and personnel to the Indian residential schools of Canada.

The mid-1980s ushered in an age of lament and apology in many parts of the Western world,[112] and certainly in the UCC. In 1982, the General Council apologized to James Endicott "for the hurt that the church may have brought upon him in the past."[113] The 1986 "Apology to Native Congregations" marked the beginning of a new consideration of the church's theology of sin. The church itself had sinned, in the very act of evangelizing.[114] Since then the UCC has continued to repent of institutional sins. "We have violated our sacred trust through acts of sexual, racial, and cultural oppression," stated a report on sexual abuse in 1992.[115] The hymn book *More Voices*, published in 2006, features a section of songs of "lament."

A New Song for an Older (but Wiser?) Church

"The following service is not a magical nor a superstitious act." This tantalizing assertion prefaces the service "To Resist Evil" in the UCC worship resource *Celebrate God's Presence*, published in 2000.[116] It is intended to help worshippers deal with the experience of "evil" in their lives—an admission that sin and forgiveness can be accompanied by deeper and even less tangible moments of bleakness and despair.

Fifteen years later, Canada's Truth and Reconciliation Commission uncovered countless incidents of just such evil within the church-run residential schools. Justice Murray Sinclair, who chaired the commission, noted in 2015 that while the TRC mandate gave a detailed explanation of what getting at the "truth" of the Indian residential school experience would entail, it gave no definition of reconciliation. He went on to say that the government, churches, and survivors had different and conflicting views of reconciliation.[117] Part of the challenge, at least for the UCC, may be that it has paid little heed to its own understanding of reconciliation. "Reconciliation" is for both sinners and those sinned against—and the UCC includes both. Indigenous members of the UCC consistently remind the church that they, too, are members of the institution. This complex web of institutional sin, evil, and multi-layered reconciliation helped to foster the need for a new, "timely and contextual" theological statement. *A Song of Faith* was born.[118]

Song is the church's longest statement of doctrine. It is not actually a "song," but its poetic shape gives it a hybrid quality: somewhere between the articles of 1925 and 1940 and the simple and inviting phrases of *A New Creed*. With regard to sin, *Song* attempts to explain the terseness and paralysis of the earlier doctrinal statements. Rather than asking us simply to accept that "we cannot save ourselves," it gathers up the threads of several decades of UCC reflection on the many ways human beings have broken with the goodness of creation, and articulates these with a frank clarity that helps believers realize why they cannot save themselves—they are dug in too deep. Sin is both personal and systemic; it is both ingrained and learned; it is both commission and omission. "Sin" is not distinguished from "evil." It invites "lament and repentance."[119]

In terms of redemption, *Song* views the gift of human restoration through several lenses. First, it is simply "God" who forgives, reconciles, and transforms. As the wonder of this new "fullness of life" unfolds, we become aware of the "Spirit … animating all energy and matter / and moving in the human heart."[120] It is through the experience of the loving and corrective power of the Spirit that we come to "sing of Jesus," where more redemption is on offer: Jesus "forgave sins and freed those held captive"; through the incarnation "God makes all things new"; and we celebrate the Risen Christ as "the transformation of our lives." Further, even at our birth into the world's brokenness, "we are surrounded by God's redeeming love." And in response to God's redeeming love "we participate in God's work of healing and mending creation."[121]

This cluster of restorative actions is reminiscent of the cluster of the 1925 *Twenty Articles of Doctrine* on redemption. However, it differs in two ways.

Initially, we are presented simply with God's "grace." Only later do Jesus's suffering, death, and resurrection appear as redemptive activities. This ordering of the work of salvation helps to undermine the problematic notion that suffering is redemptive,[122] but it may weaken the understanding of Jesus's role in bringing believers to new life. Second, "Christian perfection" is not on the menu, and the church becomes rather "a community of broken but hopeful believers," challenged to "live by grace rather than by entitlement." For a church born out of an entitled, activist vision, that challenge may prove the one that most tests and ultimately transforms UCC identity.

Conclusion

The United Church of Canada has rarely, as a denomination, been unsure about what is wrong in human behaviour. Disunity, spirituous liquor, gambling, untrammelled capitalism, communism, premarital sex, homophobia, bottled water, racism, sexual exploitation, empire, colonization: these have stood at various times alongside more general acknowledgements of human alienation from God as "sin." That the list has shifted over time—and even contradicted previous approbations—has perhaps helped to give the UCC the reputation of being "soft on sin," or simply letting the tide of current affairs set its norms. This is the price of being a church that, from the outset, understood itself to be vigorously engaged with its culture, not content with the "old type of Evangelism." The UCC has been less officially explicit about what "redemption" looks like, often describing reconciled relationships as the result of its theological positions, but rarely helping the membership to grasp God's action in the midst of that reconciliation.

Further, it is not clear to what extent UCC members have been willing to own for themselves what the church has called sin or sinfulness, or what their redemption might entail. Not that they have been silent on these issues. They have sung about sin and redemption, and prayed corporate prayers of confession throughout the church's history. In recent decades, UCC congregations have adopted the practices of the repentant seasons of Advent and Lent. The UCC has also embraced ecumenical agreements about the meaning of baptism, which have led to more explicit liturgical renunciations of evil,[123] and this development may have assisted believers in embracing theologies of sin and redemption in life and worship. But UCC congregations have rarely demanded personal public testimony, so individuals have generally made their own contracts with God around sin, forgiveness, and reconciliation.

Over the decades, the UCC has become officially more contrite, humble, and openly apologetic. This creates a quandary for a theology of redemption. In 1925, church doctrine continued, however gently, to posit the Wesleyan conviction that the redeemed could "go on to perfection." Recognizing the church's hubris, UCC theologians have encouraged church members to act as the redeemed children of God without assuming that such actions represent any hint of Christian perfection. In 1928, T.B. Kilpatrick wrote of the "thrilling note of wonder and surprise" with which the New Testament authors describe their new life with Christ.[124] Phrases scattered through the *Song* echo that "thrilling note," as it sounds in "moments of unexpected inspiration" and "experiences of beauty, truth and goodness." It will be the ongoing task of the church *both* to remind its members of the wonder of their redemption and to help them balance that joy with an appropriate humility about their capacity as forgiven sinners to act for good in the world. In its worship, study, and formal processes of reconciliation, perhaps that way forward will emerge, and the UCC will hear "the new song Christ is giving" and so "keep singing."[125]

NOTES

1 T.A. Moore to H.W. Dobson, June 16, 1919. Archives of the UCC, Hugh Dobson fonds, box A4, file M01, reel 10.

2 Peter Foster, "Nonsense on Tap over Bottled Water," *National Post*, November 24, 2006, FP15.

3 Thomas Buchanan Kilpatrick, *Our Common Faith* (Toronto: Ryerson, 1928), 115.

4 *The Manual*, 2013, 36th rev. ed. (Toronto: UCPH, 2013), 11–15.

5 Ibid., 15–19.

6 Ibid., 20.

7 Ibid., 20–28.

8 Sinclair Ross, *As for Me and My House* (Toronto: McClelland & Stewart, 1989 [1941]), 7.

9 *The Manual*, 12.

10 Ibid., 11–44.

11 George C. Pidgeon, *The United Church of Canada: The Story of the Union* (Toronto: Ryerson, 1950), 36. See also Brian J. Fraser, "Christianizing the Social Order: T.B. Kilpatrick's Theological Vision of the United Church of Canada," *Toronto Journal of Theology* 12, no. 2 (1996): 189–200; John Webster

Grant, *The Canadian Experience of Church Union*, Ecumenical Studies in History No. 8 (London: Lutterworth Press, 1967), 33, 36.

12 See, for example, E. Lloyd Morrow, *Church Union in Canada: Its History, Motives, Doctrine, and Government* (Toronto: Thomas Allen, 1923), 117; and C.E. Silcox, *Church Union in Canada: Its Causes and Consequences* (New York: Institute of Social and Religious Research, 1933), 137–38, who quotes Morrow appreciatively.

13 Morrow, *Church Union*, 121.

14 Ibid., 115.

15 *The Manual*, 12.

16 Kilpatrick, *Our Common Faith*, 116–17.

17 Article 2.3.5, *The Manual*, 12.

18 The Confession of Faith used in the English congregation at Geneva, 1556, in Arthur C. Cochrane, ed., *Reformed Confessions of the 16th Century* (Philadelphia: Westminster, 1966), 132–33.

19 *The Manual*, 13.

20 Kilpatrick, *Our Common Faith*, 175.

21 Morrow, *Church Union in Canada*, 117.

22 Grant, *The Canadian Experience*, 36.

23 UCC Archives, S.D. Chown fonds, fonds 3009, 86.008C-box 16-files 455, 456, S.D. Chown, "My Life," typed manuscript, 39–44. Chown was the General Secretary of the Methodist Church (Canada) at the time of church union.

24 UCC Archives, T. Albert Moore fonds, fonds 3248, 1986.257C-box 1-file 4, Resolution of the Alberta Branch, Lord's Day Alliance, recognizing T.A. Moore's resignation as General Secretary of the Lord's Day Alliance.

25 Richard Allen, *The Social Passion: Religion and Social Reform in Canada, 1914–28* (Toronto: University of Toronto Press, 1973), 13.

26 Arthur S. Morton, *The Way to Union, Being a Study of the Principles of the Foundation and of the Historic Development of the Christian Church as Bearing on the Proposed Union of the Presbyterian, Methodist, and Congregational Churches in Canada* (Toronto: William Briggs, 1912), 8.

27 See, for example, Morrow, *Church Union in Canada*, 105–8.

28 N. Keith Clifford, *The Resistance to Church Union in Canada, 1904–1939* (Vancouver: UBC Press, 1985), 224–26.

29 See "Mending the World: An Ecumenical Vision for Healing and Reconciliation" (UCC, 1997).

30 See, for example, *The Book of Common Order*, 2nd ed. (Toronto: UCPH, 1950), 4.

31 *The Hymnary of The United Church of Canada* (Toronto: UCPH, 1930), 820;

also Thomas Reginald Harding and Bruce Harding, *Patterns of Worship in The United Church of Canada, 1925–1987* (Toronto: Evensong, 1996), 7.

32 Harding and Harding, *Patterns of Worship*, 37.

33 *The Hymnary,* #476, #481, #484.

34 Ibid., #486.

35 See the prayer of humble access and the "exhortation" suggested for the Celebration of the Lord's Supper in *Book of Common Order*, 114, 123.

36 Ian M. Manson, "Religious Revival and Social Transformation: George Pidgeon and the United Church of Canada in the 1930s," *Toronto Journal of Theology* 12, no. 2 (1996): 213.

37 Kevin Kee, *Revivalists: Marketing the Gospel in English Canada, 1884–1957* (Montreal and Kingston: McGill-Queen's University Press, 2006), 109.

38 Richard Roberts, "The Oxford Group," *Christian Century*, February 1, 1933, quoted in David B. Marshall, *Secularizing the Faith: Canadian Protestant Clergy and the Crisis of Belief, 1850–1940* (Toronto: University of Toronto Press, 1992), 225.

39 Kee, *Revivalists*, 137.

40 Richard Roberts, *The Contemporary Christ* (New York: Macmillan, 1938), 143–45. Quoted in Marshall, *Secularizing the Faith*, 246.

41 Roy Andrews, interview by author, Nipper's Harbour, NF, October 2, 1991.

42 United Church of Canada, Proceedings, GC7, 1936, 85.

43 *The Manual*, 15–19.

44 *The Manual*, 16–17.

45 Ibid., 17.

46 Ibid., 19.

47 "Man" or "men" appears eight times in Articles 2.4.5 and 2.4.6, but only three times in the six comparable *Twenty Articles of Doctrine*: 2.3.5, 2.3.6, 2.3.9–2.3.12 (*The Manual*, 12–17).

48 John Dow, *This Is Our Faith: An Exposition of the Statement of Faith of The United Church of Canada* (Toronto: BESS, UCC, 1943), 107–31.

49 Ibid., 131.

50 Ibid.

51 Phyllis Airhart, *A Church with the Soul of a Nation: Making and Remaking the United Church of Canada* (Montreal and Kingston: McGill-Queen's University Press, 2014), 120–24.

52 Kee, *Revivalists*, 172.

53 UCC, Proceedings, GC15, 1952, 340.

54 See, for example, John H. Young, "A Golden Age: The United Church of

Canada, 1946–1960," in *The United Church of Canada: A History*, ed. Don Schweitzer (Waterloo, ON: Wilfrid Laurier University Press, 2012), 77–95.

55 Ibid., 342.

56 *A Companion to The Catechism* (Toronto: UCPH, 1945), 18.

57 Robert Clark, "Christian Love and Daily Work," in *Calling Canada to Christ*, ed. W.G. Berry (Toronto: National Evangelistic Mission Committee, UCC, 1957), 67.

58 Richard H.N. Davidson, *YOU and the Devil* (Toronto: BESS, UCC, 1958), 4, 64.

59 Kee, *Revivalists*, 164.

60 Ibid., 173.

61 Ibid., 174.

62 Ibid., 168.

63 Ibid., 175.

64 Ruth Bradley-St-Cyr, "The Substance of Things Hoped for": Peter Gordon White and the New Curriculum of The United Church of Canada," *Studies in Book Culture* 6, no.2 (Spring 2015), http://www.erudit.org/revue/memoires/2015/v6/n2/1032711ar.html.

65 Donald M. Mathers, *The Word and the Way: Personal Christian Faith for Today* (Toronto: UCPH, 1962), 117–30; J.S. Thomson, *God and His Purpose: The Meaning of Life* (Toronto: UCPH, 1964), 119–34; Arthur B.B. Moore, *Jesus Christ and the Christian Life* (Toronto: UCPH, 1965), 154–65.

66 Mathers, *Word and the Way*, 143, 145.

67 Robert K.N. McLean, Agnes Campbell Craig, Olive D. Sparling, and Margaret McLean, *The Kindergarten Teacher's Guide* (Toronto: UCPH, 1964), 127–268.

68 Audrey McKim, *God Is Always with Us* (Toronto: UCPH, 1964), 33–37, 79–89.

69 Paul Laverdure, *Sunday in Canada* (Yorkton, SK: Gravelbooks, 2004), 183.

70 Proceedings, GC15, 1952, 345.

71 F.W. Bailey, *A Modern Approach to Gambling* (Toronto: BESS, UCC, 1949), 19.

72 Report of the Commission on Temperance Policy and Program, UCC, Proceedings, GC19, 1960, 265–300.

73 Ibid., 283, 58.

74 See Sandra Beardsall, "And Whether Pigs Have Wings: The United Church in the 1960s," in *The United Church of Canada: A History*, 101–2.

75 "A Christian Understanding of Marriage Breakdown, Divorce and Remarriage," *Report of the Commission on Marriage and Divorce*, Proceedings, GC20, 1962, 159.

76 Arthur G. Reynolds, *What's the Difference? Protestant and Roman Catholic Beliefs Compared* (BESS and the Board of Christian Education, UCC, 1962), 3.

77 Ibid. (1962 printing), 20–23.

78 Ibid., 23–24.

79 Airhart, *Church with the Soul of a Nation*, 122–23.

80 Reinhold Niebuhr, "God's Design and the Present Disorder of Civilization," in *The Church and the Disorder of Society: An Ecumenical Study Prepared under the Auspices of the World Council of Churches*, vol. 3 in *Man's Disorder and God's Design*, ed. Willem Adolph Visser't Hooft (New York: Harper, 1948), 13–28.

81 Jonathon Herzog, "America's Spiritual-Industrial Complex and the Policy of Revival in the Early Cold War," *Journal of Policy History* 22, no. 3 (2010): 338.

82 Kee, *Revivalists*, 168.

83 Stephen Endicott, *James G. Endicott: Rebel out of China* (Toronto: University of Toronto Press, 1980), 289–302.

84 Ibid., 300.

85 Proceedings, GC 15, 1952, 65.

86 Ted Reeve, *Claiming the Social Passion: The Role of the United Church of Canada in Creating a Culture of Social Well-Being in Canadian Society* (Toronto: UCC, 1999), 92–105.

87 *Proceedings*, GC 11, 38.

88 *Proceedings*, GC 14, Appendix, ii.

89 Ibid., 83, passim.

90 Proceedings, GC 14, 1950, 352.

91 *Globe Magazine*, March 8, 1958, 6, quoted in Kee, *Revivalists*, 184.

92 *United Church Observer*, April 2016, 48.

93 *Creeds: A Report of The Committee on Christian Faith* (Toronto: Ryerson, 1969), 5.

94 See John Young's Introduction to this volume for an account of the development of *A New Creed*.

95 Stuart Macdonald, "Death of Christian Canada? Do Canadian Church Statistics Support Callum Brown's Theory of Church Decline?" *Historical Papers: Canadian Society of Church History*, 2006, 150.

96 Ibid., 139.

97 Ray Hord, "Where Is the Church in Canada Going?" *Canada and Its Future*, BESS, 42nd Annual Report, 1967, 11.

98 *Creeds: A Report*, 17.

99 *The Manual*, 20.

100 *Time*, April 8, 1966, cover.

101 Statement of Faith, article 2.4.6, *The Manual*, 17.

102 *The First Latin American Encounter of Christians for Socialism* (Toronto: Latin American Working Group and the Student Christian Movement, 1972), paragraph 1.3.

103 *To Seek Justice and Resist Evil: Towards a Global Economy for All God's People* (Toronto: Division of World Outreach, UCC, 2001), 12.

104 "Reconciling and Making New: Who Is Jesus for the World Today?" (UCC Committee on Theology and Faith, 1997), 20–21, https://commons.united -church.ca/Documents.

105 See Matthew Fox, *Original Blessing: A Primer in Creation Spirituality* (Santa Fe, NM: Bear, 1983); *Mending the World: An Ecumenical Vision for Healing and Reconciliation*, http://www.united-church.ca/sites/default/files/resources/ report_mending-the-world.pdf.

106 Proceedings, GC24, 1971, 160–61.

107 Proceedings, GC28, 177–285.

108 "Contraception and Abortion: A Statement of the Twenty-Eighth General Council of The United Church of Canada, August 1980" (Toronto: United Church of Canada, Division of Mission in Canada, 1982), 1.

109 *Membership, Ministry, and Human Sexuality*, Proceedings, GC32, 1988, 95–112.

110 Ibid., 103.

111 *To Seek Justice and Resist Evil* invites readers, through the document, both to name their complicity in the global market, and to work for change.

112 For example, the government of Canada apologized in 1988 for the internment of Japanese Canadians during the Second World War.

113 Proceedings, GC29, 1982, 75–76.

114 Proceedings, GC31, 85.

115 Proceedings, GC34, 1992, 329–30. Other apologies include one to Indian residential school survivors, their families, and communities (1998), and one to Japanese United Church members (2009).

116 *Celebrate God's Presence: A Book of Services for The United Church of Canada* (Toronto: UCPH, 2000), 680.

117 Murray Sinclair, "Big Thinking" Seminar, Congress of the Humanities and Social Sciences, Ottawa, May 21, 2015. Author's notes.

118 *A Song of Faith,* Appendix C, 14, http://www.united-church.ca/community -faith/welcome-united-church-canada/song-faith.

119 *The Manual*, 22.

120 Ibid., 22–23.

121 Ibid., 24–26.

122 "To place stress and salvific value on the death of Jesus, a death of great cruelty and unnecessary suffering, is not credible in a world where unnecessary

suffering abounds." Pamela Dickey Young, "Beyond Moral Influence," *Theology Today*, October 1, 1995, 355.

123 *Baptism, Eucharist, and Ministry* (Geneva: Faith and Order Paper No. 111, World Council of Churches, 1982), §4. A baptismal liturgy in *Celebrate God's Presence* asks, "Will you turn from the forces of evil and renounce their power?" (Toronto: UCPH, 2000), 332.

124 Kilpatrick, *Our Common Faith*, 163.

125 Lyrics from Robert S. Lowry, "My Life Flows On," *Voices United* #716.

CHAPTER FIVE

THE CHRISTOLOGY OF
THE UNITED CHURCH OF CANADA

Don Schweitzer

This chapter studies how the person, work, and relationships of Jesus Christ have been understood in The United Church of Canada. It will look at what the UCC has officially taught concerning this in its four subordinate standards and elsewhere. It will also study Christological titles, images, or understandings that have not been officially endorsed but which have been popular or significant in the UCC. The four subordinate standards will provide a periodization for this study: from 1908 to 1936 (*Twenty Articles of Doctrine*), 1936 to 1965 (*A Statement of Faith*), 1965 to 1995 (*A New Creed*), and 1995 to 2014 (*A Song of Faith*).

1908 to 1936

The *Twenty Articles of Doctrine* in the United Church's *Basis of Union* made several affirmations that provided templates for the denomination's understanding of Jesus Christ for years to come. The introduction to the *Twenty Articles of Doctrine* described Jesus Christ as the "chief cornerstone"[1] of the church's understanding of the faith. This is borne out in what follows, where Jesus Christ is referred to in seventeen of the twenty articles and often as the main reference point for the doctrine being discussed. The introduction acknowledged "the teaching of the great creeds of the ancient Church," and claimed that the following articles maintained the "evangelical doctrines of the Reformation."[2] Presumably the great creeds were the Apostles' and Nicene Creeds and the Chalcedonian Definition, which are reflected in the Trinitarian understanding of God in Article 2.3.1 and in the understanding of Jesus as fully human and fully divine in Article 2.3.7.[3] The latter affirms the virgin birth and that Jesus is the "Eternal Son of God" who became "truly man" and was without sin.[4] Here Jesus Christ is affirmed as the incarnation of the second person of the Trinity.

The official commentary on Article 2.3.7 set a pattern for how the UCC tends to understand the person of Christ when it noted that this article "does not presume to enter" the "profound mystery of the relation of the Divine to the human in the person of Christ," but merely "sets the facts side by side," as did the Chalcedonian Definition.[5] In many of its publications, the UCC has understood Jesus Christ as fully human and fully divine, the two natures united yet not confused in his one person, as the Chalcedonian Definition did. Yet its official statements and materials have generally refrained from speculating about how the divine and human natures were united but distinct in him. Themes from the three Christological traditions that flowed into the Chalcedonian Definition are present in the *Twenty Articles of Doctrine* and the official commentary on them.[6] But the commentary adds a criticism of the ancient creeds: these stressed the divinity of Jesus so much that they lost sight of his humanity.[7] Against this, the commentary stresses that Jesus was truly human. It notes that because Jesus Christ was without sin, he reveals not only God, but also the fullness of humanity.[8] This emphasis on Jesus being truly human and revealing what it means to be fully human recurs in many subsequent UCC statements.

The commentary on Article 2.3.7 interprets the virgin birth as maintaining the divine origin of Jesus and describes it as a "historic fact."[9] Subsequent subordinate standards have continued to affirm that, in Jesus Christ, God became present within creation in a new and decisive way, but none mention the virgin birth. Few subsequent UCC publications that discuss the virgin birth have affirmed it as a historic fact.

In keeping with this emphasis that in Jesus, God entered the human condition in a new way, and with the introduction's designation of Jesus Christ as the "chief cornerstone" of the UCC's understanding of the faith, Article 2.3.2 (on revelation) describes God as having been perfectly self-revealed in Jesus.[10] This article makes four interrelated affirmations that have been repeated in most UCC materials dealing with Christology. First, Jesus Christ is designated as the chief or decisive source for the church's knowledge of God. This article acknowledges other sources of revelation but states that for the UCC, Jesus Christ surpasses these. Second, Jesus Christ is described as the culmination of revelation in Scripture. Third, Scripture is described as a trustworthy source of knowledge and testimony concerning Jesus Christ. Finally, it is Jesus who is described as the Word of God, not Scripture. Scripture bears witness to Jesus Christ, but is not identical with him.

The official commentary on Article 2.3.2 acknowledged that the Holy Spirit can be at work in people of other faiths so that their message "comes to their hearers as none other than the Word of God."[11] But it did not encourage interreligious dialogue. The commentary states that Christianity "has a direct spiritual ancestry" in the Hebrew prophets. Article 2.3.6 affirms a reciprocal relationship between Jesus Christ and the church. God has given Jesus to the world as its saviour. In turn, God has given to Jesus "a people, an innumerable multitude, chosen in Christ unto holiness, service, and salvation."[12] Jesus gives to humanity, but also receives a new spiritual body in history—the church—which continues aspects of his work.[13]

Article 2.3.7 describes Jesus as the only mediator between God and humanity who saves by revealing God's will and dying sacrificially. Substitutionary atonement is presented as the chief mechanism of salvation.[14] The commentary interjects a critical note here. It argues that although the phrase "satisfied Divine justice"[15] used in Article 2.3.7 has a long history in Western Christian thought, it is "not well suited" to its purpose, even though a substitute for it "might be hard to find."[16] It argues that the "atonement is not made by another to induce God to be merciful."[17] The forgiveness of sin is God's will, achieved through God acting in Christ. The idea that God forgives sin and accepts sinners unconditionally is affirmed, but the notion that God required the sacrifice of an innocent victim for this to happen is repudiated. This combination of affirming the saving significance of Jesus's death that substitutionary models of atonement attempt to express, with criticism of the mechanism by which these seek to explain this, is repeated in many later UCC publications.

Article 2.3.7 affirms Jesus's resurrection and exaltation and his indwelling presence in the hearts of believers. It includes the Reformed notion of Christ as Prophet, Priest, and King.[18] In the Twenty Articles of Doctrine, Jesus is the divine Lord and Saviour.[19] The commentary describes the meaning of this in two ways. First, Jesus's exaltation and sovereignty reveal that "love is on the throne of the universe."[20] This was a key motif in the interpretation of Jesus's death and resurrection in the UCC at this time. Jesus's public ministry revealed that God is love. Jesus's death and resurrection revealed the ultimacy of that love: his death revealed the extent to which God's love will go to reconcile and redeem, and his resurrection revealed that God's love is more powerful than sin and death. The culmination of Jesus's resurrection was first that the risen Christ was exalted in heaven, and second that he dwells within a Christian's heart. The commentary describes this belief as "the heart of Christianity."[21] Through the indwelling presence of the risen Christ, the love that is on the throne of the universe shapes a believer's thoughts and actions. Here is another hallmark of ucc Christology: Jesus came to make a difference in people's lives.[22] The incarnation has a clear goal, which includes the transformation of people and the formation of the church.

This notion of the risen Christ dwelling in believers' hearts is closely related to the term "the Master," which was a popular unofficial title for Jesus in the ucc during this time and up into the 1960s. It was used by women and men, and had an activist bent. It was popular in social gospel networks and beyond. It was a term of endearment. It conveyed an active sense of discipleship to Jesus, and of serving God and the world by following Jesus's call, his teaching, and example—empowered by his grace and presence. A meaningful worship service was considered to be one in which participants felt the Master's presence.

1936 to 1965

A call arose in 1936 to develop a statement of faith that would express the ucc's denominational identity. The resulting 1940 *A Statement of Faith* took shape in the shadow of the Great Depression and the Second World War. It was a time of theological ferment. The ucc was challenged by a naturalism—one that saw humanity as self-sufficient, able to transform itself and achieve a meaningful life without God—and by Karl Barth's theology, which stressed God's radical transcendence and that God can truly be known only through Jesus Christ.[23]

Though *Statement* often uses different language from the *Twenty Articles of Doctrine*, it repeats many of the same Christological affirmations. For instance, while the *Twenty Articles of Doctrine* describe Jesus Christ as the "chief cornerstone"[24] of the church's theology, the "Introduction" to *Statement* states that the object of the church's faith is the "Gospel of God's holy, redeeming love revealed in Jesus Christ."[25] The affirmations of Jesus as the incarnation of the second person of the Trinity, as truly human and the exemplar of a fully human life, are repeated in Article II on Jesus Christ. Official commentaries on *Statement* stress Jesus's moral perfection. Emphasis on this was characteristic of ucc Christology from the time of the 1925 union until the 1970s. The commentaries maintain the central affirmation of the Chalcedonian Definition[26] and the conviction that Jesus Christ must be understood in a Trinitarian context.[27] One commentary described Jesus's cross as a revelation of God's eternal being,[28] and thus as a further expression of it in time and space and in the context of a world distorted by sin.

When *Statement* asserts that on the cross Jesus "bore the burden of sin" and "that the Cross is for all time the effectual means of reconciling the world unto God,"[29] it affirms what substitutionary models of atonement seek to communicate. But it does not state that Jesus's death satisfied divine justice, as did Article 2.3.7 of the *Twenty Articles of Doctrine*. Instead it speaks of Jesus's cross having a communicative and transformative function. It reveals "God's abhorrence of sin and His saving love."[30] It "moves men to repentance, conveys forgiveness, undoes the estrangement, and binds them to Himself in a new loyalty."[31] The notion that Jesus's death satisfied divine justice—as expressed in the *Twenty Articles of Doctrine*—is denigrated as "Mediaevalism" in a ucc publication of this time, and Anselm's under-standing of how Jesus's death effected atonement is similarly critiqued in an official commentary on *Statement*.[32] But while these materials disavow the mechanism of substitutionary atonement, they maintain what it sought to express: Jesus's death effects a permanent and unconditional reconciliation for sinners with God. Jesus's example and teaching convey God's love for the world[33] and how this should be lived out. His death reveals the depth of this love. His resurrection reveals its ultimacy[34] and so gives people the courage and hope to embody it in their own lives.

Statement denied that humanity is able to be all it is meant to be on its own.[35] Yet it did not simply repudiate the humanism of its time. It stated that Jesus's teaching and example show that devotion "to the will of God and the service of man"[36] coincide. *Statement*, the official commentaries on it, and some ucc preaching of this era all affirmed the humanistic goals of greater justice, peace, and human fulfillment, but also proclaimed that faith in the risen Christ was essential to achieving these.[37] For *Statement* and its commentaries, as with the *Twenty Articles of Doctrine*, Christ was a living presence, dwelling within believers' hearts, particularly present to them in worship and the celebration of communion. Christ was the basis by which God would judge people and their chief source of hope.

Regarding Jesus's relationships, *Statement* describes the church as "the organ of Christ's mind and redemptive will, the body of which He is the Head."[38] An official commentary described the church as "the extension in time of the incarnation and an integral part of God's entire act of recon-ciliation,"[39] through which Jesus remains present in history. While the two are not confused, the church is described here as intrinsic to the ongoing being and work of Jesus Christ. The relationship of Jesus to other religions is not discussed in *Statement* itself. One official commentary described this in supersessionist terms, stating that the Old Testament "finds its completion in the New," and that if "in Christ God did something for men that was utterly unique, there cannot be many ways to salvation, but only one."[40] But in another UCC publication of this time, R.C. Chalmers criticized this as dishonouring Christ and being untrue to Scripture.[41] Chalmers acknowledged that God is present and at work in other sources of revelation and in other religions, arguing that "God's revelation is to be found wherever He has been at work, and supremely in Christ."[42]

UCC publications dealing with Christology in the post–Second World War era, up until 1965, tended to make many of the same basic affirmations about Jesus Christ as *Statement*. Typical of this is the way UCC authors tended to discuss substitutionary atonement. Articles in the series "What the United Church Believes," which ran in *The United Church Observer* from 1946 to 1947, often mentioned that Jesus's death on the cross reveals the depth of God's love and that sin is forgiven, but typically refrained from endorsing a substitutionary mechanism as an explanation of atonement. Similarly, in the first book published in the *New Curriculum* series, Donald Mathers noted that Anselm and Calvin's understanding of substitutionary atonement seems "to oppose the love of God to his justice and his holiness, and even to suggest that Christ has to work against his angry and wrathful Father in order to save men."[43] Yet Mathers affirmed that this understanding "sets forth the gravity of sin, the predicament of men and the fact that Christ does for us what we could not do for ourselves."[44] This critique of substitutionary atonement—while affirming its meaning—is a consistent theme in UCC Christology, from the commentary on the *Twenty Articles of Doctrine* up until the mid-1960s. An exception to this was James Thomson's *God and His Purpose*,[45] the first in the series of Adult Basic Books in the *New Curriculum*. Thomson described Jesus as offering himself on the cross in the place of sinful people, paying a terrible penalty for their sins, thus making his death "his sacrifice to the Father for the sins of men."[46] Apart from exceptions like this and the affirmation of substitutionary atonement in the *Twenty Articles of Doctrine*, materials published by the UCC typically present the position put forth by Mathers: Jesus's death did not placate the wrath of God, but achieved what substitutionary models of atonement sought to express through revealing God's eternal love.

Arthur Moore's *Jesus Christ and the Christian Life*, the adult-level book on Christology for the *New Curriculum*,[47] departed from *Statement*'s mould somewhat in emphasizing the importance of the proclamation of the coming reign of God for Jesus's ministry and for understanding Jesus as the Christ.[48] But Moore continued *Statement*'s approach to understanding the saving significance of Jesus's death. Jesus's death on the cross demonstrated that the reign of God was present in his person, in his perfect obedience to God. It served the coming of God's reign in that it revealed the nature and depth of God's love in a way that wins others to its cause. [49] The empowerment that Jesus's disciples and later Christians experience in the forgiveness communicated through Jesus's death on the cross is matched by the assurance and hope that come from his resurrection.

Few authors writing for the UCC between 1945 and 1965 said much about Jesus's relationship to other religions. Those who discussed this tended to argue that the revelation of God in Jesus Christ surpassed any revelation available in other religions, but most acknowledged that aspects of what was revealed in Jesus could be seen in other religions too. Jesus's relationship to other religions remained a minor theme in the UCC's Christology until after the 1960s. Virtually all saw the church as intrinsic to Jesus's work as the Christ, and stressed that Jesus remains a living presence in history who calls and empowers people to find fulfillment in service to others.

In the early 1960s, Mathers and Moore expounded their understandings of Jesus against the backdrop of the challenge that the natural sciences posed to Christian faith.[50] They recognized the midrashic character of some miracle accounts in the New Testament but insisted that Jesus did perform miracles and that these and his resurrection could not be fitted into the secular world view of Western modernity. Here a criticism can be made of the UCC's Christology from its formation until the mid-1960s. It was largely developed in relation to the concerns and world view of the Western middle class, but not in relation to the concerns and world views of the victims of Western modernity, the "nonsubjects" of Western history.[51] However, there was at least one important non-official exception to this: the Christology in the book produced by the Fellowship for a Christian Social Order, *Towards the Christian Revolution*.[52]

The FCSO, formed in 1934, was a Christian response to the economic and spiritual crisis of the Great Depression. In 1936, it published *Towards the Christian Revolution*, which articulated the group's outlook and provided a basis for study and discussion at its meetings. The original edition had a foreword by former moderator Richard Roberts, and all the contributors belonged to the UCC.[53] *Towards the Christian Revolution* interpreted society in conflictual terms[54] and Jesus Christ as a prophetic figure with what is now known as a preferential option for the poor, whose teaching demanded a socialist alternative to capitalism. In light of this, following a trajectory in Karl Barth's theology, affirming the deity of Jesus Christ led to asserting that God judges the world and takes sides in the conflicts of history.[55] The Depression had opened the contributors' eyes to how capitalism oppressed the poor and created sinful social structures[56] that only collective action could adequately address.[57] Jesus was seen to have carried forward the prophetic tradition of Israel. He identified with society's victims, preached the coming of an egalitarian reign of God, and called his followers to seek God's reign and to find their lives through losing them in service to its coming.[58] Jesus's cross was both an example of this and a revelation of the depth of God's love. The reign of God was a transcendent spiritual reality with concrete ramifications for the organization of society and the economy. In relation to the capitalist economy of the 1930s, Jesus's social ethic was revolutionary.[59] It demanded a new socialist social order. His cross and resurrection provided empowerment to seek this.

These Christological themes—Jesus standing in the tradition of the prophets of Israel; Jesus calling others to find their lives through losing them in service to others; the cross as an example of this; and so on—are present in earlier UCC writings as well as others of this era. But the contributors to *Towards the Christian Revolution* gave them a radical interpretation that set their position apart. This was not the Christology of an established church that blessed current social structures. Instead, the FCSO tried to understand Jesus in relation to the suffering and needs of the non-subjects of history: the marginalized and the oppressed.

The FCSO flourished in the 1930s but collapsed after the onset of the Second World War. It may only have been "a marginal voice"[60] within the UCC. Yet its approach to understanding Jesus in relation to the underside of history would be taken up again in the UCC after the 1960s, in response to concerns expressed by overseas partners and the influence of liberation, Black, and feminist theologies.[61]

A New Creed, 1965–1995

The 1960s were a time of creative chaos[62] that ended the privileged status of Protestantism in English-speaking Canada. Denominations like the UCC became targets of widespread public criticism and were challenged, sometimes at their own instigation, to adapt to the times by shedding beliefs that conflicted with the ethos of modernity; to reorient their ethical teachings to a more liberal view of a person as an autonomous moral agent whose life choices should be respected; and to address social issues such as the nuclear arms race and racism more forthrightly.[63] What the UCC taught about Jesus Christ changed as a result. However, the first major change in the denomination's official Christology in this period came in its understanding of Jesus's relationship to other religions, and resulted more from knowledge gained through its overseas missions than from domestic criticism.

The 1966 report *World Mission*[64] introduced a fundamental change into the UCC's understanding of Jesus's relations to other religions. The report was continuous with previous UCC understandings of Christology in affirming that God had sent Christ to redeem the world and that Christ had founded the church to carry on aspects of Christ's mission.[65] This mission continued to be understood as involving both evangelism and social service. But the report called for some "reconceptualizing of traditional attitudes"[66] toward other religions. Previous UCC materials understood the revelation of God in Jesus Christ to surpass that available in other religions. *World Mission* moved the UCC's official understanding of this relationship dramatically towards a more respectful attitude towards other world religions and provided a Christological basis for this. As God's action in Christ had respected the rights of other people to accept or reject the gospel, so Christians should respect the integrity of a non-Christian's choice of religion. Mission was now broadened to include dialogue with other religions, which might lead Christians to a better understanding of their own faith.[67] *World Mission* also introduced a note of ideological critique into the UCC's understanding of Christology, arguing that what antagonized Hindus, Buddhists, and others were not so much claims for the uniqueness of Christ, but "claims about the uniqueness of a westernized Christ."[68] It recognized that Western cultural values were often fused with the UCC's understanding of Jesus Christ so that the denomination's Christology provided ideological support for Western cultural imperialism. This recognition would come to fuller expression in the UCC's 1986 apology to First Nations peoples. The report called for Christians to disassociate their understanding of Jesus Christ from Western interpretations of the same and to be open to the inculturation of Christology into non-Western cultures.[69] The impulse for these changes came from the UCC's overseas work and studies in comparative and world religions.

As this shift was happening in the UCC's understanding of Jesus's relation to other religions, the cultural and religious ferment of the 1960s had ruptured the relationship of some within the denomination to traditional confessions of Christian faith such as the Apostles' Creed. The substantial

Christological expositions in the *New Curriculum* by Donald Mathers[70] and A.B.B. Moore[71] were controversial because of their use of contemporary methods of biblical criticism. But they affirmed understandings of Jesus's person that were substantially in line with the Chalcedonian Definition. However, by the mid-1960s, some laypeople and clergy were objecting to repeating the Apostles' Creed as a confession of faith and not simply because of its affirmation of the virgin birth.[72]

The first draft of *A New Creed* described Jesus as the "true Man," who had come to reconcile and make new, and "who works within us and among us by his Spirit."[73] But it made no direct mention of Jesus's death and resurrection, or of his divinity. A motion of General Council asked the Committee on Christian Faith to revise it to more adequately express "the Christian Gospel for our time."[74] A commentary on the initial draft by Gregory Baum, a prominent Roman Catholic social ethicist, was brought to the committee's subsequent meeting in October 1968. Baum noted that the draft did not adequately state how Jesus Christ judges human sin, calls for repentance, and empowers people to seek justice.[75] Baum also noted several times that the draft made no mention of Jesus's cross and resurrection. The committee deleted the line that the church was called to proclaim Jesus's Kingdom. Against a self-secularizing trend in the UCC at that time—a trend that one-sidedly emphasized the humanity of Jesus—it offered these replacement lines, which were later adopted:

> to proclaim Jesus, crucified and risen,
> our judge and our hope.

Designed for use in worship, *A New Creed* was initially controversial. New here was a lack of insistence on Jesus as the sole source of salvation. The line "who works in us and others by his Spirit" can be read as in keeping with the new understanding of Jesus's relationship to other religions found in *World Mission*. No explicit mention is made of Jesus's divinity, but his resurrection is affirmed, which historically lies at the root of this belief. The line "our judge and our hope" confesses that for the church Jesus is the qualitative centre of history, the bearer and medium of God's final and decisive revelation by which the church discerns God's presence in history. There is no explicit Trinitarian confession, but there is mention of the three persons of the Trinity and statements about their intrinsic relations.[76] *A New Creed* continued the UCC's tendency to stress Jesus as a moral exemplar who reveals what it means to be fully human, and to confess him as the head of the church and as a living presence in history. The Christology of *A New Creed* changed when it was revised in 1979–80: "who has come in the true Man, Jesus" was changed to "who has come in Jesus, the Word made flesh." This replaced the emphasis on Jesus revealing what it means to be fully human with an affirmation of the divinity of Jesus, of Jesus as the incarnation of the second person of the Trinity.

Pierre Berton had criticized established Canadian churches for being turned in upon themselves and not prophetically involved in Canadian society.[77] The Committee on Christian Faith saw *A New Creed* as responding to the "lostness and loneliness" that people experienced in modern industrial societies, but also to the attitude of human "self-sufficiency in world affairs"[78] that Berton's writing represented. Perhaps in response to Berton's criticism, a Christological affirmation in the originally accepted version of *A New Creed* (Jesus as "the true man") was modelled partly after Bonhoeffer's notion of Jesus as the man for others.[79] The section on the calling of the church was said to affirm that following Jesus "entails political-social involvement against evil, on behalf of just treatment for all people."[80]

A New Creed was intentionally drafted so that people across a broad range of theological perspectives could profess it with integrity.[81] At this time, the spectrum of belief between theological liberals and conservatives in the UCC was widening and becoming contentious.[82] This can be seen partly as a reflection within the denomination of a broader movement in post–Second World War North Atlantic societies away from adherence to understandings of the faith defined by ecclesiastical institutions, towards an understanding of the faith in one's own terms.[83] This movement led to a pluralization of attitudes towards religious belief and an increasing number of options for it,[84] and may have contributed to a broadening of the spectrum of understandings of Jesus Christ within the UCC.

In 1974, Temiskaming Presbytery memorialized the 26th General Council, asking that the theological position of the UCC regarding the lordship of Jesus Christ be clarified.[85] The "Whereas" section of this memorial stated that while "'Jesus is Lord' was an early Christian creed, *A New Creed* did not mention this,"[86] and that the challenge of religious pluralism, a theme of *World Mission*, had introduced confusion into the UCC's understanding of Jesus's lordship. The memorial called for a reaffirmation of Jesus's lordship in a "pluralistic and secular world."[87] Toronto Conference conveyed this memorial to General Council with non-concurrence. General Council passed it with the added recommendation, "that the Committee on Christian Faith ... prepare for the Church a considered and full statement on the meaning of the Lordship of Christ and His humanity for our time."[88] The report, entitled *The Lordship of Jesus Christ*, was received by the 1977 General Council.

The Lordship of Jesus stressed that Jesus's lordship cannot be appropriately affirmed by simply repeating New Testament understandings of this in the present. Instead the church must struggle to interpret what Jesus's lordship meant in relation to the world in his day, and then what this means in the present.[89] This idea that Jesus must be understood contextually, in relation to the time and place in which the church lives, has been a consistent mark of the UCC Christology since *Statement* in 1940. *The Lordship of Jesus* affirmed that as Jesus is recognized as a figure of his time, his non-contemporaneity can give Christians a critical perspective on the ideologies of their time.[90] Implicit here was an affirmation of the importance of historical biblical criticism for the UCC's understanding of Jesus Christ, which has been a hallmark of the United Church's Christology since *Statement*.

The report represented a dialectical response to the kinds of criticism that Berton had made of established Canadian churches and their beliefs. In opposition to Berton's restriction of the importance of Jesus to simply being a moral teacher, it affirmed Jesus as the centre of history, the fulfillment of the hope of Israel, and the Chalcedonian understanding of Jesus as fully human and fully divine. The report argued that the truth of such traditional affirmations was not being disputed.[91] Against Berton's claims that affirmations such as "Jesus is Lord" were out of date and that modern Westerners did not need such authority figures, the report responded that "the plight of modern humanity is not in having no lords, but in having too many," often false and destructive, and failing to recognize their enthrallment to them.[92] The pressing issue was not assent to traditional Christian creeds, but the question of their application—how they should be lived out.[93] Here the report said "yes" to Berton's call for the church to become involved in pressing social issues. It recognized that the church is "constantly tempted to turn the Gospel into a theologia gloria,"[94] and that it may deny Christ's lordship by becoming turned in upon itself. Against this, it argued that "the Lordship of Jesus involves a prohibition from isolating ourselves from any aspect of life."[95] It stressed that Jesus was a real human being, "who identified himself with the pain and suffering of humanity in the form of a servant," and through whom God had identified with the pain and suffering of the world.[96] This marked a turn in official UCC Christology toward trying to understand Jesus in relation to the victims of history. *The Lordship of Jesus* maintained the affirmation of *World Mission* that as

Christians acknowledge Jesus's lordship by following him into the world, "in the contemporary situation, dialogue is a better model than proclamation"[97] in relation to other religions.

In recent decades, a typology of exclusivism, inclusivism, and pluralism has been used to categorize understandings of Jesus's relation to other religions.[98] Exclusivism emphasizes the differences between religions and the claim that Jesus Christ is the only source of salvation. Inclusivism typically argues that while truth and salvation can be found in other religions, what they offer can be found more fully in Jesus Christ. Pluralism tends to affirm that different religions represent various ways to the one transcendent God, and that while religions have many differences, none is clearly superior to another.

The Lordship of Jesus is somewhat unclear as to how it understands Jesus's relationship to other religions. Its statement—that "dialogue is a better model than proclamation" for Christians in relation to other religions in the present[99]—could be read as representing a pluralistic approach. Yet the report also recognizes a place for proclamation after and in the midst of dialogue. This and its emphasis that Jesus is lord seem to represent a more inclusivist understanding of Jesus's relationship to other religions.

During this time there were two unofficial depictions of Christology that were popular or widely discussed in the ucc. The first was Willis Wheatley's drawing entitled *Jesus Christ—Liberator*, also known as "the laughing Jesus." Wheatley worked for the ucc and did many illustrations for the *New Curriculum*. In the early 1970s, he was commissioned by the United Church to create four drawings of Jesus. One of these, entitled *Jesus Christ—Liberator*, was a picture of Jesus laughing, and it was particularly popular in the ucc. A second, widely discussed Christological depiction was the statue *Crucified Woman* created by Almuth Lütkenhaus-Lackey and displayed in Bloor Street United Church in Toronto during Holy Week in 1979. This generated considerable discussion in the ucc and beyond.[100] While immigrants to the ucc from Ghana, Zimbabwe, and Congo tend to find the statue's depiction of a nude woman obscene, many women and men experienced it as a powerful Christological statement. These two depictions of Christ can be seen as attempts to locate the ucc's understanding of Jesus more deeply amid the laughter and tears of the world.

If these two works of art are interpreted in light of the ancient Christian principle that "that which is not assumed is not healed,"[101] they can be seen as attempts to deepen the appreciation of the fullness of Jesus's humanity and of how the human nature assumed by the Word embraces female as

Figure 5.1   *Jesus Christ—Liberator*, by Willis Wheatley, 1972. Copyright The United Church of Canada. Reproduced with permission.

Figure 5.2   *Crucified Woman* by Almuth Lutkenhaus-Lackey, Emmanuel College, Toronto. Photograph courtesy of Paul Gillingham.

well as male gender. Wheatley's drawing showed a Jesus truly human and alive in the world. The *Crucified Woman* identified Jesus with the suffering of women and portrayed Christ as present within them. It was displayed in Bloor Street United Church at the end of a decade that had seen considerable discussion of feminist issues in the UCC and a year after the denomination had elected its first female moderator.

During this period, Douglas John Hall developed a Christology that also tried to deepen Canadians' appreciation of Jesus's humanity and their own. Drawing on the theology of Martin Luther, Hall understood Jesus as representing humanity to God and God to humanity, most profoundly in his suffering and death on the cross.[102] In Christ, people can see that God is with them and accepts them as they are. From this, people can find the courage to accept and rejoice in their own humanity, and live creatively within the possibilities this affords, rather than destructively trying to master nature and deny their finitude.

A Song of Faith, 1995–2015

Throughout the 1980s, there was a sense that the UCC was due for a new articulation of its faith.[103] The 1988 General Council decision regarding the eligibility of gay and lesbian persons for ordination came near the end of two decades during which the UCC revised many of its teachings regarding gender roles and sexuality. The theological spectrum within the denomination now openly ranged from the theologically conservative to those greatly distanced from the UCC's more extended statements of faith such as the *Twenty Articles of Doctrine*. The UCC's Christology was also affected by its grappling with ethical issues such as the environmental crisis and globalization, the increasing religious pluralism of Canadian society, and the attempts by many Western churches following the Holocaust to expunge anti-Semitic elements from their teachings. There were three major Christological discussions in the United Church during this time: the first is found in the series of interfaith statements which the UCC issued; second was the controversy about Bill Phipps's interview with the *Ottawa Citizen*; and third was the publication of *A Song of Faith*.

The UCC's interfaith statements were all developed through extended processes of consultation with church members, each lasting several years. The first was *Mending the World*.[104] This included sketches of various New Testament images of Jesus, which, the report argued, directed the church toward a whole-world ecumenism of care for the entire creation in partnership with others. Its acknowledgement of the diversity of images of Jesus in the New

Testament set a precedent for subsequent statements. Following the lead of *The Lordship of Jesus*, the report payed particular attention to Jesus's Jewish heritage and the historical circumstances and concrete injunctions of his public ministry and teaching. Jesus was affirmed to be fully human, living out of his Jewish heritage and exemplifying for Christians how they should live.[105] *Mending the World* also affirmed that Jesus was fully divine. Through his humanity he gives Christians direction. Through his divinity he gives hope and empowerment.[106] New here was an emphasis on the cosmic nature of Christ as the author and redeemer of all things.[107] This extended the UCC's understanding of Jesus's saving significance to include all of creation.

Next came *Bearing Faithful Witness*,[108] a statement by the UCC about its relationship to Judaism. This was received in 2003. It emphasized that Jesus's teaching and ministry could be understood only in relation to his Jewish heritage. It repudiated any notion of supersessionism that understood Christianity as replacing Judaism or rendering it obsolete,[109] and argued that Jesus extended the breadth of God's promises and blessing to include gentiles. It provided a post-Holocaust reading of major New Testament traditions and concluded that Jesus probably understood himself as a prophet but not as the Messiah.[110] It argued that the correct answer to the question "Is Jesus the Messiah?" was "For Jews, no; for many Christians, yes."[111] This moved the UCC's Christology to a more pluralist position.

A subsequent statement—this one on the UCC's relationship to Islam, *That We May Know Each Other*[112]—affirmed Jesus as fully human and fully divine, but noted that while Jesus is the full and normative revelation of God, "Jesus defines God's Spirit but does not confine it."[113] It affirmed the "'prophetic witness' of Muhammad" but maintained that for Christians Jesus Christ remains the centre of history. This moved the UCC's Christology to somewhere between inclusivism and pluralism.

An interfaith statement in regard to Hinduism is currently being developed. The study document for this, *Honouring the Divine in Each Other: United Church Hindu Relations Today*, affirms the uniqueness of Jesus and proposes that the UCC should adopt an orientation of "acceptance, respect, and openness to mutual transformation" towards Hinduism.[114] Like other interfaith statements that immediately preceded it, it holds that interreligious dialogue can lead to a transformation of the church's understanding of its faith.[115]

Up until the 1960s, the UCC typically took an inclusivist position in its understandings of Jesus's relationship to other religions. Since then, it has typically affirmed the uniqueness of Jesus as the Christ but also the need for dialogue with other religions. As Jesus Christ embodies virtues like love, hope, and faith, to fail to recognize and value these virtues as they appear in other religions is to fail to acknowledge the presence of Jesus's Spirit at work therein. Faithfulness to Jesus Christ impels Christians to recognize these values as they are manifest in other religions and to seek the truth through respectful dialogue with them.[116] At the same time, "Christ" in the New Testament is an evaluative term. It designates Jesus as having a unique saving significance for the whole of creation. A pluralist understanding of Jesus's relationship to other religions does not do justice to this aspect of the New Testament witness. Faith in Jesus Christ places one within the tension of affirming both "the enriching facts of cultural and religious plurality, and 'commitment' as a clear advocacy of the distinctive symbols and perspectives of the Christian tradition centered in Jesus the Christ."[117] The UCC has tended to stand within this tension and in recent decades has adopted a more respectful, dialogical approach to other religions, while still affirming Jesus's uniqueness.

The uniqueness of Jesus Christ was central to a public Christological discussion that happened after Bill Phipps (Moderator from 1997 to 2000) was interviewed by the *Ottawa Citizen* on October 24, 1997. In the interview, Phipps emphasized how faith in Jesus connects to work for social justice. The interviewer was uninterested in this and repeatedly posed questions about the divinity and resurrection of Christ from a theologically conservative perspective. Phipps affirmed that "Christ reveals to us as much of the nature of God as we can see in a human being" and that Christ is risen in the hearts of Christians; but he stated that he didn't believe that Christ was God and declined to engage in Trinitarian speculation.[118] The interview attracted national media attention, created a minor furor in the UCC, and was discussed by its General Council Executive. In a subsequent news release, Phipps said his remarks were within "the broad mainstream of United Church belief."[119] They were in keeping with *A New Creed*, albeit on the theologically liberal side. However, Phipps tended to speak of God's presence in Jesus in quantitative terms. In a videotaped discussion with Phipps, Peter Wyatt responded positively to Phipps describing Jesus as the Word made flesh, but suggested that the Nicene Creed and the Chalcedonian Definition made a qualitative, not quantitative distinction between Jesus and other people.[120]

The responses to Phipps's remarks demonstrated the importance of Jesus Christ to many in the UCC and revealed the breadth of opinions about him. This was also apparent in responses to the study resource, *Reconciling and*

Making New: Who Is Jesus for the World Today? commissioned by the 33rd General Council in 1990 and distributed by the Theology and Faith Committee in 1997. The committee reported to the 37th General Council in 2000 that while most who responded to the study documents understood salvation to be inseparable from Jesus, there was a wide range of understandings in the UCC of who Jesus was, what salvation is, and how he effects it. The General Council then asked the committee to produce a draft of a new statement of faith to be circulated throughout the church for study and response. This process produced *A Song of Faith*, which was affirmed by the 39th General Council in 2006.

Song attempted to reflect how the gospel was understood in the denomination at the start of the new millennium. It is not restrained about affirming Jesus's resurrection or the incarnation in the way that the first draft of *A New Creed* was, and it is not reticent about Trinitarian understandings of Jesus in the way that Bill Phipps was. Instead, *Song* responded to a postmodern demand for recognition of God's transcendence and otherness[121] with a Trinitarian understanding of God as revealed in Jesus Christ. It is a contemporary expression of faith, filled with echoes of Scripture and the ancient creeds.

Song responded to the diversity of Christological understandings in the UCC by describing Jesus and his saving significance along the two trajectories of a Word and a Spirit Christology.[122] Its overall presentation of Jesus Christ is structured as a Spirit Christology. Jesus of Nazareth is portrayed as the epicentre in the great arc of the Spirit's life-giving and redemptive work. Jesus is described as so "filled with the Holy Spirit"[123] that people experienced the presence of God in him. But this presentation is punctuated by affirmations of a Word Christology, as when Jesus is described in Trinitarian terms like "God the Christ, the Holy One embodied."[124] *Song* begins with a Trinitarian affirmation of God, which it states in several ways.[125] Similar affirmations occur throughout it. Its presentation of Jesus stresses that he was Jewish and truly human. It outlines his public ministry and understands his death in two ways: first as that of a martyr for justice (Spirit Christology), then as an atoning death (Word Christology) through which "God bears the sin, grief, and suffering of the world."[126] The risen Christ is affirmed as a present source of hope, and the Christological section ends with an echo of the Chalcedonian Definition: Jesus is "the one in whom God and humanity are perfectly joined" who effects "the transformation of our lives."[127] *Song* affirms that Jesus and the church go together. The church seeks "to continue the story of Jesus by embodying Christ's presence in the world."[128] But the two are distinct. The church celebrates Christ, acts in his name, and is comforted and empowered by his presence. But the church's hope lies in God, and in what God has done in Christ and is doing in the Holy Spirit, not in itself. Near the end of *Song,* there is a mention of Jesus's second coming.[129] This was noted in Article 2.3.19 of the *Twenty Articles of Doctrine*[130] and appears periodically in UCC literature over the years. Its appearance here indicates the unapologetic tone of *Song.*

Popular among many people in the UCC at this time were the understandings of Jesus generated by New Testament scholars such as John Dominic Crossan and Marcus Borg, and popularized by John Shelby Spong.[131] These authors tended to see the eschatological elements in the gospel accounts of Jesus's public ministry as later, inauthentic accretions and the resurrection narratives as fictional representations of the church's beliefs. They understood Jesus as an inspired person whose message was distorted by later church teaching. While these portrayals of Jesus were sometimes potentially radical in their social implications, they refused to see Jesus as anything more than an inspired person. This put them at odds with the New Testament and made it difficult for them to explain how faith in Jesus Christ survived his crucifixion. There are echoes of these portrayals in the section of *Song* describing Jesus's upbringing and public ministry. But *Song* insists on also understanding Jesus in Trinitarian terms, and acknowledges Jesus's resurrection as an intervention of God that overcame Jesus's death.

Conclusion: Some Broad Themes

The United Church of Canada has typically sought to understand Jesus in a way that is faithful to Scripture and the ancient creeds, and open to what it hears the Spirit saying to it in the present. Throughout its history and in its official teachings, it has tended to understand Jesus's person along the lines of the Nicene Creed and the Chalcedonian Definition, and so understands Jesus in a Trinitarian way. Yet it has always insisted on fleshing out the affirmations of these ancient creeds with attention to Jesus's public ministry, usually emphasizing that Jesus was truly human and that he models what it means to be fully human. Since *Statement* in 1940, the denomination has emphasized the need to understand Jesus in relation to its current context. This has led to affirming the teachings of the ancient creeds in an open way. The UCC's statements of faith do not mechanically repeat their teachings, but instead employ them as guidelines for articulating who Jesus is and what he means in the present.

While the UCC affirmed an understanding of substitutionary atonement in Article 2.3.7 of the *Twenty Articles of Doctrine*, it has had an ambivalent relationship to this. Forgiveness of guilt is essential for a church that was involved with running residential schools. The UCC has always affirmed what this atonement model seeks to express about God's mercy and forgiveness, yet its official literature has repeatedly stressed an antipathy to the barbarism of the mechanism used to explain Jesus's saving significance in traditional versions of this understanding of atonement.[132] The UCC typically affirms that the ultimacy of God's love is revealed in Jesus's death and resurrection, seeing in this a source of hope that empowers people to love others and follow him. UCC literature and statements of faith typically see Jesus's reigning in one's heart to be as important as his reigning in heaven. In keeping with this, they typically emphasize that the church continues aspects of Jesus's ministry.

Jesus Christ was described as the "chief cornerstone"[133] of the UCC's understanding of the faith at the time of its formation. Decades later, in a very different context, this remains true. The UCC continues to see Jesus Christ as central to its understanding of God, itself, and its calling as a church.

NOTES

1   *Twenty Articles of Doctrine, The Manual*, 2016, 37th rev. ed. (Toronto: UCPH, 2013), 11.

2   Ibid. The official commentary on the *Twenty Articles of Doctrine* notes that Article 2.3.7 sets forth the uniqueness of Jesus Christ as the person in whom God has acted to reconcile and redeem creation and humanity and sees this as maintaining a theme that was at the heart of the Reformation. See Thomas Kilpatrick, *Our Common Faith, With a Brief History of the Church Union Movement in Canada* by Kenneth Cousland (Toronto: Ryerson Press, 1928), 134.

3   *The Manual*, 12.

4   Ibid.

5   Kilpatrick, *Our Common Faith*, 135.

6   The description of Jesus as the Word made flesh in Article 2.3.2 reflects the Alexandrian tradition. The emphasis on Jesus as fully human ("truly man") in Article 2.3.7 reflects the Antiochean tradition. Kilpatrick's commentary reiterates a theme from Augustine's Christology, which through the Latin tradition helped shape the Chalcedonian Definition: the fullness of Jesus's humanity is

as essential as his divinity for his saving significance. It is the combination of both in his one person that mediates salvation. See Kilpatrick, *Our Common Faith*, 136.

7 Kilpatrick, *Our Common Faith*, 136–37.

8 Ibid., 137.

9 Ibid., 138–39.

10 *The Manual*, 12.

11 Kilpatrick, *Our Common Faith*, 94.

12 *The Manual*, 12.

13 For a discussion of the import of this two-way relationship between Jesus and the church, see Don Schweitzer, *Jesus Christ for Contemporary Life* (Eugene, OR: Cascade, 2012), 177–97.

14 Articles 2.3.7 and 2.3.9, *The Manual*, 12–13.

15 Kilpatrick, *Our Common Faith*, 94.

16 Ibid., 141–42.

17 Ibid., 144.

18 *The Manual*, 12.

19 Ibid., 2.3.15, 14.

20 Kilpatrick, *Our Common Faith*, 149. George Pidgeon frequently used this phrase in his sermons to describe the meaning of Jesus's resurrection and exaltation. For example, George Pidgeon, *The Indwelling Christ* (Toronto: Clarke, Irwin, 1948), 50.

21 Kilpatrick, *Our Common Faith*, 148.

22 This may reflect John Wesley's emphasis on sanctification, part of the UCC's Methodist roots. However, in the Reformed tradition, John Calvin also insisted that there is no justification without sanctification.

23 For discussions of this naturalism, see Randolph C. Chalmers, *See the Christ Stand! A Study in Doctrine in The United Church of Canada* (Toronto: Ryerson Press, 1945), 165–76, and Phyllis D. Airhart, *A Church with the Soul of a Nation*, 112–16. For the influence of Barth's theology on *A Statement of Faith*, see Airhart, *A Church with the Soul of a Nation*, 121. For a reading of Barth's theology and Neo-Orthodoxy in general at the time from within the United Church, see Chalmers, *See the Christ Stand*, 177–97. Chalmers taught theology at Pine Hill Divinity Hall In Halifax from 1957 to 1974.

24 *The Manual*, 11.

25 Ibid., 15.

26 Ibid., 21; The Commission of Christian Faith of The United Church of Canada, *Highways of the Heart* (Toronto: BESS, UCC, 1941), 17–18.

27 John Dow, *This Is Our Faith: An Exposition of the Statement of Faith of The*

United Church of Canada (Toronto: BESS, UCC, 1943), 78. Dow taught theology at Emmanuel College in Toronto.

28 *Highways of the Heart*, 47.

29 *The Manual*, 17, 16.

30 Ibid., 16.

31 Ibid., 17.

32 Chalmers, *See the Christ Stand*, 127; Dow, *This Is Our Faith*, 112.

33 *The Manual*, 16.

34 Ibid., 16, 17.

35 Article V declares that man [*sic*] lives "in a world of confusion and distress, and is unable of himself to fulfil God's high purpose for him," *The Manual*, 16–17.

36 *The Manual*, 16, 19.

37 Ibid., 17, 19; *Highways of the Heart*, 16; Dow, *This Is Our Faith*, 221; George Pidgeon, *The Vicarious Life* (Toronto: Cumberlege/Oxford University Press, 1945), 77–78.

38 *The Manual*, 17.

39 *Highways of the Heart*, 55; Dow, *This Is Our Faith*, 140, 32.

40 Dow, *This Is Our Faith*, 173, 171.

41 Chalmers, *See the Christ Stand*, 248. He would later write: "whatever element of truth is to be found in other religions is already seen in Christ in a more complete and perfect manner." Chalmers, *A Gospel to Proclaim* (Toronto: Ryerson Press, 1960), 16.

42 Chalmers, *See the Christ Stand*, 253.

43 Donald Mathers, *The Word and the Way: Personal Christian Faith for Today* (Toronto: UCPH, 1962), 123; see also 130.

44 Ibid., 123.

45 James Sutherland Thomson, *God and His Purpose* (Toronto: UCPH, 1964).

46 Ibid., 130. See also 114, 117 129–30, 132.

47 Arthur Moore, *Jesus Christ and the Christian Life* (Toronto: UCPH, 1965).

48 Ibid., 66.

49 Ibid., 163–64.

50 Ibid., 93–94.

51 This is a criticism that Gustavo Gutierrez directed at most of modern Western theology. Gustavo Gutierrez, *The Truth Shall Make You Free: Confrontations* (Maryknoll, NY: Orbis, 1990), 23–25.

52 *Towards the Christian Revolution*, edited by R.B.Y. Scott and Gregory Vlastos, with an Introduction by Roger Hutchinson (Kingston: Ronald P. Frye, 1989). Originally published by Willett Clark in 1936.

53 "Preface," in ibid.

54 John Line, "The Theological Principles," in *Towards the Christian Revolution*, 48.

55 Ibid., 48–49.

56 R.B.Y. Scott, "The Biblical Basis," in *Towards the Christian Revolution*, 96.

57 Line, "The Theological Principles," 34.

58 Gregory Vlastos, "The Ethical Foundations," in *Towards the Christian Revolution*, 54–56.

59 Ibid., 52.

60 Eleanor Stebner, "The 1930s," in *The United Church of Canada: A History*, ed. Don Schweitzer (Waterloo, ON: Wilfrid Laurier University Press, 2012), 51.

61 Exemplary of this is Harold and Patricia Wells, *Jesus Means Life* (Toronto: Division of Communication, UCC, 1982). See also Harold Wells, "Jesus the Christ: Centre and Norm for a Life-Giving Critical Theology," in *Intersecting Voices*, edited by Don Schweitzer and Derek Simon (Ottawa: Novalis, 2004), 168–85.

62 Douglas John Hall, "Christianity and Canadian Contexts: Then and Now," in Schweitzer and Simon, *Intersecting Voices*, 19.

63 These criticisms were expressed in Pierre Berton, *The Comfortable Pew* (Toronto: McClelland & Stewart, 1965).

64 *World Mission*, UCC, *Proceedings*, GC22, 1966, 299–493.

65 Ibid., 341.

66 Ibid., 351.

67 Ibid., 352.

68 Ibid., 354.

69 Ibid., 355.

70 Mathers, *The Word and the Way*.

71 Moore, *Jesus Christ and the Christian Life*.

72 See John Young's Introduction to this volume for more about the development of *A New Creed*.

73 UCC, *Proceedings*, GC23, 1968, 322–3.

74 Ibid., 56.

75 Gregory Baum, "A New Creed," *The Ecumenist* 6, no. 5 (July-August 1968): 166–67.

76 The Committee's report, *Christian Faith*, stated that in *A New Creed*, the "answer to the question, 'Who is this God?' is expressed in triune form as the One who takes the initiative in creating, in coming, in working—Father, Son and Holy Spirit." UCC, *Proceedings*, GC23, 1968, 323.

77 Pierre Berton, "Out of This World," in *Why the Sea Is Boiling Hot* (Toronto: UCPH, 1965), 1–2.

78 *Creeds: A Report of the Committee on Christian Faith*, The United Church of Canada (Toronto: Ryerson Press, 1969), 17.

79 Ibid. The Committee also saw this as an affirmation of the incarnation of God in Jesus, but this became much more apparent when the phrase "the Word made flesh" replaced the description of Jesus as "true Man."

80 Ibid.

81 UCC, *Proceedings*, GC23, 1968, 323.

82 Airhart, *A Church with the Soul of a Nation*, 273–76.

83 Charles Taylor, *A Secular Age* (Cambridge, MA: Belknap Press of Harvard University Press, 2007), 475.

84 Ibid., 513.

85 UCC, *Proceedings*, GC26, 1974, 111–12.

86 Ibid., 111.

87 Ibid., 112.

88 Ibid., 60.

89 David Lochhead/Committee on Christian Faith, *The Lordship of Jesus* (Toronto: Division of Mission in Canada, UCC, 1978), 3. Lochhead, the main author of this report, taught theology at the Vancouver School of Theology.

90 Ibid., 51.

91 Ibid., 26, 8.

92 Ibid., 5, 6–7.

93 Ibid., 9.

94 Ibid., 33.

95 Ibid., 47.

96 Ibid., 5.

97 Ibid., 48.

98 For a discussion of this typology, see Harold Wells, *The Christic Center* (Maryknoll, NY: Orbis, 2004), 182–84.

99 Lochhead, *The Lordship of Jesus*, 48.

100 Doris Jean Dyke, *Crucified Woman* (Toronto: UCPH, 1991). The *Crucified Woman* statue was eventually moved to the grounds of Emmanuel College in Toronto, where it remains.

101 Gregory of Naziansus, *On God and Christ: The Five Theological Orations and Two Letters to Cledonius* (Crestwood, NY: St. Vladimir's Seminary Press, 2002), 158.

102 Douglas John Hall, *Professing the Faith: Christian Theology in a North American Context* (Minneapolis, MN: Fortress Press, 1993), 363–548; *The Cross in Our Context* (Minneapolis, MN: Fortress Press, 2003), 111–33. Hall taught theology at St. Andrew's College in Saskatoon from 1965 to 1975 and then at McGill University from 1975 until his retirement.

103   Ross Bartlett, "1990–2003: The Church into the New Millennium," in Schweitzer, *The United Church of Canada: A History*, 170.

104   *Mending the World: An Ecumenical Vision for Healing and Reconciliation* (Toronto: United Church of Canada, 1997).

105   Ibid., 10.

106   Ibid., 11.

107   Ibid., 12–14.

108   *Bearing Faithful Witness: United Church–Jewish Relations Today* (Toronto: Committee on Inter-Church Inter-Faith Relations, UCC, 2003).

109   Ibid., 17.

110   Ibid., 26. However, aspects of Jesus's ministry, such as his gathering of twelve disciples, can be seen as making a "monumental though implicit" claim about his person and role in the coming of God's reign. John Meier, *A Marginal Jew: Rethinking the Historical Jesus*, vol. 2 (New York: Doubleday, 1994), 144. This suggests that he saw himself as more than a prophet.

111   Ibid., 25.

112   *That We May Know Each Other: United Church–Muslim Relations Today* (Toronto: Committee on Inter-Church and Inter-Faith Relations, UCC, 2004 [approved 2006]).

113   Ibid., 36.

114   *Honouring the Divine in Each Other: United Church–Hindu Relations Today*, Theology and Inter-Church Inter-Faith Committee (Toronto: UCC, 2014), 39.

115   Ibid., 47.

116   John B. Cobb Jr., *Transforming Christianity and the World* (Maryknoll, NY: Orbis, 1999), 60.

117   Mark Lewis Taylor, "Introduction: The Theological Development and Contribution of Paul Tillich," in *Paul Tillich: Theologian of the Boundaries*, edited by Mark Lewis Taylor (London: Collins, 1987), 32. For discussions of the relationship of Jesus Christ to other religions by United Church theologians, see Pamela Dickey Young, *Christ in a Post-Christian World* (Minneapolis, MN: Fortress Press, 1995); Wells, *The Christic Center*, 181–210; Schweitzer, *Jesus Christ for Contemporary Life*, 222–60.

118   "An *Ottawa Citizen* Q & A: Is Jesus God?" in Bill Phipps, *Cause for Hope* (Kelowna, BC: Copperhouse, 2007), 222–23.

119   "Responses from the Moderator," in Phipps, *Cause for Hope*, 225.

120   *Who Is Jesus for You today?* (Toronto: Berkeley Studios, UCC).

121   This postmodern demand is described in David Tracy, *On Naming the Present* (Maryknoll, NY: Orbis, 1994), 41.

122   For a sketch of these, see Lisa Sowle Cahill, *Global Justice, Christology and Christian Ethics* (New York: Cambridge University Press, 2013), 129–33. Cahill

notes that both these trajectories are present in the New Testament and argues that both are necessary to sustain Christian discipleship today (126, 133). For a Spirit Christology by a United Church theologian, see Paul Newman, *A Spirit Christology: Recovering the Biblical Paradigm of Christian Faith* (Lanham, MD: University Press of America, 1987).

123   *The Manual*, 24.

124   Ibid.

125   Ibid., 21.

126   Ibid., 24.

127   Ibid., 25.

128   Ibid.

129   Ibid., 27.

130   Ibid., 15.

131   Representative texts are John Dominic Crossan, *Jesus: A Revolutionary Biography* (New York: HarperCollins, 1995); Marcus Borg, *Meeting Jesus Again for the First Time* (New York: HarperCollins, 1995); and John Shelby Spong, *Jesus for the Non-Religious*, 2nd ed. (New York: HarperCollins, 2008).

132   For an attempt to reinterpret substitutionary atonement in a way that avoids what UCC materials have criticized about it, see Don Schweitzer, "Understanding Substitutionary Atonement in Spatial Terms," *Touchstone* 31, no. 2 (June 2013): 7–17.

133   *The Manual*, 11.

CHAPTER SIX

THE HOLY SPIRIT

Adrian Jacobs

A theological understanding of the person and work of the Holy Spirit is no small subject to explore. Within the broad range of The United Church of Canada, this doctrine has been expressed and explored through official statements like the *Twenty Articles of Doctrine* (1925), the *Statement of Faith* (1940), *A New Creed* (1968), and *A Song of Faith* (2006), as well as in many other publications and in the lives and practices of members of the church. In this chapter, I will offer a focus on the way the Holy Spirit is distinctively understood—experientially and traditionally—among Indigenous peoples, and cross-reference those understandings to the teaching of the UCC. In this exploration, both commonalities and differences are visible. Cultural and linguistic differences, together with diverse relationships to Creation, have historically complicated what should be understood in greater harmony among all peoples.

Pre-Columbian Work of the Spirit

Indigenous people had their own theology of the Spirit from time immemorial. Even though Indigenous cultures varied they all had an understanding of spirit and spiritual matters. Connection to the land is a common element of the Indigenous Turtle Island world view (*Turtle Island* is a shared Indigenous name for the North American land mass). The land informed our languages. Elders learned the lessons of our "faculty," the Earth. Within our language families, our elders shaped our cultures and gave us our unique national governance. Confederacies and treaties between nations guided our relationships with each other. This is the work of the Spirit from the beginning. We believe that the energy of our world is from Our Elder

Brother the Sun and the deep subterranean heat of Our Mother the Earth.[1] Our generations emerged from the rhythm and warmth of Our Mother and mothers. The waters of regeneration have been overseen by Our Grandmother the Moon. Our Grandfathers the Thunders brought the rain that fed Our Three Sisters (corn, beans, and squash). We learned to live in reciprocity with our lands, giving thanks for what we harvested and taking only what we needed. We made decisions honouring our elders back to the seventh generation[2] and providing for our "faces coming from the ground" (future generations) to the seventh generation. This is the work of the Spirit in this world. Our women were strong and were the backbones of our communities. Our men stood as defenders and gave their lives in service for the good of our communities. Our children were the centre of our sacred circle. Child abuse was almost non-existent. If it did happen, the abuser was banished from the community. They lived only months at the most, because no other community wanted them and they were so much a part of community that living alone was death.[3] This is the work of the Spirit in community.

Indigenous people were not without fault. That is why we had cleansing ceremonies. We talked about keeping things in balance, because things got out of balance and we needed help to bring things back to the way they needed to be. Haudenosaunee people remember a time of great unbalance when the Peacemaker came to restore things to the way the Creator intended. People turned from war and fighting to peace, and to the dignity of consensus-based decision making. Haudenosaunee people look for the return of the Peacemaker in this time of crisis and chaos brought by disrespect toward Our Mother and The People.[4] This is the work of the Spirit in restoration.

A Community Preamble

Even though Indigenous people had their own understanding of spiritual matters, to the European Christian colonizers, it was in error and needed to be replaced by "correct" European Christian doctrine. Roman Catholic, Anglican, Presbyterian, Methodist, and Congregationalist denominations all found Indigenous adherents throughout Canada. I grew up in the traditional Handsome Lake Longhouse religion of my Cayuga ancestors. I came to Christian faith at age twenty and was enculturated into a middle-class Canadian charismatic church with roots in Methodism. Indigenous followers of the Jesus way had to adopt the values and sensibilities of denominations from the Western European groups that settled in Canada, and so did I. Denominations utilized the policy of assimilation to remake Indigenous followers of Christ into their denominational images. A good Indigenous Christian was one who thought and acted like them, but was brown. In less than a year, I burned all things native, including poetry not expressive of Western Christian sensibilities as I understood them. This kind of inherent distrust of Indigenous ways expresses itself in Indigenous communities that burn down sweat lodges[5] and expel Indigenous ceremonial practitioners.[6] I was never satisfied with this, though, and continued to read all I could about my people, history, and culture.

As a young follower of the Jesus way, I embraced the UCC's approach to the Bible as it is expressed in the *Twenty Articles of Doctrine*: "Holy Scripture ... contain[s] the only infallible rule of faith and life."[7] Western Christianity in general, and the UCC in particular, was not shy about knowing what this "only infallible rule of faith and life" was. Many Indigenous followers of the Jesus way absorbed the missionaries' view and ruled out Indigenous spirituality as pagan and something to be abandoned. Burning and abandoning native things became an act of discipleship in this assimilationist model. Some UCC Indigenous elders maintain this kind of stance. Western missionaries have been very effective in replacing Indigenous world views with Western ones.

In 1986, the UCC apologized for this Eurocentric, Western-ethnocentric, and Western-Christian approach to discipling Indigenous church members: "We did not hear you when you shared your vision ... we were closed to the value of your spirituality.... We tried to make you like us and in so doing we helped destroy the vision that made you what you were. As a result, you, and we, are poorer and the image of God in us is twisted, blurred, and we are not what we are meant by God to be."[8] The first fruit of this apology resulted in the creation of All Native Circle Conference with four Presbyteries.[9] Indigenous communities of faith were invisible in the original 1925 union of denominations, as acknowledged by the 41st General Council in revisions to the introduction to the *Basis of Union*.[10] Now the UCC seeks to "live into right relations" with Indigenous people as an ongoing follow-up to the original apology.[11] Keewatin Presbytery was formed with this thought in mind: "We are drawing aside to find out who we are and then we will be back."[12] The Indigenous faith community of the UCC never desired to leave the church but wanted to find its own identity, and to have this respected. This quest for personal identity within the Jesus way has been important to me personally and to many others. While reading

Bruce Olson's autobiography, *Bruchko*, I came to a *kairos* moment[13] in my understanding of Christian mission when Olson prayed, "Jesus, become Motilone."[14] I wept and prayed similarly, "Jesus, become Onkwehohweh."[15] Shortly after this, I met a number of Indigenous followers of Jesus who were also seeking an authentic Indigenous expression of Christian faith. I had experienced a time when I felt an invisible blanket cover my head and I could not think; it covered my eyes and I could not see; and then it covered my mouth and I could not speak. After a deep struggle I finally was able to throw off this muting, dampening, and deafening influence. I realized I was being shaped by a way of thinking that was destroying my identity as an Indigenous person. I said to myself, "I am abandoning Western Christianity as my self-expression of faith in Jesus and my followership of Jesus. I hang on to Jesus and the Word of God but I have no idea what this will mean for me." We in the Indigenous faith community of the UCC have a comfortable place to pursue our unique identity as Indigenous followers of the Jesus way.

Political and land claim conflict has galvanized Indigenous people to stand up and fight for identity, recognition, and control. On Victoria Day in 2006, the Six Nations community radio station CKRZ sent out a call that people were needed at the Caledonia, Ontario, land claim conflict site. Police were there to possibly arrest Six Nations people who were standing up for their lands, which were being developed for a housing division. While I stood on the front lines with our people, about eighty police in riot gear stood facing a mob of more than five hundred Caledonians, keeping them away from us. At one point a backhoe began to dig up Argyle Street and I began to weep. I said inside, "We are finally saying NO! to abuse of our people." My propositional faith became fully embodied that day and I began an intense reorganization of my spiritual perspective. As I have continued this journey with my network of friends, and in the context of the UCC's movement among Indigenous people, I see that I have evolved through the UCC statements of faith and am most comfortable with *A Song of Faith*. There is a future beyond this latest iteration of the faith that is emerging from a broad Indigenous reaffirmation of identity. The loss of language, culture, and Indigenous identity in the colonization and denominational process is being rectified, and a new vision that will bless the UCC is coming. The Spirit is increasingly evident not just in the Indigenous faith community but in the whole church.

The Final Report of the Truth and Reconciliation Commission and its ninety-four Calls to Action (with sixteen Calls specifically citing the church) has opened a conversation long overdue in the Canadian public. The 1996 Royal Commission on Aboriginal Peoples Report recognized the churches' unique role in getting a national conversation going. The UCC at its 42nd General Council adopted the United Nations Declaration on the Rights of Indigenous Peoples as a framework for reconciliation.[16] This has added to the public dialogue on Indigenous rights to self-determination and access to the resources for sustainability. This is a *kairos* moment for the church in Canada to address the outstanding grievances of Indigenous people, and to make things right and live into right relations. The work of the Spirit is seen in the convergence of many strands like these, woven together in the fabric of these times. Each brings an added dimension of the work of the Spirit that is embodied in all things and continually at work everywhere. Where human flourishing is, there is the Spirit. Where human happiness is promoted through dignity, there is the Spirit. Where the cycle of life is embraced with all of its feeling, from joy and celebration to comfort in mourning, there is the Spirit.

An Indigenous Comfort with Mystery

When I first heard the term "Holy Ghost," I had trouble with the word *ghost*. I associated this term with the mysterious, otherworldly dimension of fear as it was expressed in Hollywood movies. New to Christian faith at the age of twenty, I took it for granted that my church leaders knew what this was all about. Jesus was cool and not to be feared, and I concluded this must be true of the Holy Ghost too. As a unilingual English-speaking child, I grew up influenced mostly by school and television for grand ideas, and by my Indigenous family for social norms. My parents were not philosophical teachers, so I had no strong shaping of big ideas from them. Most of what I have from my parents has been absorbed by living in their gracious presence. Since I was not taught the ancestral language, I was not shaped by the world view encoded in the Lower Cayuga Longhouse, which is the modern context of the Handsome Lake religion of my Cayuga ancestors. I did experience the longhouse phenomenologically, though. I sat for hours, with no books or toys, and listened to the speakers speak for hours in the Cayuga language. I joined my dad in the dances and ate the food distributed after the ceremonies. I attended the feasts in homes and observed the rituals of my traditional community. I often asked my dad what they were doing and saying, but in the sacredness of the moment, and since my dad was not a great explainer, I gathered but meagre crumbs of understanding. Growing up with an awareness of the spirit dimension and a belief in God or Creator is normal in Indigenous communities. This spirit dimension is not some place "over there somewhere," but is right here, right now, and a normal part of life. It is not always evident, but every now and then we would experience something of it. People in our community seemed to have a special ability to engage it too. The UCC has provided a comfortable and supportive environment to explore an Indigenous understanding of spiritual matters.

The Spirit Disembodied

Being enculturated into a Western Christian understanding of the Holy Spirit has been detrimental to Indigenous people and is at the heart of a larger Western problem.[17] Western Christianity has disembodied the Spirit from physicality. Spirit has been extracted from the body, moved to a distance, and is no longer a practically animating force in the here and now. This secularization is a fundamental result of Western Christianity.[18] Indigenous people have preserved and are restoring a pre-contact integration of spirit and physicality. Christian faith is embodied in action.[19] You can see faith.[20] Faith reveals itself in a life lived by it. To the Indigenous person, faith or belief is not some esoteric idea but an embodied ceremony. Our dance is our prayer. Our smudging is our cleansing. Our dropping of tobacco is our thanksgiving. We can tell what someone believes by what they do. The Canadian state believed in breaking promises because that is what it did with treaties. The church and state believed Indigenous communities could not parent their children and removed them to Indian residential schools. The church and state believed Indigenous spirituality was not good, outlawed it, and replaced it with Western Christianity. This reminds me of the teaching of the Bible: "How can you say you love God whom you have not seen, when you do not love your brother whom you have seen?" (1 John 4:20). It was not Christian faith that abused our Indigenous children in Indian residential schools. It was not Christian faith that stood by and let it happen. It was not Christian faith that treated elders, chiefs, clan mothers, and Indigenous parents with such contempt. What perpetrated these atrocities was something masquerading as Christian faith.

A disembodied Western Christian faith is this altogether different thing. It proved quite capable of incredible indignity. It is an aberration of Christian faith to deny the physicality of spirituality. If there is no physical resurrection of Jesus from the dead, then faith is useless and there is nothing worth preaching. Christian faith that does not tell the story of Christ's resurrection, his re-embodiment, is not being true to the story of the gospel. This disembodied faith and spirit does not have the ability to animate goodness in a deep and fundamental way. When it comes to laying down its life for the vulnerable, this disembodied faith and spirit stands idly by while atrocities are committed. When the top leadership trained in the highest ministry capacity in Western Christianity can abuse an Indigenous child (and tens of thousands were), the impotence of this disembodied spirit and faith training is clear. Another way to understand the Spirit must come into view and be embodied. The current environmental crisis of climate change would be radically impacted by an Indigenous embodiment of Spirit and reconciliation that includes all of our relations in creation. Stan McKay Jr., Cree and former moderator of the UCC, said: "The urgent need for all of us to care for the earth would give us a common base from which we could converse. Reconciliation is more than people getting along."[21] People or beings, in the Indigenous way, includes Creation seen and unseen. This is Indigenous embodiment of being. As I gain a greater understanding of my people's understanding of spiritual matters, my phenomenologically based fear from my non-Indigenous-speaking childhood is being mitigated. This Indigenous embodied spirituality is an expression of an authentic spirituality witnessed to within the text of Scripture. This also informs my understanding of the Holy Spirit and has led me to conclude there is great harm in the Western Christian world view. This is one reason why Indigenous people have suffered so greatly in colonialism and denominationalism.

Methodist and Presbyterian Mission History

Indigenous churches that joined the UCC were primarily from the Methodist tradition, although some communities in British Columbia represented Presbyterian missions. Both Arminian and Calvinistic views are represented in this history. These theological positions represent polar viewpoints highlighted in an either/or Western way of thinking. Reductionist processes are used in a rhetorical debate model to create discrete, intrinsic categories of objects. This colonial way of thinking is representative of classical Greek philosophies pervasive in Western churches. The Western academy, which is the norm for the theological schools of the Roman Catholic and Protestant traditions, operates this way. These schools train ministers and missionaries how to think and reason in this paradigm. Western pedagogical approaches place the teacher as expert and the student as child-learner who needs the knowledge of the expert to come to a place of peer competency.

Indigenous ways of thinking are very different. The left-brain-dominant Western thinking described above contrasts with the more whole-brain way of thinking that is common in Indigenous communities. A holistic big-picture view and an emphasis on relationship are familiar to most Indigenous communities. In this way of thinking, elders tell stories that serve as myth, a "grand story" that explains why things are as they are. Questions posed to elders are responded to by stories, while each one focuses on the central fire in their communion experience. Each person contemplates the meaning and implications of the story. Each one is given adult dignity (including youthful learners) to gain the insights they need. These insights often come to them by "a-ha!" moments. The wisdom of our Indigenous elders is passed on generation to generation for thousands of years, just like the stories of the Bible were passed on by word of mouth before they were written down.

Compartment or Embodiment

Pneumatology, the doctrine of the Holy Spirit, emerges from the dichotomous, either/or, reductionist approach to theologizing about the Holy Spirit. This approach emphasizes nouns and adjectives. Verbs and adverbs then describe the movement and actions of nouns. Who the Holy Spirit is, and what the Holy Spirit does, are the foci of inquiry in this way of processing. The central question asked is "What are in these compartments of theological ideas?" Indigenous ways of thinking, however, are fundamentally not about the separation of spirit and matter, but take the view that spirit and matter are integrated here and now. The ancestors are addressed in prayer and ceremony. The future generations are consulted in development projects.[22] The other side is here and just over there. Creation is seen as a relative, and plant and animal beings are spoken to, just as humans are.[23] Spirit imbues creation. Spirit may not be readily perceived by human senses, but the senses can see evidence of Spirit all around. This is embodiment. Embodiment is spirituality as described in Scripture. The spirit/breath/wind of God was imparted to the clay body of the proto-human. Human spirit is embodied. The Holy Spirit filled believers and the internal witness proclaims familial connection: "the Spirit bears witness with our spirit that we are the children of God" (Romans 8:16). The Holy Spirit imbued Jesus and was at work in him in works evidenced by powerful sensory experiences, such as healings and "miraculous" works. When the Holy Spirit is present, that presence is evident to the senses, with varying human abilities to perceive.

A UCC minister, Greta Vosper, though she does not believe in an interventionist or personal God of any kind, speaks of an embodied love in empathy.[24] This thing, the only thing that matters, is expressed in our care and interaction with others. She does not look to God, or some abstract conception of God revealed through the text of Scripture, for inspiration to do good, but sees the profound logic of relationship in the here and now. This is an approach very similar to Indigenous embodiment of spirituality. If the priests and teachers in the Indian residential schools thought and acted like Vosper in matters of love and empathy, I do not think Indigenous children would have been raped and abused as they were.

Western Abstracts and Indigenous Concretes

A creed is a summary of the most important aspects of a belief system. Most often, when Indigenous people meet, there are two questions we ask, "Where are you from?" and "Who are your relatives?" An Indigenous creed for followers of Jesus would answer, "Where are you from?" with geography. The question "Who are your relatives?" would answer the Indigenous concern about genealogy. An Indigenous creed of followers of Jesus would be full of mentions of place and relatives. It would also be a creedal song and creedal dance. It would be a feast over several days with teaching, prayer, and ceremony. Western creeds, in contrast, are full of abstract words with a whole universe of esoteric meaning behind them. Seeking to understand the Trinity, conclaves of Greek-speaking church theologians, pastors, and bishops gathered to parse out the fine distinctions between Greek words like *homoousia* (same substance) and *homoiousia* (similar substance). These fine distinctions between words arise from the Greek language and the fine-tuned abstract distinctions that exist in the Greek way of thinking.

Article 2.3.1 of the UCC's *Twenty Articles of Doctrine* describes the Holy Trinity as "three persons of the same substance." We honour this iteration of early Christian faith as it is expressed in the UCC's foundational history. The concerns answered by these fine distinctions in nouns, however, are not those of Indigenous ways of thinking. They are fine for Western/Greek thinkers, but these efforts do not need to be applied to other peoples who think differently. When new to the faith, I did not dig down this deep, and later I struggled to see why these fine distinctions mattered when I began to teach other ministry students. Being filled with the Holy Spirit for prayer and prophecy is all about relationship and the integration of Spirit and matter (or body) right here, right now.

The Haudenosaunee language family utilizes metaphor, which works so well in story communication. The Bible is fundamentally a story tradition. It is a book of stories. It is myth, the grand story that explains why things are the way they are. Metaphor is the illustration methodology of story. We see what we are saying. Ours is a language of poetry and oratory. This fits well the narrative and poetic genres of the Scriptures. Other Indigenous languages emphasize the verb, and everything flows from movement. Relationship is very important, and in some languages you cannot say anything until you reference it. Christian experience in the Western/Greek world view is a legitimate concern for those who live there, but it is not the standard to measure every other culture's experience of Christ. The New Testament is preamble, not prescription, for other cultures. It is just the first example of the contextualization of a Hebrew spirituality into another culture. It is simply a gift that is offered to future generations. Each new receiving culture is left to receive this gift and whatever treasure they can as each culture decides what this gift means for them. The gift of the Holy Spirit who is with us, like Jesus was with his disciples, is easy to understand for an Indigenous audience.

Western cultures lean to the left brain in their dominant way of thinking. Indigenous cultures lean to the right brain, but also, through the strong influence of women, operate in a more whole-brain fashion. These generalizations are always fraught with exceptions or even greater simplifications. The actual functioning of societies and the brain are more complex. No function of the brain is neatly compartmentalized in any one section of the brain, and continuums are better models of understanding. It is helpful here, however, to make some broad observations rooted in respect. Binary thinking is ubiquitous in Western discourse. This is a natural result of either/or thinking. The Indigenous community looks at issues in a more both/and assessment. There is plenty of grey, instead of simple black-and-white judgments. I have worked in Indigenous interdenominational settings for thirty years and rarely, almost never, have I been in a theological debate. There were strongly held positions, but respect—not rancour—marked people's attitude toward differing opinions. This is the unity of the One Spirit that the apostle Paul wrote about.

A local story will help to illustrate what I am talking about. A grass-roots Indigenous church support group met monthly. This group consisted of a Baptist church on the Tuscarora Indian Reserve, New York; an independent Indigenous Baptist church in Buffalo, New York, and its daughter church in Fort Erie, Ontario; and an independent charismatic church and an independent Oneness Pentecostal church from Six Nations, Ontario. This group of about twelve to fifteen lay, ordained, and licensed Indigenous leaders met for more than ten years to pray together, support each other, to hold a men's retreat and children camps together, and to exchange preachers on special occasions. Such a diversity of faith expressions was able to cooperate with each other without hurting each other by doctrinal differences through the influence of the Indigenous Spirit. Western denominational communities less commonly encourage true fellowship with other denominations, and though many confess the "one catholic church" on Sunday, they rarely live that out. The top leaders in denominations often discourage interdenominational fellowship and try to provide everything they think their members need by stand-alone programs in their churches. Western churches focus on their distinctives and the "denominational family" values that set them apart from their near spiritual relatives. This is not the uniting Spirit of the Bible.

The Sandy-Saulteaux Spiritual Centre's Learning Circle in January 2016 called for the subject of Systematic Theology to be taught. Western "systematic theology" is the *problem* in Indigenous communities, and not what needs to be taught. However, helping our ministry training students understand the Western Christianity they have dealt with all their lives, and that of the UCC in which they are immersed, is necessary. The title of the Learning Circle was modified to "Western Systematic Theology and Indigenous Theologies." The singular "theology" term arises from the pervasive way of thinking in the West. The multiple "theologies" term expresses the fundamental intra-cultural realities of the Indigenous community. Alf Dumont, an Ojibwa minister in the UCC, when discussing the teachings, history, stories, and experiences of the Bible and Indigenous people, said, "These do not have to be unified into one system of thought."[25] It is the Greek New Testament that is most distinctive from Indigenous ways of thinking. There is much more in common between Indigenous and Hebrew peoples with their clans, tribes, confederacies, genealogies, land, and seasonally based ceremonies and rituals. The Western Christian church owes more to the ancient Greek writings with their abundant abstract conceptions than to the more visual earthiness of Hebrew writings. Indigenous people, with their Original Instructions, find a comfortable milieu in the Hebrew frame of reference. Even given this similarity, Indigenous elders and leaders said, "the traditional ways and teachings of their people could walk side by side with Christian ways and teachings."[26] Walking side by side is an expression of peer respect and means trusting the Holy Spirit to guide each other.

The Great Commission speaks of disciples being made in "all nations." The book of Revelation, in a final image of the Creator's purpose on earth, pictures the city of God descending out of heaven and united with the earth. This city has twelve gates on it, four sides, and the "kings of the nations enter with their glory."[27] Nations survive the Great Commission of Jesus. Indigenous nations have been disappeared by Western denominations and governments through their policy of assimilating non-Western people into citizenship in the colony and membership in the denomination. This assimilation is not the inevitable end of "making disciples of all nations." For each nation, each unique world view, there is a special theology expressive of the heart of that nation. It takes God the Holy Spirit to be the teacher of such diverse nations. The world should move away from denominations and policies of assimilation to seeing followers of Christ (via the Holy Spirit as Teacher) as peoples and nations.

Indigenous Nationhood and the Great Commission

"The Land is our Language, Our Language is our Land," read the banner at the Keewatin Presbytery meeting at Raymond Flett Memorial Church in Winnipeg in February 2014. "The Earth is Our Faculty," is the motto of Sandy-Saulteaux Spiritual Centre. The land speaks and teaches us the lessons we need to live in a good way with "all our relations"—the tree folk, the four-footed people, the bird people, the medicine families, and all. Our languages encode the values our elders have learned from the land. We have differing lands and therefore differing lessons, so each of our cultures is unique: from the West Coast, the Mountains, the Sub-Arctic, the Arctic, the Plains, the Woodlands, the Great Lakes, the River Country, the East Coast, and all the Islands. The land shapes our languages, cultures, and nations. There has never been a National Elder for the Aboriginal Ministries Council of the UCC because no Elder from one territory wants to lead in another people's land. We have decided that the answer to the protocol question "How do we do this?" is "Whoever's land we are in, it is the host community who will decide how we proceed with protocol." We all are connected to the earth and we all respect our Mother, so we honour this by honouring our hosts. Our elders have read the lessons of the land and have shaped our cultures. The special lands of every nation have taught our people their special wisdom. How we survive the elements, how we harvest Mother Earth's bounty, how we move about on the land, rivers, oceans, mountains, and plains, and how we make decisions have been determined by long years of contemplation and experience by our elders.

Each Indigenous nation has its own governance—political, spiritual, familial, and so on. Among Haudenosaunee people, our Clan Mothers choose the Chiefs. Women have top leadership and land stewardship roles. Among other groups, decisions have been made since time immemorial according to the customs and values of each nation. Some have strong consensus-achieving structures. Others have a communal voting system. In others, protegés are chosen by leaders and take over when training is deemed sufficient. Each Indigenous nation had its own land, language, culture, and leadership. If the church had respected this, Indigenous nations would have remained intact to finally enter into the New Jerusalem City of God with the glory of each nation. Our lands would have flourished. The spirit of our lands would have been happy. Our languages would have flourished. The spiritual inspiration reminiscent of the Day of Pentecost that began the church with its praise of God in every language would have joined with the chorus of the earth. Our culture would have flourished. The spirit infusing our life and ceremonies would have been honoured. Our governance would have been respected and the Holy Spirit's work among our people would have been affirmed.

Instead of this grand vision of national fulfillment, the colonial state stole Indigenous lands through fraudulent treaties, forced English or French languages on Indigenous children and communities, outlawed Indigenous culture, and supplanted traditional governance with colonial elected systems under the direct control of the Minister of Indigenous Affairs and the Prime Minister. This has been accomplished by the policy of assimilation. The Western church (Roman Catholic and Protestant) did the same thing to Indigenous people. Christian clergy softened up Indigenous communities and helped overcome resistance in the treaty process that stole Indigenous land. Our languages were beaten out of our children in the Indian residential school system. Our cultures and spiritual traditions were condemned and vilified by the churches. We were treated as children, and our traditional teachers, elders, chiefs, clan mothers, community and extended family leaders were ignored as uncivilized, unchristian, and unworthy of this sacred leadership role. The final insult has been church governance and policy imposed upon us by each of the denominations. We are told in this process, "You Indigenous children cannot govern yourselves. You must learn from us and do it our way (even though all of the hundreds of Western denominations claim they are the true church). You cannot govern yourselves without us as your leaders. You cannot make the agenda. You cannot control the money. We will put our main leaders on every circle, council, or board you create so we can keep an eye on you and make sure you don't get too Indigenous for us." The work of the Holy Spirit as teacher, guide, enabler, and source of inspiration was denied to us.

And yet, the Holy Spirit has always spoken to us. The Spirit speaks through all of creation.[28] When our Mother the Earth speaks, we listen. When the eagle cries, we are alerted. When our Mother trembles, we are humbled. When the wind whistles, we find our way. When the stars sing, we hear them tell us which way to go and when to do what is important. When we dream of our relatives, we know we are not alone and that we must honour their memory and presence. When our medicines heal or help us to die well, we know that this is the Spirit animating all of creation. The Holy Spirit has always spoken to us. When our elders speak and tell us the old stories, we sit and weep. No one moves until the time is right. When we hear the creation stories, we begin to understand why the things are as they are now in this world. We see the past and how things have changed, sometimes permanently, and at times we have hope that renewal can come. Our elders paint pictures. They are our televisions. They are our internet. They are our prophets, warning us, and our priests, comforting us. The Holy Spirit speaks and we hear what we need to hear.

When the donkey spoke to the prophet,[29] the Western person asks, "How can the donkey speak?" He will take the donkey to the lab and examine its vocal chords and perform a randomized trial with a control herd of donkeys. The Indigenous person asks, "What did the donkey say? What does this mean for us and our world?" When the fish produces money to pay taxes, the Western person says, "That was a coincidence," or "Let's fish some more." The Indigenous person says, "Cool," and drops tobacco. When the storm rages, the travelling Western person opens the weather app and looks online for a hotel. The Indigenous traveller prays for safety in the storm, because they have no extra money for a hotel. Scripture provides charismatic or Holy Spirit answers to the power questions of Indigenous people. The energy of the Holy Spirit has always been present in all of creation and is not limited by abstract theologizing or human imagining. When there is sickness beyond human coping, hands are laid on the sick and the efficacy of prayer is evidenced by the life-giving Spirit.[30] Spiritual dreams and visions come to the seeking souls who are blindly and deafly stumbling about. When adversarial powers and circumstances block, hinder, and attack, pillars of fire and smoke arise, people walk on water, and Jesus stands up and welcomes us home.

The human conscience is a product of genetics and nurture. Down through the ages, the soft voice of guidance and affirmation, usually a mother's voice, has shaped us, and this shaping has been encoded in our DNA and conduct. We are our engagement with parenthood. From a primordial place, we respond to the competing calls of circumstance, guided by a seemingly innate impetus from the deep regions of our being. This is our survival genetics speaking. This is our nurturing mothers and fathers speaking to us. This is the teacher within.[31] This is the voice of the Holy Spirit. In the pain of the inexplicable affairs of nations, with their bloody boundaries, comes the voice of revelation guiding the future of human survival.[32] Human dignity is negotiated at the margins of encounter. There is nothing like competing interests to reveal the values and violations of human expectations before an altruistic and fully comprehending Creator God. Human choice meets an exemplar evaluator in the long history of sowing and reaping. It is in this liminal place that a mother's voice and a father's voice find their awful and awesome conclusions, lessons taught by the Holy Spirit.

UCC Teaching about the Holy Spirit in Light of Indigenous Teaching

The UCC began in 1925 with a statement, the *Twenty Articles of Doctrine*, that used terminology from the Bible. It followed Western conceptions and approaches to summarizing the teaching of the Bible. It was fundamentally concerned with defining terms and describing actions. The Holy Spirit was the focus of this effort that reflected an agreement among Methodist, Presbyterian, and Congregational factions. A rigid view of the Bible was evident in "the only infallible rule of faith and life" statement in Article 2.3.2. The Holy Spirit was identified as male in Article 2.3.8 and throughout. The person and work of the Holy Spirit are clearly stated in biblical language, which is written from an overwhelmingly male perspective. A feminine perspective is largely absent from the Bible and therefore misses half of humanity's voice. There is no genealogy or geography in this creed-like summary. The two questions Indigenous people ask when they meet are not answered: "Where are you from?" and "Who are your relatives?" This statement of faith does not summarize matters important to Indigenous people. An Indigenous summary would include geography (Nazareth, Bethlehem, Egypt, Jerusalem, Sea of Galilee, the Decapolis, and so on) and genealogy (the Abraham to David to Solomon to Joseph to Jesus genealogy of Matthew 1, and the Jesus to Mary to Nathan to David to Abraham to

Noah to Adam to God genealogy of Luke 3). An Indigenous creed would be a dance and teaching in a multi-day celebration with feasting. The Holy Spirit would be understood as the embodiment of all that is good and of Creator in the people, in the ceremonies, in the dances, in the prayers, in the feasting and in the good care of the people for one another.

The 1940 *Statement of Faith* says it is a brief summary of the church's teaching, but is longer than the 1925 *Twenty Articles of Doctrine*. It is a restating in the new context. The Preamble says the statement uses "the language of Scripture, a language which matches the supreme facts it tells of, God's acts of judgment and of mercy."[33] These supreme acts of God are firstly "judgment" and then "mercy." This is at odds with the Indigenous understanding of the Bible story beginning with the goodness of creation. The Holy Spirit's *person* (Lord and Giver of life, eternal personal Spirit, one God in Holy Trinity) is less evident, but the Holy Spirit's *work* is clearly prominent (at work in the hearts and minds; inspiring right desire and effort; moving people to confession and repentance; enabling witness; filling people with love and hope; sustaining; guiding; empowering; fortifying; building up; teaching; cleansing in baptism and giving gifts and graces; enabling love, righteous living, and death to sin). *Statement* is of the same spirit as the *Twenty Articles of Doctrine* and compartmentalizes the Holy Spirit even more.

A New Creed (1968) was a mere 116 words. This radical simplification and summary of the faith reduced the teaching on the Holy Spirit to "God ... who works in us and others by the Spirit." The pendulum has swung from a very academic expression to a simple poem. The doors of acceptance were swung wide open, but toward whom or what those doors were opened to was not substantively stated. *A New Creed* may have been more easily translated in Indigenous languages, but the metaphors and nuances of the faith needed to wait for *A Song of Faith*.

A Song of Faith (2006) is a lyric with more than 2,400 words. As a poem, it is dense with meaning and full of metaphor and passion. It is nuanced with contemporary issues and has a clear call to justice, environmental care, art, and music. Creation is seen as ongoing and an engaging partner in the dance of life. It is much more amenable to Indigenous sensibilities, even though it still lacks geography and genealogy. It is an improvement and a move toward a relevant and motivating expression of faith. *Song* speaks of the Holy Spirit in terms of "Mother" and "comforter," and this aspect of the feminine is pervasive in the Indigenous world. Mother Earth is a commonality, and the respect accorded mothers and grandmothers is widely shared in Indigenous ways. All of creation is alive, and, among Haudenosaunee people, future generations are spoken of as "faces coming from the ground" or from Mother Earth. *Song* also speaks of the Holy Spirit "animating all matter and energy, moving in the human heart." This Holy Spirit is embodied in creation and in humanity. This is similar to the Haudenosaunee concept of *orenda*,[34] the good and creative animating power present in all creation. Children are born with it and puberty enhances it for the life journey of that child. The idea of the Holy Spirit coming upon the prophet to do prophetic work is similar to the idea of enhanced *orenda*.

Song speaks of the followers of Christ "carrying a vision of creation healed and restored."[35] It continues, "And so we sing of God the Spirit, who from the beginning has swept over the face of creation, animating all energy and matter and moving in the human heart."[36] In this song, we see the Holy Spirit in embodied animation of the whole range of human personality and sexuality. The Indigenous world sees children as coming from the Sky World of Creator and Mother Earth with gifts and *orenda* to be a blessing. The Indigenous world is comfortable with being led by the genius of children. The Holy Spirit breathes the revelation of Scripture "in the life of community."[37] The Spirit is with the church to effect "creation healed and restored" and "creation's mending," making the church an "instrument of the loving spirit of Christ."[38] This community dynamic of the Holy Spirit's work, however, is extended to the whole of the Indigenous creation family: the rock people, the tree folk, the fish family, our Elder Brother the Sun, our Mother Earth, our Grandmother Moon, our Grandfathers the Thunders. *Song* is a beginning, but it requires more development in its teaching about the Holy Spirit; it needs a fuller and clearer expression of embodiment. Connection to the land, including specific places, is the story of Scripture and of Indigenous people. It matters where you are and it matters whom you are relating to, including all of our non-human families. When the UCC wipes away the blood of oppression, sops up the tears of indignity, and stands in the pain of dispossessed people in the lands of restoration and reparation, then the next step of embodied Christian spirituality will be evident enough for Indigenous people in community to see. Perhaps then the Indigenous communities of faith in the UCC will be able to say, "We accept your apologies because we now see what they mean embodied in the actions that are clear to all. The Spirit we have known since time immemorial embodied in our people, lands, and relatives is the same Holy Spirit we see and feel embodied in you."

An Evolution

It is encouraging to see in the evolution of the faith statements of the UCC a gradual move from abstract, context-less, and timeless concepts of the Holy Spirit to more concrete expressions of spiritual embodiment, the use of metaphor, and the work of the Holy Spirit in the here and now. The extension of this evolution would result in a fully embodied expression of spirituality that is comfortably "geographic" and embracing of genealogy and physicality. This will mean a sudden, exponential accumulation of narratives, characters, and events, and would require not just more recording of the stories of spirituality, the work of the Holy Spirit in humanity and creation, but also the development of oral communication skills and community memory. This is a primary work of the Holy Spirit, who continues the work of the canonization of sacred story, both oral and written, for the future guidance and comfort of the followers of Christ. This is the living nature of an embodied faith, constantly adapting and evolving in new environments and societal development.

NOTES

1   The terms *Elder Brother the Sun, Our Mother the Earth, Our Grandmother the Moon, Our Grandfathers the Thunders,* and *Our Three Sisters* (corn, beans, and squash) convey the idea that all of creation are our relatives. "All my relations" is the meaning of the Mohawk phrase *Akwe Nia'Tetewá:neren* on the UCC crest.

2   *Seventh generation* is a concept that honours the past and the future so that selfish decisions for expediency are avoided.

3   This teaching about banishment was shared by Resource Person Pat McLeod at Sandy-Saulteaux Spiritual Centre, Beausejour, Manitoba, during the "Traditional Medicines and Healing" Learning Circle, January 27–31, 2014.

4   The Haudenosaunee Peacemaker story is part of the Original Instructions given to the Six Nations Haudenosaunee people. See http://www.onondaga nation.org/history/.

5   See http://aptn.ca/news/2011/01/17/crees-ban-sweat-lodges-fns-spirituality -from-community/.

6   Sandy-Saulteaux Spiritual Centre board member Rev. John Thompson from Oxford House, Manitoba, tells the story of an Indigenous ceremonialist who came at the invitation of the Social Welfare agencies at Oxford House and who was expelled by the Christian Band Councilors. Their version of Christian faith had no room for Indigenous ceremony.

7   *Twenty Articles of Doctrine*, Article 2.3.2.

8   *The Manual*, 4.

9   *Mandate: The United Church of Canada's Mission Magazine*, Special Edition, May 2005.

10 The text of the 1986 Apology is available online at http://www.united-church .ca/sites/default/files/resources/1986-1998-aboriginal-apologies.pdf.

11 See https://commons.united-church.ca/Documents/Programming%20 and%20Education/Aboriginal/Living%20Into%20Right%20Relations%20 Report.pdf.

12 Conversation with All Native Circle Conference elder Evelyn Broadfoot, February 2015.

13 *Kairos* is a Greek New Testament word for "time" in the sense of opportune time. It is the time to act rather than simply another moment in the *chronos* understanding of day-to-day, minute-to-minute chronological time.

14 Bruce E. Olson, *Bruchko* (Altamonte Springs, FL: Creation House/Strang Communications, 1973/1978), 136.

15 *Ongwehohweh*, "the original beings who live forever," is the name Six Nations people give themselves.

16 See http://www.united-church.ca/news/united-church-responds-call-action -un-declaration.

17 *Western* is a European cultural pattern that fundamentally assumes a way of thinking based on Greek philosophy with its dichotomous and reductionist processes, resulting in discrete, intrinsic categories.

18 Paul Hiebert notes that "Lesslie Newbigin has argued ... that Western Chris- tian missions have been one of the greatest secularizing forces in history." Hiebert, "The Flaw of the Excluded Middle," *Missiology: An International Review* 10 (January 1982): 35–47.

19 See Romans 10:9–10, in which Paul refers to believing in your heart and con- fessing with your mouth.

20 James challenged the idea of a faith that did not move by the evidence of his faith that did (James 2:14–18).

21 Stan McKay Jr., *From Truth to Reconciliation* (Ottawa: Aboriginal Healing Foundation, 2008), 104

22 Paul Hiebert recounted a story of Hopi people and a development project. The Hopi said they consulted the future generations, who said, "What will be left for us?" and told the developers no to their project. Hiebert, "Lecture [Phenomenology and Folk Religion course]," Fuller Theological Seminary, Pasadena, CA, 1995.

23 The Haudenosaunee Thanksgiving Address refers to earth as Mother; corn,

beans, and squash as Three Sisters; the thunders as Grandfathers; the sun as Elder Brother; and the moon as Grandmother.

24   See http://www.grettavosper.ca/answers-questions-ordination/.

25   Alf Dumont and Roger Hutchinson, "United Church Mission Goals and First Nations Peoples," in *The United Church of Canada: A History*, ed. Don Schweitzer (Waterloo, ON: Wilfrid Laurier University Press), 222.

26   Ibid., 224.

27   Revelation 21:26.

28   Psalm 19:1–4; Romans 1:18–20.

29   Numbers 22:21–33.

30   James 5:14–15.

31   Romans 12:1–11.

32   Acts 17:24–28.

33   *The Manual*, 15.

34   See http://www.metanexus.net/archive/conference2005/pdf/macdougall.pdf.

35   *The Manual*, 27.

36   Ibid., 23.

37   Ibid., 23.

38   Ibid., 27, 26.

CHAPTER SEVEN

ECCLESIOLOGY:
"BEING THE UNITED CHURCH OF CANADA"

Gail Allan and Marilyn Legge

What is the church and what is it for? This chapter assumes that ecclesiology is a doctrinal practice through which "the church rethinks the meaning of its self-understanding as a community of Jesus Christ in every changing circumstance."[1] As followers of the Way of Jesus, the church is the community of those whose purpose is remembering and hoping in Jesus Christ, signifying the gospel in life and action, in work and worship oriented by the promise of the kingdom, a kin-dom fulfilled and realized in "abundance of life" for all (John 10:10).[2] The New Testament is confident that nothing can separate us from the love of God and the eschatological promise of that love. The church is called to be a transfigured mode of living communal witness to this new creation founded on the life, death, and resurrection of Jesus Christ. And yet ...

Questions of ecclesiology are rife in The United Church of Canada as it struggles to respond faithfully and creatively to the gospel in this time and place. As Douglas John Hall has hauntingly noted, the church as centre of the social fabric has shifted because community life has all but disappeared. In turn, this decentring of the church has provoked unrequited nostalgia and deep loss for those who cannot be liberated from a past of Christendom à la Protestantism.[3] The church finds itself disestablished and marginalized, diminished and soul-searching to be the UCC that is heterogeneous, amid severe dislocations in a pluralist world where a globalized capitalist economy, ecocide, terrorism, and violence prevail. Once assured of a central place in the nation as the UCC, is it any wonder that this "humiliation of the church" has provoked fear of identity loss, conflict, and dying as a community of faith?[4] Given the perennial and pervasive questions about being church, we explore in this chapter key images and examples of how the UCC has understood itself and its task in particular embodiments since its formation in 1925 with this originating intention:

> In the minds of those who laboured to form the United Church it was intended to play a decisive role in shaping the moral ethos of Canadian society by infusing the values of Evangelical British Protestantism into Canadian citizens through evangelism, social service, public activism, and advocacy. This intention was reflected in its chosen name: The United Church of Canada.[5]

The *Basis of Union* has a preamble, then a short doctrine section, and a very long polity section. Some would hold that the church operates more by ethos (character and disposition) than by doctrine. Most would agree that the UCC is shaped by its conciliar nature, which requires taking counsel together and working out its ecclesiology amid the various relations and accountabilities of congregations/Presbyteries/conferences/General Council; local/national; and national/global. As a liberal, mostly white denomination, the UCC also assumes that for faith to seek understanding, "human experience of faith and life" is a necessary and fundamental site of authority, along with Scripture, tradition, and reason. Therefore, the diversity of faith experiences in the range of lived eco-social situatedness makes a significant difference in how the church understands itself and how it articulates, witnesses, and takes up its mission.

To excavate the ecclesiology of each doctrinal era, we must pose key questions: What has the UCC understood to be the nature and the purpose of the church? What has been the relationship of the UCC with Canada, with other denominations, with ecumenical organizations, with various religions, and with the rest of the world? What particular emphases were taken in the different eras and why? What metaphors and images shaped its self-understanding as "church"? For example, some of those metaphors and images have been Body of Christ; Fittingly National; Conscience of the Nation; Conciliar Church: United and Uniting by Taking Counsel Together; The Whole People of God; People on the Way: Building Communities of Reconciliation, Inclusive Diversity, and Justice; and "Akwe Nia'Tetewá:neren," in the Mohawk language, which was recently added to the UCC crest, signifying "All My Relations."

This chapter is organized following the four subordinate standards of the UCC's doctrine: first, the 1925 *Twenty Articles of Doctrine*, which guided a new denomination until 1939; second, the 1940 *Statement of Faith* responding to the crisis of the Second World War; third, 1968's *A New Creed*, which sought to embrace the call to be church in shifting economic, global, national, social, and political contexts; and fourth, the 2006 *A Song of Faith: A Statement of Faith for the United Church of Canada*, which affirms a theological vision and framework for new ways to be church in a globalized, diverse, fraught, broken, beautiful, and intricately complex world. Each doctrinal statement articulates an ecclesiology (self-understanding of the nature and task of the church) in each generation.

Notions of being church are also connected to other key UCC actions and events as found in official documents, reports, and statements. For example, the Board of Evangelism and Social Service's *Commission on Christianizing the Social Order* (1934), *That All May Be One* (2004), and *Towards 2025: A Justice-Seeking, Justice-Living Church* (2012) are fruits of ecclesial struggles to respond faithfully and creatively to the gospel for its time and place.

"A Canadian Christianity, a Christian Canada"[6]—
The *Twenty Articles of Doctrine* of the *Basis of Union*, 1925 to1939

We begin with the founding vision of the UCC: "It shall be the policy of the United Church to foster the spirit of unity in the hope that this sentiment of unity may in due time, so far as Canada is concerned, take shape in a Church which may *fittingly be described as national*."[7] Phyllis Airhart argues that this preamble to the 1925 BOU "captured remarkably well the hopes of the founders and the vision which shaped the new church's understanding of its mission. In this aspiration to create a "national church" was a vision that was both complex and comprehensive."[8] The gathering that founded the first organic church union in the Western world and Canada's largest Protestant denomination consisted of Congregationalists, Methodists, two-thirds of the Presbyterians in Canada, and the Association of Local Union Churches.[9]

While the founders assumed its members to be white Protestant descendants of immigrants from the British Isles, Wenh-In Greer Anne Ng cogently assesses how this complexity hid from view "the victims of these imaginings[:] Aboriginal peoples, French Canadians, non-Protestants, non-Christians, and recent immigrants." Thus to be comprehensive and "fittingly national" in response to historical changes in/as "Canada" and in relation to global impacts, the new church would over time find it necessary to name, face, and respond to the harmful and changing effects of its founding vision in struggles to be faithful and fittingly national, as this chapter will present.[10]

An ecclesiology of nineteenth-century evangelical Protestantism was enshrined in the *Twenty Articles of Doctrine*. Three in particular—Article XIV "Of the Moral Law," Article XV "Of the Church," and Article XX "Of Christian Service and the Final Triumph"—frame what the UCC was meant to be and to do. These Articles teach unity not as uniformity but as being "integral parts of one visible catholic church of Christ" and seeking true spiritual fellowship.[11] The UCC has understood itself to be constituted by what God has done, particularly in Jesus Christ. Article XV of the *Twenty Articles of Doctrine* acknowledges "one Holy Catholic Church, the innumerable company of saints of every age and nation, who being united by the Holy Spirit to Christ their Head are one body in Him and have communion with their Lord and with one another." Being the body of Christ and seeking true spiritual fellowship grounded the very being of the UCC from its originating vision. The church continues to embrace this in its subsequent doctrinal eras, grounding who it is and what it is being called to do.[12] A strong sense of mission was key to the formation of the UCC. This has remained constant throughout its history.

While the *Twenty Articles of Doctrine* specify that the church was called to be active in the world, this document leaves the specifics of *how* this is to be done or to be worked out on the ground. From its beginning, the UCC sorted out its conciliar polity—to uphold the roles, rules, and relations of each court (congregations, Presbyteries, conferences, General Council as the "supreme Court")[13]—to understand its being and mission in new situations. One key example was the perennial question of how to translate Christian responsibility into public and national influence. The Board of Evangelism and Social Service assigned this to the Commission on Christianizing the Social Order. At the 6th General Council in 1934, the commission's report identified that because God seeks "a community of people" united for "justice, humility and benevolence," Christian people should move as one body for the creation of Christian social order. Common to each of the antecedent churches coming into union was a social gospel tradition of shared responsibility for the good of all. As Roger Hutchinson elucidates, the Commission on Christianizing the Social Order embraced a threefold task—transformation of persons, of social structures, and of culture.[14] This approach to social change linked theological, economic, and political issues to personal and cultural values.

The report identified the immediate task as the promotion of fellowships where conflicting views could search for consensus. The social gospel involved not just "salvation of society" but a different understanding of the "salvation of individuals," who are to be seen in "webs of connection" between the personal and the institutional—that is, the social, worldly, and local aspects of being the church were inseparable.[15] Therefore it was necessary to create and sustain church practices to "enshrine peace, justice, and co-operation as the society's core values."[16] In the context of the dire and deepening economic crisis in the 1930s, and while a national church was not to be a "state church," it claimed special political and cultural authority as necessary for its mission.

Taking pride in its place and status of the time, the UCC understood itself to be the conscience of the nation.[17] Given this role, "the Church dare not be found lacking in the power of moral leadership."[18] Note that Article XIV ("Of the Law of God") emphasizes the Christian moral purpose of manifesting the kingdom of God:

> We believe that the moral law of God, summarized in the Ten Commandments, testified to by the prophets and unfolded in the life and teachings of Jesus Christ, stands for ever in truth and equity, and is not made void by faith, but on the contrary is established thereby. We believe that God requires of every man to do justly, to love mercy, and to walk humbly with God; and that only through this harmony with the will of God shall be fulfilled that brotherhood of man wherein the kingdom of God is to be made manifest.[19]

In keeping with this moral law, the Commission on Christianizing the Social Order took the immediate task of the church "as the Body of Christ and the organ of His Spirit, [to] actively foster understanding, self-criticism and insight begotten of fellowship among those of contrasted traditions." The success of this enterprise relied on several specifics: "the 'absolute' freedom of prophesying, participation in intimate groups for fellowship, [and] formation of judgement arising from corporate spirit ... in the face of social change."[20] To this end, their report was received and made available to Presbyteries, congregations, and young people's groups for study because it was "in substance a statement of the Christian attitude and approach to the economic question."[21]

Action/study and faith/worship became inseparable strands of the nature and purpose of being church. The same Board of Evangelism and Social Service that commissioned *Christianizing the Social Order* had also tasked its Committee on Evangelism to write a *Report on Evangelism*. In it, religious revival was linked to economic and social revival, and it sought to reform society beginning with strengthening personal faith.[22] While this report cited the diversity of emphasis regarding the purpose of the church found in the gospels, the love of God found its objective in the fellowship created by sharing the Holy Spirit and in "a concrete society of people ruled by Love [which] was the first outcome of the Gospel given and embodied by Jesus."[23] The report promoted active membership in the Christian church and its new life, joined by baptism.[24]

According to Articles XIV "Of the Moral Law," XV "Of the Church," and XX "Of Christian Service and the Final Triumph," the UCC aimed, therefore, to be an agent of evangelism, which included the process of enlisting people into the Kingdom of God as the first fellowship of Christian church. The church must also be rich in "things of the spirit" to awaken and sustain dependence and responsibility, because the priesthood of all believers was vested in the whole church.[25] The *Report on Evangelism* also considered the urgency of confronting the social evils of the day, specifically "greed, exclusive nationalism, and love of domination [that] threaten the continuance of what we call society." The corporate church was to transmit and enrich religious life—which included the importance of naming the threats, such as "possession of riches as attesting human worth, ... arrogant retention of privilege and power," and "sins fostered and protected by institutions designed to foster, protect, and satisfy evil desires"—that contradict "God's mission for our nation."[26] Overall, although the work of evangelism had different emphases, it would be consistent with the directions and work of the church for a Christian social order because both evangelism and social service were seen as serving the same end: the *missio Dei* (God's mission).[27] In the *Twenty Articles of Doctrine*, the church was imagined to be united by the Holy Spirit to Christ their Head, to be one body in Him. All are to do justly, love mercy, and walk humbly with God and thus be in harmony with "the will of God that will fulfill the brotherhood" wherein the kingdom of God is made manifest.

For this purpose and in response to this calling, the UCC has been reforming itself through "adaptive changes," especially by weaving together evangelism and social service through various programs and partnerships. For example, in its early years, the UCC was challenged to find enough resources to fulfill its ecclesial rubrics as noted above, especially ministers to tend its far-flung congregations. Nevertheless, more than a decade of delay and debate preceded the 1936 decision to ordain women. The story of Lydia Gruchy,[28] the first woman to be ordained in the UCC, underlines how meeting practical needs of the day has shaped the theology, policies, and practices of the UCC. It also underlines the role of women and of local congregations to press the national church to change its ecclesiology. This innovation of the ordination of women reflects a Reformed ecclesiology: the church reformed is always in need of reform. Other issues of inclusion and justice would continue to challenge the church in terms of its self-understanding as capable of changing. Therefore it has been able to understand that God has been calling the church to do a new thing as befits the needs of the day.

In summary, the developing ecclesiology of the UCC with its liberal-evangelical social gospel roots attended in this era to being church with a conciliar motif expressed in a constant refrain of "discernment in community." Reforming itself became a vital expression of understanding itself: faithfulness to its Christian calling by interweaving the tasks of evangelism, Christian education, social service, public activism, and advocacy for justice, peace, and the integrity of creation.[29]

"Being Church in Secular Society, in a Decolonizing World with Other Religions"—*A Statement of Faith*, 1940–1967

It is important to note that the social, political, and economic turmoil between 1908 and 1936 led many Christians to reassess their beliefs about, for example, how God is revealed and the depth of human sinfulness. By the middle of the 1930s, many in the UCC had begun the kind of theological reassessment expressed in *A Statement of Faith*, as in Article VII: The Church—"We believe that the Church, the society of the redeemed, was brought into existence by God Himself through the work and risen power of Christ, Who in calling men into fellowship with Himself calls them by the same act into fellowship with one another in Him."

As John Dow stated in the official interpretation of *Statement*, God brought the church into existence after Jesus's crucifixion. By the work of the risen power of Christ "borne on the tide of mysterious urgency" and the power of the Holy Spirit at Pentecost, people experienced the self-communication of the Divine which is the strength of the church. As Dow reflected on this ecclesial doctrine, "Christians are heirs to the joys, privileges, and responsibilities of the new order and insight through Christ's standards and values."[30] As Article VII put it, "We believe that the Church is the organ of Christ's mind and redemptive will, the body of which He is the Head. Under Him the Church is called to the proclamation of the everlasting Gospel with its offer of salvation, to the worship of God, Creator and Redeemer, to the loving service of mankind, and to the care and nurture of the flock."

In comparison to the BOU era, the new *Statement* urgently framed the UCC more in terms of God's acts of judgment and mercy. It encouraged churches and "the whole Church of ecumenical spirit" with images of the church as Body of Christ, household, and family of God.[31] The church was called to proclamation, worship, loving service, care, and nurture for the sake of the world under threat of deepening violence and war and a nation experiencing economic depression. Therefore, it imagined that

> Christian life is lived in fellowship and called to abide in fellowship with Christ and His Church ... and called to live as those who are of the Kingdom of God and to seek his righteousness both in individual and social life, serving their fellow men in love for Christ's sake and striving and waiting in prayer for an ordered common life where the will of God for the well-being and peace of men shall be done over all the earth.[32]

Therefore, in the midst of intensifying world crisis and the "national anguish" of the Second World War, the task of the church was to do the will of God and be "one of persistence in well-doing."[33] Also, picking up the prophetic theme of Jeremiah and Isaiah, these images of being a church "for Christ's sake" manifested a spiritual core of "an ordered common life where the will of God for the well-being and peace of men shall be done over all the earth." Given the context, this doctrinal era embraced a theology of humanity as humbled, flawed, and always in need of repentance, forgiveness, and grace, and thus saw Christians being reconciled to God and to one another in Christ and by the Spirit.

In 1942, amid national anguish and in search of hope for new community, a Commission on Church, Nation, and World Order was established and presented its report to the 10th General Council in 1944.[34] It examined the causes of the crisis and affirmed the basic moral principles of a Christian society and the role of the church; affirmed the spiritual and social dimensions of life; named far-reaching reforms for full employment and adequate production of goods serving basic needs (e.g., education, employment, food, health, housing); and called for systems of just distribution and basic security for all through state involvement in Crown corporations, fair taxation, labour relations, and the provision of medicare and social insurance. It boldly countered the amassing of huge profits, declaring that the Canadian public interest was at stake.[35] As Phyllis Airhart and Roger Hutchinson describe, "The 1944 report of the Commission on Church, Nation and World Order dealt with the changing role of mainstream Protestant churches in the prewar society that was passing away, in the 'Christian society' the youth of the nation were expected to fight and die for and in the new world order that would emerge after the war."[36] The character of God and God's purpose were "the foundation of the Church's message in all its applications." This report stressed the role of the ecumenical movement for the church, "to open up the way for a new and passionate emphasis of the appeal and proposal of Jesus to the whole world."[37] Therefore the UCC was a founding member of the new Canadian Council of Churches in 1944 and of the World Council of Churches in 1948, and participated in the development of the WCC's "responsible society" criteria.[38] In this era, ecumenism (which was a key element of the UCC's originating identity) came to the fore, and the church now elaborated and developed its ecclesiology through its evolving commitments to "well-doing" in national and global contexts.

Questions of evangelism also continued alongside this persistent commitment to serving the *missio Dei*, and in 1945, on the UCC's twentieth anniversary, *Crusade for Christ and His Kingdom* was launched. As Ian Manson explains, "As the war drew to an end, the United Church became more clearly convinced that a spiritual revival was required in order to re-establish the church in the minds of Canadians and instill Christian values in a new generation of citizens.... This campaign aimed to 'win to Christ and his Church those not yet reached by the Gospel message,' to recruit returning service men and women and wartime workers to the church's work, and to encourage larger numbers of young people to enter the ministry." Manson also discerns that "the process of reassessing its theology, developing a blueprint for postwar society, and launching a spirited evangelical campaign had left the church *cautiously optimistic* that it could continue to play a central role in transforming the country's spiritual and social fabric."[39] This ecclesial task of influencing public affairs and society was indeed challenged as postwar Canada became increasingly secular.

So the church continued to struggle with its vocation as a church with a mission to the nation. For example, in 1950, the UCC examined its social situation in the *Report of the Commission on Culture (Church and the Secular World)*.[40] The report's bracketing of ecclesiology makes clear that it was not about the church per se but about the Canadian context shaping the church of Canada. The church was therefore aiming to become alert to the cultural crisis and the relation of Christian faith to it. While the church experienced itself as being challenged by secularism, it still held to its vision of being and becoming a national church and playing a role in shaping the conscience of the nation.

Undertaking this mammoth task—notably concurrent with the Canadian government's Royal Commission on National Development in the Arts, Letters and Sciences (the Massey Commission) of 1949–51—the commission set out to evaluate both the history of Western culture in general and the condition of modern culture in particular, according to norms and principles derived from the Christian faith. Affirming a theological anthropology rooted in *imago Dei,* human beings as co-creators are called on to connect to the arts and other cultural resources as key to being church and moral agents in society. That is, the church could be the church only if it understood, critiqued, and engaged its cultural milieu.

Another major contribution to understanding the ucc as being the church was the *Report of the Commission on World Mission* received by the 22nd General Council in 1966. It confirmed how the 1960s altered the way in which Christians related to one another and their attitudes towards members of other "living faiths and ideologies." Indeed, "the unfinished and continuing task of the Church [and] the essence of its whole life and being" needed evangelism, teaching, healing, and social welfare to express "Christian concern for human need wherever it be."[41] It offered insight into the context of a pluralistic world and the nature of the church, including self-critical awareness of the church's complicity in colonial and imperial relations, as well as the need for dialogue and partnerships of mutual understanding and co-operation to repent and join with others to meet the needs of the world. The report recommended that "the United Church of Canada acknowledge its share of guilt and be determined to cleanse itself based on repentance with God's help from all arrogance whether racial, cultural, or ecclesiastical ... and disown all forms of ecclesiastical colonialism." Envisioning "moving toward full partnership with other churches in all countries in service and witness," the report asked for recommitment to church unity and ecumenical collaboration as necessary to God's mission. Therefore, mission is to the "whole world" and committed to the "whole church."

The report's attention to relations with other religious communities demonstrated a crucial shift in the ucc's ecclesiology that saw the church as the "sole source of salvation." Instead of a supersessionist or exclusivist notion of being church, "the church should recognize that God is creatively and redemptively at work in the religious life of all mankind."[42] This report initiated particularly active engagement in dialogue and working together with people of other faiths. Thus, ecumenical partnerships, interfaith dialogue, and co-operation in every sector and aspect of human life to meet human need are considered connected and necessary for being church, for being Christians faithfully doing God's work in the world.

In sum, the UCC in this era responded to its context of rapid changes in society and around the world with various commissions and programs of evangelism, participation in building "a responsible society" alongside other churches and communities, education for faith and action, and the embrace of ecumenism and interfaith dialogue as constitutive of being church in Canada and for the whole world. Thus, in marked contrast to the church's self-understanding as the sole vehicle of salvation, this doctrinal shift taught about a church of worship and proclamation that served Christ through work with those who served God's purpose of abundant life for all.

"Called to Be a Responsible Church with Others for Justice and Sustainable Life for All"—A New Creed, 1968–2005

In this doctrinal era, diverse social movements struggling for radical change and for recognition and respect for different marginalized groups in public and in law continued to challenge the church's ecclesial character and conduct. For example, Indigenous peoples, racialized immigrant communities, sexual minorities, and middle-class and marginalized women demanded systemic changes to address issues that were previously considered to have few public moral dimensions, such as domestic and unequally paid labour, marriage, domestic violence, rape, and reproduction. Such contestations also preoccupied the UCC and effectively challenged its ecclesiology.

As a creative response to this context, A New Creed set the doctrinal compass for this era.[43] Presented to the 23rd General Council in 1968 as a brief, modern profession of faith, its ecclesiology was elegantly expressed as follows:

> We are called to be the church:
> to celebrate God's presence,
> to love and serve others,
> to seek justice and resist evil,
> to proclaim Jesus, crucified and risen,
> our judge and our hope.

Taking Jesus as authority came with action imperatives rooted in *metanoia*, ongoing creative transformation that characterizes the church as being people of the Way of Jesus. *A New Creed* encouraged and galvanized engagement to meet serious challenges to the very being and purpose of the church and how it should relate to the wider world.

"To seek justice and resist evil"—as a mark of being church in its particular time and place in Canadian context and with its global partnerships—involved responding to calls to address white settler colonization of Aboriginal peoples, divestment in South Africa, care for the earth, and economic, ethnic, gender, racial, and sexual justice. Therefore, for example, the creed was made gender-inclusive in 1980. In 1994, "to live with respect in Creation" was added to remind the church of its vocation to live out its 1986 apology to First Nations peoples and their calls for creation care.

The process of accountability for ecclesial complicity in the use and abuse of power holds the UCC responsible for a history "for which it must repent."[44] The General Council in Sudbury in 1986 offered an "Apology to Native Congregations" for having failed to respect the depth and richness of Aboriginal spirituality and vision, and for confusing the gospel of Jesus Christ with Western institutions and cultures.[45] The All Native Circle Conference established in 1988 by the 32nd General Council created some symbolic and institutional space to tackle the redress of these wrongs within the church. In 2003, the report of the Residential Schools Steering Committee to the 38th General Council, *Building toward Right Relations*, presented principles for the UCC to be a church guided by "A Vision for Reconciliation."[46]

Another significant intervention in the self-understanding of the UCC was the creation in 1985 of the Consistoire laurentien de l'Église Unie, a francophone presbytery in Montreal and Ottawa Conference. This structure respected the desire of francophone members of the UCC to "se faire reconnaître, de prendre en charge leur avenir dans cette Église majoritairement anglophone. Ce consistoire offre le soutien et les ressources nécessaires au fonctionnement et au développement de ses paroisses où les francophones désirant s'épanouir dans la foi chrétienne sont accueillis."[47]

Also in this doctrinal era, the 1984 *Report of the Task Force on Changing Roles of Women and Men in Church and Society* contributed concerted focus, energy, and resources to the ongoing process of ecclesial *metanoia*. It resolved that

> Whereas sexism is manifested and perpetuated through the traditions, structures and policies of the church and thereby supports and encourages the sexist patterns of society; and whereas sexism is evil and contrary to the intention of God for creation; and whereas other forms of oppression will be not be eradicated until sexism is eliminated and whereas to work against the evil of

sexism is to enter more fully into the process of transformation [*metanoia*] and therefore to act more faithfully as the people of God; therefore be it resolved that the General Council 1) declare its complicity in sexism; 2) commit itself to address sexism in all spheres of the church's life and stand in solidarity with those in society and within the church who experience sexism.[48]

The UCC continued this commitment to tackle the sin of sexism by participating in the WCC's *Ecumenical Decade of Churches in Solidarity with Women* (1988–98). Alternative images of being church emerged, such as living a gospel that discomforts and leads to action; bringing worship into the world and the world into the churches; creating communities of "co-equal disciples" where patterns of domination are resisted; and generating new kinds of knowledge and ways of speaking to transform the church.[49]

Meanwhile, the UCC also grappled intensely in this era with its complicity in homophobia and heterosexism. After multitudinous expressions of deep pain and prayer, conflict, and petitions, the General Council adopted in 1988 the *Membership, Ministry and Human Sexuality* statement declaring that "all persons, regardless of sexual orientation, who profess their faith in Jesus Christ are welcome to be or become members of the United Church of Canada" and that "all members of the Church are eligible to be considered for ordered ministry."[50] This decision became a line in the ecclesial sands of the UCC. Some rejoiced and reconciled, but some left. While the General Council had received the report in order to heal and continue to build community, in the wake of the decision it also directed that "there be further church-wide study of the authority and interpretation of scripture and the theological and cultural premises that inform our understanding."[51]

The Theology and Faith Committee of the General Council took up this task of clarifying how Scripture is used as a necessary yet always interpreted source of Christian life, and in 1992 delivered *The Authority and Interpretation of Scripture* report to the 34th General Council. It underscored the vital conviction that the church is a community in a constant process of discernment about being church in relation to where God is calling it to engage, and that the church becomes church by seeking God's community with all people, living creatures, and the earth.[52] Thus the process of moving toward full inclusion affirmed the heritage of the UCC as "reformed and reforming," capable of repentance and change for the sake of wholeness and right relations.

Another crucial feat of ecclesial discernment was the creation of the Ethnic Ministries Council. Having been approved by the 35th General Council in 1994, it was inaugurated in 1996 with lament and hope:[53]

Re-membering our brokenness,
Re-naming God and ourselves,
Rediscovering our identities and authenticity;
Reclaiming our names and identities
Among the whole people of God.

We, the racial and ethnic minorities of The United Church of Canada,
Invite the whole church to join us
As we pursue this vision.[54]

By this action, the church accepted that "theology that does not address the structural issues of today is a theology of the oppressor, the sin of the wrongdoers."[55] In naming and lamenting how the church is *not* whole, that it is broken by the sins of ethnocentrism and racism and by pressures toward assimilation, segregation, and rejection, the church acknowledged the need of the majority-white church to repent of its sinful complicity. The church was challenged to confront ethnocentrism and racism in personal and systemic relations, and to be willing to listen, to learn from, and to act with those persons and groups marginalized by racial and ethnic identities. To enact the implications of this vision, the UCC was called to examine more deeply its systemic racism. *That All May Be One: Policy Statement on Anti-Racism* was adopted by the 37th General Council in 2000 as a resource to provide "the basis for the creation of a church where all are welcome, where all feel welcome and where diversity is as natural as breathing."[56]

As the UCC became committed to learning about negotiating respectful difference and diversity as nurturing faith, it was similarly challenged to do so in its ecumenical, interfaith, and global relations. As previously noted, the UCC has been committed from its beginnings to Christian unity and has been active in the ecumenical movement at local, national, and global levels. There is a history of ecumenical work to celebrate in Canada—work that is ongoing despite occasional dire predictions of an "ecumenical winter."

Beginning in the 1970s, more than a dozen ecumenical coalitions were formed to focus work on particular justice issues including peacemaking, human rights in different regions of the world, economic justice, and Indigenous rights in Canada. Coalitions gave important leadership in research and analysis, advocacy, and education and animation in local communities.[57] In 2001, in the context of changing ecumenical dynamics and decreasing resources, the work of most coalitions was integrated into one organization: KAIROS: Canadian Ecumenical Justice Initiatives. The UCC was also active in ecumenical bodies addressing various aspects of mission and ministry, including the Women's Interchurch Council of Canada, the Canadian Churches' Forum for Global Ministries,[58] and the Churches' Council on Theological Education.

Lively discussion and concerted action on a range of questions continue to take place through KAIROS, the Canadian Council of Churches, and a number of smaller organizations and projects. At the same time, the UCC maintains an active involvement in global ecumenical bodies. The WCC is primary, but there is also significant engagement with the World Communion of Reformed Churches and, to a lesser degree, the World Methodist Council. All of these ecumenical commitments represent both the church's continued effort to be guided by a vision of Christian unity as well as a conviction—present since church union—that a social gospel vision is best lived out in partnership with other Christians.

While engaging in these broad ecumenical endeavours, the UCC has also explored intensely how to continue as a "united and uniting church." To this end, from 1943 to 1972, union talks were undertaken with the Anglican Church of Canada and the Christian Church (Disciples of Christ) in Canada. The resulting *Plan of Union* (1972) envisioned a denomination that would be "a new manifestation of the Church which in its faith and witness, worship and ministry, structure and mission, will help to make visible the God-given unity of the Church."[59] However, the union vote failed in 1975, and another proposal for mutual recognition of ministry, presented in 1983, was also defeated. One fruit of these conversations was a joint hymn book that remained in use long after the union vote. Twenty years later, in 2003, in the context of growing numbers of ecumenical shared ministries across Canada, bilateral dialogue with the Anglican Church was renewed. Along with focused work on guidelines for ecumenical shared ministries, this dialogue continues "to explore what is at the heart of our traditions, the obstacles these self-perceptions have created and create, and the gifts they share with society," "to pursue the way forward on mutual recognition of ministry," and to hold a vision of full communion as a model for church unity in the twenty-first century.[60]

In contrast, the long-running Roman Catholic–United Church Dialogue has focused since 1975 on "increas[ing] understanding and appreciation between the Roman Catholic Church and the United Church of Canada."[61] This has involved a series of dialogues and reports on issues emerging in their relationships in the Canadian context. Topics have included baptism, authority, evangelism, sin and reconciliation, marriage, and theologies of creation. The dialogue's 2012 report on marriage noted the gifts of this ecumenical encounter:

As dialogue participants, we are convinced that Roman Catholic and United Church members can, with God's help, learn from each other's strengths, even when they differ on issues held to be revealed truth. Our experience has renewed our conviction that ecumenical dialogue—with openness to new insights and in the presence of the Holy Spirit—is an important means by which God's Church can advance understanding and carry on the work of Jesus Christ.[62]

An often-forgotten aspect of the 1970s union talks was the participation of the Christian Church (Disciples of Christ). Talks with the Disciples continued until 1985. Although this initiative also ultimately failed, recent recognition that a deeper relationship of mission and ministry together would be fruitful for both churches has led to conversations toward a full communion agreement, expected to be enacted in 2019. This agreement follows on the Full Communion Agreement with the United Church of Christ (US), adopted in 2015. The two churches have found a variety of ways to witness to their declared intention to "pursue with intention ways of expressing the unity of the Church," including "ways of manifesting the common mission of witness and service."[63] An example was the February 2018 launch of a joint commitment to the United Nations International Decade for People of African Descent. Acknowledging the challenge to find new ways of being church in an age of global migration contributed to the development of these agreements. Agreements for mutual recognition of ministry with global partners such as the United Church of Christ in the Philippines and the Presbyterian Church in the Republic of Korea, as well as new models of "associate relationship" with migrant churches, have been important responses to this challenge.[64]

A vital dimension of ecumenism occurs at the local level, where congregations join across denominational lines to minister and witness in their context. In ecumenical shared ministries, people from two to four denominations join in a worshipping community without losing ties to their home church. Congregations are also working together in response to poverty, refugees, environmental destruction, and other concerns. The challenges for the UCC are to find effective ways to encourage and support this local ministry and witness, and to enable people across the church to see how ecumenical work can be a source of empowerment and hope.

Responding to a mandate to develop a wider understanding of ecumenism, *Mending the World: An Ecumenical Vision for Healing and Reconciliation* was adopted in 1997 at the 36th General Council as a "lens through which all the work of the General Council is reviewed on an ongoing basis" and for use by "individuals and households, congregations and other mission units, Presbyteries, and Conferences."[65] Rooted in the conviction that justice and healing are necessary for the church to be church, the report named "whole world ecumenism" as being intentional about "making common cause with all people of good will, whether they be of faith or not, for the creation of a world that is just, participatory, and sustainable."[66] This "whole world ecumenism" has shaped the UCC into being church by nurturing partnerships with people of different faiths. *Mending the World*, with its salvific notion of God who loves the world, has served as a framework for further interfaith study, beginning in 2003 with *Bearing Faithful Witness: United Church–Jewish Relations Today*, and followed in 2006 by *That We May Know Each Other: United Church–Muslim Relations Today.*[67]

The long-standing conviction that the nature of the church is reflected in its commitment to economic well-being and the common good was most clearly stated in this doctrinal era in the 37th General Council report in 2000, *To Seek Justice and Resist Evil: Towards a Global Economy for All God's People.*[68] Responding to the voices of global partners regarding the devastating impact of economic globalization on their lives and communities, the report insisted on the fundamental connection of economic justice to the life of faith. It led the General Council to affirm that "global economic justice is essential to the integrity of our faith in God and our discipleship as Christians.... [U]nrestrained global market capitalism ... is thus a sin against God, against our neighbour, and against creation."[69] Justice in all relations can be seen as another mark of being church.

That to be church included living with respect in creation was further emphasized in 1992 when the 34th General Council adopted the policy statement *One Earth Community*. The fruit of over forty years of dedicated work on ecological issues and their ecclesial significance, the report affirmed twelve key ethical principles for the church's work on ecological issues. These principles include economic justice, human responsibility, sustainable lifestyles, the protection of biodiversity, and ensuring the rights for future generations.[70] The statement has been followed by numerous policy and action initiatives that affirm that the "protection of Earth's vitality, diversity, and beauty is a sacred trust."[71]

In light of its mission of eco-justice, partnership, and inclusion of all in and for the world, the 36th General Council, in *Seeking Transformation: Congregational Mission in a Changing Canada Report*, took up in 1997 the question of the conciliar nature of the UCC's ecclesiology.[72] The report affirmed that courts are partners with one another in God's one mission within Canada and the world. The conciliar system serves the mission best when it fosters collaboration among the courts of the church. The mission of congregations is to proclaim the Good News and to gather people into faith communities that worship, evangelize, educate, and serve in mission and justice seeking in their communities. The report asked the perennial question of how disciples of Christ can reinvent practices of social responsibility with their neighbours and engage in today's world. The church was again challenged to integrate outreach and evangelism, to resist the tendency to be "private" Christians, or to view the relationship between congregational mission and the mission of the denomination as one of competition, rather than as linked or related.[73] These concerns, challenges, and hopes are also alive in the next doctrinal era.

"A Church in Canada on Earth for Right Relations of Justice, Peace and Integrity of Creation"—A Song of Faith, 2006–2016

In *A Song of Faith* the purpose of the church is vividly articulated as follows:

> We sing of a church
> > seeking to continue the story of Jesus
> > by embodying Christ's presence in the world.
> We are called together by Christ
> > as a community of broken but hopeful believers,
> > loving what he loved,
> > living what he taught,
> > striving to be faithful servants of God
> > in our time and place.
> ...
> The church has not always lived up to its vision.
> It requires the Spirit to reorient it,
> > helping it to live an emerging faith while honouring tradition,
> > challenging it to live by grace rather than entitlement,
> for we are called to be a blessing to the earth. [74]

In *Song*, the metaphorical "head, heart, and guts" of being the UCC has three expressions: its ecclesiology rooted in the interpretation of Scripture, its affection for the concept of inclusivity, and its passion for social justice.[75]

Song reflects an image of church as being committed to all people as family of God in its naming of diversity as a blessing; in its honouring of Jesus as one who crossed barriers of race, class, culture, and gender; and in its criticism of biblical interpretations that abuse Scripture by turning it into a "tool of oppression, exclusion, or hatred." The church's self-understanding as an advocate for social justice in society and in the world is reflected in *Song*'s vision of God's reign as "a commonwealth not of domination but of peace, justice, and reconciliation"; in its naming as sinful those "systemic forms of injustice, violence, and hatred" that threaten human community and the integrity of creation; and in its call to the church to "stand with the oppressed" and offer "resistance to the forces that exploit and marginalize."[76]

The UCC has struggled to act faithfully in response to calls for it to be an "inclusive" church. While not uniformly embraced throughout the church, seeking right and respectful relations of negotiated and shared power remains nonetheless a significant part of the church's self-image:

> We sing of God's good news lived out,
> a church with purpose:
> > faith nurtured and hearts comforted,
> > gifts shared for the good of all,
> > resistance to the forces that exploit and marginalize,
> > fierce love in the face of violence,
> > human dignity defended,
> > members of a community held and inspired by God,
> > corrected and comforted,
> > instrument of the loving Spirit of Christ,
> > creation's mending.
> We sing of God's mission.[77]

In this doctrinal era, the church continued to wrestle with living its mission of "a church with purpose," believing its members are faithful when Spirit-inspired, Scripture-rooted, and Scripture-formed, inclusive, justice-seeking and justice-living.

Simultaneously, a manifestation of this ecclesial vision was also presented in 2006. A healing model of church was proposed to the General Council, elaborated as *Partnership of the Aboriginal Peoples in Healing the Church and the World*:

that we too were a very spiritual people of the same Creator ... with our own gifts to offer.... We come here with a proposal ... a plan and a way of moving ahead, walking together ... beyond the grief, beyond the lament to become fully active partners in the work of The United Church of Canada. We are here to help transform our historical legacy to that of a Healing Model for the world to see, to follow, and to use in practicing peace and faith in a diverse world.[78]

The General Council responded with vehicles of ecclesial transformation: the formation of the national Aboriginal Ministries Council and the Aboriginal Ministries Circle as a unit in the General Council Office.

As the church enacted these decisions, further impetus for transformation in relation with Aboriginal peoples was generated by the church's participation in the process established by the federal Truth and Reconciliation Commission (2008–15). Across the UCC, some became deeply engaged in the hearings and deliberations of the TRC. Also, the UCC participated in the release of an ecumenical statement expressing the commitment of a diverse group of churches to enact the commission's Final Recommendations and Actions. In response to the TRC's *Call to Action to Faith Communities #48*,[79] the UCC agreed to use the principles, norms, and standards of the *United Nations Declaration on the Rights of Indigenous Peoples* as the framework for reconciliation. These combined commitments and actions require the church "to revisit its identity as a church, and how that identity does or does not foster relationships of mutuality, equality, and respect, both within and beyond the walls of the church."[80] These criteria serve to guide prayer and action, work and worship along the journey of reconciliation that at least formally has been integrated into the life and purpose of the church.

Also strengthening and keeping this vision, the Ethnic Ministries' Council report in 2006, *A Transformative Vision for The United Church of Canada* (in relation to becoming an intercultural church), acknowledged: "We are the body of Christ rising on Native land, rising in humbling respect for First Peoples to a resurrection hope for respectful diversity, differences, and an openness to God doing a new thing in The United Church of Canada."[81] Becoming intercultural in the UCC rests on recognizing and encountering social difference that is a source of injustice for those who are the victims of white-settler colonialism and racism so that all are involved in resisting and transforming the practices and assumptions that reproduce racism. Being intercultural also involves creating structures that enable full participation of all who have been marginalized in a church where those who reflect Canada's white, Anglo-Saxon settler society have been dominant. The vision affirmed that:

> in the company of God and one another, our community [of The United
> Church of Canada] can be transformative ... and live out its commitment
> to racial justice as an intercultural church where there is mutually respectful
> diversity and full and equitable participation of all Aboriginal, francophone,
> [Deaf Ministries],[82] ethnic minority, and ethnic majority constituencies in the
> total life, mission, and practices of the whole church.[83]

Thus in an anti-racist, intercultural church people participate fully, organize for diversity, act justly, speak to the world.[84] One of the seeds planted by Indigenous and other marginalized groups in the UCC may well be seeking in a world of difference and diversity an alternative interpretation of *national* in a world where "nation" becomes an idol.[85] Hence, as the United Church continues to wrestle with "which church in which Canada" as the taproot of our ecclesiology, the challenge for this doctrinal era is "whose church in whose Canada?"

What indeed is the United Church *of Canada*? The 41st General Council (2012) received the Permanent Committee on Programs for Mission and Ministry Task Group report on *Intercultural Ministries: Living into Transformation* with its in-depth policies and processes for ecclesial transformation. The theological bases were named as welcoming, relational, adaptive, justice-seeking, intentional, and missional. Ecclesial marks of covenant—equality, mutuality, respect, empowerment, reciprocity, and love—were also given as action guides. The Task Group also addressed the question of how to put these marks into practice, including the complex discernment required to enact inclusion in the midst of diversity.[86]

"Inclusion" is a contested term because when one is included, it means that someone else has the power to include—and exclude. The task group therefore astutely acknowledged that "inclusion" is not necessarily mutual, and it is not always transformative. Therefore, the task group called for a theology for intercultural ministries in Canadian contexts.[87] "Becoming an intercultural church is the call to live together in intentional ways where there is the mutual recognition and understanding of difference through intentional self-examination, relationship building, and equitable access to power; it is also our attempt to respond faithfully to such a call."[88] And in particular contexts in Canada, uniformity of church is no longer assumed or lauded. The idea of unity is good, however, if and when it encourages the vision of living in transformed relations among and across difference—and doing something towards right relations.

The *Theologies of Disabilities Report* (2015) discusses how the UCC's commitment to becoming an intercultural church prompts its members to ask: What social and material arrangements enable all minds, bodies, and souls to worship, grow spiritually, and contribute to the community of justice, peace, and the integrity of creation? A radically intercultural faith community is also by definition an accessible one in which Christians with disabilities are active, self-identified members in the body of Christ and their vulnerability makes the church whole.[89] Disability is also about difference. "Practices of welcoming people with disabilities and their allies as full participants in churches have their roots in a theological imagination that understands disability neither as flaw nor defining characteristic, but instead as part of the variation that makes up our communities across the range of human experience."[90]

The biblical images in the *Theologies of Disabilities Report* offer theological horizons for being church:

> Accordingly, the church—the body of Christ—is that place where welcome, access, and accommodation are central features of life together, through which all members "have the same care for one another" (1 Cor. 12:25). The church is a household of God (Eph. 2:19) in which "dividing walls" based upon human ordinances are abolished (Eph. 2:14–15) and gifts are received from all members of the body (Rom. 12:4–5; 1 Cor. 12), some of whom may be assumed to be weaker but who are in fact indispensable (1 Cor. 12:22).... The church is a place where all might give and receive gifts. All belong. Since God's image includes disability, and this image dwells in all human beings, the church is summoned into a radical kind of belonging, as if welcoming each other is to welcome the divine in our midst.[91]

This intervention in a world structured by ableism resonates with the way in which God calls people to a bold confession and renewed profession and practice of faith as well as transformation of policies and practices.[92]

Another strand of ecclesial formation in this doctrinal era was developed in *Living Faithfully in the Midst of Empire* (2006), the report of the Permanent Committee on Programs for Mission and Ministry Empire Task Group.[93] It focused on how power relations of "empire" have co-opted the church and rejected the gospel, which is centred on freedom for God, for the world, for the neighbour, and for the earth. The report identified empire as "the convergence of economic, political, cultural, geographic, and military imperial interests, systems, and networks that seek to dominate political power and economic wealth."[94] Because we are entangled in and complicit with the very systems we are called to change, living gospel in the midst of empire requires "our boldest and most passionate humanity."[95]

As affirmed in the 2008 *Statement on Partnership Principles*, "Creation, Christ, and the early church provide models of interrelationship, interdependence, and the development of radically inclusive communities that challenge empire by working toward right relations and the mending of creation, and that, by the power of the Spirit, take part in a different future."[96]

Covenanting to live faithfully in the midst of empire invites the UCC and its partners into a process of assessing relations of empire, invoking every aspect of church life: from congregations to the General Council, from outreach ministries to one's own particular discipleship, and from worship patterns and forms to stewardship and governance models. Each dimension needs to be centred on how people of the church can more fully embrace the transformative gospel of Jesus.[97]

Conclusion

In each doctrinal era, the UCC understands its nature to be a unifying presence and a vehicle and sign of God's grace—the promise of the kingdom/kindom of God, the promise of redemption of the torn, divided, and wounded world and creation, humans' one earth home. The *Towards 2025: A Justice-Seeking, Justice-Living Church* report to the March 2012 General Council Executive concludes with these insights into the current ecclesial understandings of the UCC:

> Woven together these areas of [our] work produce a new vision of a diverse
> justice-seeking–justice-living church engaged in the world for love, justice,
> and the integrity of creation, transformed from the inside out and from the
> outside in. It is a compelling vision of a church willing to risk discipleship
> in today's world and seeking to embody the transformation it has already
> proclaimed, open to and inviting others to join in and change the journey. It
> unites areas which have defined the United Church as a denomination—the
> apology to Aboriginal peoples, the honouring of diverse sexual orientations,
> and social justice, with new and growing areas of challenge for the church such
> as becoming an intercultural church, honouring all gender identities and our
> commitment to the inclusion of all peoples. It is justice-seeking in that it seeks

to become a different kind of church in the future; it is justice-living in that it takes concrete actions to change and begin to live into that reality now.[98]

A Church with Purpose: Towards an Ecclesiology for The United Church of Canada in the 21st Century, the report to the 41st General Council (2012), identified five ecclesial themes arising from the four doctrinal statements of faith and their eras that have been discussed in this chapter:

- The church does not belong to humans but to God through Christ.
- The UCC is governed by scripture and secondly by contextually expressed doctrine.
- The UCC is an expression of universal church.
- All ecclesiology in the UCC is provisional.
- The UCC seeks to act in solidarity with God's mission, which is greater than the church and includes people of other faiths and no specific faith.[99]

This ecclesial imaginary of the UCC has been nurtured only by concrete involvement and struggles with the actual dilemmas, suffering, and joys of specific challenges in particular regions and historic locations.

The church's purpose is the *missio Dei*—the mission of God. To be church requires seeking right relations through repentance of wrongdoing and responding to calls to transform the church as well as social relations. For example, Pamela Dickey Young presents a theological vision of the church as "a diverse collection of communities of *eros* who find their common identity in the shared memory and presence of Jesus Christ and seek to embody God's transforming grace by fostering flourishing and right relationship for all creation."[100]

In conclusion, we recall the pertinent symbolic action of the 41st General Council in 2012 in the context of the *Covenant with Aboriginal Ministries Council*. It was decided to add materials to the introduction of the BOU in *The Manual* that would include Aboriginal people as signatories, and also to revise the denomination's crest. The crest was changed to include the Indigenous church and to recognize Aboriginal spirituality. It now incorporates the four colours of the Aboriginal medicine wheel and the Mohawk phrase "Akwe Nia'Tetewá:neren," which means "all my relations." The challenge remains for the UCC to discover and live into this covenant as "a community which exists to announce and give social form to what God hopes and strives for, for all creation, as this has been glimpsed in Jesus of Nazareth and experienced in the Spirit,"[101] who grants courage and grace for taking part in the healing of the whole inhabited earth for abundant life for all.

NOTES

1 Letty M. Russell, "Ecclesiology," in *Dictionary of Feminist Theologies*, ed. Letty M. Russell and J. Shannon Clarkson (Louisville, KY: Westminster John Knox Press, 1996), 78–79.

2 "The word *kin-dom* makes it clear that when the fullness of God becomes a day-to-day reality in the world at large, we will all be sisters and brothers— kin to each other." Ada-Maria Isasi-Diaz, "Solidarity: Love of Neighbor in the 1980s," in *Lift Every Voice: Constructing Christian Theologies from the Underside*, ed. Susan Brooks Thistlethwaite and Mary Potter Engel (San Francisco: Harper, 1990), 306n8.

3 Douglas John Hall, *The Future of the Church: Where Are We Headed?* (Toronto: UCPH, 1989), 17–18.

4 Douglas John Hall, "Christianity and Canadian Context: Then and Now," in *Intersecting Voices: Critical Theologies in a Land of Diversity*, ed. Don Schweitzer and Derek Simon (Ottawa: Novalis, 2004), 18–32.

5 Don Schweitzer, "Introduction," *The United Church of Canada: A History*, ed. D. Schweitzer (Waterloo, ON: Wilfrid Laurier University Press, 2012), xi.

6 We are indebted to Greer Anne Wenh-In Ng for this phrase. See Ng, "The United Church of Canada: A Church Fittingly National," in *Christianity and Ethnicity in Canada*, ed. Paul Bramadat and David Seljak (Toronto: University of Toronto Press, 2008), 204–46.

7 *BOU*, General Preamble, 2; emphasis added.

8 Phyllis Airhart, "Christianizing the Social Order and Founding Myths— Double Vision?," *Toronto Journal of Theology* (special issue) 12, no. 2 (1996): 170–71.

9 The UCC considered itself a uniting church. In keeping with this, at the 4th General Council in 1930, the Wesleyan Methodist Church of Bermuda joined Maritime Conference.

10 See Greer Anne Wenh-In Ng, "The United Church of Canada: A Church Fittingly National."

11 T.B. Kilpatrick, "Church and Fellowship," in *Our Common Faith* (Toronto: Ryerson Press, 1928), 90.

12 *BOU*, Article 15 "Of the Church."

13 Commission on Christianizing the Social Order, UCC, *Proceedings*, GC6, 1934, 245.

14 Roger Hutchinson, "Christianizing the Social Order: A Three-Dimensional Task," *Toronto Journal of Theology* (special issue) 12, no. 2 (1996): 227–36.

15 Ibid., 176–77.

16 Ibid., 223.

17 Phyllis Airhart, *A Church with a Soul of the Nation: Making and Remaking the United Church of Canada* (Montreal and Kingston: McGill-Queen's University Press, 2015), 171–73.

18 Commission on Christianizing the Social Order, UCC, *Proceedings*, GC6, 1934, 248.

19 *BOU*, Article 14, "Of Law of God."

20 Commission on Christianizing the Social Order, UCC, *Proceedings*, GC6, 1934, 248.

21 Ibid., 64.

22 *Report on Evangelism*, UCC, *Proceedings*, GC6, 1934, 252–62.

23 Ibid., 254.

24 Ibid.

25 UCC, *Proceedings*, GC6, 1934, 257.

26 Ibid., 261–62.

27 See Airhart, *A Church with a Soul of the Nation*.

28 For more details on this, see HyeRan Kim-Cragg's account of Lydia Gruchy's journey to ordination in chapter 9 in this volume.

29 Schweitzer, "Introduction," xi.

30 John Dow, *This Is Our Faith: An Exposition of the Statement of Faith of The United Church of Canada* (Toronto: Board of Evangelism and Social Service, United Church of Canada, 1943), 14–41.

31 GC9, 1940, *Statement* Article VII: Church.

32 GC9, 1940, *Statement* Article XI: Christian Life and Duty.

33 Dow, "Church," 134.

34 *Report of Commission on Church, Nation and World Order*, UCC, *Proceedings*, GC11, 1944. This report was eighty pages long and not included in the Record of Proceedings. It was mailed to commissioners and regional groups of the commission, to all ministers and theological students, to members of the House of Commons and Senate, Legislative Assemblies, and Councils.

35 Ibid., 6–24.

36 Phyllis Airhart and Roger Hutchinson, "Introduction to Christianizing the Social Order: A Founding Vision of the United Church," *Toronto Journal of Theology* (special issue) 12, no. 2 (1996): 156.

37 *Report of Commission on Church, Nation and World Order,* UCC, *Proceedings*
GC11, 1944, 36.

38 Airhart and Hutchinson, "Introduction to Christianizing the Social Order,"
156.

39 Ian Manson, "The UCC and Second World War," in Schweitzer, ed., *The
United Church of Canada: A History,* 70–72; emphasis added. Manson is cit-
ing "Crusade for Christ and His Kingdom, *"Doers of the Word,"* UCC, BESS,
Twentieth Annual Report, 1944, 62–63.

40 *Report of the Commission on Culture (Church and the Secular World),* UCC,
Proceedings, GC14, 1950, Appendix, i–100.

41 *Report of Commission on World Mission,* UCC, *Proceedings,* GC22, 1966, 135–36;
emphasis added.

42 Ibid., 136–37.

43 "A New Creed," *Report of the Committee on Christian Faith,* UCC, *Proceedings,*
GC23, 1968, 311.

44 Stan McKay, "The Church Has Some History for Which It Must Repent," in
Stories of Survival: Conversations with Native North Americans, ed. Kathleen
and Remmelt Hummelen (New York: Friendship Press, 1985), 64.

45 *Apology,* UCC, *Proceedings,* GC31, 1986, 85.

46 *Building toward Right Relations,* Residential Schools Steering Committee,
UCC, *Proceedings,* GC38, 2003, 167–73.

47 http://justicepaix.org/repertoire/consistoire-laurentien-de-leglise-unie/.
(Editor's translation: "to be recognized, to take charge of their future in this
majority anglophone Church. This consistory offers the necessary support
and resources for the operation and development of its pastoral charges
where francophones wishing to flourish in the Christian faith are welcomed.")

48 "Sexism is the unequal distribution of power, personal and institutional,
between men and women, where men are in a position of control; any attitude, action, or institution which discriminates against a group of people on
the basis of gender; any attitude, practice or policy or institution that ignores,
denies, or violates women's self-affirmation and self-determination as moral
and social agents." Task Group on Changing Roles of Women and Men in
Church and Society, UCC, *Proceedings,* GC30, 1984, 2, 15.

49 "Being Church: Women's Voices and Visions," *Making Waves* 2, no. 1 (Fall
2001): 12–24.

50 "Membership, Ministry and Human Sexuality," UCC, *Proceedings,* GC32, 1988,
275–76.

51 UCC, *Proceedings,* GC32, 1988, 275–76, 306–12; UCC, *Proceedings,* GC34, 1992,
215–18.

52 *Authority and Interpretation of Scripture Report*, UCC, *Proceedings*, GC34, 1992, 215–71.

53 UCC, *Proceedings*, GC35, 1994, 241–59.

54 Ibid., 245.

55 Ibid.

56 Ethnic Ministries, UCC, *Proceedings*, GC37, 2000, 724–26.

57 Christopher Lind and Joe Mihevc, eds, *Coalitions for Justice: The Story of Canada's Interchurch Coalitions* (Ottawa: Novalis, 1994).

58 Formerly Ecumenical Forum of Canada, Ecumenical Institute of Canada, Canadian School of Missions and Ecumenical Institute, and The Canadian School of Missions.

59 The Anglican Church of Canada, Christian Church (Disciples of Christ) in Canada, and The United Church of Canada, *Plan of Union and By-Laws* (Approved by the General Commission on Church Union, November 1972) (n.p., 1973), 11.

60 *Drawing from the Same Well: The St. Brigid Report. A Report of the Anglican–United Church Dialogue 2003–2009* (Toronto: General Synod of The Anglican Church of Canada and The United Church of Canada, 2009), 42; *Called to Unity in Mission: A Report of the Anglican Church of Canada–United Church of Canada Dialogue 2012–2016* (Toronto: The General Synod, Anglican Church of Canada, 2016), 19.

61 Roman Catholic Church/United Church of Canada Dialogue, *Marriage: Report of the Roman Catholic/United Church Dialogue, October 2004–April 2012* (n.p., 2012), 2. https://commons.united-church.ca/Documents/What-We-Believe-and-Why/Ecumenical-and-Interfaith-Relations/Report-of-the-Roman-Catholic-United-Church-Dialogue-Marriage.pdf.

62 Ibid., 20.

63 UCC, *Proceedings*, GC42, 2015, 251.

64 Ibid., 245–48.

65 *Mending the World*, Inter-Church and Inter-Faith Committee, UCC, *Proceedings*, GC36, 1997, 195–227.

66 Ibid., 206.

67 *Bearing Faithful Witness*, Inter-Church and Inter-Faith Committee, UCC, *Proceedings*, GC38, 2003, 210–16; *That We May Know Each Other*, Inter-Church and Inter-Faith Committee, UCC, *Proceedings*, GC39, 2006, 553–55, 757–58.

68 *To Seek Justice and Resist Evil: Towards a Global Economy for All God's People*, Division of World Outreach, UCC, *Proceedings*, GC37, 2000, 184–85, 197–200, 784–857, 1182–84.

69 Ibid., 845–46.

70   *One Earth Community*, UCC, *Proceedings*, GC34, 1992, 501–5.

71   UCC, *Proceedings*, GC38, 2003, 480, http://earthcharter.org/discover/
the-earth-charter/.

72   *Seeking Transformation: Congregational Mission in a Changing Canada
Report*, UCC, *Proceedings*, GC36, 1997, 539–59.

73   Ibid.

74   Committee on Theology and Faith, *A Song of Faith: A Statement of Faith of
The United Church of Canada / L'Église Unie du Canada*, UCC, *Proceedings*,
GC39, 2006, 433.

75   Ibid., Appendix D: "On the Identity of the United Church as Reflected in the
Statement of Faith," 442–43.

76   Ibid., 428–35.

77   Ibid., 433–34.

78   *Partnership of the Aboriginal Peoples in Healing the Church and the World*,
UCC, *Proceedings*, GC39, 2006, 95–96.

79   Truth and Reconciliation Commission of Canada, *Truth and Reconciliation
Commission of Canada: Calls to Action* (2015), 5, http://www.trc.ca/websites/
trcinstitution/File/2015/Findings/Calls_to_Action_English2.pdf/.

80   See UCC, "Statement on the United Nations Declaration on the Rights of
Indigenous Peoples Rights as the Framework for Reconciliation," March 31,
2016. http://www.united-church.ca/sites/default/files/resources/undrip
-united-church-statement.pdf.

81   *A Transformative Vision for The United Church of Canada*, Ethnic Ministries'
Council, UCC, *Proceedings*, GC39, 2006, 587.

82   Deaf ministries were added to the intercultural vision in 2007. Deaf ministries were visible and tangibly foregrounded as stakeholders at the "Behold!"
Intercultural Conference held by the UCC in Toronto, October 30–November 2,
2008.

83   *Transformative Vision*, UCC, *Proceedings*, GC39, 579–80.

84   UCC, *Ending Racial Harassment: Creating Healthy Congregations* ([Toronto],
2008).

85   Ng, "The United Church of Canada: A Church Fittingly National."

86   *Intercultural Ministries: Living into Transformation*, UCC, *Proceedings*, GC41,
2012, 312–14, 524–33. See also Ethnic Ministries Re-Visioning Task Group,
A Transformative Vision for the United Church of Canada, UCC, *Proceedings*,
GC39, 2006, 579–90.

87   In this vein of continuing ecclesial work on "critical inclusion" of varied identities, see the Church in Mission Unit Resource, *Moving toward Full Inclusion:
Sexual Orientation in the United Church of Canada*, 1st ed. 2012; 2nd ed. 2014.

88 *Living into Transformation*, UCC *Proceedings*, GC41, 2012, 312; 524–33.

89 Theology and Inter-Church Inter-Faith Committee, *Theology of Disabilities Report*, UCC, *Proceedings*, GC42, 2015, 604–13.

90 Ibid., 610

91 Ibid., 613.

92 Ibid., 604–13.

93 Empire Task Group, Permanent Committee Programs on Mission and Ministry, *Living Faithfully in the Midst of Empire*, UCC, *Proceedings,* GC39, 2006, 596–657.

94 Ibid., 601, citing World Alliance of Reformed Churches, *Covenanting for Justice in the Economy and the Earth*, 2004.

95 Ibid., 625.

96 Justice, Global and Ecumenical Relations Unit, *Reviewing Partnership in the Context of Empire* (Toronto: UCC, 2009), 28.

97 Permanent Committee Programs on Mission and Ministry, Empire Task Group, *Covenanting to Live Faithfully in Midst of Empire*, UCC, *Proceedings*, GC40, 2009, 777.

98 *Towards 2025: A Justice Seeking / Justice Living Church*, UCC, *Proceedings*, GCE, March 24–26, 2012, 130d.

99 Theology and Inter-Church Inter-faith Committee, *A Church with Purpose: Towards an Ecclesiology for The United Church of Canada in the 21st Century*, UCC, *Proceedings*, GC41, 2012, 434.

100 Pamela Dickey Young, *Re-Creating the Church: Communities of Eros* (Harrisburg, PA: Trinity Press International, 2000), 4.

101 Larry Rasmussen, "The Near Future of Socially Responsible Ministry," in *Theological Education for Social Ministry*, ed. Dieter Hessel (New York: Pilgrim Press, 1988), 28.

CHAPTER EIGHT

WHAT ARE PEOPLE FOR?
IN CHRISTIAN LIFE, DISCIPLESHIP, AND MINISTRY

HyeRan Kim-Cragg

The question "What are people for?" in Christian life is not easy to answer. It is a question that goes to the core of what it means to be human beings as people of God. There are many possible answers. One that runs throughout materials produced by The United Church of Canada is stated in the words of *A New Creed*: "We are called to be the church, to celebrate God's presence."[1] Celebration has been central to the life of the people of the UCC. It is what they believe they are created for. This chapter will explore this calling, as well as two virtues, namely courage and humility, that are important if the Christian life is to be celebrated faithfully.

Purpose of Christian Life: Being Celebratory

In *Voices and Visions*, a publication marking the 65th anniversary of the UCC, Peter Gordon White cautions readers not to be swayed by the problems and difficulties they face but to "learn to celebrate" because it is "an opportunity to know ourselves more truly as a believing people."[2] This emphasis on "learning to celebrate" as UCC people was made early on. In 1943, Richard Davidson argued that the church is to be an educator that embodies the celebratory way of life through worship, and that this was key if the Christian faith was to be passed down to its children. People learn to become Christian as they experience God's presence and encounter God's grace. This formative experience is enacted as the Scripture is remembered and embodied in worship. Davidson writes: "Architectural lines, light and shade, colour, windows, hangings, pictures, texts of Scripture, the font, the pulpit, and the Holy Table—in all the symbolism nothing is omitted that will help the child to understand and feel in whose *presence* he [*sic*] is when he [*sic*] comes" to worship.[3] Davidson's view is further echoed in *A New Creed*. This profession of faith indicates that Christian life and identity are most clearly expressed when Christian people celebrate God's presence in life as a gift of God. *Celebrate God's Presence*, the most recent service book of the UCC, affirms this view.[4] Its Preface begins with a poem exhorting the church to "celebrate its experience of God's presence."[5] *A Song of Faith* proclaims that "we cannot keep from singing" as "we celebrate [Jesus Christ] as the Word made flesh."[6] Church members learn to do so because celebrating Jesus Christ enables them to experience the grace of God, a freeing and unconditional gift. Walter Brueggemann, referring to the tradition of the Psalms, says that the human vocation is to praise.[7] The fundamental purpose of human life is to celebrate. The act of praise is a response to God's work as Creator. The act of celebration as Christian is giving thanks to God, who created us in God's image. Furthermore, to claim the human vocation is to praise is a constitutive act. It makes us human, giving purpose to human existence.

This human existence of being celebratory is not a solitary act. Human purpose in life manifests itself in fellowship through diverse relationships. The church calls people to socialize with others as a way of communicating the gospel.[8] The Bible records how the early church connected the celebratory life of praise to God with fellowship: "Day by day, as they spent much time together in the temple, they broke bread at home and ate their food with glad and generous hearts, praising God and having the good will of all the people" (Acts 2:46). The celebratory life of the early church has continued to evolve in ordinary communal activities of Canadian churches such as quilt making, baking, bazaars, potlucks, ham and turkey suppers, prayer meetings, and Bible studies. These are concrete examples of how UCC people practise a theology of celebration through fellowship, *koinonia*.[9] Such examples affirm the belief in *A Statement of Faith* (1940) that "the Christian life is the life lived in fellowship with Christ and His Church."[10] Such examples also show the UCC's desire to form a community of people in relationship, relationship with God, self, and neighbour. "One of the best things about going back to the pastorate ... was the fellowship with the congregations," one retired minister said of returning to the pastorate. "I want people."[11] God's desire for relationship is poured out into all people. The UCC teaches that people of God long for relationship because they know that we cannot live without God or others. To take the Trinity seriously is to claim that humans are made to be relational. Humans desire relationships because God made us that way. This truth is most strongly captured in the first words of *A New Creed*: "We are not alone."[12]

Celebration in this sense is at the very heart of the UCC's understanding of what it means to be human. The church upholds the human desire to celebrate life, and to celebrate even those aspects of life that include suffering and death. That is why the UCC believes that the focus of a funeral should be "to celebrate the life of the person who has died, while praising God and proclaiming hope."[13] This, it believes, is a very human thing to do. Being able to celebrate life deepens one's understanding of what it means to be human. Throughout the UCC's history, this understanding of what it means to be human has penetrated various aspects of the denomination's life as church and has encouraged the people to articulate their reasons for particular actions and decisions. While the UCC has always understood that humans have a sinful nature that God redeems,[14] it has also always affirmed human goodness with a belief that people are made in the image of God. Such affirmation is rooted in Reformed theological anthropology: we are sinners yet saved. Sanctification is another theological concept of importance in terms of understanding the UCC's theological anthropology, human nature as sinful and good.

The Process of Becoming Christian:
Living a Life toward Sanctification

Affirmation of the goodness of human living is the goal of Christian life and of evangelism,[15] a goal that points to change and conversion, a turning to God in the process of Christian perfection. This affirmation calls for sanctification because sanctification affirms the goodness of people. Christians celebrate the goodness of God and creation as they learn and practise to live a life towards sanctification. Sanctification, the Christian attainment of Christlikeness, was an important part of the Methodist tradition in particular, and thus found its place in the UCC theology as well. For instance, Nathanael Burwash, anticipating church union, argued that Methodist views, which emphasize the importance of the Holy Spirit, Christian perfection, and the testimony of experience, would not be lost in the new church.[16] These views are captured in Article 2.3.12 of the *Basis of Union*: "We believe that those who are regenerated and justified grow in the likeness of Christ through fellowship with Him, the indwelling of the Holy Spirit, and obedience to the truth; that a holy life is the fruit and evidence of saving faith.... And we believe that in this growth in grace Christians may attain that maturity and full assurance of faith whereby the love of God is made perfect in us."[17] This doctrine of sanctification got little attention during the Second World War and in the postwar years, but it was there. For example, J.S. Thompson, one author of *The New Curriculum*, wrote, "Becoming like Christ" means "growing towards a new kind of goodness."[18] One might argue that the teaching of sanctification was translated into a quest for social righteousness that spurred the denomination's social justice work. The doctrine of sanctification was lived out as people sought the empowerment of those at the margins. The Christian goal of sanctification was connected with the cherished value of human dignity and challenged the systematic oppression that deprives human goodness. Therefore, the doctrine of sanctification not only was expressed through a dogmatic set of beliefs but embraced experiential aspects of practice and action. Sanctification requires right relationships with others and with God. Living the relational life leads to sanctification. Here we see the connection between sanctification and the communal nature of the Christian life of celebration. For John Calvin, sanctification is manifested as grace as the individual Christian life is woven into the communal and relational ways of being. In reading Calvin, Serene Jones describes "the church as a communal context in which people are pulled together and given defining practices and institutional form by a sanctifying grace."[19]

To be sanctified is to grow into one's full potential. This growth includes facing difficult realities and knowing one's own limits. There is no growth without growing pain. Celebration is especially needed when we face unfamiliar and uncomfortable realities. *Song* captures this point well: "The Spirit challenges us to celebrate the holy not only in what is familiar, but also in that which seems foreign."[20] The ordination of women was one case of that which was unfamiliar. It required the church to face an untried reality and embark upon a journey that they had never taken before. Living out a celebratory life towards sanctification as Christian people, as the following case study demonstrates, means embracing struggles, even if that means going against the status quo with regards to women's leadership in the church.

Case Study: The Ordination of Lydia Gruchy

Lydia Gruchy was the first woman student to graduate at the Presbyterian Theological College (now St. Andrew's College), Saskatoon, in 1923. Upon her graduation, she did everything that ordained men would do in Veregin, Saskatchewan. In 1926, Kamsack Presbytery requested her ordination.[21] When a motion was made at the General Council in 1926 (the first Council following church union) to grant this request, the meeting "exploded."[22] It was almost impossible for many people at the time to imagine women in leadership roles in the church with a position of authority over men. The postwar reality contributed to the disruption of the old social and family networks. As more mothers worked outside the home, the emphasis on the family as religious educator decreased.[23] This dismantling of a family role was felt as a loss. For some this led to strong resistance, to the point where the idea of women working outside the home was seen as anti-Christian. Even J.R. Mutchmor, who believed in the role of the church as "the conscience of state," publicly opposed women working outside the home.[24] Many women did so, nevertheless, and many also performed the work of ordained ministers within the church without being recognized as such.[25] The issue of women's ordination was, therefore, closely related to culturally accepted understandings of gender roles within the family, the basic unit of Christian life for society at that time. That is why the 1926 General Council took no action, though it passed the motion that "there is no bar in religion or reason to such ordination."[26] This rather ambiguous position required a further report.[27] A 1928 report tapped into biblical wisdom in which Jesus considered men and women to be spiritually equal. The report also acknowledged that some passages spoke against women in public leadership (1 Corinthians 14:34–36). However, it invoked the teachings of Jesus and Paul to put contradictory biblical passages such as Eph. 5:21–33 and 1 Tim. 2:9–15 in context.[28] The report demonstrates how the UCC heeded the biblical call for human equality and exercised evangelical freedom of counterbalancing the weight of passages that seem to be against "the general tenor of the Gospel."[29]

In short, the story of Lydia Gruchy indicates that the UCC clearly teaches that women are created in the image of God and are equal before God and responsible to God.[30] This teaching is a cause to celebrate, which moves human beings one step closer toward the goal of becoming like Christ, who calls people to follow him to denounce sexism. This celebratory theology of sanctification affirming human goodness and equality has helped the church move toward the inclusion of women in ordained ministry and the recognition of their many leadership roles. The decision to ordain women in 1936 paved the way to deal with the issue of sexual orientation and eligibility of ministry for those who belong to sexual minority communities in 1988. Following Gruchy, other women led the way. Lois Wilson was the first ordained woman moderator; Anne Squire was the first laywoman moderator; and Jordan Cantwell was the first lesbian moderator.[31]

Celebrating Christian Life Courageously: A Call for Discipleship

Celebrating Christian life means practising discipleship—following Jesus. As the Bible witnesses, and as Christians today know too, following Jesus is not easy. It takes courage. It requires risks. It often brings pain and causes loss. The following two case studies will highlight the challenges of practising discipleship. They will show how celebration requires courage and humility.

Case Study: *The New Curriculum*

The New Curriculum was courageous in its theological and biblical approaches. Prior to the 1960s, Christian education was mainly interested in teaching methods and skills and was preoccupied with theories of Christian education without sufficient theological content.[32] Taking scientifically informed historical biblical criticism seriously, *The New Curriculum* embraced a "new" knowledge for exploring the theological and ecclesial inquiries under the headings *God and His Purpose, Jesus Christ and the Christian Life*, and *The Church and the World*.[33] *The New Curriculum* boldly claimed that the Bible does not have to be defended or explained scientifically, and that Christians have no need to "make a choice between scientific truth and religious faith."[34] What was needed instead was a biblical literacy, aided by historical criticism in conversation with traditional and emerging critical theologies.

Its pedagogical approach was also courageous because it was geared not only children but also to adults. "For many, the idea of Christian nurture among adults is novel," the chief editor of *The New Curriculum* acknowledged.[35] This notion of Christian nurture for adults was revolutionary thinking for some in the UCC. It planted the view that Christian education is a lifelong learning process, involving all ages. Discipleship, as a calling to follow the way of Jesus, did not stop at a young age after all. Christian nurture for all was to become the "preeminent method of evangelism" if the church was to have an assured future foreseen by its forebears in the early twentieth century.[36] In hindsight, it was perhaps unrealistic to imagine "having all ages studying similar topics together over a three-year cycle," but *The New Curriculum* was nonetheless a courageous move in its educational approach.[37]

This gradual process was not without big hurdles.[38] The momentum for a nationwide comprehensive church curriculum had been building since the 1950s, a period during which every sector of the church saw growth.[39]

In this context, the General Council in 1952 approved the development of a new curriculum for the church.[40] When *The New Curriculum* came out in 1964 after twelve years of preparation, the controversy over this curriculum was so strong that some were worried that the church would split apart.[41] The church's teachings about scientific evolution and biblical interpretation were difficult to swallow for many Christians. *The New Curriculum* was under attack to the point where there were calls for all of its books to be "banned and burned."[42] It generated unanticipated controversies mostly from people outside the UCC. Despite this strong reaction, the UCC was patient and persistent. This work was accompanied with a courageous call for discipleship to discern how to follow Jesus by way of growing biblical and theological knowledge relevant to the twentieth-century context.

For some people, *The New Curriculum* rekindled their vocation of Christian discipleship. Anne Squire, for example, reflecting on its legacy, stated that it transformed her ministry as she journeyed from the role of a seasoned Sunday school teacher to become the first female lay moderator.[43] But for others, the teaching of Genesis as a collection of myths went too far. For them "myths meant fiction, or worse, something not true." Though they were a minority, some felt neglected by the church's "lack of pastoral care." They demanded the "dismissal of the editors and faculty people" who wrote such heretical materials.[44] The negative reactions and strong resistance continued.[45] While the backlash and negative criticism were strong, the General Council of 1964 courageously approved *The New Curriculum* in its biblical and theological grounding and its teaching.[46] Even though this move resulted in emotional, spiritual, and financial losses,[47] there were also priceless gains for growth. The "cost of discipleship"[48] that requires courage echoes the vocation of ministry understood as service to God by serving people through education and empowerment. *The New Curriculum* enhanced and renewed the understanding of ministry as empowerment of the whole people of God. It challenged a clergy-centred notion of ministry as it celebrated the inclusion of laity for ministry.

One of the theological and educational legacies of *The New Curriculum* that continues to impact the lives of the people in the UCC today is the notion of ministry as the empowerment of the whole people of God. *The New Curriculum* saw the purpose of Christian life as inclusion of people who have been ignored and unnoticed in the church. In order to reach out to the marginalized in the church, a central role was envisioned for the laity. In *The New Curriculum*, ministry was seen as primarily the responsibility of the laity while the clergy were to empower others in that ministry to the world. That was the intention behind the idea to create *The New Curriculum*: "to bridge the gap between clergy and laity" and to create a more theologically literate membership.[49] That is also why *The New Curriculum* focused on adults as well as children.

The emphasis on empowering laity found conceptual expression in the 1980s with *Envisioning Ministry* (1985).[50] In the same year, the Division of Mission in Canada wrote *Future Directions of Christian Education*, which called for lifelong learning of both lay and ordered members of the church.[51] The 1986 report *Learning on the Way* also stressed the importance of education for all ages.[52] Not only did adults become the focus of Christian education, but children, previously understood as passive observers in church, began to be regarded as active participants in worship and other parts of the life of the church as well. The *Report of the Project Group on Christian Initiation* explored a theology of baptism out of which came the 1982 policy that all baptized children will be welcomed to receive the Lord's Supper.[53] The empowerment of laity, including children, rooted in a theology of the whole people of God, shaped the UCC's eucharistic practices and led to an "open table" where, regardless of baptism or confirmation, all are now regarded as welcome to receive communion.[54] Given that most mainline churches today still restrict communion to those who are fully baptized members of that particular church, the UCC's eucharistic practices are another example of courageous discipleship. Its inclusive and egalitarian view of ministry is clearly captured in *Song*: "the work of the church requires the ministry and discipleship of all believers."[55] A theology of the whole people of God, following a long "tradition of theological inclusion"[56] helped to tune in erstwhile unheard voices. *The Planner for Lifelong Learning* (in its revised edition of 1991) stated that "in our educational programmes ... we take seriously the needs and aspirations of those in the United Church who have been marginalized: racial, cultural, linguistic minorities; the poor, the disabled, seniors, singles, gays and lesbians."[57] To advocate for the people at the margin is to echo a theological anthropology of each person as made in the image of God. Thus "the dignity" of the oppressed must be "defended." And that is what "God's good news is."[58]

Case Study: Marriage, Sexual Orientation, and Eligibility for the Order of Ministry

In 1988, the General Council made a decision that "in and of itself, sexual orientation should not be a factor in determining membership in the Order of Ministry of The United Church of Canada."[59] This decision on the eligibility for the order of ministry was the culmination of the previous reports that explored and examined gender justice, marriage, and sexuality.[60] While this decision was basically an endorsement of the *Report on Sexual Orientation and Eligibility for the Order of Ministry* (1984), it was a culmination of decades of study, struggle, and soul-searching.[61] Thus it is worth tracing these decades.

One may go back to 1946, ten years after the ordination of Lydia Gruchy, to see the beginnings of this spiritual undertaking.[62] A report on Christian marriage contested Augustine's teaching that original sin that came from Eve, a notion that has supported a gender hierarchy and unequal marriage relationships for centuries. Instead, the 1946 report interpreted the Genesis account of Adam and Eve as a story about "comradeship" and of the two first humans' need for each other.[63] Almost twenty years later, this interpretation had stuck. The author of the first-year theme of *The New Curriculum* took a similar interpretation to that of the 1946 report but drew it out even further: "there is nothing wicked in being tempted: in fact, it is the way we can really grow up into real strength of character." Far from viewing Eve as the cause of the original sin, Thomson described Eve as someone who "stands for powerful and attractive elements in our nature, our attachment to others, and particularly to those whom we specially love."[64] These two materials reflect the *Twenty Articles of Doctrine* that speak of both Adam and Eve (not Eve alone) as "out first parents, being tempted."[65]

By the 1970s, human sexual relationships including marriage were primarily understood as an expression of intimacy rather than as a means of procreation, and views of women's domestic role as inferior to that of men's were dismissed.[66] This shift was a sign that the UCC was moving its understanding of marriage to partnership and human sexuality to "a primarily relational sexual ethic."[67] The movement to affirm human sexuality and its various orientations was certainly a gradual and contested process. The General Council of 1980 identified the church as the people who "stand with the oppressed as they struggle for justice, to oppose personal, social, and systematic injustices" and who "work for the reconciliation between God and humanity in Church and society."[68] In the world where heterosexuality is dominant and regarded as the norm, people of sexual minority status have been oppressed. The church was thus moved to stand with them rather than against them.[69] Such a view was helped by liberation, feminist, and Black theologies that offered critical analyses of multilayered systematic oppressions.[70] These theologies have advanced our understanding of how the oppression of sexuality is intertwined with that of gender, race, and class in colonial Christian history. In this regard, "sexuality and intimate relations are not private matters, but critical sites for investigating the surveillance of colonial boundaries and production of desire."[71]

Disclosing the sites that have been veiled for so long prompts troubles and public outcry. Similar to the negative reactions *The New Curriculum* generated, a study document of 1980 entitled *In God's Image ... Male and Female* and the follow-up document, *Gift, Dilemma, and Promise*, also generated controversies. The UCC required strength of character and courage to work its way through these documents as well. It did so by understanding the opposition and heated discussion that resulted in an opportunity for spiritual discernment about the call to discipleship: what it means to follow Jesus.[72] The UCC was again faced with the spectre of a split, as it had been over the introduction of *The New Curriculum*. Indeed, 25,000 members left the church in the 1980s.[73] But the church was again ready to work through the controversy and to rediscover its call to discipleship, which requires courage and faith. The decision to be fully inclusive was argued partly on the basis that "this is the faithful thing to do"—the best way the church knew to follow Jesus, the way to celebrate Christian life faithfully. So following Jesus is more important than doing easy things or opting for the popular opinion of the day. Following Jesus is core to understanding how the UCC understands what it means to be human and how to celebrate its theological anthropology through embodiment and empowerment.

The 1988 decision on sexual orientation and eligibility for ordered ministry posed a question about the authority of Scripture and of the interpretation of the Bible. The 1984 *Report on Sexual Orientation and Eligibility for the Order of Ministry* shows that the authors of this report wrestled with the question as they confronted the biblical texts that condemn homosexuality. The UCC has drawn from the well of its own tradition, "seeking always to be faithful to Scripture," with awareness that "no statement of ours can express the whole truth of God."[74] Taking *A Statement of Faith* from 1940 further, *Song* even says that Scripture contains "contrasting points of view held in tension."[75] Such points of view exist because when we engage Scripture, we cannot avoid "interpretation," and this interpretation is always "influenced by and entangled in the world views" that are limited.[76] This fact, however, is not an excuse for turning our back on the Bible and/or emerging contexts.[77] By seeking biblical wisdom, and responding to and learning from the world,[78] the 1988 decision was to affirm that each person's sexuality is not a choice but an orientation, and that such orientation is natural, which means all sexual orientations are intended to be good, for they are created in the image of God.[79] To the UCC, this was another courageous act of discipleship toward becoming "a justice-seeking, responsive, and inclusive church."[80]

In short, both case studies—*The New Curriculum* and the decisions about marriage and sexual orientation and eligibility for the Order of Ministry—demonstrate that the UCC has prayerfully discerned and responded to the call to follow Jesus in ways that require courage. This courageous Christian life has allowed UCC people to celebrate their Christian life where other Christians have feared to tread. It deeply explored its scriptures and beliefs, holding to the conviction that what belongs to the world (scientific knowledge, philosophy, and diverse world views) belongs also to God. This is nothing new, but it affirmed what was made clear in *A Statement of Faith*.[81] It also means that the UCC has been able to embrace the world and uphold that "all creation is good."[82] This is in line with its theological anthropology that no matter how different or marginalized one is we are all fearfully and wonderfully made in the image of God (Psalm 139:14). Thus the denomination proclaims, "we cannot keep from singing," and celebrates life by praising God.

Sober Celebration: A Call for Humility

The UCC has not always succeeded in celebrating courageous life. Although it has acted courageously as a response to sanctifying grace, it has made mistakes and acted out of fear and cowardice. Such acts reveal humanity as both good and imperfect, sinners yet saved. *Song* is clear on the theological conviction that humans readily "surrender ourselves to sin."[83] Behind redemptive history, there is also a sinful history. Ironically, recalling the church's not-so-courageous history also takes courage. It is only by acknowledging its failures that the UCC people truly rise to the fullness of what it means to be Christian. To live towards sanctification means to live a life that holds both human goodness and human failing in tension. That is the key to celebrate the Christian life by affirming the paradox of the theology of discipleship. To some extent, humans celebrate Christian life as broken vessels through which God's grace shines. Thus the celebratory life for the Christian can be truly celebratory only as long as there is also humility.[84] When Christianity finds itself in privileged places of power, humility is particularly important. Even as Christianity has become less significant in Canadian society, humility is still important. Humility helps Christians ground themselves in God. How is humility embodied in Christian life, discipleship, and ministry? It is embodied first through naming and acknowledging wrongdoing, continuing to renew and reform its life towards sanctified life. The following examples, tracing the previous decades from 1920s up to 2009, are some of the ways the church has named its sinful acts as well as acknowledged its renewed commitment to live up to the gospel in its fullest sense. They are examples of courage and humility in fulfilling the Christian calling of living out the life celebrated faithfully.

One of the external forces that drove church union was the arrival of new immigrants. This external force was alarming for S.D. Chown, a church union leader. "If the major Churches of Protestantism cannot unite, the battle which is going on now so definitely for the religious control of our country, will be lost within the next few years."[85] The arrival of new Roman Catholics was perceived as a threat to the goal of creating a Protestant Christian nation. There were also underlying views about the importance of "racial purity and the European inheritance."[86] Chown's fears about non-European Protestant immigrants were widely shared by socially progressive Christians, including J.S. Woodsworth. He made no secret of his opposition to immigration from non-British, non-English-speaking, and non-European places.[87]

Religious and racial prejudice from the Eurocentric world view reared its head many times over the years. During the Second World War, the Canadian government displaced 20,000 citizens of Japanese descent fearing they might be enemies collaborating with the Japanese army. Some church bodies protested such action while providing assistance to those who were interned. Others justified and acquiesced to this action. In the case of European Jews, the church supported Jewish refugees, pressuring the government to loosen the rigid restriction imposed on them. But, again, attitudes towards Jews were ambivalent, with many people expressing fear and distrust of them.[88] The UCC suffered from "the toxins of religious and ethnic bigotry."[89]

As the UCC began to realize in the 1960s that it was losing numbers and prestige, it began to ask how it could still celebrate Christian life in a society that no longer assumed religion as an integral part of individual and social life. In 1961, the report of the Board of Evangelism and Social Service's committee on church membership contemplated a religiously pluralistic future and the end of Christendom. The report, however, regarded this end as a cause to celebrate because the UCC was finally beginning to be free from "European domesticity"[90] and was instead embracing a world that consisted of non-European and non-Christians more fully. Yet, in the 1960s and 1970s, the UCC continued to hold a paternalistic attitude towards so-called ethnic ministries and "Indian" missions.[91] Again, it had a double standard. On one hand, the UCC made a statement that condemned racism in southern Rhodesia, South Africa, and Portuguese colonies of Africa in the 1970s.[92] On the other hand, it regarded the Board of Home Missions as a "transitional vehicle" to assist non-Anglo and non-white groups to "assimilate into Canadian society."[93] It was viewed as "transitional" because it was understood that once immigrant children learned English they would no longer need to maintain their ethnic, linguistic, and racial differences. The Board of Home Missions was incorporated into the Division of Mission in 1972. Until the Ethnic Ministry Council was established in 1996, ethnic and racial minority congregations struggled to gain recognition because, as Stan McKay has noted, "racism is at the bottom of the list of priorities of Canadian Christians." Though many might feel "liberal guilt," what is needed is "active repentance."[94]

Once the UCC took the first step of confessing sins through naming and admitting its wrongdoings, humility took the next tangible step of embodiment through the Christian life of responsibility and accountability. After many decades of struggle, the UCC undertook a more committed step in its journey toward "reconciliation and healing."[95] The 1986 General Council's "Apology to Native Congregations" was one of these steps.[96] The 2006 General Council marked the twentieth anniversary of the apology by recommitting to this humble yet courageous journey. This General Council also made a decision to become "an intercultural church" after much prayerful review from the Ethnic Ministry Council (EMC). The establishment of the EMC in 1996 signalled a shift from the church's paternalistic ways to a respectful engagement with ethnic minority and Aboriginal people. A review of the EMC's ten years of work made it clear that an intentional effort would be necessary to more fully disclose the power dynamics inherent in racism and Eurocentric cultural imperialism in the UCC. Now the vision of the church union with its underlying assumptions about the preferability of a white, Anglo, English-speaking, Protestant society over Indigenous, non-European, French-speaking people, was clearly redressed with a "transforming vision" of an intercultural church, where Aboriginal, francophone, Deaf, and racialized communities were fully included as part of the church.[97] The 2006 report underlined the scope of the transformation it envisioned: "Not one thing will be left untouched in God's transformative power."[98] The next General Council in 2009, reflecting on this report, confirmed that the commitment to becoming an intercultural church means change for all and "that no one would be left unchanged" in this process.[99]

The intercultural vision of the UCC stresses interdependence. *Song* makes a point of this interdependence and stretches the church beyond a human-centred world view as it sings of "finding ourselves in a world of beauty and mystery, of living things, diverse and interdependent."[100] A Korean/Chinese cosmological anthropology may help us understand the idea of interdependence. The word for human is made with two characters, 人 and 間. 人 represents "person" with two lines, each leaning on each other. These represent the reality that being human means finding support from others. 間 stands for "in between space," or "inter" as it depicts the opening in a door or gate (門) through which the sun (日) shines. Thus humanity, the very core of who we are as persons, is discovered in the space or relationship between and among different individuals who lean on one another for survival and support. Human beings are fully human only when they are dependent on and related to one another, including non-human beings.[101] This intercultural vision based on interdependent life has sought to correct the church's dominant missional position of "one-way communication,"[102] recognizing that mission is the work of listening and leaning on each other, recognizing power differentials and inequity through self-examination and self-critique.

What constitutes a challenge for the UCC is not only the sinful history that lies behind it, but the fact that (positive steps to address the problems notwithstanding) Eurocentric world views, racist attitudes, and colonial practices continue to be active in the present. Thus there is a need to continually revisit the past in order to reshape the present and the future. This is precisely why it is so important to continue to courageously and humbly celebrate both human brokenness and human goodness in the light of a God who calls Christians to be something more.

Concluding Remarks

The question posed in this chapter—"What are people for?"—may seem strange, because it conjures the image of someone rummaging through a box of old things, and upon finding something unfamiliar asking themselves, "What's this for?" People are not known for what they are for but for who they are. Through reviewing the issues of the ordination of women, *The New Curriculum*, and marriage and sexual orientation, however, we have learned that the tasks of how the people in the UCC have practised and articulated their Christian life are deeply related to the church's theological conviction that God created each human being with intrinsic value. Life is sacred, as Christians live toward a sanctified life. Thus, what people are for and who they are can find one answer: the celebration of being created in the image of God.

This study of the theological anthropology of the UCC has helped us realize that God created humans for a purpose. That purpose is to celebrate life as a gift by serving God and serving others in love, especially those who are oppressed and marginalized. It has taken courage to celebrate in times of suffering and brokenness, but the church has often persevered—but not always. Therefore humility is necessary as the UCC continues to celebrate its life in discipleship and ministry through a careful consideration of the complexities of the past as a way to discern future directions. These directions point at seeking interdependent relationships among people, with creation and with God, for "the one eternal God seeks relationship."[103]

NOTES

1 *A New Creed, The Manual,* 2016, 37th rev. ed. (Toronto: UCPH, 2013), 20.

2 Peter Gordon White, "An Introduction," in *Voices and Visions: 65 Years of the United Church of Canada,* ed. John Webster Grant, Steven Chambers, Diane Forrest, Bonnie Greene, SangChul Lee, and Peter Gordon White (Toronto: UCPH, 1990), vii.

3 Richard Davidson, *A Faith to Live By* (Toronto: UCPH, 1943), 29; emphasis added.

4 William S. Kervin, "Worship on the Way: The Dialectic of United Church Worship," in *The United Church of Canada: A History,* ed. Don Schweitzer (Waterloo, ON: Wilfrid Laurier University Press, 2012), 188.

5 *Celebrate God's Presence: A Book of Services for The United Church of Canada* (Toronto: UCPH, 2000), xiii.

6 *A Song of Faith, The Manual,* 20, 25.

7 Walter Brueggemann, *Israel's Praise: Doxology against Idolatry and Ideology* (Minneapolis, MN: Fortress Press, 1988), 11.

8 German practical theologian Christian Grethlein suggests the goal of practical theology as "communication of the gospel." See Grethlein, *An Introduction to Practical Theology: History, Theory, and the Communication of the Gospel in the Present,* trans. Uwe Rasch (Waco, TX: Baylor University Press, 2016).

9 Maria Harris, *Fashion Me a People: Curriculum in the Church* (Louisville, KY: Westminster/John Knox, 1989), 16, 75.

10 *A Statement of Faith, The Manual,* 18.

11 A.C. Forrest, "What's Happened in the Church in the Last Ten Years," *United Church Observer*, May 15, 1968, 16.

12 Phyllis D. Airhart, *A Church with the Soul of a Nation: Making and Remaking the United Church of Canada* (Montreal and Kingston: McGill-Queen's University Press, 2014), 274. Airhart interprets *A New Creed* as capturing "a longing for fellowship."

13 Charlotte Caron, *Eager for Worship: Theologies, Practices, and Perspectives on Worship in The United Church of Canada* (Toronto: UCC, 2000), 166.

14 *Twenty Articles of Doctrine, The Manual*, 12; *Statement*; *Song*.

15 Phyllis D. Airhart, *Serving the Present Age: Revivalism, Progressivism, and the Methodist Tradition in Canada* (Montreal and Kingston: McGill-Queen's University Press, 1992), 23.

16 Nathanael Burwash, ed., *Wesley's Doctrinal Standards: The Sermons, with Introduction, Analysis and Notes* (Toronto: William Briggs, 1881), 172–73, cited in Airhart, *Serving the Present Age*, 137.

17 *The Manual*, 13.

18 J.S. Thompson, *God and His Purpose: The Meaning of Life* (Toronto: UCPH, 1964), 215.

19 Serene Jones, *Feminist Theory and Christian Theology: Cartographies of Grace* (Minneapolis, MN: Augsburg, 2000), 165.

20 *The Manual*, 23.

21 Mary Hallett, "Lydia Gruchy—The First Woman Ordained in The United Church of Canada," *Touchstone* 4, no. 1 (January 1986): 20.

22 C.T. McIntire, "Unity among Many: The Formation of The United Church of Canada, 1899–1930," in Schweitzer, ed., *The United Church of Canada: A History*, 29.

23 Airhart, *A Church with the Soul of a Nation*, 182.

24 Ibid., 161–62.

25 Charlotte Caron, "A Look at Ministry: Diversity and Ambiguity," in Schweitzer, ed., *United Church of Canada: A History*, 206. Even a few decades after Lydia's ordination, until 1964, it was a long and difficult road for married women to be ordained or to become deaconesses.

26 UCC, *Proceedings*, GC2, 1928, 120.

27 UCC, *Proceedings*, GC3, 1928, 362–400.

28 HyeRan Kim-Cragg and Don Schweitzer, *An Intercultural Adventure Part II: The Authority and Interpretation of Scripture in The United Church of Canada* (Daejeon, Korea: Daejanggan, 2016), 90.

29 Harold Wells, "The Making of the United Church Mind—No. II," *Touchstone* 8, no. 1 (January 1990): 26–27.

30 *The Manual*, 12. As Article 2.3.4 puts it: being "made in His own image ... and free and able to choose between good and evil and responsible to his Maker and Lord."

31 http://www.ucobserver.org/pogue_blog/2013/05/famous_five/.

32 A.C. Forrest, "The Crisis and the New Curriculum, *United Church Observer*, February 15, 1965, 21.

33 White, "Magnifying Voices, Sharing Visions," in *Voices and Visions*, 107–9. The original proposal that contains the inquiry "Who is God?, Who is my neighbour? and Who am I?" was not approved.

34 Forrest, "The Crisis and the New Curriculum," 16.

35 Peter Gordon White, "Introduction," in J.S. Thomson, *God and His Purpose*, x–xi.

36 Airhart, *Serving the Present Age*, 134.

37 Yvonne Stewart, "From One Thing to Another," in *Fire and Grace: Stories of History and Vision*, ed. Jim Taylor (Toronto: UCPH, 1999), 224.

38 The Presbyterian Church (US) launched a new curriculum called "Christian Faith and Life" in 1948. Its approach is similar to what the UCC undertook. A.C. Forrest, "The Crisis and the New Curriculum," 19–21.

39 Airhart, *The Church with the Soul of a Nation*, 167. For example, *The United Church Observer*'s subscriptions increased. The Women Missionary Society set a new record for fundraising in 1950, and the highest number of young people became candidates for ordination in 1954.

40 Forrest, "The Crisis and the New Curriculum," 19.

41 SangChul Lee, "United in Faith," in *Voices and Visions: 65 Years of the United Church of Canada*, ed. John Webster Grant et al. (Toronto: UCPH, 1990), 157.

42 Forrest, "The Crisis and the New Curriculum," 19.

43 Anne Squire, "Who Will Teach the Children?," in *Fire and Grace: Stories of History and Vision*, ed. Jim Taylor (Toronto: UCPH, 1999), 220.

44 White, "Magnifying Voices, Sharing Visions," 109.

45 To some of the more conservative members, theologically speaking, *The New Curriculum* was heretical. Forrest, "The Crisis and the New Curriculum," 18. A survey by *The United Church Observer* (September 1970) noted ongoing animosity six years after it was published.

46 White, "Magnifying Voices, Sharing Visions," 109.

47 There is a study of the direct link between *The New Curriculum* and the decline in attendance. See Kevin Neil Flatt, "The Survival and Decline of the Evangelical Identity of the United Church, 1930–1971," PhD diss., McMaster University, 2008, chapter 3.

48 Dietrich Bonhoeffer, *The Cost of Discipleship* (London: SCM Press, 1959).

49 "Recommendation on the New Curriculum," UCC, *Proceedings*, GC20, 1962, 419.

50 Anne M. Squire, *Envisioning Ministry* (Toronto: Division of Ministry Personnel and Education, UCC, 1985).

51 *Future Directions for Christian Education* (Toronto: Division of Ministry Personnel and Education, UCC, 1985).

52 UCC, *Proceedings*, GC31, 1986, 438–521. *Learning on the Way* (Toronto: Division of Ministry Personnel and Education, UCC, 1986).

53 UCC, *Proceedings*, GC29, 1982, 187–206. The same year the WCC published *Baptism, Eucharist, and Ministry*: Faith and Order Paper No. 111 (Geneva: WCC, 1982).

54 UCC, *Proceedings*, GC33, 1990, 514.

55 *The Manual*, 26.

56 Airhart, *A Church with the Soul of a Nation*, 272.

57 *The Planner for Lifelong Learning: Part of the Future Directions Project* (Toronto: Division of Mission in Canada, UCC, 1991), 3.

58 *The Manual*, 26.

59 UCC, *Proceedings*, GC32, 1988, 186.

60 "Toward a Christian Understanding of Sex, Love, Marriage" was approved by the 19th General Council in 1960. *In God's Image … Male and Female* was released as a study document in 1980. *Gift, Dilemma and Promise: A Report and Affirmations on Human Sexuality* was approved by General Council in 1984.

61 For example, the UCC asked many congregations to study sexuality in 1982. St. Thomas–Wesley UC was one of the first congregations to study this issue, which led to it to it being the first to become an affirming ministry in Saskatoon in 1997. Jill Doepker, "St. Thomas–Wesley United Church: Importance of Church in the City," *Folklore* (Spring 2016): 14.

62 "Commission on Christian Marriage and the Christian Home," UCC, *Proceedings*, GC13, 1946, 105–62.

63 Ibid., 109.

64 Thomson, *God and His Purpose*, 63–64.

65 *The Manual*, 12.

66 Airhart, *A Church with the Soul of a Nation*, 262.

67 Tracy J. Trothen, *Linking Sexuality and Gender—Naming Violence against Women in The United Church of Canada* (Waterloo, ON: Wilfrid Laurier University Press, 2003), 62.

68 UCC, *Proceedings*, GC28, 1980, 155.

69 UCC, *Proceedings*, GC30, 1984, 186.

70 UCC, *Proceedings*, GC30, 1984, 90. Tracy J. Trothen, "1980s: What Does It Mean to Be The United Church of Canada? Emergent Voices, Self-Critique, and Dissent," in Schweitzer, ed., *The United Church of Canada: A History*, 141.

71 Kwok Pui-lan, *Postcolonial Imagination and Feminist Theology* (Louisville, KY: Westminster/John Knox, 2005), 143.

72 *United Church Observer*, October 1980, 6.

73 Ross Bartlett, "1990–2003: The Church into the New Millennium," in Schweitzer, ed., *Th United Church of Canada: A History*, 165–66.

74 *The Manual*, 15.

75 *The Manual*, 24.

76 *The Authority and Interpretation of Scripture* (Toronto: UCPH, 1992), 11–12.

77 UCC, *Proceedings*, GC30, 1984, 195. *Moving toward Full Inclusion: Sexual Orientation in The United Church of Canada* (Toronto: UCC, 2010). This is an example of not avoiding emerging contexts but responding to a need arising from ecumenical partners.

78 UCC, *Proceedings*, GC30, 1984, 201. The knowledge that was influential for this decision included the American Psychiatric Association, which no longer considered homosexuality to be a disease.

79 UCC, *Proceedings*, GC30, 1984, 206.

80 UCC, *Proceedings*, GC39, 2006, 579.

81 *The Manual*, 15.

82 *The Manual*, 21.

83 *The Manual*, 22.

84 Don Schweitzer, "The Changing Social Imaginary of The United Church of Canada," in Schweitzer, ed., *The United Church of Canada: A History*, 286.

85 S.D. Chown, "Church Union," *Christian Guardian*, June 28, 1922, 13.

86 Airhart, *The Church with the Soul of a Nation*, 7.

87 J.S. Woodsworth, *Strangers within Our Gates* (Toronto: Missionary Society of the Methodist Church, 1909), 7.

88 Ian McKay Manson, "The United Church and the Second World War," in Schweitzer, ed., *The United Church of Canada: A History*, 67–69.

89 *The Manual*, 22.

90 *Church Membership: Doctrine and Practice in the United Church of Canada*, 8–9. This document was the result of the consultation that began in 1960. The final report was presented to General Council as "The Doctrine and Practice of Church Membership," UCC, *Proceedings*, GC20, 1962, 458–510.

91 Greer Anne Wenh-In Ng, "The United Church of Canada: A Church Fittingly National," in *Christianity and Ethnicity in Canada*, ed. Paul Bramadat and David Seljak (Toronto: University of Toronto Press, 2008), 208.

92 Joan Wyatt, "The 1970s: Voices from the Margins," in Schweitzer, ed., *The United Church of Canada: A History*, 120.

93 Ng, "The United Church of Canada," 208.

94 Stan McKay, "Canadian Churches Have Their Own Racism," *United Church Observer*, September 1980, 17.

95 UCC, *Proceedings*, GC36, 1997, 892–94.

96 UCC, *Proceedings*, GC31, 1986, 85.

97 Ng, "The United Church of Canada," 204.

98 UCC, *Proceedings*, GC39, 2006, 588.

99 Adele Halliday, "Introduction: A Transformative Vision," in *Intercultural Visions: Called to Be the Church*, ed. Rob Fennell (Toronto: UCPH, 2012), xi.

100 *The Manual*, 21.

101 HyeRan Kim-Cragg, *Interdependence: A Postcolonial Feminist Practical Theology* (Eugene: Pickwick, 2018), 28. HyeRan Kim-Cragg and Joanne Doi, "Intercultural Threads of Hybridity and Threshold Spaces of Learning," *Religious Education* 107, no. 3 (2012): 268.

102 John W. Grant, *Moon of Wintertime: Missionaries and the Indians of Canada in Encounter since 1534* (Toronto: University of Toronto Press, 1984), 189.

103 *The Manual*, 20.

CHAPTER NINE

SACRAMENTS AND SACRAMENTALITY IN THE UNITED CHURCH OF CANADA

William S. Kervin

Each of the four subordinate standards that serve as the touchstones of this volume are more substantially connected to the history and theology of United Church of Canada worship and sacraments than is often appreciated. The ecumenical concord of *Twenty Articles of Doctrine* is evident in the liturgical consensus of *Forms of Service* (1926), the first service book of the UCC. The origins of *A Statement of Faith* can be traced in part to questions about the theological integrity of infant baptism and its liturgical expression in *The Book of Common Order* (1932). Similarly, the genesis of *A New Creed* in the 1960s was a call for more contemporary creedal language in the baptismal services that were being prepared for the *Service Book* (1969). Subsequent revisions to *A New Creed* reflected feminist and Indigenous perspectives, which in turn helped transpose the impact of the ecumenical liturgical movement and emerging contemporary theologies into a United Church key, as further explored in the liturgical pluralism of *Celebrate God's Presence* (2000) and the theopoetics of *A Song of Faith* (2006).

This chapter will explore these and other dimensions of sacramental theology in the UCC. Portions of each subordinate standard will be considered in relation to relevant material from the denomination's primary liturgical resources. The resulting doctrinal and liturgical case studies will serve as lenses through which to view features of its theology of sacraments. The subsequent picture suggests an evolution from a dominically instituted origin of sacraments to a more broadly understood sacramentality, an expanding and expansive theology of "the sacred in the midst of life."[1]

Twenty Articles of Doctrine and the Sacraments

It is widely acknowledged that the *Twenty Articles of Doctrine* drew liberally upon other sources of the period.[2] Of these Articles, only two appear
to be entirely original to the work of the Joint Committee.[3] On the subject
of sacraments, the sources and content of Article 2.3.16 illustrate what John
Webster Grant called "blending traditions,"[4] a sign of the theological consensus and sacramental convergence of the founding traditions:

> We acknowledge two sacraments, Baptism and the Lord's Supper, which were
> instituted by Christ, to be of perpetual obligation as signs and seals of the cov-
> enant ratified in His precious blood, as a means of grace, by which, working in
> us, He doth not only quicken but strengthen and comfort our faith in Him, and
> as ordinances through the observance of which His Church is to confess her
> Lord and be visibly distinguished from the rest of the world.[5]

This language evokes theological themes that would have been well known
among the founding traditions. The use of the term "Lord's Supper" for
Holy Communion or Eucharist reflects classic Reformed Protestant terminology. Far removed from the context of Martin Luther's sixteenth-century
railings against the Roman Church, modern mainline Protestants tended
simply to emphasize the imperative of dominical institution (instituted by
the Lord, *dominus*), a reflection of the Reformed principle of *sola scriptura*
(by the authority of Scripture alone). Put simply, the church baptizes and
breaks bread, first and foremost, because Christ said to do so. Article 2.3.16's
definition of sacraments as visible "signs and seals of the covenant" evokes
a well-worn Presbyterian phrase, traceable to the *Westminster Confession
of Faith*.[6] Similarly, "means of grace," while also familiar to Presbyterians,
would have particular resonance with Methodists via the teachings of John
Wesley.[7] That God acts through sacraments to "not only quicken but also
strengthen and comfort our faith in Him" is language drawn directly from
the Anglican and Methodist *Articles of Religion*.[8]

There is also a confessional dimension to sacramental "obligation," a
sign of evidence by which Christians are to "be visibly distinguished from
the rest of the world." While to contemporary ears this can sound like an
exclusionary or spiritually elitist claim, it can also be understood as affirming the kind of public witness so important to a prophetic social gospel.
This doctrinal articulation comes directly from the *Westminster Confession*, but Anglicans—and, later, Methodists and Congregationalists—took

it further. Wesley agreed with Anglicanism on this point in their article of faith, "Of Baptism": "Baptism is not only a sign of profession and mark of difference whereby Christians are distinguished from others that are not baptized; but it is also a sign of regeneration or the new birth."[9] However, this notion of baptismal regeneration was not without controversy. Does baptism automatically result in a regenerated new life? By the time of union, Presbyterians, Methodists, and Congregationalists each affirmed the general value of regeneration in their theology while uncoupling it from baptism per se, connecting it instead to the ongoing work of the Holy Spirit in the life of faith.[10] Thus, the UCC's Article 2.3.9, "Of Regeneration," takes a broad approach: "We believe in the necessity of regeneration, whereby we are made new creatures in Christ Jesus by the Spirit of God, who imparts spiritual life by the gracious and mysterious operation of His power, using as the ordinary means the truths of His word and the ordinances of divine appointment in ways agreeable to the nature of man."[11] Understood this way, the "necessity" of regeneration and transformation "in Christ Jesus by the Spirit of God" comes about through a variety of "ordinary means" and "ordinances of divine appointment"—which could include baptism but is not limited to it. When, to this day, the integrity of baptism for infants or adults is questioned, whether due to lack of individual conversion or little evidence of commitment to social transformation, one wades into the depths of the relations between baptism and the Holy Spirit, regeneration, and sanctification.

Subsections 2.3.16.1 and 2.3.16.2 of the *Twenty Articles of Doctrine*, on baptism and the Lord's Supper respectively, offer further exposition and a summary of the nineteenth-century Reformed Protestant theological consensus and pastoral principles. With respect to baptism, two emphases stand out: method and meaning. The method entails the classically defined matter (water) and form (Trinitarian formula): "with water into the name of the Father and of the Son and of the Holy Spirit." The meaning is covenantal—"union with Christ and participation in the blessings of the new covenant"—and inclusive of both "believers" and "infants" of believing parents or guardians (though no age of discretion is defined). The context of familial and congregational nurture is assumed, but neither profession of faith nor the rite of confirmation is mentioned.

In 2.3.16.2, the Lord's Supper is also called "the sacrament of communion," but the communion emphasized is not so much a matter of the taking of consecrated elements as it is a question of "communion with Christ and His people," expressing a "communion" theology more than a "consecratory" theology, and reminiscent of the Methodist "Supper of the Lord" as "a sign of the love that Christians ought to have among themselves."[12] The elements are "bread and wine" (though grape juice was quickly becoming the norm), "given and received in thankful remembrance of Him and His sacrifice on the Cross." The presence of Christ in the sacrament is defined simply as "spiritual": participants receive "in faith" in order to "partake of the body and blood of Christ" "after a spiritual manner" (as in Methodist articles) for the purpose of "comfort, nourishment, and growth in grace." Finally, signalling the origins of the UCC's tradition of an "open table" and in keeping with classic Reformed understanding, the closing sentence specifies that "all may be admitted to the Lord's Supper who make a credible profession of their faith in the Lord Jesus and of obedience to His law."

In summary, these articles emphasize a Reformed theological focus on dominical institution and covenant theology as a means of strengthening God's grace, all set within an overall appreciation for the confessional witness of regeneration and sanctification. The manner in which the theological themes are sounded advances an amicable consensus. The opening paragraph of Article 2.3.16 seems to suggest that the founding traditions are all talking about the same thing—whether Presbyterian "sacraments," Methodist "means of grace," or Congregationalist "ordinances." In another context and time, the use of these terms would have pointed to significantly different, if not inherently contradictory, sacramental theologies—from the more sacerdotal, to the experientially pneumatological, to a simple memorial, respectively. But in the new denomination, they were blended, united.

The liturgical expression of this doctrinal approach is evident in the UCC's first service book, *Forms of Service*. Quickly assembled by the Committee on Church Worship and Ritual in time for the second General Council of 1926, it was a compendium of orders of service or liturgical "forms" drawn from the service books of the founding traditions and "authorized" by the General Council "for voluntary use in the three uniting Churches."[13] Of the twenty-one orders provided, *Forms* included five for sacraments: two for the baptism of infants, one for the baptism of adults, and two for the Lord's Supper. The two services for infant baptism in *Forms* would be a study in conflicting contrasts were it not for the force of the consensus about theological essentials noted above. The more lengthy liturgical style of the "First Order," drawn from the Presbyterian *Book of Common Order* (1922), stands in stark contrast to the simple brevity of the "Second Order" from the *Book of Congregational Worship* (1920). In these services, the emphasis is on God's love and acceptance of children. They speak generally of "welcome," "blessing," "dedication," and "reception." However, in the case of adult baptism, *Forms* includes the traditional Presbyterian language and theology, and even a measure of baptismal regeneration: "The Sacrament is a sign and seal of the cleansing of our hearts by the grace of Jesus Christ; of the renewal of our nature by the Holy Spirit; of adoption into the household of faith, and admission, by Christ's appointment, into His Church." But this exception seems only to prove the general rule that dominical institution with water and the Trinitarian formula, set within a covenant theology of reception of the individual into the Church, is sufficient.

A similar modus operandi is used in the two services of the Lord's Supper, combining traditional Presbyterian liturgical structures with more liberal Congregationalist theological content. Both services take the principle of dominical institution to extremes, reciting the Institution Narrative twice—once before the communion prayer as a scriptural warrant, then again at the fraction. Other liturgical features combine to defy easy categorization. For instance, ample use of Scripture sentences is combined with the Anglican/Methodist Collect for Purity ("cleanse the thoughts of our hearts") and classic liturgical forms (e.g., Sursum Corda / "Lift up your hearts," Sanctus / "Holy, Holy, Holy"). Heartfelt scripturally based invitations mingle with classic Reformed calls to confession and repentance. The first (Presbyterian) order defines the sacrament as a "perpetual remembrance of the sacrifice of [Christ] in His death." Notably, the second (Congregationalist) order concludes with a compelling recollection of Jesus washing the disciples' feet and closes with Jesus's exhortation, "ye should do as I have done to you." One might wonder how the UCC's theology of the Lord's Supper might have evolved had this practice been carried forward in its liturgical tradition. In this paradigm, the grace of baptism is remembered in the Lord's Supper as manifested in lives of service to others.

How are we to understand the convergence and coexistence of such varied theological articulations and diverse liturgical traditions of sacramental doctrine and practice in the newly formed UCC? That which in other circumstances might have seemed contradictory is here affirmed as complementary. As others have noted, the ethos of this union spirit was more concerned with "practical matters" than with "theological issues."[14] The ease with which the tasks of compiling the *Twenty Articles of Doctrine* and *Forms* were completed and embraced bears this out. As summarized in the Introduction to this volume, the confluence of liberal theology's "inherent optimism," with its increased passion for social engagement, and historical criticism's critique of the perceived biblical foundations on which many of the traditional denominational divisions had been erected, combined to give rise to a form of liberal evangelicalism that animated the founding traditions of the ucc towards union. Moreover, church-building went hand in hand with nation building, to the point where the Canadian approach was as much a "national gospel" as a "social gospel."[15] In referring to the ucc as an "evangelical church," the First General Council appealed to the principle of an Evangelical/Protestant church that identified with the "evangelical doctrines of the Reformation."[16] The denomination understood itself as part of "one Holy Catholic Church" (Article 2.3.15) living into its "reformed" and "reforming" character (*ecclesia semper reformanda est*—"the church is always to be reformed"). "That all may be one" (*ut omnes unum sint*—as it appears on the ucc crest) spoke of a "united and uniting" church for the sake of the Kingdom of God on earth.[17]

This context is the setting in which the doctrinal, liturgical, and sacramental eclecticism of both the *Twenty Articles of Doctrine* and *Forms* is best understood. If the theological ethos of the day was *evangelical*, the corresponding liturgical ethos was *experimental*—a term that carried connotations and meanings very different from today. As George Pidgeon put it in the Foreword to Thomas Kilpatrick's commentary on the articles, *Our Common Faith*:

> In so far as it is theology, it [the *Twenty Articles* document] is experimental, rising out of the experience of God in Christ. Experts in technical theology will notice at once that a great deal which enters into the older credal [*sic*] statements is missing here.... The whole aim of the book is to make a synthesis of experimental truth. These doctrines are accepted by all evangelical Christians. There is nothing here to alienate believers from one another or to perpetuate divisions.[18]

By "experimental" is meant what we might today call "experiential." Today's popular association of experimental with the contemporary or exploratory is also suggestive. For Kilpatrick, sacraments embody the experience of "the saving work of Christ, and ... the Covenant ... [the] relation between God and His people." As "signs," or "pictorial presentations or typical illustrations of the simplest kind," they point to the "reality" of what Christ has done for us. Like "seals," they are "appended to ... the Word of promise, attesting" to "the Gospel of His grace." As "means," this is how grace is "communicated," "apprehended," and "appropriated." Furthermore, Kilpatrick argues, while "the doctrine of transubstantiation is sometimes described as 'high,'" this

"Protestant claim is 'truly 'high,'" for in it the fullness of Christ's grace is experienced more closely "than … can be conceived."[19] The reality of spiritual experience is the epistemological linchpin around which his expository apologetics revolves.

Just as the theological congruence among nineteenth-century mainstream Protestants was evangelical, its sacramental theology was experimental—in both senses of that word: experiential and exploratory. Thus, the *Twenty Articles* and *Forms* fuse diverse theological subtleties and different liturgical practices aimed at "our common faith" as a *basis* of (or for) union. It is an intentional blending of traditions, committed to the value of such "diversity" and confident in "the sharing that the union would bring."[20] In liturgical terms, this approach came to be known as "ordered liberty" in worship, a liturgical ethos rooted historically in John Knox's liturgically liberal strategy of "forms" of prayer with "directories" to provide direction for "common order"—as distinct from "common prayer."[21] To summarize these correlations succinctly: the *Twenty Articles of Doctrine* are to United Church theology what *Forms* is to United Church worship.

A Statement of Faith and Infant Baptism

A 2016 issue of the *United Church Observer* featured the following in its popular column, Question Box: "Our worship committee recently met and is very divided around the issue of baptism. We baptize babies and small children, and then we never see the families again. What can we do about this?"[22] In response, columnist Christopher White noted the persistence of this concern, the ongoing problem of what is sometimes irreverently referred to as "the splash and split." Over eighty years earlier, in Our Readers' Forum in *The New Outlook*, the precursor to *The United Church Observer*, the issue took a slightly different form: "[A] baby is taken to church, forcibly baptized, its name placed on the cradle roll of the Sunday School, then it is advanced from class to class, until it is finally told to join the church. Obediently it takes the step, without, in too many cases, knowing anything about being 'born again.'"[23] This would seem to be the inverse problem, not so much "the splash and split" as perhaps "wash and whatever." But both scenarios point to the integrity of the practice of infant baptism, whether challenged by absence or apathy. The history and theology of baptism in the UCC has been dogged by this challenge. A brief survey of the UCC's liturgical theology of Christian initiation provides a window on some persistent themes.[24]

Within five years of union and the publication of *Forms*, the General Council was already receiving requests to clarify the meaning of church membership, particularly in relation to infant baptism. When placed in the context of a world shaken by the horrors of the First World War, the devastation of the Great Depression, and the rise of fascism, it is perhaps not surprising that people were in need of greater social and salvific clarity. *A Statement of Faith* was received and approved at General Council in 1940. Its section on baptism signals significant developments:

> We believe that in Baptism men are made members of the Christian society. Washing with water in the name of the Father, the Son, and the Holy Spirit signifies God's cleansing from sin and an initial participation in the gifts and graces of new life. The children of believing parents are baptized and nurtured in the family of God so that they may in due time take upon themselves the yoke of Christ.... So we acknowledge Baptism as God's appointed means of grace at initiation into the Christian fellowship.[25]

Note the lack of explicit reference to dominical institution. While it may have been assumed, the absence of specific comment corresponds with the services of *The Book of Common Order*. There, the scriptural warrant for infant baptism is solely Mark's account of Jesus's blessing of the children (Mark 10:13–16).[26] As the Commission on the Christian Faith later put it, "The formula of the threefold name has caused some scholars to doubt that this is a true word of Jesus and to infer that it comes from a later period in the life of the Church and mirrors the practice of that time." Nevertheless, they concede, "the tradition of the early Church was to baptize and its tradition also was that Jesus gave instructions to do this. We have no alternative but to accept the tradition."[27] Thus, the criterion of dominical institution has been broadened beyond scriptural warrant to include the consensus of tradition in an effort to demonstrate a biblical foundation for infant baptism.

Statement also understands baptism more as a communal process than as an individual event. Baptism is how persons are "made members of Christian society." While God's action is certainly not absent, this is only an "initial" step. As such, it is inclusive of children, but also based on the assumption that they will be "nurtured in [and by] the family of God" into order to "take upon themselves" the burden, responsibilities, and privileges ("yoke") of Christian life and work in the world. In this spirit, BCO introduced a charge to the congregation, which in subsequent generations of baptismal liturgies evolved into explicit communal vows, thereby enacting the conviction that baptism is a public and corporate act of the Church.[28] While it is still a salvific "means of grace," baptism is here understood as "*initial* participation in the gifts and graces of new life" and for the purpose of "initiation into Christian fellowship." Thus, theological themes that *Forms* and the *Twenty Articles of Doctrine* were content to blend, BCO and *Statement* now seek to delineate.

An impressive array of supporting denominational bestsellers took great pains to defend infant baptism by asserting this communal perspective through an appeal to covenant theology. In *Highways of the Heart*, H.B. Hendershot argued that in the early church it was "unthinkable that children should be denied the privileges of those who were 'heirs according to the promise'" (Gal 3:29).[29] John Dow, in *This Is Our Faith*, reasoned: "The idea that a parent should enter a religion or covenant-relation with God as an individual merely, *i.e.* by himself as distinct from his immediate family, would never occur to the ancients, least of all to a Jew."[30] Or as the widely used *Catechism* taught: "The children of believing parents are baptized in infancy because they are born within the fellowship of the Church and Christ claims them for His own."[31] Yet questions persisted. In 1952, *The Doctrine and Practice of Infant Baptism* concluded that "children who are part of that fellowship which is believed to be within the covenant of grace cannot be excluded from the Sacrament which denotes entrance into that covenant."[32]

While a covenant ecclesiology may have been able to make theological sense of infant baptism, questions of polity remained. In 1956, the General Council instructed the Committee on Christian Faith "to make a careful study of Church Membership in all its aspects."[33] The first two recommendations, approved in 1962, were "that the traditional order of Baptism, Confirmation, First Communion, be the accepted order of initiation into The United Church of Canada" and "that 'confirmation' continue to be the term applied … to the service used for the reception by Profession of Faith of baptized persons into full communion with the church."[34] This represents a significant development in baptismal theology in the UCC. *Forms* was consistent in its Reformed emphasis on profession of faith.[35] A "Confirmation," consisting of laying on of hands with prayer for the Holy Spirit, would not have been countenanced by Reformed traditions that traced their lineage to John Calvin and his critique of the "sacrament" of Confirmation and his defence of a profession of faith as sufficient for admission to the Lord's Supper. Nevertheless, in BCO, the term "Confirmation" was subtly introduced.

"Confirm" was used in reference to God's strengthening and in an optional laying on of hands by the minister.[36] As the *Catechism* put it: "When those baptized in infancy profess their faith in Christ, God confirms and equips them as soldiers of the Cross, and the Church receives them into full communion with all its rights and duties."[37]

After *Church Membership* was published, the UCC's understanding of profession of faith takes on a more explicitly pneumatological—even sacramental—connotation, becoming a specific rite with action and prayer for strengthening by the Holy Spirit as a means of admission to the Lord's Supper. In the 1969 *Service Book*, the word "confirmation" appears throughout—in the questions to parents, the exhortations, prayers, and laying on of hands. *Church Membership* and the draft orders of the *Service Book* went so far as to refer to confirmation as "the ordination of the laity."[38] The danger in a confirmation-based paradigm of Christian initiation is that one can lose sight of the primacy of baptism. The church's collective formation by and witness to God's grace can devolve into an individualistic, pedagogical focus on salvation by education.[39]

It would be left to another reformation to shift the paradigm again, this time ecumenical in scope. The evolving theology and practice of baptism and the rise of confirmation took yet another turn with the ecumenical liturgical renewal movement precipitated by the Second Vatican Council and the explosion of scholarship on Christian initiation. Together with the World Council of Churches' *Baptism, Eucharist and Ministry*, the theological scope of baptismal theology was broadened biblically and enriched liturgically. BEM summarized this biblical palette with five clusters of scriptural themes: dying and rising with Christ; forgiveness, conversion, cleansing, and grace; the gifts and fruits of the Holy Spirit; incorporation into the Body of Christ, the Church; and the sign of the Kingdom or Reign of God.[40] Ruth Duck argues that "recovering all these meanings of baptism is essential to revitalizing worship and renewing the church."[41] This recovery of a breadth of meaning can also be seen as a means of moving beyond a reductionist conception of dominical institution in baptism to a more holistic biblical ecclesiology rooted in the life and witness of the body of Christ in the world.

The UCC's efforts to this end entailed yet another study of baptism. Again, questions about the theology and practice of baptism and the adequacy and integrity of confirmation resources came to the General Council. Beginning in 1977 with the Task Group on Confirmation and concluding in the late 1980s with The Project Group on Christian Initiation, the baptismal landscape of the UCC was both enriched and rendered more complex.[42] As one person put it several years into the process, "This all grew out of a request for new filmstrips!"[43] Along the way, the publication of a new generation of optional liturgies, including *Baptism and Renewal of Baptismal Faith*,[44] was complicated and overshadowed by other issues facing the denomination, including human sexuality, liberation and feminist theologies, and inclusive language. The "Covenant of Baptism" services of *Celebrate God's Presence* also reflect the UCC's theological and liturgical advances as well as its juridical and pastoral ambiguities.[45]

At the risk of doing a great disservice to the decades of complex work that began with *Statement* and extended well into the 1980s, perhaps the best summation of the present state of baptismal theology is that of the "Theological Affirmations" from the Report of the Project Group on Christian Initiation, as approved by the 1980 General Council:

1. We affirm that the Sacrament of Baptism with water in the Triune Name of God is the visible sign and seal of the covenant love of God, of incorporation into Christ and of entry into membership in the Christian Church.

2. We affirm that Baptism is the single rite of initiation bringing one to full membership in the Church. While it requires no further ritual to make it complete, we recognize it as the initial step in an ongoing process of Christian maturity. It grants admission to the Sacrament of the Lord's Supper and introduces the recipient into a life of witness, priesthood and ministry.

3. We affirm that there is one baptism as the rite of initiation into the Christian Church whatever the age at which it is administered. The baptizing of people at varying stages of maturation variously reflects both divine gift and human appropriation, of corporate and individual response, of child-like trust and mature responsibility.

4. We affirm the theological validity within the church of rites which acknowledge that the response to God's grace set forth in Baptism will be, to the end of the Christian's pilgrimage, an ongoing, developing response, varying with the time and place in which Christian disciples find themselves in their life's journey.

5. We affirm that, while the sacrament of Baptism is a visible sign that sets forth the reality of God's love, all persons are within the scope of God's saving love and power, whether baptized or not.[46]

While such affirmations may raise as many issues as they resolve, they have come to represent the overall theology and ethos of present-day UCC baptismal theology and practice. As *A Song of Faith* poetically states it: "Before conscious thought or action on our part, we are surrounded by God's redeeming love."[47] Baptism remains a sign of this prevenient grace, lived out in the covenant community of the church.

A New Creed, Inclusive Language, and the Trinitarian Formula

Before "inclusive" language was on the UCC's radar, "contemporary" language was the issue. When Pierre Berton in *The Comfortable Pew* described how he ended up having his children baptized in the UCC, he credits the "simple, clear and to the point" language in the service of infant baptism as a primary reason.[48] Work on the revision of BCO began in 1958 by the Committee on Church Worship and Ritual. The issue of contemporary language dogged their work. Advocates of "contemporary worship" argued that new translations of the Bible and the historical-critical methods of the New Curriculum demanded a new vernacular in worship, a demythologizing of a transcendent God from "Thou" to "you," a "new worldliness and secularity" that spoke of God "not on the fringe of life, but at the centre." Immanence and incarnation in theology called for immediacy and intimacy in worship. "Contemporary" and "new" were key watchwords.[49]

A New Creed emerged from the same climate as an expression of the need for contemporary theology and language in the sacrament of baptism.[50] The first approved version of *A New Creed* appeared on the inside front cover of the *Service Book*, yet the orders for "Public Worship" in the *Service Book* contained no reference to any creeds. It is ironic that *A New Creed*, having originated as a result of revisions to the services of baptism in the *Service Book*, ended up virtually absent from its baptismal liturgies. Even more ironic is the fact that *A New Creed* seems to have become more popular in the UCC than the Apostles' Creed ever was.

By 1980, the attention had shifted from "contemporary" language to "inclusive" language. "Guidelines for Inclusive Language" identified strategies for consciousness raising and called for inclusive language in reference to persons and God. Changes were made to *A New Creed* to reflect the policy: "Man is not alone" was changed to "We are not alone"; "the true Man, Jesus" became "Jesus, the Word made flesh"; and the male pronouns for God were eliminated. While the focus in the 1980s was mostly on gender-inclusive language, broader concerns were also in view.

> What do we mean by "inclusive language"? We mean, of course, language that does not exclude any person on the basis of sex, colour, age, religion, physical

condition, or any other thing. It is not easy to be totally inclusive because our language, which is rich in symbols, uses many words in a symbolic sense, and we learn to understand more deeply by the use of symbols. However, when our word-symbols consistently and obviously favour certain groups of people at the expense of others, they become exclusive. This kind of exclusivity poses a problem for many people.[51]

As church policy sought to keep pace with feminist and liberationist theological perspectives, "at the grassroots level there was significant dissension" and resistance.[52] The question of language for God placed the issue in particularly bold relief. Miriam Tees spoke of her experience in *The Words We Sing*: "the first time a pastor visited our church and prayed, 'O God, our Father and Mother,' my heart leapt with joy and recognition. A whole new dimension opened for me.... [S]uddenly my God grew to double the size."[53] Hers was testimony to the experiential truth of "just language."[54] As Ruth Duck has summarized it:

> No serious theologian claims that God is literally male. Constantly using male language for God supports male dominance by implying that men are more like God than women are; such language also renders women invisible. Language that identifies a dominant group (males, masters, parents) with God and makes others (women, slaves, children) invisible or submissive shapes the way we think and subtly condones coercion, violence, and injustice. Jesus Christ demonstrated mutual respect and not domination between males and females. In contrast to cultural values, Christian worship should also reflect God's love and justice for all.[55]

Or, in Mary Daly's trenchant feminist proposition, "if God is male, then the male is God."[56]

However, as a member of PLURA, the UCC was also a signatory to a 1975 ecumenical agreement "acknowledging the historic and common value of the 'matter of baptism' (water) and its 'form' (the traditional Trinitarian Formula), and granting mutual recognition for baptism performed under these signs in each denomination."[57] Moreover, the use of the Trinitarian formula was again affirmed by the General Council in 1984 and used in the "optional" liturgy *Baptism and Renewal of Baptismal Faith* in 1986.[58] In the same year, the UCC's official response to BEM noted the tension:

> The use of the Trinitarian formula in baptism would seem to be fundamental to any ecumenical consensus. However in many churches, including our own,

the formula is questioned as intrinsically "sexist." This is a problem that is critical for many Western churches like ours but barely exists as an issue for many churches elsewhere. As we, the United Church of Canada, struggle with this issue, we become aware that it is more complex than a question of language, but involves our basic understanding of God.... [T]he Trinitarian formula, while central to ecumenical consensus, is experienced by many Christians as a source of alienation.[59]

With the publication of the UCC's new hymnal, *Voices United*, in 1996, inclusive language in congregational song received further support, benefiting also from a larger number of baptismal hymns that appealed to a broader range of baptismal theology and imagery. In the same year, *Services for Trial Use* used the traditional naming of the Trinity in baptism but also invited "prayerful consideration" of two alternative formulas:

N___, I baptize you in the name of the triune God: Creator, Redeemer, and Sustainer.

and

N___, I baptize you in the name of God, Source of love,
in the name of Jesus Christ, love incarnate,
and in the name of the Holy Spirit, love's power.[60]

However, by 2000 and the publication of *Celebrate God's Presence*, the Judicial Committee had ruled that "a Remit is required to alter the wording of the baptismal formula in The Basis of Union, section 2.16.1."[61] As a result, CGP employs the Trinitarian formula in the action of baptism, but "in keeping with established General Council policy on just and inclusive language, it also provides for the optional use of a variety of Trinitarian blessings following Baptism in the Name of the Triune God."[62]

What can be said of the theological complexities and institutional contradictions of the UCC's commitment to inclusive language and its use of the Trinitarian formula in baptism? Writing at the time of these developments, feminist liturgical theologian Marjorie Proctor-Smith identified "three possible ways to respond to the problem of androcentric liturgical language ... nonsexist, inclusive, and emancipatory." Proctor-Smith writes, "Nonsexist language seeks to avoid gender-specific terms. Inclusive language seeks to balance gender references. Emancipatory language seeks to transform language use and to challenge stereotypical gender references."[63] Though "distinct," they often function in combinations. "Non-sexist" language uses gender-neutral terms. The language changes to *A New Creed* in 1980 were essentially non-sexist—e.g., "Man is not alone" became "We are not alone." The strategic advantage of non-sexist language is that it achieves inclusion with a minimal amount of linguistic or conceptual disruption. But the disadvantage of non-sexist language is also related to its relative neutrality. For example, by simply replacing He or Him with "God," hearers can continue to harbour their default (male) image of God. As Procter-Smith puts it, "daily experience encourages the hearing of male reality as normative, even when it is not specifically stated."[64]

In the case of the Trinitarian formula, the results of non-sexist language can be similarly mixed. "Creator, Redeemer, and Sustainer," a popular favourite in the early reform of liturgical language, does an effective job of avoiding gender-specific terms and alluding to important theological characteristics of God. However, while it is strong on the "economic" Trinity—the action of God—it is weak on the "immanent" Trinity—the being and nature of God. As such, it suffers from modalism in that it speaks only of three modes of God's action but lacks relational categories that point to the interrelationships within the being and nature of God. Furthermore, to put it bluntly, there is nothing identifiably Christian about it; it could also be used in Jewish or Muslim contexts.[65] Conservative and feminist theologians alike agree it is an inadequate naming of God in the act of baptism, where it is incumbent upon the church to speak of the grace of God as revealed in and through Jesus Christ.[66] In contrast, "God, Source of love; Jesus Christ, love incarnate; and the Holy Spirit, love's power," while also largely non-sexist, is arguably more effective due to its explicit naming of Jesus Christ.[67]

In Procter-Smith's typology, "inclusive" language "recognizes [the] problem with non-gender-specific language and answers it by including female references explicitly, normally balanced with male references." "He" becomes not simply "one" but "he or she." "Mankind" becomes not "humanity" but "women and men" or "brothers and sisters." While this approach predates today's critiques of the binary social construction of gender, its strength is that it unmasks exclusion, restoring important dimensions of variety, diversity, clarity, and colour to language. Its weakness "lies in its assumption that male and female images are symmetrical." As Procter-Smith notes, for example, "Mother carries wholly different connotations from Father."[68] On the other hand, perhaps such language no more absolutizes mothering than the traditional formula does with fathering, thus providing a necessarily disruptive counterpoint. Alternatively, Lois Wilson's blessing is an example of how biblical language can enrich and bypass the metaphysical constraints of economic and immanent categories:

> May the blessing of the God of Sarah and Hagar,
> as of Abraham,
> the blessing of the Son, born of the woman Mary,
> and the blessing of the Spirit, who broods over us
> as a mother her children,
> be with you today and always.
> Amen.[69]

By naming God in relation to diverse characters in the narrative of faith, by pointing to the incarnation in the particularity of "the woman Mary" rather than absolutizing motherhood per se, and by evoking the maternal compassion of the Spirit in biblical terms, the result is both familiar and disruptive, moving beyond non-sexist and inclusive strategies towards more emancipatory results.

"Emancipatory" language seeks to move beyond both gender-free and gender-inclusive strategies towards the proclamation of gender-related liberation: "Emancipatory language assumes that God is engaged in women's struggles for emancipation, even to the point of identifying with those who struggle."[70] Again, while Procter-Smith's methodology is helpfully placed in the context of early feminist theology and its focus on women's experience, the point of emancipatory language is best understood theologically: it is about God's identification with particular struggles for emancipation. Emancipatory language seeks to do more than include: it strives to bear witness, liberate, and heal.

In the meantime, as the ecumenical boat of the Body of Christ sails slowly onward, the findings of the Roman Catholic/United Church dialogue may offer the most responsible and practical options for an ecumenically recognized Trinitarian articulation in baptism. Out of that five-year process of dialogue, UCC participants recommended, first, that the traditional words be maintained ("if we are to avoid further schism in the Church of Jesus Christ, who prayed that 'they all may be one'"), but they also "strongly commended" augmenting them "with inclusive language."[71] Reminiscent of the UCC's response to BEM, they also recommended that "the whole service of worship in which a baptism occurs" embody "gender balance" and that "intentional conversation with our ecumenical partners" continue.[72]

Inclusive language and the use of the Trinitarian formula in baptism are best understood as ongoing developmental processes in UCC theology and practice. One can dare to hope that, given what we now know of the social construction of gender, the language of liturgy and sacraments will continue to proclaim new dimensions of the freedom of the Gospel—e.g., God as Transgender, Jesus as Two-Spirit, the Holy Spirit as Queer. Clearly, the fullness of baptismal identity as "neither Jew nor Greek, slave nor free, male nor female" in Christ (Gal 3:28) is still being discovered.

A Song of Faith, Eucharist, and Sacramentality

It may help to remember that the inaugural service of the UCC was a communion service. It was no surprise to anyone that it culminated in the Lord's Supper, "that all may be one." On that day, members of the new UCC enacted this sacramentally with what was to become a beloved tradition: simultaneous communion—in which members of the congregation partake of each of the elements together as one.[73] Years later, at the twenty-fifth anniversary of union, George Pidgeon, the presider at table in that very service and the UCC's first moderator, recalled: "The Bread of Life ... had a new meaning for us.... Partaking together for the first time, as we did, our union was sealed in Christ."[74]

However optimistic or joyous that first service may have been at the time, or however naive or triumphalist it may seem from the vantage point of today, the theology of communion in this period was reverentially penitential. The two orders for Lord's Supper in Forms contain no strident indictment of sin. The emphasis is more invitational, for the sake of "spiritual refreshing," and "the renewal of ... strength," in order "to lead a new life, following the commandments of God."[75] The experimental/experiential warmth of communion in Forms gets chilled somewhat by the liturgical formalism of BCO.[76] With the publication of the Service Book, it was clear that the early stages of the Liturgical Movement had begun to shift the theology of communion from penitence to celebration. As the compilers put it, the communion services "emphasize the element of thanksgiving. Stress is laid upon the resurrection and victory of Christ."[77] The recovery of a more explicitly "eucharistic" sensibility (from the Greek eucharistia meaning thanksgiving) shows up in many other aspects of the communion orders as well, where liturgical forms of praise and thanksgiving dominate.[78] But perhaps more importantly, in order to connect eucharistic and liturgical action to social action, a "commissioning" was introduced, immediately preceding the benediction at the end of the service. Turns of phrase like "go into the world with a daring and tender love. The world is waiting,"[79] quickly set down deep roots in the fertile soil of the UCC's liturgical and social consciousness. By the time CGP was published, eucharistic prayer forms had evolved in diverse directions. CGP contains eleven eucharistic prayers, from the early church example attributed to Hippolytus to UCC originals at the turn of the millennium, from feminist to intercultural perspectives, and encouragement for extemporaneous and contextual improvisation.[80]

BEM presented a five-fold ecumenical consensus on eucharistic theology: giving thanks to God (*eucharistia*); remembering Jesus (*anamnesis*); invoking the Spirit (*epiclesis*); communing with God and one another (*koinonia*); and rehearsing God's future (*eschatos*).[81] A Song of Faith takes a similarly multivalent approach. Holy Communion is "a vision of creation healed and restored"; it is inclusive welcome, hospitality, feeding, friendship, commissioning, forgiveness, love, remembrance of Jesus, brokenness, promise, and hope; eschatological vision is inseparably linked to justice, just as the "Holy Mystery" is manifest in "Wholly Love."[82] It would seem that in UCC theological methodology, there is as much value placed on multivocal description as on univocal definition. *Song* implies not so much a systematic definition of sacraments as a poetic description of the phenomenon of sacramentality.

Liturgical historian James White uses the term "sacramentality" generally to "mean the concept that the outward and visible can convey the inward and spiritual. Physical matters and actions can become transparent vehicles of divine activity and presence. In short, sacraments can be God's love made visible."[83] For Luther it came down to the confluence of "promise" and "sign." Only in "baptism and bread," he concluded, do the commands of Jesus—"Go ... baptizing" (Matt 28:19) and "Do this" (1 Cor 11:24)—reveal the promises of God with "signs attached to them."[84] Or as White summarizes it, "sacraments are scriptural promises to which Christ has given a visual sign." In contrast, Swiss Reformer Ulrich Zwingli, a skilled linguist, emphasized the etymology of the Latin word *sacramentum*, meaning an oath of allegiance. "The sacraments," he argued, "are signs or ceremonials ... which inform the whole Church ... of your faith."[85] Sacraments are professions of faith—given by Christ, to be sure—but human memorials nonetheless. For Calvin, it was Augustine's definition of a sacrament that was most helpful—"a visible sign of an invisible grace"—but the point here was to remind us that such signs are acts of gracious condescension to our frailty by an absolute sovereign God.[86] With the advent of eighteenth-century Enlightenment rationalism, Immanuel Kant argued that any claim that the sacraments are "means of grace" with any real connection to divine action was an "illusion."[87]

Sacramental theology continues to wrestle with age-old questions. How is the visible related to the invisible, a living body related to the Risen Body, the earth related to its Maker? Is it by a divine promise as sacred sign (Luther), a memorial profession of faith (Zwingli), a gracious divine conde-scension (Calvin), or a human moralistic ceremony (Kant)? Perhaps there is a sense in which it is all of these, as in the polyphonic *Song*:

> To point to the presence of the holy in the world,
>> the church receives, consecrates, and shares
>> visible signs of the grace of God.
>
> In company with the churches
>> of the Reformed and Methodist traditions,
> we celebrate two sacraments as gifts of Christ:
> baptism and holy communion.
> In these sacraments the ordinary things of life
> —water, bread, wine—
> point beyond themselves to God and God's love,
>> teaching us to be alert
>> to the sacred in the midst of life.[88]

However, White's definition of sacramentality as a belief that "the outward and visible" conveys "the inward and spiritual"—and even Augustine's notion of a "visible sign of an invisible grace"—do not go quite far enough. Sacramentality describes not simply a binary relationship between the out-ward and inward, the visible and the invisible. It asserts the presence of one in the other, the deeply embedded reality of God's presence "in the midst of life." This is not about figuring out how two disconnected realms can be connected; it is about living in concert with their "integral connection." While it has become something of a cliché to prefer both/and interrelation-ships in contrast to either/or dualisms, Christians would do well to take their mandate for sacramentality from the Christ event itself, from the mys-tery of the incarnational Word-made-flesh, the perichoretic dance of the Trinity, and its reaffirmation of the sanctity of all life in God's good earth.

There is also evidence of increasing sacramentality in the UCC's overall gravitation towards a eucharistic *ordo* or structure in worship. *Forms* provided no orders for the Sunday service of the Word. As a result, the orders for Lord's Supper took on particular significance, especially in light of the widely admired inaugural service. BCO placed the directories for public worship first in the collection, providing two for Public Worship—the first being a preaching service (with the sermon at the end), the second based on "the structure of the Lord's Supper" (with the sermon more central).[89] In the *Service Book* the directories for Lord's Supper were placed first in the book, and the priority of particular structures was reversed, making the *ordo* of Lord's Supper "normative." As the compilers put it, "Our concern is to emphasize the unity of word and sacrament. Implicit here is acceptance of the sacrament of the Lord's supper [*sic*] as the basic Christian service and as such normative for Christian worship."[90] In CGP, this principle is again affirmed in the "Pattern for Sunday Worship" structured as Gathering-Word-Thanksgiving-Sending Forth:

> In Christian worship there are two primary focal points or "meeting places": word and table.… As the Word is proclaimed and interpreted, we encounter the living Christ and discern the working of the Spirit. As we gather around the table, God's grace is ritually enacted and embodied. Words and symbols are human means by which God speaks to us and touches us. Story and supper, sermon and sacrament belong together—both Bible and bread, broken open.… In worship, the Church gathers to celebrate God's presence and to respond by going out into the world as followers and friends of Jesus Christ.… Worship and mission belong together. [91]

Thus, the order of service is here understood as inherently formative. The shape of worship is the shape of Christian life, and this shape is eucharistic, sacramental. Sacramentality is the term that describes this collective Christian posture, consciousness, and witness in the world.

The argument for the integrity of such sacramentality in UCC worship is supported by its key liturgical scholars, from R.B.Y. Scott, who connected the activism of the Social Gospel to the premise that "all worship is sacramental" and "all life is sacramental,"[92] to HyeRan Kim-Cragg, who challenges the traditional conception of baptism as "belonging" by proposing a model of "crossing," where "the mystery of dying and being born again" transforms the identity of the church as much as the candidate.[93] Engagement with liturgical structures is not accidental to revelation, but formative of the community's experience of "the sacred in the midst of life." Sacramentality assumes that we are standing on holy ground.

Conclusion: From Sacraments to Sacramentality in the UCC

George Lindbeck, in *The Nature of Doctrine: Religion and Theology in a Postliberal Age*, identifies three approaches to doctrine: propositional, experiential-expressive, and cultural-linguistic.[94] The propositional view is typical of traditional orthodoxies, which rely on largely propositional tests of orthodoxy to define the scope of faithful belief and practice. The experiential-expressive approach is characteristic of liberal theologies, where theological reflection serves as an interpretation of or correlation to human experience. The cultural-linguistic model can be described as a post-liberal approach, where doctrines function neither primarily as propositional truth claims nor as expressive symbols, "but as communally authoritative rules of discourse, attitude, and action." While one is tempted to see in these three approaches to theology and doctrine an ascending hierarchy of validity, it is important to recognize that all three perspectives can be (and usually are) at work in any tradition, even within any one person within a tradition.

For our purposes, Lindbeck's schema suggests a way of understanding the evolution of the theology of sacraments in the UCC. As we have seen, *The Twenty Articles of Doctrine* included a healthy dose of propositional foundations acceptable to the founding traditions, especially the assertion of dominical institution in sacraments, as well as other important principles of Reformed sacramental theology. Such orthodoxy provided the pragmatic basis on which the union could be built. *Forms* gathered these and other assumptions in its compendium of interdenominationally acceptable liturgical forms. However, from before its conception, the UCC also contained a strong experiential-expressive dimension within its ethos, an experimental evangelicalism that rooted doctrinal convictions in the experience of God in Christ. Doctrinal affirmations such as an ecclesiology of covenant, the "necessity of regeneration," and the "fruit" of sanctification in service to the world gave the UCC an affective liberal flavour.

Statement continued this blending of orthodoxy and liberalism, as evident in the efforts to articulate the efficacy of infant baptism and church membership in the context of church growth and changing social realities. The *Service Book* forms of worship ended up on the front lines of an effort to negotiate tensions between liturgical orthodoxy and liberal socio-cultural pressures. Confirmation was employed to negotiate a way forward, but contextual changes were so constant that institutional efforts to renew Christian initiation persisted until the eve of the millennium. Meanwhile, as the impact of the Liturgical Movement was felt, eucharistic structures began to re-form the work of the people in the shape of increased sacramentality—but this hint of a cultural-linguistic way forward would take time to be translated into a uniquely UCC dialect.

A New Creed can be understood as the beginning of an explicit move beyond experiential-expressive forms towards a more cultural-linguistic approach. What begins as a creative liberal restatement of the faith for contemporary purposes soon takes root and grows into a new kind of language for UCC theology. A New Creed's amendments and additions signal key emerging values and consciousness. Non-sexist terms give way to inclusive language and in turn lead toward more emancipatory articulations. Its vocabulary and syntax become hallmarks of the UCC's liturgical ethos, theological reflection, and institutional culture—not merely as propositional claims, or even liberal expressions, but as cultural-linguistic touchstones of ecclesial identity.

Song pushes UCC sacramental theology to the level of sacramentality. Propositional claims and experientially expressive symbols are not absent, but its poetic and lyrical style shifts the mode of discourse from the definitive towards the evocative, from systematics to theopoetics. "More *descriptive* than *prescriptive*,"[95] it is a kind of poetic "thick description"[96] of UCC theological culture, embracing many "unresolved (and possibly unresolvable) tensions."[97] If the enthusiasm with which Song has been embraced by the church is any indication, it seems well on its way to fulfilling Lindbeck's criteria of a cultural-linguistic approach to doctrine, increasingly functioning as a dynamic set of "communally authoritative rules of discourse, attitude, and action." Admittedly, this particular subordinate standard strikes a unique, if sometimes hard to define, post-liberal posture. But, liturgically speaking, this posture can be understood as the stance of sacramentality. Finally, it is worth considering that the ultimate goal of sacramentality is the emancipation of sacraments themselves. Here faithfulness is about not only orthodox sacramental observance, or liberal sacramental expression, but sacramental living.

NOTES

1   *A Song of Faith, The Manual, 2016,* 37th rev. ed. (Toronto: UCPH, 2013), 26.

2   For a discussion of these sources see John Young's account of the *Basis of Union* in the Introduction to this volume.

3   *The Manual,* 11–15. Cf. the "Brief Statement of the Reformed Faith" (1905) of the Presbyterian Church in the United States of America; "The Twenty Four Articles of the Faith" of the Presbyterian Church of England (1890); and "Statement of Doctrine and Confession of Faith" of the Congregationalist Union of Ontario and Quebec (1886). The sources are well documented in E. Lloyd Morrow, *Church Union in Canada: Its History, Motives, Doctrine and Government* (Toronto: T. Allen, 1923), and Claris Edwin Silcox, *Church Union in Canada: Its Causes and Consequences* (New York: Institute of Social and Religious Research, 1933).

4   John Webster Grant, "Blending Traditions: The United Church of Canada," in *The Churches and the Canadian Experience: A Faith and Order Study of the Christian Tradition* (Toronto: Ryerson Press, 1966), 135–38.

5   *The Manual,* 14.

6   "Chapter XXVII. Of The Sacraments," *Westminster Confession of Faith* (1647), in *Sacraments and Worship: The Sources of Christian Theology,* ed. Maxwell E. Johnson (Louisville, KY: Westminster John Knox, 2012), 22.

7   John Wesley, "The Means Of Grace," in *The Wesley Centre Online,* http://wesley.nnu.edu/john-wesley/the-sermons-of-john-wesley-1872-edition/sermon-16-the-means-of-grace/. See also James F. White, *Protestant Worship: Traditions in Transition* (Louisville, KY: Westminster John Knox, 1989), 154.

8   Cf. "Of the Sacraments," in the *Articles of Religion* (1563) in *The Book of Common Prayer* (1784) and John Wesley's *Sunday Service of the Methodists in North America,* in *Sacraments and Worship,* 20.

9   John Wesley, "Of Baptism," *Sunday Service,* in *Sacraments and Worship,* 167.

10 For a fuller discussion of Methodist baptismal regeneration see William S. Kervin, *The Language of Baptism: A Study of the Authorized Baptismal Liturgies of the United Church of Canada, 1925–1995* (Lanham, MD: Scarecrow, 2003), 20–23.

11 *The Manual,* 13.

12 John Wesley, "Of the Lord's Supper," *Sunday Service,* in *Sacraments and Worship,* 243.

13 *Forms of Service for the Offices of the Church* (Toronto: UCPH, 1926), i–iii, v. Unless otherwise noted, references to the orders of service for baptism and Lord's Supper are from the respective orders in *Forms,* 1–32. For a more

detailed discussion of what follows, see Kervin, *The Language of Baptism*, 28–36, and *Ordered Liberty: Readings in the History of United Church Worship*, ed. William S. Kervin (Toronto: UCPH, 2011), 30–33, 315–21.

14   John H. Young, "Sacred Cow or White Elephant? The Doctrine Section of the Basis of Union," *Touchstone* 16, no. 2 (May 1998): 31–32; John Webster Grant, *The Canadian Experience of Church Union* (London: Lutterworth, 1967), 34.

15   Phyllis D. Airhart, *A Church with the Soul of a Nation: Making and Remaking the United Church of Canada* (Montreal and Kingston: McGill-Queen's University Press, 2014), 21; Phyllis D. Airhart, "A 'Review' of The United Church of Canada's 75 Years," *Touchstone* 18, no. 3 (September 2000): 22–24.

16   *The Manual*, 11. See also Airhart, "A 'Review,'" 21–22.

17   *Ecclesia semper reformanda est* is the Latin of the Reformers' principle, "the church is always to be reformed." *Ut omnes unum sint*, Jesus's prayer "that all may be one" (John 17:21) is on the United Church crest and animated the inaugural service of the UCC. See also C.T. McIntire, "Unity among Many: The Formation of The United Church of Canada, 1899–1930," in *The United Church of Canada: A History*, ed. Don Schweitzer (Waterloo, ON: Wilfrid Laurier University Press, 2012), 20–23.

18   George Pidgeon, "Foreword," in Thomas Buchanan Kilpatrick, *Our Common Faith* (Toronto: Ryerson Press, 1928), vi.

19   Kilpatrick, *Our Common Faith*, 93–94.

20   Grant, "Blending Traditions," 136–37.

21   For a fuller discussion of "ordered liberty" see William S. Kervin, "Worship on the Way: The Dialectic of United Church Worship," in *The United Church of Canada: A History*, 188–91, and *Ordered Liberty*.

22   Christopher White, "Question Box: The 'Splash and Split,'" *United Church Observer*, June 2016, 44.

23   Anonymous, "'The Book of Common Order' in Our Readers' Forum," *New Outlook*, 6 June 1934, 430.

24   For more details see Kervin, *The Language of Baptism*, 102–8.

25   2.4.10, *The Manual*, 18.

26   "An Order for the Baptism of Children," *The Book of Common Order of The United Church of Canada* (Toronto: UCPH, 1932), 97–103. For a detailed documentation of its sources see Kervin, *The Language of Baptism*, 54–79.

27   *The Doctrine and Practice of Infant Baptism* (Toronto: Commission on the Christian Faith, 1954), 3.

28   *Common Order*, 101; *Service Book for the Use of Ministers Conducting Public Worship* (Toronto: Canec Publishing and Supply House, 1969), 43, 53.

29   *Highways of the Heart: A Devotional Book Based on "The Statement of Faith"* [*sic*] (Toronto: BESS, 1941), 85.

30   John Dow, *This Is Our Faith: An Exposition of the Statement of Faith* [sic] *of the United Church of Canada* (Toronto: BESS, 1946), 52, quoting J.V. Bartlet, 192.

31   *Catechism* (Toronto: BESS, 1944), 6.

32   *Doctrine and Practice of Infant Baptism*, 7

33   *Church Membership: Doctrine and Practice in The United Church of Canada* (Toronto: Committee on Christian Faith, 1963), 5.

34   Ibid.

35   *Forms*, 40, 43.

36   *Common Order*, 104–5, 111.

37   *Catechism*, 6.

38   *Church Membership*, 30; Kervin, *The Language of Baptism*, 131.

39   E.g., Donald M. Mathers, *The Word and the Way* (Toronto: UCPH, 1962), 205–9, 223; Kervin, *The Language of Baptism*, 195.

40   *Baptism, Eucharist, and Ministry*, Faith and Order Paper No. 111 (Geneva: WCC, 1982), 2–3.

41   Ruth C. Duck, *Worship for the Whole People of God: Vital Worship for the 21st Century* (Louisville, KY: Westminster John Knox, 2013), 172.

42   For a detailed examination of the work see Kervin, *The Language of Baptism*, 231–49.

43   Patricia Clarke, "Now What's Happening to Baptism?" *Observer*, March 1980, 12.

44   *Baptism and Renewal of Baptismal Faith: For Optional Use in The United Church of Canada* (Toronto: UCC, 1986).

45   *Celebrate God's Presence: A Book of Services for The United Church of Canada* (Toronto: UCPH, 2000), 319–73.

46   ROP 1982, 58–59, 188–89. See also "Theological Affirmations," in *Ordered Liberty*, 111–12.

47   *The Manual*, 27.

48   Pierre Berton, *The Comfortable Pew: A Critical Look at Christianity and the Religious Establishment in the New Age* (Toronto: McClelland and Stewart, 1965), 24–25.

49   See Kervin, *Ordered Liberty*, 329; Ronald Atkinson, "Factors in the Preparation of a 'Contemporary' Liturgy," in *Ordered Liberty*, 224; Young in the Introduction to this volume.

50   See the Introduction to this volume for an account of the development of *A New Creed*.

51 *The Words We Sing: An Inclusive Language Guide to The Hymn Book* (Toronto: UCC, 1984), in *Ordered Liberty*, 88.

52 Tracy J. Trothen, "1980s: What Does It Mean to Be The United Church of Canada? Emergent Voices, Self-Critique, and Dissent," in *The United Church of Canada: A History*, 144.

53 *The Words We Sing*, in *Ordered Liberty*, 89–90.

54 *Just Language: A Guide to Inclusive Language in The United Church of Canada* (Toronto: UCC, 1997).

55 Duck, *Worship for the Whole People of God*, 102–3.

56 Mary Daly, *Beyond God the Father: Toward a Philosophy of Women's Liberation* (Boston: Beacon, 1973/85), 19.

57 CGP, 322–23. PLURA is the ecumenical network of Presbyterian, Lutheran, United Church, Roman Catholic, and Anglican churches in Canada.

58 See "Recommendations of The Report on Christian Initiation," in *Ordered Liberty*, 112–13, 121–22.

59 "United Church of Canada," in *Churches Respond to BEM*, vol. 2 (Geneva: WCC, 1986), 279.

60 *Voices United: Services for Trial Use 1996–1997* (Toronto: UCPH, 1996), 59.

61 CGP, 323.

62 Ibid.

63 Marjorie Procter-Smith, *In Her Own Rite: Constructing Feminist Liturgical Tradition* (Nashville, TN: Abingdon, 1990), 63.

64 Ibid.

65 *In Whose Name? The Baptismal Formula in Contemporary Culture* (Toronto: UCC, 2001), in *Ordered Liberty*, 171.

66 E.g., Ruth C. Duck, *Gender and the Name of God: The Trinitarian Baptismal Formula* (New York: Pilgrim, 1991), 171–76; Procter-Smith, *In Her Own Rite*, 64, 108–9; Laurence Hull Stookey, *Baptism: Christ's Act in the Church* (Nashville, TN: Abingdon, 1982), 198–200.

67 This formulation received significant affirmation by the RC/UCC dialogue. "In Whose Name?," *Ordered Liberty*, 169–70.

68 Cf. Procter-Smith, *In Her Own Rite*, 64–65, 109–11.

69 CGP, 348.

70 Procter-Smith, *In Her Own Rite*, 66.

71 "In Whose Name?," *Ordered Liberty*, 173.

72 Ibid., 168, 172.

73 Simultaneous communion was also made possible by the recent introduction of individual cups and pasteurized grape juice. Thomas Reginald Harding

and Bruce Harding, *Patterns of Worship in The United Church of Canada, 1925–1987* (Toronto: Evensong, 1996), 14–15; Kervin, *Ordered Liberty*, 14.

74   Harding and Harding, *Patterns,* 14–15.

75   *Forms,* 1, 11.

76   BCO, 76, 77, 78, 91.

77   *Service Book,* 1.

78   E.g., the Sursum Corda ("lift up your hearts"); acclamations such as "Glory be to thee, O Lord"; a contemporary paraphrase of the Sanctus; and the exchange of Peace. Ibid., 1, 9, 10, 17, 18.

79   Ibid., 186.

80   CGP, 237–311.

81   BEM, 10–17. The parenthetical Greek terms, correlating with the BEM themes, are my additions. For other approaches see also Duck, *Worship for the Whole People of God,* 185–88; Charlotte Caron, *Eager for Worship: Theologies, Practices, and Perspectives on Worship in the United Church of Canada* (Toronto: UCC, 2000), 64.

82   *The Manual,* 27–28.

83   James F. White, *The Sacraments in Protestant Practice and Faith* (Nashville, TN: Abingdon, 1999), 13. What follows is based on White's overview in *Sacraments,* 18–22.

84   Luther, *Babylonian Captivity,* in *Sacraments and Worship,* 12–13, 18–19.

85   Ulrich Zwingli, *Commentary on True and False Religion* (1525), in *Sacraments and Worship,* 16.

86   John Calvin, *Institutes of the Christian Religion* (1559), in *Sacraments and Worship,* 17–18.

87   Immanuel Kant, *Religion within the Limits of Reason Alone* (1793), in *Sacraments and Worship,* 24–25.

88   *The Manual,* 26.

89   BCO, V.

90   *Service Book,* 3.

91   CGP, 1–2.

92   R.B.Y. Scott, "The Cultus of the Community," in *Ordered Liberty,* 215–21.

93   HyeRan Kim-Cragg, "Baptism as Crossing beyond Belonging?" in *Liturgy in Postcolonial Perspectives: Only One Is Holy,* ed. Cláudio Carvalhaes (New York: Palgrave Macmillan, 2015), 201–11.

94   For what follows see George A. Lindbeck, *The Nature of Doctrine: Religion and Theology in a Postliberal Age* (Louisville, KY: Westminster John Knox, 2009), 16–18.

95   "Appendix A: On the Purpose and Status of the Statement of Faith," in *A Song of Faith: A Statement of Faith of The United Church of Canada, L'Église Unie du Canada* (Toronto: UCC, 2006), 10. For a strong sense of its cultural-linguistic approach, note especially appendices explaining its "intended audience," "language and form," "context," and relationship to United Church "identity" (10–18).

96   Clifford Geertz, *The Interpretation of Cultures: Selected Essays* (New York: Basic Books, 2000), 1–32.

97   "Appendix D: On the Identity of the United Church as Reflected in the Statement of Faith," in *Song*, 17.

CHAPTER TEN

PRACTISING GOD'S MISSION BEYOND CANADA

Hyuk Cho

On May 23, 1914, a Japanese ship, the *Komagata Maru*, carrying 376 passengers, mostly Sikhs, arrived at Vancouver harbour. The ship had made the long journey from Hong Kong via Shanghai, China, and Yokohama, Japan, with a mission to challenge Canada's immigration rule of the "continuous journey regulation" of 1908 that required all immigrants to arrive directly from their point of origin. Since the main immigration routes from South Asian countries did not offer direct passage to Canada, it was an almost impossible task for people from there who wanted to emigrate to Canada to meet the rule. Upon arrival, the passengers were refused entry. While they languished in the harbour for two months, suffering from a lack of water and food, the song "White Canada Forever"[1] was gaining popularity. Upon their forced return to India, twenty-six were shot by the British army, and an estimated two dozen were missing. William Scott, who had just graduated from Westminster Hall (the Presbyterian theological college in Vancouver), was an astute observer of the incident. It caused him "deep concern" for the Indian people and fired his determination to work as a missionary.[2] Scott's first choice was India, but since there was no opening in that country, the Foreign Mission Board suggested Korea. He arrived in Korea with his wife Katie in December 1914 and worked there for thirty-eight years.

Scott, originally from the Presbyterian Church in Canada, along with 638 out of 655 foreign missionaries, entered church union to form the United Church of Canada in 1925.[3] The UCC inherited well-established overseas mission work from three uniting denominations. The result was a tremendous mutual widening of horizons as each of the denominational mission societies brought precious links with a rich variety of Christian

Figure 10.1   Mission Fields of The United Church of Canada in the 1930s

Source: John T. Taylor, *Our Share in India: The Story of the Central India Mission, The United Church of Canada* (Toronto, ON: Department of Missionary Education, UCC, 193?), 78.

communities abroad. Into the UCC the Presbyterians brought the missions in Trinidad (South America), India-China-Korea (Asia), and New Hebrides (now Vanuatu the south Pacific), the Methodists in China and Japan (Asia), and the Congregationalists in Angola (Africa).

This chapter will trace the history of why and how UCC missiology changed from the time of church union in 1925 until the middle of the first decade of the twenty-first century, and the implications of that change for the church's relationships and mission practice with ecumenical and global partners and other faith communities. Important sources include the five major policy statements or reports on world mission in the UCC issued during that time period: "The Report of the Special Committee on Policy Appointed by the Board of Foreign Missions and The Woman's Missionary Society of the United Church of Canada" (1936), *World Mission* (1966), "Dual Mandate" (1977), "Seeking to Understand 'Partnership' for God's Mission Today" (1988), and *Mending the World* (1997). All five statements or reports, written in different contexts, define the changing missiology that influenced UCC mission policy and practice. This chapter will also consider the relationship between these reports and the UCC's four doctrinal statements.

"I am not Come to Destroy but Fulfill": The Report of the Special Committee on Policy (1936)

Aspects of the doctrine section of the *Basis of Union* are important for understanding leading themes in the UCC's approach to mission policy and practice. For example, Article XX, "Of Christian Service and the Final Triumph," reflects two central tenets of late-nineteenth- and early-twentieth-century Evangelical Protestantism's approach to mission. First, the BOU locates its affirmation of Christians' various duties "as disciples and servants of Christ"—including the duty "to further the extension of His Kingdom"—within the final article on eschatology. Mission, then, was one part of the larger project of building the Kingdom. Second, in its profession that "we joyfully receive the word of Christ, bidding His people go into all the world and make disciples of all nations," it reflected the widespread contemporary influence of the Great Commission of Matthew 28:18–20 on English-speaking Evangelical Protestants' understanding of world mission.[4]

Similarly important is Article 2, "Of Revelation," which affirms Jesus Christ as the perfect revelation of God and the Bible as "containing the only infallible rule of faith and life," but also acknowledges other sources of revelation such as nature, history, and the human heart. It also affirms that God "has been graciously pleased to make clearer revelation of Himself to men of God who spoke as they were moved by the Holy Spirit." Such "men of God," however, were not limited to those reported in biblical and subsequent Christian history. As T.B. Kilpatrick explained in his discussion of Article 2, through the working of the Holy Spirit God also speaks through people of various faiths: "We need not deny to the ethnic faiths the possession of men who belong to this class; and in the great literature of the nations we may read moral and religious truth which can have had no other Source than God's self-communications."[5] Thus, while upholding the call to "go into all the world and make disciples of all nations," the UCC affirmed the validity of the spiritual truth already present in those nations.

"The Report of the Special Committee on Policy Appointed by the Board of Foreign Mission (BFM) and the Woman's Missionary Society (WMS)" (hereafter *Report of the Special Committee*), adopted in 1936 at the 7th General Council,[6] became the basis of the mission policy of the UCC. The institutional context for the *Report of the Special Committee* was as

follows. From the late 1920s to the mid-1930s, the church had been facing financial challenges on account of the Great Depression. Further, the
annual allocations to the BFM from the Missionary and Maintenance Fund
(MMF) had been greatly declining each year, so that, by 1935, the fund was
reduced to less than half.[7] As a result the BFM had undertaken the necessary but painful reduction of expenditures and withdrawal of missionaries
from the fields.[8] In April 1935, the BFM appointed a Policy Committee to
review the financial situation and report to a special meeting of the BFM
in September of that year. Based on its financial review, the Policy Committee recommended a further reduction of its expenditures amounting
to $100,000 to take effect in 1936.[9] In authorizing the proposed reduction,
the BFM faced another challenge—how to reduce expenditures other than
making percentage cuts on all forms of mission work.[10] The committee
identified the need for guidelines in case further reductions were required.
Apart from the financial difficulties, the Policy Committee recognized that
since there had been no thorough study of its whole work and the relationships among its various parts since church union more than a decade
before, an extensive study of mission and the establishment of a policy as
a basis for a sound and forward-looking mission was needed.[11] In this context, the BFM appointed the Policy Committee to make an extensive study
of its mission work.

As a result, the *Report of the Special Committee* stated that the central
task of mission was "to establish a Christian Church which will be truly
indigenous, self-governing, self-supporting and self-propagating: a Church
with a vision of its task of creating a Christlike society."[12] In line with the
central task, one of the most important principles governing missionary
expenditure was "to give first place to the support of those phases of missionary effort which contribute directly to the development of a self-propagating and self-supporting Church on the field."[13] The goal of building up
the indigenous church was not new to the UCC. Since 1922, before church
union, it had also been the mission policy of the Presbyterian Church in
Canada.[14] It was also the main argument of the book *New Days in Old
India* published in 1926 by the Committee on Missionary Education and
the WMS.[15] The increasing demand for an anti-colonial, independent, and
indigenous church from the missionized churches drew the attention of the
Western churches. Chinese Christians were voicing their concerns about
Western ecclesiological domination and denominationalism.[16] Indian
Christians too urged that the fundamental aim of Christian missions was to
develop an "indigenous Christianity."[17] One of the UCC leaders of the time

and its first moderator, George C. Pidgeon, also supported the indigenous church movement in China and India.[18] The *Report of the Special Committee* pointed out that the church in the field was too Western and often regarded as an alien organization.[19] Struggling from a lack of finances to support world mission, the goals of the Three-Self Movement, particularly the establishment of a self-supporting church, must have been a welcome task for the Western churches including the UCC. Money had been a great source of power for the Western churches, but now that power was decreasing, just as the money was.

The rise of powerful forces such as nationalism, communism, militarism, and fascism characterized worldwide tensions in the late 1920s and early 1930s, the period between the First and Second World Wars. The prevalent tendency of this period was also described as materialism, secularism, and atheism.[20] The atmosphere of the day seemed to threaten a Christian universalism. In this context, the *Report of the Special Committee* identified two urgent reasons for supporting world mission: first, to keep the vision and experience of a universal God by sharing it with the whole world, and second, to transplant Christianity in order to inspire a new vitality.[21] These two reasons reflected both unchanging and changing interpretations of mission in the UCC at that time.

The unchanging attitude toward mission is observed in the argument that the vision of a universal God is important for the unity needed to challenge the rising aggressive nationalism of the day. It was used to provide a reason to maintain an outdated policy of mission work. However, history suggests that in the early 1920s, nationalism was promoted as a form of anti-Western nationalism,[22] while communism in China and Mahatma Gandhi's *swaraj* (self-government) movement were ways of resisting the economic and political domination of Western nations.[23] In the context of resistance, the universal God of Christianity was undoubtedly identified with the God of empire. The *Report of the Special Committee* may be seen as an extension of the doctrine of BOU in the call to "go into all the world and make disciples of all nations."[24] Further, that unchanging Christological conviction, expressed in the statement "Christ came into the world to save all men or to bring all men and peoples to completion"[25] led to an ambivalent position in the relationships with others in mission—an unwillingness to abandon the traditional conviction of Christian universalism as the only truth, while indicating the need to collaborate with all men and women of faith in the struggle against materialism and secularism, a position consistent with the stand of the Jerusalem Conference 1928.[26]

Less positive views of other faith traditions appeared in other elements of the UCC's work. The same 7th General Council that adopted the *Report of the Special Committee* also authorized the development of a new statement of faith. Written by a commission under the auspices of the Board of Evangelism and Social Service, and reflecting the influence of the Neo-Orthodox theology that had arisen and grown following the First World War, the *Statement of Faith* was approved by the 9th General Council in 1940. While *Statement* does not explicitly deny the *BOU*'s affirmation of revelation in nature, history, the human heart, and people moved by the Holy Spirit, its Article IX, "The Holy Scriptures," mentions only the Bible, understood in relation to Jesus Christ and the Holy Spirit, as a source of revelation. What *Statement* implied, however, John Dow made explicit in his discussion of Article IX when he expressed doubt about the possibility of revelation in nature, history, and the human heart.[27] As evoked in the words of the *Report of the Special Committee*, "I am not come to destroy but fulfill,"[28] non-Christians are no longer to be seen as enemies to be destroyed but still as lacking something that needs to be fulfilled. As the *Report of the Special Committee* remarked, "It is also to be recognized that the conception of God held by many people is very primitive, and in the case of others, many of whom have lacked religious training, the idea of God is not seriously considered."[29] The supremacy of Christianity is maintained, and mission is understood as fulfilling what is lacking in others and doing something *for* others.

The changing attitude toward mission, however, is observed in the thought that world mission might benefit the donors to the mission funds of the UCC. Influenced by the discussion of the International Missionary Council (IMC) held in Jerusalem in 1928, and inspired by Asian spiritual leaders such as Mahatma Gandhi and Toyhiho Kagawa, the *Report of the Special Committee* noted, "More men like Kagawa can come to us to strengthen us where we are weak and to bring us all nearer to the Kingdom of God on earth."[30] It is interesting to note this self-critical view in comparison to that of Christianity in other places:

> Our type of Christianity is too individualistic, too much inclined to accept the distinction of secular and sacred, too closely allied with competitive forces that have come to grief. Now is the time to transplant it, to give it the benefit of new soil, to let it spring up into newness of vitality because of a new richness that will come to it. We of the West have no right to assume that our form of Christianity is final, or that our minds are better qualified to understand the Son of Man than is the Oriental mind.[31]

This openness to the possibility of receiving from "younger churches" is a much different attitude toward mission than that reflected in the BOU and can be seen as a step toward mutual respect and partnership in mission.[32]

As discussed above, the main task of mission was understood in that time period to be the building up of self-supporting, self-governing, and self-propagating churches. The major reasons for the policies suggested in the *Report of the Special Committee* were the financial crisis facing the UCC and the resistant voices of global churches. The church was not ready to support truly indigenous churches because of its unchanging attitude towards others. This is indicated clearly in its distinct definitions of mission and church in the *Report of the Special Committee*: "We must distinguish between the Mission which is a temporary foreign institution and the Church which is indigenous and permanent and between the limited aim of the Mission and the complete Christian programme of the Church."[33] Although this distinction meant to emphasize the importance of the indigenous church, it reveals an understanding of mission as belonging to the church of the West: the UCC, as the *subject* of mission, provided medical, educational, and evangelical services to the *objects* of mission who needed them. Mission, from the 1920s to the mid-1960s, was understood as "service" for and to others through a spirit of sacrificial giving and helping. There was not much recognition of what the UCC had already received in mission.[34]

"To Share in God's Concern for All": The Report of the Commission on World Mission (1966)

After 1925, the world mission enterprise of the UCC was undertaken by two organizations—the renamed Board of Overseas Missions (BOM)[35] and the Board of the Woman's Missionary Society (WMS)[36]—until the two were integrated in 1962 (table 10.1). Often both organizations served in the same area. While they operated separately in the mission fields, missionaries sometimes worked for the other Board.[37] In 1956, at the 17th General Council, the executives of the BOM and the WMS jointly recommended the "real possibility of closer integration in the administration of all overseas work."[38] Acting on this recommendation, the next General Council in 1958 approved the report of the Committee on Integration of Overseas Missions Work.[39] With their history of over thirty years of working separately yet together, why did the organizations want to be integrated? The report of the Committee on Integration notes that a desire for a closer union between the BOM and the WMS came from the overseas mission fields.[40] The missionaries of each

Table 10.1   Expenditures on overseas missions, 1926–1960

Year	BOM	% of total	WMS OM*		% of total	Total
1926	$1,159,340	68.20	$540,596	(797,201)	31.80	$1,699,936
1930	$859,683	60.49	$561,547	(903,892)	39.51	$1,421,230
1935	$562,675	56.81	$427,813	(665,178)	43.19	$990,488
1940	$453,167	51.52	$426,447	(664,834)	48.48	$879,614
1945	$473,774	51.19	$451,691	(813,974)	48.81	$925,465
1950	$599,094	48.54	$635,215	(1,006,842)	51.46	$1,234,309
1955	$844,914	56.60	$647,900	(1,237,706)	43.40	$1,492,814
1960	$1,336,322	62.00	$818,914	(1,518,055)	38.00	$2,155,236

Source: UCC, *World Mission: Report of the Commission on World Mission* (Toronto: UCC, 1966), 181–84, and UCC, *Year Book.*

*WMS OM = money used for overseas mission (OM). Numbers in parentheses indicate total money raised by the WMS.

Board were almost unanimous in favouring a closer union. They believed that union would benefit the whole overseas missionary program by providing a broadened outlook of interest to all UCC members.

To gain a deeper understanding of why the WMS approved institutional integration, one needs to go back to 1953. From that year, women's related organizations within the UCC such as the WMS, the Deaconess Order and Women Workers, and the Woman's Association began to work toward an incorporation into a united women's organization in order to participate fully in the life and work of the church. One of the goals of the promotion of a united women's organization was "further full partnership of women and men in the Church."[41] Since the WMS actively participated in the amalgamation of the women's organizations, it is probable that they related it to their perceived necessity for the integration of their overseas mission work with the BOM. The WMS often heard the growing voices within the organization and the mission fields: "'I think it is good to have just one voice on the mission field.' ... The overseas people were confused and wondering why there were two parallel [organizations]."[42] To solve these concerns, a unified women's origination was formed on January 1, 1962: the United Church Women. At the same time, the WMS and BOM were integrated into the newly named Board of World Mission (BWM). The BWM decided that in the rapidly changing context within and outside the UCC, it needed a new policy, direction, and understanding of mission, and new methods of working ecumenically both in Canada and beyond with its global partners.[43]

With this goal in mind, in 1962, during the same year that the Second Vatican Council (1962–65) of the Roman Catholic Church was convened, the UCC approved the creation of a Commission on World Mission to conduct "an independent and fundamental study of how the United Church of Canada can best share in the World Mission of the Church."[44] Among the twenty members, seven were former missionaries or had a variety of overseas experiences.[45] After two and a half years of study and consultation, the Commission on World Mission presented its report, *World Mission: Report of the Commission on World Mission* (hereafter *World Mission*), to the 22nd General Council (1966). The most extensive mission consultation in the history of the UCC, *World Mission* became and remains the foundation for its missiology and mission practice.

World Mission indicates that the compelling motive for the study approved in 1962 was the rapidly changing context of mission. What were the changes facing the UCC at that time? In the section titled "Revolutionary Changes in the Twentieth Century Challenging Conventional Approaches to Missions"[46] *World Mission* took note of the association of Christian mission with Western political imperialism. "The imperial ties of the mission were doubtless most obvious in countries governed by the west, but even elsewhere the forces making for westernization easily shaded into each other."[47] It points out that, as a result, missionary enterprise erected an enormous structure that could be maintained only with continued Western help. As mentioned above, in the early twentieth century the most significant change was the movement toward independence from the colonial context. The spread of communism and its revolutionary changes in China and Angola are examples of the resistance against colonial powers.[48] In the context of rising independence movements in many countries, the UCC was painfully aware of the ties between Christian mission and Western colonial powers.

With the emergence of younger churches, the report raised the central question "How can mutual respect be achieved?"[49] This question led to the adoption of the phrase "Partnership in Obedience," which became the mission theme of the IMC held at Whitby, Ontario, in 1947. To express its intention to work toward sharing the task of world mission between "younger and older" churches, the IMC rejected the "colonial" approach to mission in favour of the concept of partnership.[50] The paradigm change in mission from a parent–daughter relationship to one of equality was recognized. This understanding differs from previous faith statements such as the doctrine of *BOU* and *Statement*, in which mission was mainly understood as social service to others.[51] To reflect this change, *World Mission* declared that "our church disowns all forms of ecclesiastical colonialism. It seeks no extension abroad of existing ecclesiastical structures under its own control."[52] It recommended that "the United Church of Canada continue its policy of moving toward full partnership with other churches in all countries in service and witness."[53] In the 1960s, the concept of partnership became key to the understanding of mission as a way to overcome colonialism and has remained central to UCC mission practice ever since. Further, *World Mission* serves as an example of how UCC theology developed through specific areas of the church's work, and how such theological developments shaped later faith statements. For example, *A Song of Faith*'s affirmation that God "is creatively and redemptively active in the world" explicitly echoes the *World Mission*'s recommendation that "the church should recognize that God is creatively and redemptively at work in the religious life of all mankind."[54]

Another change in the UCC's overseas mission from the early 1960s was the diversification of mission fields. In the 1930s, 80 percent of UCC's missionary work was carried out in Asia, but with the expansion into African, Caribbean, and Latin American locations such as Brazil, Angola, Kenya, Congo, Zambia, Jamaica, and Trinidad, that was reduced to 60 percent.[55] After the mission fields in China closed in 1951, the UCC allocated its resources to other parts of the world. The establishment of new mission fields was carried out through ecumenical work with global partners with which the UCC had not had a previous tradition of co-operation. A small number of missionaries were appointed upon the request of partner churches and worked under the direction of these churches.[56] Table 10.2 depicts the areas where missionaries worked with global partners.

The writers of *World Mission* located the UCC in the context of a religiously pluralistic world. Before the commission began its work, Wilfred C. Smith delivered a series of lectures aired by the *Ideas* program on Canadian Broadcasting Corporation Radio in 1961, and published in 1962 under the title *The Faith of Other Men*.[57] Smith later became a member of the commission. The commission accepted Smith's notion of the "'evolving global religiousness of men,' within which God must be seen to be at work within the church as well as in other identifiable religious communities."[58] Thoroughly infused by Smith's pluralistic understanding of religion, *World Mission* states, "The church has always lived in a religiously plural world, though it is now becoming more genuinely aware of this fact and of some of its implications. Perhaps the most important implication is that the church must be involved in this religiously plural world."[59] A pluralistic understanding of

Table 10.2   Work areas of missionaries, 1964

Work areas*	Persons**	% of total
Education (teachers, theological education, student work, adult education)	40	21.74
Health (doctors, nurses, pharmacists, physiotherapists)	50	27.17
Evangelism (ministers, women in church work)	75	40.76
Social work	3	1.63
Special projects (agriculture, technology, broadcasting, business administration)	16	8.70
Total	184	100.00

Source: *World Mission*, 141–42.

* Some of the work, especially special projects, was carried out by short-term appointments starting from the early 1950s, as requested by partner churches.

** Sometimes the professionally qualified spouse of a missionary was assigned to a particular work, but their numbers are not included here.

religion appears later in *A New Creed*: "We believe in God ... who works in us and others by the Spirit."[60] *A New Creed* affirms that God works in a variety of ways, perhaps even through other faiths. *Song* would later reflect a similar pluralistic understanding.

Along with situating the UCC in the context of religious pluralism, *World Mission* proposed a new missiology. It noted that the theological ferment of the twentieth century had challenged the UCC to rethink the nature of mission as a whole.[61] *World Mission* adopted the concept of *missio Dei* (the mission of God) as God's activity that embraces the world, humanity, and the church.[62] For example, Finding Seven of *World Mission* states: "The mission in which the church is engaged is a mission from God to man—to man in all continents—and not a mission from men in the west to men in the east."[63] In 1967, C. Douglas Jay, the secretary of the commission, reiterated this in his series of lectures, "World Mission and World Civilization." *Missio Dei* understands that God is primarily related to the world, not to the church; the church is invited to discern and practise God's mission in the world with others.[64] *World Mission* boldly recommends that "the United Church of Canada broaden its awareness of mission, seeking to relate its performance of each task at home and abroad to its understanding of God's mission as embracing the whole world and as committed to the whole Church."[65] In *missio Dei*, the church's mission is the singular mission of God, not a matter of church mission fields.

When mission is understood as belonging to God, the viewpoint of mission relationships with other churches shifts. The UCC is no longer to be seen as the subject or agent of mission, but a participant in God's mission along with other churches in the world; the former parent-and-daughter relationship is to be transformed to one of partners; and bilateral relationships are intended to grow multilateral patterns of co-operation. In God's mission, relationships with non-Christians also shift from seeing Christianity as fulfilling other religions to accepting religious plurality, and the process also shifts from proclamation to dialogue. Mission no longer moves from West to East, serving others who are waiting to be served, but working together in God's mission in a world of mutual respect and acceptance for human betterment in God's world.

Further, *World Mission* articulated a process for working mutually with Christians and those of other faiths or of no faith for the common good in a pluralistic world.[66] It recognizes that although there may be no points of contact between "Christianity as a system and, say, Hinduism as a system," there are almost limitless points of contact whenever a Christian meets a *person* of another faith and they share their life concerns together. *World Mission* identifies "shared concern" as that which brings people together to live into God's mission in a pluralistic world. Religious plurality provides the context for the UCC's creative work with others beyond all differences. Such a context evokes the question, How can Christians create just relations with others when the partners are of different faiths or of no faith? Pluralism is often misunderstood simply to mean a diversity of faiths. *World Mission* pushes the UCC to move beyond a pluralistic approach that is merely descriptive, one that acknowledges diversity without seeking a shared bond. It states: "Shared concern is of more fundamental importance than the existence of elements of thought or belief. Where, for instance, there is a shared concern that the eternal reality of things unseen should be recognized as distinct from the temporality of things seen, there will be opportunities for honest and persuasive dialogue, and any dialogue which is honest must also be persuasive if it is about things that deeply concern us."[67]

World Mission develops its missiology out of its "shared concern" rather than in a common definition of faith or in a descriptive acknowledgement of the diversity of faiths. It moves from a religious to a "humanitarian approach" in its dialogue and mission practice.[68] In this way *World Mission* breaks through ecumenical and religious boundaries to work with people of different faiths and of no faith. This approach of mission focuses on shared praxis, a *process* of working together, not necessarily on doctrinal features—a paradigm shift in missiology in the UCC. With the concepts of partnership, pluralism, *missio Dei*, and mutuality ("shared concern"), *World Mission* provides a firm foundaion upon which the next generations may develop contextually appropriate missiology for ministry.

"Doing Justice is a Central and Indispensable Element of Doing Mission": Dual Mandate—Doing Mission and Doing Justice (1977)

In the 1970s, the UCC received many requests from partner churches around the globe.[69] People in Korea, for example, were struggling for human rights in the context of a repressive military dictatorship. The 26th General Council in 1974 expressed "its solidaridy with the Christian community of Korea in every possible way," and the next General Council in 1977 resolved to endorse a signature campaign with its partner, the Presbyterian Church in the Republic of Korea (PROK) in its struggle for human rights.[70] Katharine Hockin recalled that the UCC faithfully responded to the "calls from partner churches for solidarity in support for human rights and the struggle for freedom and democracy, as in Korea, the Philippines, Central America, and several nations in Africa."[71] In this context, the policy document, "Dual Mandate," was created as a response to the requests for advocacy and solidarity by partner churches facing challenging situations.

The 27th General Council of 1977 adopted "Dual Mandate: Doing Mission and Doing Justice" as UCC mission policy and as the theme of the Divison of World Outreach (DWO).[72] "Dual Mandate" means "solidarity with Jesus Christ by joining in work and witness with the world Christian family (doing mission), and in structuring Christian love and action toward the global human family (doing justice)."[73] The words "Christian family" indicated that doing mission involved co-operative work with, at that time, other people of faith, mostly Christians,[74] while "global human family" indicated that doing jusice implies identification and action on issues of justice with people regardless of their faith.[75]

In the preamble to "Dual Mandate," "doing mission" is expressed as partnership, maintaining the continuity of the concept from *World Mission*. "Partnership with Christians is an authentic way of carrying out mission around the world today. We respect overseas initiatives and we strive for patterns of mutual decision-making. We seek to avoid all paternalism and cultural imperialism."[76] At this time, mission initiatives are understood to be taken by the global partner churches and agencies in their contexts, with the UCC playing a responding role. No longer would the UCC make decisions for the partner churches; rather, it would respect the other's integrity.

In response to global mission partners who asked the UCC to seek justice with them, a renewed effort was directed to the "doing justice" aspect of the "Dual Mandate."[77] "Dual Mandate" identifies contemporary reasons why the UCC is called to participate in the work of doing justice: first, Canadians benefit from participation in international structures of injustice; second, the power to work for just change is nurtured; third, doing justice is consistent with the teaching of the Gospel. In doing justice, solidarity with oppressed peoples seeking liberation became an important aspect of mission in the UCC.

To meet one of the objectives of doing mission/doing justice, "Mutuality in Mission," a program that had been approved in principle by the 26th General Council of 1974,[78] was presented along with the "Dual Mandate" in 1977. Mutuality in Mission was a program of exchanging people from global partners to learn from one another. In the process of "receiving" people in the years between 1976 and 1977 from various countries such as Zambia and Burma, the Division of Mission in Canada and DWO collaborated to implement the program. It was hoped that this action of interdivisional work would be reflected in the life and work of the UCC at the levels of the congregations, presbyteries, and conferences.[79]

Since the *World Mission* report in 1966, partnership has continued to be the central expression of mission of the UCC. In this mutually respectful relationship with global partner churches, the UCC carried out its mandate to participate in God's mission of doing justice in an unjust world. The mission was practised by acting in solidarity with global partners to support Christian witness in the world and, at the same time, by raising the consciousness of Canadian people about social justice issues, and by acting together to challenge them.

"Mutual Empowerment through the Sharing of Gifts": Seeking to Understand "Partnership" for God's Mission Today (1988)

In 1981, the newly established China Christian Council invited a Canadian delegation of seventeen, including Hockin, to visit China for the first time after the years of painful alienation among Chinese and Canadian Christians. Through this reconnection, which allowed her to listen to and hold many conversations with her Chinese hosts, Hockin raised this very insightful question: "How can we share the more profound gifts of joy, suffering, relationship, and prayer?"[80] At a time when Canadian Christians' understanding of mission was generally limited to sharing material resources such as funding, personnel, or management, again she took her new learning with her as she encountered Chinese Christians who had walked a different path from that taken by Western Christians over the last few decades.

How can two Christian communities share each other's gifts beyond a material sense? The meaning of partnership was reflected in the DWO statement of 1988, "Seeking to Understand 'Partnership' for God's Mission Today" (hereafter *Partnership*). There were two urgent reasons for the adoption of this statement by the 32nd General Council in 1988. First, the DWO identified the need for clarity about the meaning of partnership in the policy document of "Dual Mandate" from 1977; it was recognized that there was a communication gap between the DWO and the denomination as a whole that made it difficult to attain understanding, commitment, and supportive action from the church.[81] Second, the "Ecumenical Sharing of Resources" document of the WCC, popularly known as *El Escorial* and produced through a consultation with participants from around the world in El Escorial, Spain, in 1987, was having a strong impact on the DWO's reflection on partnership. A new understanding of sharing based on the structure of justice, mutual accountability, and mutual involvement in decision making at all levels—regional, national, and international—was being proposed to General Council.[82]

The 1988 *Partnership* statement emphasizes two major points: it defines partnership in relation to God's mission (*missio Dei*) and suggests a development of the concept of partnership to that of companionship.[83] First, the foundation of the statement is that the mission is God's: it is God who is working in the world. This missiological basis, adopted in *World Mission*, is clearly expressed: "In fact our partnership is not primarily in the life and work of our partners. It is rather a partnership *with* God in God's mission."[84] As Christians are called to be partners with God in God's mission, they also meet with others who are partners with God. Therefore, partnership is not primarily the bilateral relationship between two churches, but the meeting of partners of God. In God's mission, primary responsibility for mission in any particular place belongs to the people of that place, but not all the gifts needed for the fulfillment of mission are necessarily found in that place. Here is the definition of partnership:

Partnership means becoming involved with others in God's mission for whole-ness of life especially on behalf of the poor and powerless. Partnership brings people together in community for mutual empowerment through the shar-ing of gifts recognized as gifts freely given by God for the benefit of all, not possessions which some may control. We need the gifts our partners can share with us. They have gifts of spiritual and theological insight, of faithfulness in witness, the experience of costly discipleship.[85]

Partnership emphasizes the mutual sharing of gifts between partner churches rather than giving from one church to the other. In the practice of God's mission, the gifts needed for the fulfillment of mission are found throughout all the participants. The UCC had been sharing its gifts with its partners, but not always recognizing the contributions made by the mis-sion partners, particularly when the gifts were considered only in a material sense. For example, the contributions of persons sent by global partners in recognition of "Mutuality in Mission" had been noted from the 1970s, but the challenge was to identify ways in which global partners contrib-uted their significant gifts for mission in the UCC context.[86] In this effort to understand the implications of partnership for God's mission, part-ner churches' contributions were expressed as spiritual gifts, theological insights, faithfulness in witness, and the experience of costly discipleship, all of which carry a higher value than material gifts.[87]

Further, upon reconnection with Chinese Christians in 1981, Hockin was beginning to experience the limations of the concept of partnership. Let's hear her words:

Our Canadian church proposes a dual mandate; *doing mission and doing justice*. This mandate is an entirely faithful priority in recognition of what are Canadian priorities in relationship with partner churches in many areas of the world. But it does mean a continuing role of being the initiators in promoting justice or advocating solidarity. Being initiators, however, we are again faced with the insidious temptation to slip into a "management role," even while we are committed to the idea of "partnership."[88]

Elsewhere, in the 32nd General Council report of the DWO in 1986, Hockin proposed a missiological shift from a partnership model to a model of companionship:

Indeed the time may be ripe to shift from our emphasis on "partners," with its overload of business and operational connotations, to a term like "companions," with its implications of warm, active friendship. The companional model is, after all, the ideal we strive for, even though we know from experience how hard it is to achieve where two friends are sharing very unequal resources.… Working together toward a common vision we *can* sometimes, perhaps often, simply take pleasure in each other's company and be happy together in our common faith.[89]

Based on this growing voice for a new concept of relationship in the practice of mission, the UCC proposed the concept of "companion" for its image of journeying together in God's mission in this ever-more-interdependent global village world.[90] Companionship was lifted up as a way of fulfilling the mission of God for the wholeness of life for all, particularly on behalf of the poor and powerless. Even though the *Partnership* statement offered a new understanding of the relationships with global partners, it did not get much attention at the General Council in 1988 because the debate about the UCC's openness to ordered ministry of gay and lesbian persons dominated the Council.

Ten years after the adoption of *Partnership*, the UCC issued the "Gender Justice and Partnership Guidelines" initiated by the DWO in 1998. Continuing the work of the WCC Ecumenical Decade of the Churches in Solidarity with Women in Church and Society, and to advance systemic justice, the DWO promoted gender justice as one of the most fundamental ways to transform structures and systems consistent with the realization of God's vision for humanity and creation.[91] The "Gender Justice and Partnership Guidelines" were intended to be used to strengthen relationships between Canadians and the UCC's global partners, and to facilitate further the dialogue with partners on how to develop goals and strategies that promote gender justice. The UCC expressed its commitment to gender justice to enhance the practice of partnership/companionship in a world context of gender injustice.

"Toward a Whole-World Ecumenism": *Mending the World* (1997)

After the General Council's approval in 1988 of the *Partnership* statement, the Executive of General Council launched the "Ecumenical Agenda Research Project" (EARP) to determine future ecumenical directions for the UCC. In the process of fulfilling its mandate, the Inter-Church and Inter-Faith Committee (ICIF) interviewed dozens of people across the country and examined the literature on ecumenism. It found a clear message that the world was in trouble and that the churches should join with peoples of goodwill to work together in the common task of peace, justice, and the healing of God's creation.[92] The EARP's report of its findings became the ICIF report "Toward a Renewed Understanding of Ecumenism" (hereafter TRUE), to the 34th General Council in 1992, but it was returned to the committee for further work.[93] Despite the quality of TRUE, some commissioners of General Council, perhaps in reaction to the 1988 decision about ordination and sexual orientation, wanted to affirm a statement about the "centrality of Christ."[94] General Council recommended that ICIF further consult *World Mission*, since that "report has been and is part of an ongoing process of study and discernment."[95] It may be pondered how another report to be produced in 1997, *Mending the World: An Ecumenical Vision for Healing and Reconciling*, would incorporate the affirmation and recommendations of a General Council that wanted to affirm a world-centred approach on ecumenism over a Christ-centred one. After all, *World Mission* had already moved beyond a Christ-centred perspective. In effect, the General Council mandated that both approaches, the centrality of Christ and world ecumenism, be reflected in the ICIF report.

The affirmations and recommendations of General Council are reflected in the document reported to the 36th General Council in 1997, "Mending the World." This report on ecumenism and mission asked how the UCC related to other denominations and faith communities. In "Theological Foundations," a lengthy part of the report, Jesus is described as *representative* of humanity, God, and the whole creation.[96] Jesus, as the mediator between God and the world, brings healing and reconciliation. The UCC's ecumenical imperative to participate in God's work with others of goodwill is derived from a Christ-centred perspective. The report notes that it uses a "representative model" of Christology.[97] This approach resembles the "fulfillment model," since, in it, Jesus clearly embodies and represents the fullness of God's saving love and truth.[98] Behind this approach is the mandate of the 1992 General Council to affirm the saving significance of Jesus.

"Mending the World" may be read as an apologetic not only for those who claim a traditional understanding of atonement, but also for those who take an "inclusive" or "pluralistic" understanding as a comprehensive approach to world ecumenism. "Mending the World" recognizes a variety of voices in the church and embraces them as a "significant issue for Christians in the new ecumenical setting" in which Christology must be articulated in a religiously pluralistic world.[99] "Mending the World" echoes the *World Mission* statement that "God is creatively and redemptively at work in the religious life of all mankind."[100] At the same time, it also uses the concept "share[d] concern" with reference to working collaboratively with others for the common good.[101] To the question of how the ucc should work with other denominations and faith communities, "Mending the World" answers that the church should work in partnership and through interfaith dialogue with others. It named this approach "whole world ecumenism."[102] The intent was to shift the paradigm from a traditional church-centred to a world-centred approach that includes "other religious traditions, ideologies and secular agencies."[103] This expanded approach appears to adopt the main thrust of *World Mission*—to work with others out of a shared concern for justice.

"Mending the World" embraces partnership as the "key concept in whole world ecumenism."[104] Partnership continues to serve the church's ecumenism and mission practice based on mutuality and collaboration among religious communities and secular organizations. It is interesting, therefore, to read in the dwo's review of "Mending the World," that the title "sounds paternalistic to us. How about 'Making Common Cause to Mend the Brokenness'?"[105] The dwo hoped that the essence of the report would reflect the practice of ecumenism and mission, but the title sounds like an old paradigm of mission. Perhaps the dwo wanted to affirm that the church's mission was based on mutuality at work for a common cause, even though "Mending the World" had reflected this motivation for mission. The ucc's latest statement on missiology reinterprets *World Mission* in the context of structural injustice such as globalization and the crisis of faith found in the "institutional preoccupation" of the church to promote a shared concern for all.[106] To fulfill this mission, the ucc is seeking ways to work together with whoever shares the concern to meet the new challenges of the day.

Conclusion: God's Unending Mission

Change in the theology of overseas mission throughout the history of the ucc was initiated by challenges from church constituencies in Canada, from global partner churches and agencies, and from overseas personnel. The ucc responded faithfully to meet the challenges. Some members of the ucc may wonder why its overseas mission policies were more progressive than those of mission within Canada.[107] Many missionaries including Scott and Hockin, far from seeing the cultures of overseas partners as superstitions and thus condemned, wrote of the values of other cultures, and particularly of the courage of global partners to be faithful in the sometimes difficult situations in which they lived.[108] Indeed, some, in learning to respect the peoples and cultures with whom they lived and worked, used their professional skills to research those cultures.[109] They brought their learnings back to Canada and contributed to the creation and reformation of mission policy. Overseas missionaries were located in the in-between spaces between Canada and the global partners in whose missions they worked. They carried out their tasks by going in-between, building bridges between them. This involved a dynamic of social power relationships different from that of colonization—the sharing of power in respectful mutual relations with each other.

It took several decades for the UCC to overcome a colonial approach to mission overseas. There was a reluctance to give up the inherited power in mission and embrace the concept of partnership with global partners in God's mission, understanding that power and accountability are shared by all participants in mission. Since 1966, partnership has continued to be the principal policy conceptualization for the UCC, yet some global partners and members of the denomination have struggled to understand its meaning.[110] In spite of the explanation in the *Partnership* document, the concept still seems too narrowly confined to the sharing of material resources;[111] its business-like language suggests a bilateral relationship between two parties, rather than an attentiveness to God's mission as a participant with many global partners. While the intention of mission expressed as partnership was to move away from a colonial legacy, that legacy still lingers as a way of representing mission as service to and helping needy global partners.

The UCC's developing theology of mission has also borne fruit through its influence on the church's later faith statements. For example, we hear a different voice in *A Song of Faith* when it sings, "We participate in God's work of healing and mending creation" in seeking "right relationship with each other and with God." This latest statement of faith by the UCC sings God's mission as it strives for just relations with all people and all creatures as kin. To participate in God's mission and develop a new missiology reflecting an ever-changing context the UCC would do well to heed *World Mission*, which recommends "that the church should be prepared constantly to adapt both its organization and its programme to meet new opportunities and changing needs and conditions."[112] It suggests persistent dialogue with contemporary theology, with the rapidly changing context of the world, and with the UCC's history to develop a missiology for this time and place. On this journey of participating in God's mission, missiologist Hockin offers words of encouragement: "[Even] when the goals of justice are gained, the mission will not end."[113]

NOTES

1 See Khushwant Singh, *A History of the Sikhs*, vol. 2: *1839–1964* (Princeton, NJ: Princeton University Press, 1966), 168–69.

2 William Scott, *Canadians in Korea: Brief Historical Sketch of Canadian Mission Work in Korea* (Toronto: BWM, UCC, 1975), 232. See Hyuk Cho, "Partnership in Mission: William Scott's Ministry in Korea," *Touchstone* 31, no. 1 (February 2013): 57–66.

3 Jesse H. Arnup, *A New Church Faces a New World* (Toronto: UCPH, 1937), 97.

4 David J. Bosch, *Transforming Mission: Paradigm Shifts in Theology of Mission* (Maryknoll, NY: Orbis Books, 1991), 320–34, 341–49.

5 T.B. Kilpatrick, *Our Common Faith* (Toronto: Ryerson Press, 1928), 94–95.

6 UCC, "Report of the Special Committee on Policy," *Proceedings*, GC7, 1936, 238–304.

7 Annual allocations to the Board out of the Missionary and Maintenance Fund from 1928 to 1936 are as follows:

Year	Allocations	MMF
1928	$1,020,000	$2,885,929
1929	1,003,000	2,696,710
1930	830,000	2,721,269
1931	800,000	2,405,326
1932	681,000	1,864,355
1933	457,750	1,713,856
1934	458,500	1,585,167
1935	445,000	1,632,610
1936	417,000	1,559,008

BFM, "The Crisis in Foreign Missions" (Toronto: UCC, 1936), 1, and Scott, *Canadians in Korea*, 133.

8 BFM, "The Crisis in Foreign Missions," 1. The missionary force had been reduced by 20 percent, salaries of secretaries and missionaries reduced by 25 percent, grants to the mission fields reduced or entirely cut off, and the number of native workers in the mission field greatly reduced. During the years 1932 to 1935, the BFM drew heavily on their reserve funds, and as a result by 1935 the funds were exhausted. The mission fields had to go through the painful decision-making process of withdrawing missionary families due to a lack of funds. In the Korean mission field, for example, four missionary families had to leave. See Scott, *Canadians in Korea*, 133–34.

9 BFM, "The Crisis in Foreign Missions," 2.

10 The recommendation of the Policy Committee was accepted by the BFM

and grants to the fields correspondingly reduced, approximately on a percentage basis.

11 UCC, "Report of the Special Committee on Policy," *Proceedings*, GC7, 1936, 238.

12 Ibid., 251.

13 Ibid., 252.

14 Presbyterian Church in Canada, *The Acts and Proceedings of the Forty-Ninth General Assembly of the Presbyterian Church in Canada* (Toronto, 1923), 65–66. The 1922 Report of the BFM declared that the mission objective was to develop an indigenous and independent church. "The future of the Churches in the Orient is to be in the near future in their own keeping. The missionary must abdicate and find his place, not any longer as master or ruler but as helper and fellow-worker on equal terms, which will it is hoped contribute to the cultivation of Christian brotherhood and to a more rapid development and upon right and enduring lines.… It has been an objective of all Mission Boards that [at] the earliest date possible the Native Church should become self-controlling, self-propagating and self-supporting" (65).

15 Frank H. Russell, *New Days in Old India* (Toronto: Ryerson Press, 1926).

16 See Presbyterian Church in Canada, *The Acts and Proceedings* (Toronto, 1923), 65.

17 Russell, *New Days in Old India*, 136. Some Indian leaders claimed that the only mission work that can be carried out by people from the West is that in subordination to the Indian church and under its full direction and control.

18 George C. Pidgeon, "The Message and Mission of the United Church of Canada," Layman's Conference (Massey Hall, October 7, 1928), 20–21, UCA, 86.243C, box 52-2072.

19 UCC, *Proceedings*, GC7, 1936, 254.

20 UCC, *Proceedings*, GC7, 1936, 247–51.

21 Ibid., 249.

22 Phyllis D. Airhart indicates that difficult questions were raised about the Anglo-Saxon form of nationalism unwittingly spread by the early missionary movement in the West. Phyllis D. Airhart, *A Church with the Soul of a Nation: Making and Remaking the United Church of Canada* (Montreal and Kingston: McGill-Queen's University Press, 2014), 86.

23 Robert Wright, *A World Mission: Canadian Protestantism and the Quest for a New International Order, 1918–1938* (Montreal and Kingston: McGill-Queen's University Press, 1991), 144–45.

24 UCC, "Article XX: Of Christian Service and Final Triumph," BOU.

25 UCC, *Proceedings*, GC7, 1936, 246. Cf. 1925 "Doctrine," Article VI, Of the Grace of God: "We believe that God, out of His great love for the world, has given

His only begotten Son to be the Saviour of sinners, and in the Gospel freely offers His all-sufficient salvation to all men."

26 Ibid., 247–51 and 288–89. David Bosch, *Transforming Mission*, 480, also indicates that the "one Truth" to which it referred was the statement about the Christian faith of the Jerusalem Conference.

27 On this see Robert C. Fennell's discussion of Dow's work in chapter 2 of this volume.

28 UCC, *Proceedings*, GC7, 1936, 288.

29 Ibid., 289.

30 Ibid., 250. IMC's Jerusalem Conference discusses a new relationship and a concept of partnership between the older and younger churches: "The younger churches can serve the older at their home base by giving them a fresh inspiration and new interpretation of the Christian message through such means as deputations." This quotation is found in IMC, *The World Mission of Christianity; Messages and Recommendations of the Enlarged Meeting of the International Missionary Council held at Jerusalem, March 24–April 8, 1928* (New York/London: IMC, 1928), 34.

31 UCC, *Proceedings*, GC7, 1936, 250.

32 Jesse H. Arnup, secretary of the BFM, asserts that even though the United Church cannot be called a world power, it has a wholesome contact and helpful fellowship with its global mission partners. See Arnup, *A New Church Faces a New World*, 241.

33 Ibid., 251.

34 See "Article XX: Of Christian Service and Final Triumph," *BOU*, and "VII: the Church," *Statement*.

35 In 1944, General Council changed the name of the BFM to the Board of Overseas Missions.

36 One of the aims and objectives of the WMS was "to unite all the women of the Church for the World Mission of Christianity; to provide missionary education for children, teen-age girls and young women; to encourage study, prayer and giving on behalf of Christian Missions at home and abroad." WMS, *Manual for Missionaries* (Toronto: UCC, 1950), 5.

37 For example, in the 1940s a WMS-appointed medical doctor, Dr. Florence Murray, worked in a medical school and hospital operated by the BOM. Florence Murray, *At the Foot of Dragon Hill* (New York: E.P. Dutton, 1975).

38 UCC, "Overseas Missions," *Proceedings*, GC17, 1956, 80.

39 UCC, "Committee on Integration of Overseas Mission Work," *Proceedings*, GC20, 1958, 56.

40 UCC, "On the Integration of the Administration of the Overseas Work of the

Woman's Missionary Society and the Board of Overseas Missions, *Proceedings*, GC20, 1958, 226.

41 UCC, "The Work of Women in the Church," *Proceedings*, GC20, 1958, 214.

42 Donna Sinclair, *Crossing Worlds: The Story of the Women's Missionary Society of the United Church of Canada* (Toronto: UCC, 1992), 114.

43 At its integration the BWM stated that "to accomplish its mission today, the Board must use new methods and must work in conjunction with other Churches." UCC, "Board of World Mission," *Proceedings*, GC17, 1962, 298.

44 Ibid.

45 UCC, *World Mission: Report of the Commission on World Mission* (Toronto: UCC, 1966), 3.

46 UCC, *World Mission*, 16.

47 Ibid., 15.

48 Ibid., 18–20.

49 Ibid., 24. It was agreed that Katharine Hockin would write the section on the social, political, and economic context of mission titled, "Revolutionary Changes in the Twentieth Century Challenging Conventional Approaches to Missions." UCA, United Church of Canada General Council Committees Collection fonds, Records of the Commission on World Mission, 82.124C box 1, file 10, 1965.

50 UCC, *World Mission*, 38. There was a discussion about partnership between the older and younger churches at the IMC Jerusalem Conference in 1928; however, it received particular emphasis at Whitby, 1947.

51 See also John Dow, *This Is Our Faith: An Exposition of the Statement of Faith of the United Church of Canada* (Toronto: BESS, 1943), 145.

52 UCC, *World Mission*, 38. The BWM had a direct relationship with the autonomous church in each area; the Board sent the missionary in response to the request of the partner church; financial grants also were made in response to requests; and Block Grants to partner churches were based on their budgets and the Unified Budget Fund. All of the above reflect the effort to not make decisions for other churches or exercise control over them.

53 Ibid., 137.

54 Ibid.

55 Among the countries with which the UCC already had relationships were Trinidad (1868), Angola (1881), and Zambia (1953); in the early 1960s the UCC's mission relationships also expanded into Asian countries such as Nepal and the Philippines.

56 UCC, *World Mission*, 124.

57 W.C. Smith, *Patterns of Faith around the World* (Oxford: Oneworld, 1998; first

published in 1962 under the title *The Faith of Other Men: The Christians in a Religiously Plural World*).

58 UCC, *World Mission*, 24.

59 Ibid., 25.

60 Minutes of General Council Executive, November 5, 1968, UCA 82.001C, 3.

61 UCC, *World Mission*, 43–57.

62 Ibid., 43. The concept of *missio Dei* first emerged at the IMC in Willingen, Germany, in 1952. The UCC had adopted the concept of *missio Dei* before the WCC published two reports, *The Church for Others* and *The Church for the World* (Geneva: WCC, 1967).

63 UCC, *World Mission*, 128.

64 C. Douglas Jay, "World Mission and World Civilization" (Toronto: BWM, 1967).

65 UCC, *World Mission*, 135.

66 In this chapter the word faith denotes a system of religious belief or belief in God.

67 UCC, *World Mission*, 54.

68 Hyuk Cho, "Sharing Concern for Justice: Becoming an Intercultural Church as a Postcolonial Mission Practice in the Canadian Context of Integrative Multiculturalism" (Th.D diss., Toronto School of Theology, 2017), 125.

69 See UCC, *Proceedings*, GC26, 1974, 226–35.

70 UCC, *Proceedings*, GC26, 1974, 79, and *Proceedings*, GC27, 1977, 156.

71 Katharine Hockin, "My Pilgrimage in Mission," *International Bulletin of Missionary Research* (January 1988): 30.

72 UCC, *Proceedings*, GC27, 1977, 156. The mission policy of "Dual Mandate" was based on DWO General Secretary Garth W. Legge's focus on the concept of solidarity. The goal of the "Dual Mandate" was "raising the awareness of our own church members in understanding the implications of doing mission and doing justice in the Canadian context and at a congregational level."

73 UCC, *Proceedings*, GC27, 1977, 350.

74 Ibid., 379. The two goals of doing mission were: Goal 1: to maintain and extend the network of relationships and patterns of co-operative work with churches and Christian agencies outside Canada in evangelism, agriculture, medicine, education, etc.; Goal 2: to develop community through dialogue with people of other faiths within and beyond Canada.

75 Doing Mission and Doing Justice are not meant to be understood as separate polarities. Doing mission means doing justice and doing that together with partners.

76 UCC, *Proceedings*, GC27, 1977, 380.

77 Ibid., 352–53.

78 UCC, *Proceedings*, GC26, 1974, 137. Mutuality in Mission was a joint action of the DMC and the DWO.

79 UCC, *Proceedings*, GC27, 1977, 350. The concept of mutuality here, however, should not be confused with the "mutuality"—shared concern—discussed in *World Mission* 1966. Here, Mutuality in Mission is a program to deepen the understanding of the concept of partnership.

80 Katharine Hockin, "From 'Church to the World' to 'Church for the World,'" in *A New Beginning; An International Dialogue with the Chinese Church*, ed. Theresa Chu and Christopher Lind (Montreal: Canada China Programme of the Canadian Council of Churches, 1983), 126. Hockin served as a member of the DWO executive and its various committees from 1972 to 1988.

81 UCC, *Proceedings*, GC32, 1988, 597.

82 Ibid., 616. The document, "The World Consultation on Resource Sharing, El Escorial, 24–31 October 1987, Guidelines for Sharing" is attached to the DWO Report in UCC, *Proceedings*, GC32, 1988, 616–21.

83 For the concept of companionship, especially through the work of Katharine Hockin, see JungHee Park, "Mission as Companionship: Towards a Theology of Mission for the Diakonia of the United Church of Canada," *Toronto Journal of Theology* 25, no. 2 (2009): 257–74.

84 UCC, *Proceedings*, GC32, 1988, 615; italics in original.

85 Ibid., 616.

86 Rhea M. Whitehead, "Gift and Challenge" (unpublished, 1995), 4.

87 UCC, *Proceedings*, GC32, 1988, 616.

88 Katharine Hockin, "Some Random Missiological Musings," *China Notes* (Winter 1983–1984): 281; italics in original.

89 UCC, "DWO Theological Task Force 'Popular Statement,'" *Proceedings*, GC31, 1986, 611–12 italics in original. For an abridgement of its previous statement, see "Looking Forward in Mission in the Mid-Eighties" and a "Popular Statement" written by Katharine Hockin and edited by Pat Wells. UCA, DWO fonds, Secretary's records, 504/1, 92.150C, box 4, file 2.

90 UCC, "Seeking to Understand 'Partnership' for God's Mission Today," GC32, 1988, 615.

91 UCC, "Gender Justice and Partnership Guidelines, DWO (1998), 1–3.

92 ICIF, "Toward a Renewed Understanding of Ecumenism" (Toronto: UCC, 1992), 1.

93 The main concept of ecumenism in "Toward a Renewed Understanding of Ecumenism" reappears in "Mending the World."

94 UCC, *Proceedings*, GC34, 1992, 75.

95 Ibid.

96 ICIF, "Mending the World," 13–19.

97 Ibid., 13fn1.

98 This model concedes the presence of God in other religious traditions in which revelation and grace are experienced, but claims they are enhanced when Jesus, as the representative of God, enriches them, since all salvation is finally through Christ.

99 ICIF, "Mending the World," 17.

100 Ibid., 20.

101 Ibid., 21.

102 Ibid., 3–4.

103 Ibid., 3. The shift was suggested by the ICIF in 1992 in its discussion paper "Toward a Renewed Understanding of Ecumenism." See UCC, *Proceedings*, GC34, 1992, 287.

104 ICIF, "Mending the World," 21.

105 DWO, "Sessional Committee 'D': 'Mending the World,'" undated paper.

106 ICIF, "Mending the World," 3.

107 Loraine MacKenzie Shepherd, "From Colonization to Right Relations: The Evolution of United Church of Canada Missions within Aboriginal Communities," *International Review of Mission* 103, no. 1 (April 2014): 153.

108 Scott respected Korean religions such as Shamanism, Taoism, Buddhism, and Confucianism that formed the basis of Korean culture. See Scott, *Canadians in Korea*. As a teacher (1934–37) at Ahousaht Residential School, BC, Hockin noted the church's blindness and careless abuse of native culture, dismissing it as pagan or heathen, and its goals to assimilate the Nootka into white culture. See Sinclair, *Crossing Worlds*, 52.

109 Marion Pope, for example, studied the "Influence of the Traditional Korean Childbearing Culture on Breast Feeding" and introduced graduate nursing courses in Korean Nursing Philosophy to challenge her students to develop culturally appropriate nursing theory and practice.

110 UCC, "Reviewing Partnership in the Context of Empire" (Toronto: UCC, 2009), 17–23.

111 Ibid., 19–25. The participants of the consultation understood that the concept of partnership is often reduced to money issues even when framed in the context of mutual sharing of all kinds of resources.

112 UCC, *World Mission*, 136

113 Hockin, "My Pilgrimage in Mission," 30.

CHAPTER ELEVEN

THE UNITED CHURCH'S MISSION WORK WITHIN CANADA AND ITS IMPACT ON INDIGENOUS AND ETHNIC MINORITY COMMUNITIES

Loraine MacKenzie Shepherd

The United Church of Canada inherited well-established mission work through its Methodist, Presbyterian, and Congregational predecessors. They each brought into union a historical commitment to missions both overseas and within the Dominion of Canada. In this chapter, I will explore the UCC's theological rationale for home missions and will contrast its policies with those of foreign missions. My primary lens of inquiry is the impact of mission upon Indigenous people and ethnic minorities in Canada. I will begin with a brief overview of the types of home mission work practised.

Practice of Mission

UCC mission work was first administered by the Board of Home Missions (BHM), the Board of Evangelism and Social Service (BESS), and the Board of Christian Education. Their responsibilities lay within five primary areas: education, health care, community service, church development, and mission education. Colleges and universities were established. Day schools and residential schools were administered for First Nations and ethnic minority children. Grants and loans were given for new church buildings. UCC hospitals and medical clinics were set up in isolated communities across the country. The best-known UCC medical missions were offered on the west coast by the Thomas Crosby boat, which served isolated First Nations and fishing communities, as well as lighthouse families.

The UCC founded and staffed homes for older women and maternity homes. Inner-city missions, such as the All Peoples Missions, offered social services and ministries to ethnic minority communities. Many of these later evolved into the UCC's current community ministries. In 1925, the All

Peoples' Missions operated in five cities and two rural communities, and welcomed all people, including "Italians, Bulgarians, Finns, Magyars, East Indians, Doukhobours, and Hebrews" to hear the Gospel of Christ without prejudice of race.[1] The presumption was that everyone, regardless of race or religion, was welcome to join the evangelical Protestant mission, but only upon profession of the Christian faith.

Port ministries were established on the east coast to welcome and support "the Stranger" arriving by boat from Europe. The port chaplains kept careful records of the racial and ethnic identity of all immigrants and, where possible, directed each group of immigrants to their own religious communities.

"Indian Missions" were supported across the country and often included the dispensing of medicine and education as part of their ministry. BHM noted that Indigenous peoples were at first wary of Western medicine, preferring their traditional medicine, but by the mid-1930s there was "general acceptance of the help medical science brings to them."[2]

Much of this work was supported by the Woman's Missionary Society, which also conducted its own mission work running hospitals, school homes for Indigenous and ethnic minority children, community programs, and ministries to new immigrants.[3] The Woman's Association raised funds for both local congregations and mission work. In 1962, the WMS and the WA joined to form the United Church Women, which continued both the fundraising emphasis of the WA and the missionary work and educational programs of the WMS.

Early UCC mission work also included advocacy and education on moral and ethical issues such as preserving the Lord's Day; furthering the temperance movement; clarifying the meaning and responsibilities of Christian marriage; issuing statements against gambling, economic exploitation, poverty, racism, and capital punishment; and supporting national broadcasting, a national health care system, organized labour, and international peace and disarmament. These areas were later expanded to include issues such as violence against women, pornography, sexism, homophobia, environmental degradation, colonialism, and empire building. In 1930, the UCC affirmed a *Statement of Principles*, which included equal rights and justice for all, the right to continuous and sustaining employment, a living wage as well as a social wage, safe working conditions, the reduction of working hours, and at least one day off a week. The *Statement* also advocated assistance for families in need; support to rural communities; land use for food, raw materials, and homes rather than for speculation; national health insurance; and unemployment insurance.[4]

Funding for UCC mission work came largely from two sources: fundraising from the UCW groups, as described above, and donations to the unified fund for mission work. Originally, this fund was called the Maintenance and Extension Fund, but in 1928 the UCC changed the name to the Mission and Maintenance Fund to better reflect its support for mission. In 1968, after a restructuring of the General Council offices that combined stewardship and revenue generation into one unit, the fund's name was changed once again to the Mission and Service Fund. This last name change was intended to better reflect the purpose of the fund. The unified nature of the Mission and Service Fund encourages donors to give to the overall mission of the church at home and in the world. This allows the administrators the freedom to distribute funds according to need and to the priorities set by the General Council units. This has not been without controversy. When church members have been upset with General Council decisions, they have sometimes boycotted the Mission and Service Fund to protest. This was particularly the case when Mission and Service Fund money was used to fund the studies on sexual orientation. Many churches indicated their opposition to General Council decisions concerning sexuality by withholding their pledges to the Mission and Service Fund.

Motivation for Mission

[O]nly through ... harmony with the will of God shall be fulfilled that brotherhood of man wherein the Kingdom of God is to be made manifest.
   —*Twenty Articles of Doctrine*, Article 2.3.14, "Of the Law of God"

According to the *Basis of Union*'s doctrinal section, the church's missional purpose is to further the Kingdom of God on this earth by proclaiming the gospel of Christ and promoting kinship among all peoples. These *Twenty Articles of Doctrine* represented the evangelical position of its time that recognized Jesus Christ as the only mediator between God and humanity. At the same time, they offered a liberal understanding of revelation: although God is perfectly revealed only through Jesus Christ, a general revelation of God can be found in nature, history, human hearts, and in holy people of God. This latter was in particular reference to the prophets of the Old Testament, giving a nod to revelation found within the Jewish tradition. The *Twenty Articles of Doctrine* also supported the modern belief in progress, assuming that the kingdoms of the world were slowly becoming aligned with the values of the Kingdom of God.

Christianizing the Social Order

Initially, the overall theological rationale of UCC mission was to share the good news of Jesus throughout all lands. By the time of union, this motivation had acquired a dual purpose: redemption of the individual and redemption of society. The UCC was committed to this dual emphasis so as to avoid "an evangelism lacking in moral vigour [or] a programme of social service divorced from deep religious incentive."[5] This commitment was rooted in a post-millennialist theology, based on a belief that Christ was working through the church to gradually usher in the Kingdom of God on earth.[6] It was assumed that the Spirit would shape the hearts of Christians so that they would naturally seek a higher moral standard for themselves and for the world. The more Christian converts the church made, the sooner the Kingdom of God would be fully realized throughout the world.[7] The church acknowledged that individual conversion was not enough. Also needed was the exertion of a Christianizing influence on the governing structures to help institute a higher moral and social standard in society.

The 1930 *Statement of Principles*, mentioned above, formed the basis of the 1934 *Report of the Commission on Christianizing the Social Order*.[8] This commission gave the UCC a mandate to create a national conscience within the Dominion of Canada.[9] In other words, its task was to Christianize the social order so as to help establish the Kingdom of God on earth.[10] To Christianize the social order meant to apply "the principles of the Gospel of Jesus to the economic, political, social, and moral relations of life."[11] However, the term *Christianize* was also used in reference to conversion, such as the mission goal to "Christianize the Orientals on the Pacific Coast."[12] A report on evangelism, issued in 1934, defined the term *Christianization* as "the re-organization of life on a Christian basis."[13]

One of the assumptions underlying the Christianization of the social order was the progress of modernity. Although the world had just emerged from the First World War, the most destructive war that it had yet known, Western nations had not lost faith in modern progress. The Allied and Associated Powers were able to declare victoriously that they had won the war to end all wars. This optimistic outlook carried over into the Western churches. They believed that the world was still in various stages of openness to the "civilizing influence" of the gospel. The UCC, in particular, believed that the civilizing influence of the gospel included a call for the abolition of national armaments.[14] BESS spoke strongly of the futility of war and reports to General Council denounced war as contrary to the mind of Christ.[15]

Peace and justice were at the heart of UCC mission, and there was some urgency to it. Fascism was mounting, and the 1928 General Council urgently called the members of the UCC to a renewal of faith and mission. It believed that its mission work was crucial to world peace.[16] "Race prejudice" was understood as a significant block to peace within Canada as well as within the world.[17] Racism and fear contributed to blatant discrimination and violence. On the prairies this was manifested, in part, through the Ku Klux Klan, which targeted Eastern European and Roman Catholic communities and whose membership included UCC ministers and congregants.[18]

Apart from some individual UCC participants in the KKK, the UCC officially condemned racism in general and spoke out strongly against the rising tide of anti-Semitism in the 1930s. From its inception, the UCC made clear statements against racism, believing that all people, regardless of race, should be treated equally. One of the manifestations of the Kingdom of God was a "brotherhood of men" without distinction. Because the UCC understood itself to be a national church of Canada, it believed that its mission included responsibility for the well-being of all Canadian immigrants, regardless of ethnic or religious identity, especially if minority ethnic groups were not supported by their own religious communities. BHM stated "the United Church of Canada as the latest expression of Canadian Christianity has a definite responsibility for every community, Anglo-Saxon and non-Anglo-Saxon, of Canadian people not adequately provided for spiritually or morally by any other religious body."[19] The term "brotherhood of man" was used frequently to indicate the depth of caring relationships that the UCC sought to develop among all the nations of the world.

In alignment with its concern for the welfare of all races in the Dominion of Canada, the UCC was also attentive to the situation of the First Nations. Status Indians were deprived of Canadian citizenship, voting rights, self-governance, freedom of movement, and economic opportunity. As wards of the state, Indigenous people were particularly affected by the economic depression of the 1930s because they were not allowed to supplement their lower fur, grain, or fish prices with off-reserve work. They had no option but to depend upon government relief.[20] BHM protested this forced economic dependency of Status Indians.[21]

In spite of the UCC's pronouncements against racism, BHM's immigration reports stated a preference for Anglo-Saxon Protestants and expressed dismay when the number of British immigrants began to decline as Eastern European immigration increased. The UCC reports do not give any indication that their dismay might have strengthened the very discrimination against ethnic minorities that they were denouncing. There were also mixed messages in the UCC's statements against anti-Semitism because they actively encouraged evangelistic mission work to the Jews.[22] While the UCC supported the human rights and equal treatment of the Jews, it also worked for their conversion to Christianity.

Evangelism

Evangelism was a key component of mission work and the Christianization of the social order. However, even in the early life of the UCC there was significant disagreement over its meaning and implementation. For this reason, BESS was asked to write a statement about evangelism. The 1934 statement clarified what it did not support. It contrasted its own position with that of Roman Catholics and Unitarians. It also distanced itself from the Evangelical movement, which rejected the scientific view of the world and upheld an ahistorical interpretation of Scripture, a rigid moral code indifferent to one's culture, and a personal faith that spurned social obligation. Instead, the UCC statement on evangelism proclaimed Good News for the whole person in relationship with others.

The 1934 statement on evangelism distinguished between evangelism and evangelization, both of which were considered necessary aspects to the overall evangelistic mandate. Evangelism referred to "an emphasis on the preaching of Christ's atoning death, and faith in the same as bringing Forgiveness of Sins."[23] The object of evangelism was to encourage acceptance of the message of the gospel that would enable personal redemption. Redemption was indicated by a person's "re-organization of life" and their alignment of behaviour and thought with Christian morals and values. Because of the UCC's link between acceptance of the Good News and a lifestyle in accord with Christian standards, this understanding of evangelism was also called "Christianization."

The second aspect to the evangelistic mandate was called evangelization and referred to the "territorial expansion of the mission of the church." This provided a theological justification for colonization and empire building, even though the intent was not to conquer and overthrow a people. Rather, the practice of evangelization was intended to show respect and love for what the church believed was a nationless people, offer them a gift of new life in Christ, and help them live out that life in a manner that might provide them the best opportunity for success in a rapidly Christianizing country.

The UCC did not initially understand that First Nations were nations in their own right, with their own land, cultures, languages, and religion. They did not realize that their forms of dress, communal sharing, governance, personal interaction, and relationship to the land and all creation were aspects of a different culture to be respected. Instead, they saw the First Nations as devoid of culture and religion. They understood these differences as evidence that the First Nations needed to be "civilized" and taught Christian moral standards. They understood their ceremonies to be "cruel, heathen rites" that needed to be eliminated.[24] These assumptions led to home mission policies of assimilation that attempted to eradicate Indigenous culture, language, and traditional teachings. The 1938 WMS report stated affirmatively:

> It is difficult for us to realize how comparatively recent has been the emergence of the Indian people from savagery. They have been forced almost in one generation to adopt entirely new ideas and develop new means of industry. In our Indian Residential Schools, we have an excellent opportunity to bridge that gap and lessen the bitterness in the mind of the Indian toward the white race.[25]

This evangelistic motivation for mission is important to understand, as it has shaped UCC mission work within Canada across the decades and not only with First Nations communities. Although the UCC has always upheld diverse cultural expressions of the gospel, it confused cultural differences with what it believed were bad habits requiring eradication. It was not until decades later that the UCC would confess its own confusion of the gospel with British culture.

Supremacy of the Christian Gospel

An assumption undergirding the Christianization of the social order was the supremacy of the Christian gospel. Pre-union statements largely disparaged other religions, with such references as "the menace of Mohammedianism" and Hinduism as "a formidable foe."[26] Relationships with other religious communities within Canada over the next ten years continued to be antagonistic.[27] The UCC believed that salvation could come only through Jesus Christ, and because of this, evangelism was a driving force for mission work at home and abroad: "The Carpenter of Nazareth is still building coffins for the dead and dying religions of the world."[28]

Paradoxically, the UCC also attempted to honour the values and truths expressed through other religions. The *Basis of Union's* recognition of general revelation in other religions and philosophies was based upon a comparative study of world religions. This approach identified values within these "ethnic faiths"[29] that could be held in common with Christianity. These values were evidence of the *general* revelatory work of the Holy Spirit through "men of God" who followed other religious traditions. Still, the writers of the doctrinal section of the *Basis of Union* claimed the *perfect* revelation of God through Jesus Christ as the unique and sole source of redemption.[30] They believed that only Christianity was of universal importance and therefore the pinnacle of religious development.

However, this acknowledgement of general revelation and noble values within world religions was not extended to the "primitive, animistic" beliefs of Indigenous peoples throughout the world, such as the folk religions in China, the Bantu in Africa, and the Indigenous traditional teachings in North America. These beliefs were understood only as pagan superstition that needed to be destroyed. There was little attempt to identify values or benefits in Indigenous spiritual or cultural traditions. Frequent mention was given of the progress made in the death of the "old, deep-rooted heathen practices."[31] A Home Missions superintendent described a worship service that included two drummers: "I was inducted … with a big bass drum on each side of the pulpit and two stalwart braves with coats off and beating for all they were worth. We eliminated the drums shortly after, but retained the drummers, and better still, the drummers retained their religion and a less strenuous method of expressing it."[32] While the use of drums may have been welcomed in Foreign Mission work during this era, the cultural adaptation of the gospel within First Nations communities of Canada never seemed to be considered. When some Indigenous people attempted to follow both traditional and Christian practices, they were denounced as being "double-hearted" and were urged to drop their "repulsive" pagan practices, such as the potlatch and the role of the medicine man, and become single-hearted Christians.[33]

Belief in the superiority of Christianity was accompanied by assumptions of Anglo-Saxon superiority within Canada. Cultural practices that deviated from British practices were considered uncivilized and in need of eradication. Lying beneath this collusion of Christianity with Anglo-Saxon cultures was what later became known as the Doctrine of Discovery. The cultures and beliefs of Indigenous peoples in the Americas were considered so inferior that the land was considered devoid of culture and religion. It was determined to be *terra nullius*, a Latin term derived from Roman law that literally meant "nobody's land." This pronouncement meant that the land had never been subject to a state government and was therefore free for the taking by European explorers who "found" the land and claimed title through occupation.

Foreign Mission's Indigenization vs. Home Mission's Assimilation

Heavily influenced by the 1928 meeting in Jerusalem of the International Missionary Council, the UCC *foreign* missions policy prioritized the indigenization of the gospel. In other words, it sought to express the gospel of Christ through the local culture, language, music, and governance, including the development of local leadership. Foreign missionaries were proud of the fact that Christian converts never became members of the UCC. Rather, they discouraged denominationalism and encouraged local converts to join local churches in co-operation with other Christian bodies.[34] The UCC foreign missionaries believed that they were in the "shrinking business" of foreign missions.[35] Their goal was to help local churches become self-governing, self-sustaining, and self-propagating so as to render foreign missionaries obsolete.[36]

However, *home* missions policy within Canada was less clear in its appreciation of the indigenization of the gospel. To whose culture should the gospel be indigenized? The British settlers carried their British heritage of law, parliamentary procedures, education, religion, and custom into their churches and missions. Note in the photo on page 290 the imposition of the British flag towering over the cross, while the diverse cultures in the Church of All Nations in Montreal were being acknowledged.

The UCC did recognize that French Canadian culture must be honoured: "In questions of religion, the French Canadian must be led by men of their own race and language."[37] The UCC also knew from the beginning that ethnic minorities, especially those from Eastern Europe, China, and Japan, were best served by bilingual ministers.

In missionary work of previous centuries, local First Nations languages were learned by many of the pioneering missionaries. The creation of Cree syllabics in 1840 was attributed to Rev. James Evans, although it was Henry Bird Steinhauer, the Anishinaabe Methodist missionary who accompanied Evans, who had the initial vision of developing Cree syllabics.[38] "Many faithful missionaries and teachers since that day have burned the midnight oil while translating the Bible and Christian hymns into the Cree language," wrote Arthur Barner in 1934.[39] In addition, ministers F.G. Stevens of Fisher River and R.T. Chapin of Norway House launched a quarterly Cree paper, *Spiritual Light*. There is mention only of Cree in the Home Missions reports, however, with little recognition of other First Nations languages.

As an increasing number of Indigenous people spoke English, BHM gave less attention to language training for missionaries serving "Indian

Figure 11.1   "New Canadians Bringing Gifts to the Altar of Canada."
Source: *The United Church Observer*, October 1, 1941, 15. Reproduced with permission.

Missions." The disappearance of Indigenous languages, together with the disappearance of traditional rituals and ceremonies, was seen as a sign of progress of their Christianization and assimilation. BHM did not understand what the Board of Foreign Missions had long known: the retention of Indigenous language and culture was crucial to the identity of a people and their ability to sustain healthy, self-sufficient, self-governing, and self-propagating ministries. Although BHM did not apply this Foreign Missions rationale to Indigenous missions, they did recognize the importance of one's mother tongue with ethnic minority missions:

> With a decrease in immigration, the number of non-Anglo-Saxons who are without a knowledge of English is small; nevertheless, the language of religion is always the language of one's childhood. We can never forgo our language services. Every tongue contains phrases, idioms, shades of meaning, small colourings of thought and a knowledge of this is necessary for religious interpretation. Hence foreign language services are a necessity if we would help men to share a vital religious experience.[40]

BHM recognized that the church needed to find and train ministerial candidates from within their own ethnic minority communities.[41] This was related less to the indigenization of the gospel and more to the gradual integration of these communities into the British culture of Canada. While ethnic minority churches were encouraged to become self-sufficient, they were not encouraged to become autonomous. Rather, they were considered part of the UCC and urged to adapt as much as possible to the majority culture of the wider church and society. This was to help them become more integrated with Canadian society and to have a church that could break apart barriers of prejudice and be one united human family.[42] Over time, the UCC began to realize the importance of ethnic minority communities retaining and even celebrating their cultural roots while contributing to Canadian society. The UCC recognized that sincere friendship and understanding of different cultural traditions was an integral part of mission.[43]

There was less effort to train Indigenous leadership within the "Indian Missions." The role of the Caucasian "Indian worker" served to displace the leadership of the Indigenous elders and relocate their power and authority into the person of one white man: "He was a spiritual leader, but he did everything from pulling teeth to burying people to acting as a sort of magistrate or judge, the one who decided when to call in the police or other outside authorities."[44] Even though most UCC missionaries did not have medical training, they were entrusted to keep and dispense the stock of government-issued drugs.[45] This was an arrangement made between the church and Department of Indian Affairs and is another example of forced dependency. There seemed to be no attempt to recruit Indigenous persons for this responsibility.

On some reserves, it was the Pentecostal church that afforded an opportunity for some of the elders to break away from the "domination of the resident missionary."[46] They upset some UCC members of reserve missions by violating the "gentleman's agreement" concerning denominational territory and establishing their own churches on the same reserves, thereby competing for church members. However, Pentecostal church polity was more flexible, allowing them to honour and engage the traditional leadership of the elders.

While mission work among "non-Anglo-Saxon" communities varied in its effectiveness, mission work among Indigenous people was constantly noted as particularly challenging: "I do not know a more difficult and in many ways more discouraging piece of work in our entire Mission field."[47] Various reasons were given for this. Some blamed the natural constitution of Indigenous people;[48] others blamed their traditional practices; some blamed the "baneful and adverse influence of the unscrupulous whites of no moral sense,"[49] while others blamed government policies. There seemed to be no recognition that the church could be at fault.

In order to further their goals of Christianization and assimilation of Indigenous people into the majority British culture of Canadian society, BHM and the WMS operated day schools on reserves and residential schools in conjunction with the government, as did other Christian denominations and groups within Canada. They believed that the best way to help Indigenous children advance in Canadian society was for them to receive Christian instruction, develop Christian morals, and learn the educational basics in English. The residential schools' harsh level of discipline, forced isolation from families sometimes for a year at a time, a ban on the use of the mother tongue and the practice of traditional rituals, and the occurrence of sexual abuse have been well documented. Documentation of nutritional experiments from 1942 to 1952 among hungry Indigenous children in residential schools has recently been publicized.[50] Wayne Williams noted that the cross-denominational "gentleman's agreement" not to set up competing churches on the same reserve was not applied to children, who were divided up and sent to different residential schools run by different denominations.[51]

In addition, the level of education at the residential schools was substandard. BHM believed that the Indigenous boys were best suited for farming and girls for domestic work (cooking, laundry, and sewing), and for this reason part of each school day was spent on these tasks.[52] "The Indian population should be trained for the farm as life in the open makes the strongest appeal to the Indian mind."[53] Because of this emphasis on manual labour, the children did not receive the same level of education as non-Indigenous children, and the residential school students found themselves less qualified to seek higher education and professional careers.[54] This was diametrically opposite to the educational policy of Foreign Missions at that time, which was meant to ensure that their educational missions offered the highest level of education in each country.[55]

Ironically, due to the successful farming of some First Nations, increasingly restrictive laws urged by neighbouring white farmers prevented First Nations farmers from selling their grain on the open market.[56] In addition, First Nations people were moved, and sometimes forcibly relocated, to land that was of poor quality for farming, some of which was prone to annual flooding.[57] There were certainly mixed messages in this attempt to "help" Indigenous people succeed in the wider Canadian society. Successes were met with punitive laws, and movement toward self-sufficiency was hampered by racist assumptions regarding "the Indian mind"[58] and paternalistic attitudes of care for "our Indians." They were "treated as children by a well-intentioned Government."[59] The Second World War brought a shift in attitude that influenced a changing theology and practice of mission with Indigenous and ethnic minority communities.

Shifting Tides of War and Retrenchment

> We wait for the coming of the Kingdom.
> —*1940 Statement of Faith*, Article 12, "The Consummation"

Written as Canada was going to war, the 1940 *Statement of Faith* reflected disillusionment with the human ability to help usher in the Kingdom of God. In place of unfettered optimism in the *Basis of Union's* doctrinal section, its tone was more muted, focusing on personal sin and the need to wait for divine redemption. Emphasis was placed on God's sovereignty, Jesus's crucifixion, the Holy Spirit's conviction of sin, and the empowerment of the church to bear witness and fortify holiness. Very little is mentioned about service or active pursuit of "universal brotherhood," as emphasized in the *Twenty Articles of Doctrine*. In fact, the ministry section of the *Statement of Faith* refers only to the ordained ministry of Word, Sacrament, and Pastoral Care, deleting the additional reference in the *Twenty Articles of Doctrine* to the diaconal ministry of education, service, and pastoral care.

Fear and Personal Examination

As Canada entered into the Second World War, the UCC's strong condemnation of war shifted, and pacifists found themselves standing alone. Once again, UCC sentiment matched that of the broader Canadian society, causing the UCC to reverse its previous anti-war declarations and offer organized support for the war effort. Fear and xenophobia were heightened by the war and undoubtedly contributed to the UCC's support of the government policy to intern the Japanese living in Canada.[60] The WMS helped to solicit employment and provide education for them, but did so with the belief that internment was appropriate and that any Japanese who was a "true Christian" would carry "no resentment nor bitterness over the evacuation."[61]

Not everyone was happy with these shifts in attitude, including a group of UCC ministers who challenged church and government authorities by signing a pacifist declaration. They were still convinced that war was contrary to the mind of Christ. Alarmed individuals began to challenge other UCC members over their racist positions.[62] When the UCC realized that the government was confiscating the property of the Japanese, preventing them from owning or leasing land, blocking Japanese from their own professions, refusing to provide them with primary and secondary education, keeping them interned in deplorable housing, and refusing both their offer to enlist and their offer of blood donations, the denomination reversed its commendation and protested these discriminatory government actions.[63] By 1944, the UCC acknowledged that racist fear was growing not only within Canada but also within the church itself. BHM detected a "smugness, exclusiveness and prejudice in our Church towards the non-Anglo-Saxon."[64] There was growing awareness about the racist use of the terms "heathen" and "Jew" in The Hymnary.[65]

The Second World War, with its accompanying spread of fascism and racism, was a wake-up call to many around the world.[66] Human rights became a universal concern, resulting in the 1945 United Nations Charter, followed by the 1948 United Nations' Declaration of Human Rights. Within Canada, concern about human rights provoked a deeper, internal examination of racist attitudes that underlay a sentiment of Anglo-Saxon superiority.[67] UCC members began to ask why Canadians were demonstrating the same racist intolerance and hatred against which the Allies were fighting overseas. "Does not the passing of laws discriminating against the Japanese seem perilously like Hitler's anti-Semitic laws?" asked W.H.H. Norman.[68] BHM condemned the sentiment of many UCC ministers and members who agreed with the Canadian refusal of wartime refugees, largely because of Anglo anti-Semitism.[69] The Board recognized that racism and anti-Semitism were sinful acts that betrayed the gospel hope for the "brotherhood of man."

These self-critiques began to be extended to the UCC's treatment of Indigenous peoples. For the first time, the UCC began to consider its own role in the failure of "missions to the Indians." It realized that it should adapt its ministry to the historical and cultural identity of First Nations, rather than base it on Anglo-Saxon culture.[70] It began to recognize that First Nations' dress, language, teachings, and ceremonies constituted a culture as worthy of respect as that of other ethnic groups. This awareness led BHM to realize that it needed to provide special training in this area for ministers going to "Indian missions."[71] Perhaps because of the impressive ways in which Indigenous people offered to serve in the armed forces and to help with the harvests, fisheries, industrial shops, and other workplaces where there were shortages of workers during the war, the UCC gained a new respect for them.[72] Some may also have recalled the earlier generosity of Indian missions, which, in spite of some of the worst economic hardships in the late 1920s and early 1930s, gave impressive monetary gifts to the wider church.[73]

Personal Redemption

The end of the war signalled the beginning of an uneasy world truce, but concerns about atomic weapons were heightened with the growing tension between the east and west. Fear of communism justified control over dissident groups. The UCC warned of the evils of communism, distancing itself from the comments of Dr. James Endicott, a medical missionary in China, who suggested that the church should support the communist goals of China because of their alignment with the Christian gospel.[74] The alliance of European churches with fascist dictators during the war caused churches, including the UCC, to be more cautious in their collaboration with governments. They heeded theologians, such as Karl Barth, who urged Protestant churches to say no to any human authority that placed itself above critique. In 1948 the First Assembly of the World Council of Churches issued a frequently quoted statement that churches need to say "no" to all that flouts the love of Christ and "yes" to all that conforms to it.[75]

The shock of the human potential for great evil, as was witnessed in the war, led churches to prioritize the need for personal redemption, believing that social redemption would then follow. The Second Assembly of the WCC in 1954 stressed the hope of Christ and his return to establish the Kingdom of God. Because churches wanted to avoid identifying the Kingdom of God with any particular political system, the Kingdom of God took on an otherworldly quality rooted in the future. A similar sentiment was reflected within the UCC. Greater emphasis was placed on personal redemption. While both social service and evangelism had always been operative (and always held together with some tension) in the UCC, there was greater investment in evangelistic campaigns and goals in the 1950s. Professions of faith soared, membership increased, and personal devotion was emphasized through the widespread use of study materials accompanying the 1940 *Statement of Faith*. The 1950 *Report of the Commission on Culture* concluded that while the church must be in the world and draw upon cultural values that are sympathetic to Christian values, it must also stand against aspects of culture that are at odds with Christianity. Christ must be Lord of all the earth.

Perhaps because of this more evangelical swing, there was less evidence of the earlier UCC openness to the values of other world religions. Any reference that was given to adherents of other faiths portrayed them negatively, in need of Christian conversion.[76] Within a few years, however, there were once again calls for the recognition of values—even revelation—within other religions. L.J. Newcombe wrote "No religion could be the sole custodian of the truth, nor would the revelation of God be exclusively the possession of one race or Church."[77] At the same time, it was understood that there was no complete revelation of God apart from Jesus Christ.[78] Although debates mounted in the late 1950s and early 1960s about evangelistic methods, there was still near unanimity that the world needed to be converted to Christianity.

Racism

Self-critical questions in the early 1940s about the role of the UCC in the failure of "Indian missions," and the growing awareness of the value of First Nations' cultures, disappeared in the late 1940s and early 1950s. Although there was some awareness of the success of Indigenous lay ministers, especially in Manitoba,[79] blame was once again placed on Indigenous people for not being self-sufficient and for depending on government handouts.[80] In 1947, BHM supported the outlawing of the potlatch and community feasts.[81] Instead of respecting cultural practices for their sustenance of community, such policies viewed them as primitive practices that undermined economic progress.

At this time, the UCC was aware of racism directed against Jews, Chinese, Japanese, East Indians, and Eastern Europeans. In the late 1940s, it continued to press the government to redress their discriminatory policies against the Japanese, called for the repeal of the 1923 Chinese Immigration Act, and called upon the government to receive more refugees "without discrimination as to race, creed or nationality."[82] At the same time, however, it asked the government to prioritize immigrants who were of British stock and were healthy and able to work.[83]

When violent protests against Protestant churches broke out in Quebec in 1950, Montreal Presbytery "sent a vigorous letter of protest" to Premier Duplessis.[84] In the same year, the UCC realized that it also needed to support French language rights. It began to make its own resources available in French and to encourage its own membership to acquire a working knowledge of French.[85]

It wasn't until 1960 that *The United Church Observer* first referred to racism against African Canadians. Initially, UCC congregations and courts dismissed this as a "Baptist problem" because African Canadians were primarily Baptists in the Maritimes.[86] When the UCC began to realize that the problem lay more with society at large than with African Canadians, presbyteries and conferences began to address this in 1963, although ministers were less inclined to deal with it at a congregational level, where action was needed.[87]

As the UCC became more aware of the reality of race discrimination within its congregations as well as within society, it urged its churches to practise the principles of "brotherhood" for people of all races and to befriend new Canadians irrespective of race and country of origin.[88] General Council condemned Canadian Acts of exclusion based on race and successfully urged the enactment of national and provincial laws against racism.[89] The 1960 and 1964 General Councils called the church to repent for acts of racism.

Until 1960, the UCC recognized racial discrimination against ethnic minorities in Canada but was less aware of racism directed against Indigenous people. For instance, when the UCC condemned the British conquest of the "first settlers" of Canada and the attempts to eliminate their language, the "first settlers" were understood not as the First Nations but the French.[90] This obliviousness to the First Nations finally changed with the civil rights movement when some began to compare the treatment of Indigenous people to the enslavement of African Americans in the southern US and to the apartheid system of South Africa. However, there was still little awareness within Canada of the church's complicity with this colonization.

From Assimiliation to Integration

In 1954, the Welfare Council of Greater Winnipeg invited the Government Branch of Indian Affairs along with church leaders from the Anglican, Presbyterian, Roman Catholic, and United Churches to a conference addressing "Indian problems." It was the "first time Indians had ever been invited to discuss their own problems with the white man."[91] The conference concluded, in part, that the missionaries needed to educate the wider public on the many contributions Indigenous people had already made and would continue to make if the public were more patient and less ignorant or prejudiced. When Indigenous people were present and offered their own experiences, the critique shifted from blaming them to understanding the effects of racism on Indigenous people. Unlike this 1954 government-sponsored conference, the UCC's 1956 Commission to Study Indian Work did not include any Indigenous people on its commission. This significant study constituted a thorough assessment and review of Indian Missions conducted by BHM. Due, in part, to the absence of Indigenous representation, the conclusions were not self-critical of the church and continued to blame Indigenous people for their lack of progress.

Although the 1956 commission did not mention the training of Indigenous ministers, it did recommend better training and preparation for those in ministry with Indigenous communities, as well as the development of local lay leadership.[92] It highlighted the importance of specialized training for "Indian workers," including language. This recommendation was followed in Saskatchewan and Manitoba in the mid-1960s, when some suggested that "Indian work" was not an appropriate placement for inexperienced ordinands. Rather, a special ministry requiring ministerial experience, extra training, and cross-cultural orientation was needed.[93] The 1956 Commission to Study Indian Work also recommended the integration of Indigenous peoples into the wider community, noting the problems of poverty and forced dependency of segregated reserves on financial assistance. Integration differed from the previous emphasis on assimilation by requiring education of the non-Indigenous communities about the contributions of the Indigenous peoples.[94] Education of Indigenous children through both day schools and residential schools was still recognized as the best form of preparation for their integration.

Two years later, a 1958 report on Indian Work clarified that the term integration "does not imply the complete disintegration of any one culture or its complete assimilation by a more dominant culture."[95] The term integration was used to encourage people of all ethnic identities to celebrate, rather than deny, their particular cultures. Although the concept was promising, there was little consultation with Indigenous communities. There was also no understanding, in contrast to the revised Foreign Mission policy, that Indigenous communities needed to take the lead in this alternative approach. Instead, only particular aspects of Indigenous culture were upheld as long as this did not disrupt the white majority cultures.[96]

Listening to the Marginalized

> ... to celebrate [God's] presence, to love and serve others, to seek justice and resist evil, to proclaim Jesus ...
>
> —A New Creed

Written in the more permissive ethos of the 1960s, A New Creed reflects the relaxed mood of its time. It offers a breath of openness and acceptance, out of which the church could find the energy to love, serve, seek justice, and proclaim Jesus. Its primary emphasis is on God's presence and assurance that all will be well. It omits any reference to personal sin, saying that we need only resist evil, implying that it is external to us. This reflected a growing awareness of systemic sin located in structures of oppressive power. Resisting institutional evil began with listening to the voices of the marginalized.

It was not until the early 1960s that church leaders began to listen to and consult with Indigenous people. Through listening conferences and interviews, the church began to realize its role in the oppression of Indigenous people. The first critiques of the residential schools began to appear, including an *Observer* interview with Gloria Webster, the daughter of a west-coast chief. She explained that "residential schools have 'institutionalized' the Indian so that he may later fit into jail better than society."[97] The UCC began to rethink its mission work with residential schools and, by 1969, had ceased all operations in these schools.

A 1965 *Observer* article accused the UCC of managing Indigenous peoples instead of assisting them in their own decisions and plans for their ministry and economy. The denomination was accused of preaching "brotherhood" while practising private ownership and competition in business, and of providing Indigenous peoples with "white man's education" but little opportunity for employment in the white man's world.[98] Another *Observer* article acknowledged that Indigenous peoples rightly feared that with integration they would lose yet more of their culture, language, and identity.[99] Fuel was added to the fire of these critiques in the late 1960s with the rise of liberation movements around the world. This decade brought a questioning of authority and the status quo, as well as openness to new ideas and beliefs.

Liberation Theologies

While the cultural tenor of the 1960s in Canada was filled with messages of love and peace, this was also a tense time of civil disobedience, civil rights demonstrations, and liberation movements. The Front de Libération du Québec crisis prompted the 1971 General Council to establish a Commission on French/English Relations. The Black Panther movement in the US inspired the organization of African Canadians in Halifax to speak out as a bloc.[100] The Native Alliance for Red Power was similarly inspired to form the Beothuk Patrol in Skid Road, Vancouver, that assisted and protected Indigenous people who were living on the streets.[101] Feminist organizations were challenging the church on sexist language and practices. In 1980, the words to *A New Creed* were changed to eliminate sexist language.

Theologies of liberation, especially those from the global South, challenged the church on its own role in the systemic oppression of women and minorities, and of its collusion with colonial exploitation. Instead of starting with historical doctrines or expert opinion, liberation theologies began with the experiences of those most affected by structures of domination and oppression. Ministry among French communities needed to begin with their hopes and concerns. Mission work with Indigenous communities needed to begin not with directives but with listening to how these communities experienced the Creator working in their lives. Women reminded their male colleagues that their experiences were different from those privileged by gender, as well as by economic status and race. In the 1980s, sexual orientation was added to this list of marginalized identities that needed to be heard. Study documents on women's concerns and on sexuality, produced largely in the 1980s, helped parishioners begin to understand gender and sexual orientation as issues of justice rather than of morality. This insight was a key turning point that helped the church take significant gospel-mandated risks in decisions and statements on behalf of marginalized people.

In response to cries from the marginalized, the WCC began sending grants to minority groups to fight racism, including Canadian "Indians and Eskimos" in their struggle for land rights and survival. In spite of the UCC's surprise at Canada becoming one of the grant recipients, it, too, was contributing funds to First Nations fighting the flooding of the James Bay area by Hydro-Québec and the provincial government. As it increased its advocacy work, the UCC began to engage a more complex analysis of racism that included institutional racism and its intersection with poverty and sexism.

With its 1971 multiculturalism policy, Canada was moving away from its assimilation and integration policies. Correspondingly, in the mid-1970s, the UCC began to host national gatherings of ethnic minority ministries and by the late 1970s noted that its emphasis had moved from assimilation and integration to pluralism.[102] This included a renewed appreciation for cultural diversity. This later led to a policy on anti-racism in 2000, *That All May Be One*, and a further change of focus from pluralism to interculturalism. In 2006, General Council committed the UCC to becoming an intercultural church.[103] Mission work now needed to consider partnerships with other faith communities and ethnic minority groups as it addressed concerns of injustice.

Interfaith Policies

In the early 1970s, debates became increasingly strident between those who insisted on the supremacy of Christ with the command to make disciples of all the nations, and those who claimed that Christians should cease their mission of converting the world. Reference began to be made to particular sections of the 1966 *World Mission* document, which called for mutual respect between Christian and non-Christian religions and which acknowledged that "God is creatively and redemptively at work in the religious life of all mankind."[104] This policy had passed with ease in 1966, without General Council understanding its radical implications for evangelism.[105] It was not until the early 1970s, when this policy's interfaith mandate was pursued, that the mission of conversion began to be challenged.

The Division of World Outreach (DWO)[106] began to understand evangelism as a sequence of presence, service, dialogue, and finally proclamation.[107] The Christian's task was to serve others and speak about Christ, but it was the Holy Spirit's role to convict and convert. This differed from the Division of Home Missions' promotion of Key 73, an evangelistic program "designed to call our continent to Christ."[108] Because of this disparity, General Council requested a study of the Lordship of Jesus, which resulted in a statement of faith, approved in 1977, clarifying that Jesus was still considered to be Lord of all the earth.[109] By then, interfaith dialogue was well under way and DWO understood the Lordship of Jesus to mean that mission was larger than the church and that Christ was working through other cultures and religions.

Beginning in the early 1970s, the UCC began to uncouple Christianity from British culture.[110] Its social gospel mandate no longer required a Christian foundation. Instead, it explored relationships with other faith traditions on the basis of partnership, rather than conversion. However, it was not until 1980 when the UCC, through DWO, recognized traditional Indigenous teachings not as superstition, but as another religion with which to dialogue. These explorations of interfaith dialogue led to the 1997 document, *Mending the World*, which proposed "whole world ecumenism" that promoted respect and partnership not only with other Christian denominations but also with other religions.[111] This formed the basis for interfaith study documents, beginning with the 1997 *Bearing Faithful Witness: United Church–Jewish Relations Today*. The next interfaith study document, *That We May Know Each Other: United Church–Muslim Relations Today* was released in 2004, followed by the 2014 *Honouring the Divine in Each Other: United Church–Hindu Relations Today*.

Crossing the Divide between Home and World Missions

In the early 1970s, the Board of World Mission (BWM) realized that congregations remained stuck in an outmoded sense of mission in which "missionaries go from the west to the rest, from superior to the inferior, from the religious to the pagan" to convert and develop.[112] It recommended that the denomination should resolve the breach between world missions and home missions, foreign missionary work and congregational life. The 1966 *World Mission* report had earlier recommended that departmental fences be breached in the service of mission.[113]

Cree elder Rev. Stan McKay, who later became the first Indigenous person to be elected moderator in 1992, was one of the first to recognize this discrepancy between home and foreign missions. As he finished his first year of serving the Cree pastoral charge of Norway House, Manitoba, in 1972, he was troubled by what he saw. He had inherited a paternalistic style of mission work that had disparaged the leadership of local elders and their traditional culture. In addition, that approach had fostered dependency on charity. Hoping to find another way of doing mission, he attended the Missionary Orientation at Western University in London, Ontario, for two weeks. This orientation was sponsored by the BWM primarily for those about to serve overseas. There, McKay met Katherine Hockin, one of the leaders of the event, who was introducing the concept of partnership in mission.

McKay then realized that there was a significant disconnect between Home and World Missions. If the "Indian Missions" had been engaged with the same principles and theological rationale as World Missions, he was sure that his experience at Norway House would have been very different.[114] The missionaries would have sought the wisdom and direction of local elders and studied their language and culture. Local leadership would have been recruited and trained. The gospel would have been expressed through traditional Cree teachings, ceremonies, song, and dance. Governance structures would have been adapted to the Cree methods of consensus-based decision making. The values of listening, respecting, and learning would have been prioritized. The missionaries would have realized that, upon arrival to First Nations' communities, they were standing on holy ground. Hockin, McKay, and others were at the forefront of helping the UCC reorient its approach to mission within Canada, drawing on the lessons and conclusions of overseas mission, and attending more closely and respectfully to those with whom the church sought to serve.

In the early 1970s, UCC leadership listened to the concerns and suggestions of Indigenous people at the Indian Ecumenical Conferences and Listening Conferences. In response, the denomination began to base its mission work, programs, and priorities on the requests of Indigenous people rather than on assumptions of what would be best for them. It became clear that church policies needed to be more flexible to allow special training and ordination of Indigenous elders.[115] The church also listened to Indigenous presbyters, who were sidelined at presbytery meetings because of language barriers and decision-making processes based on British parliamentary procedures. At the request of Indigenous churches for their own consensus-based governance structures, seventeen Indigenous congregations formed Keewatin Presbytery in Manitoba and Northwestern Ontario in 1981. Seven years later, All Native Circle Conference was formed. The formation of Indigenous governance bodies and training centres for ministry supported the development of self-governance, one of the basic tenets of overseas mission policy. These initiatives helped the church realize the impact of British culture upon its own practice of ministry and its imposition of British culture upon the First Nations.

Moving Toward Right Relationship

As the UCC listened to Indigenous peoples, they began to realize their own culpability in the destruction of Indigenous culture and identity. At the end of a four-day meeting on racism against Indian and Metis peoples in 1979, Saskatchewan Conference decided to call for one year of repentance. This year gave them the opportunity to prayerfully prepare for an apology and to make amends with Indian and Metis peoples. This precedent set the stage for the 1986 General Council apology to First Nations: "We confused Western ways and culture with the depth and breadth and length and height of the Gospel of Christ. We imposed our civilization as a condition of accepting the gospel. We tried to make you be like us and in so doing we helped to destroy the vision that made you what you were."[116] At the following General Council in 1988, the All Native Circle Conference responded to this apology. They decided to acknowledge it, rather than accept it, with a hope and prayer "that the Apology is not symbolic but that these are the words of action and sincerity."[117] They did not want the church to move on from the apology to other concerns, but instead to live out the apology genuinely in action and partnership.

During this time of apology in the late 1980s, survivors of residential schools began to disclose abuse they experienced in the schools. Class-action suits were begun and the UCC was involved in legal settlements. This led to the General Council's 1998 apology for harm caused by the fifteen residential schools operated by the UCC. Moderator Bill Phipps announced, "We are aware of some of the damage that this cruel and ill-conceived system of assimilation has perpetrated on Canada's First Nations peoples. For this we are truly and most humbly sorry."[118]

While the leadership at General Council, Conferences, and Presbyteries was moving into lament and confession for the harm that the church caused to First Nations, most congregations were more hesitant. They feared litigation and the resultant associated costs. They were reluctant to acknowledge their own racism and the colonization perpetrated by their own ancestors. It was difficult to listen to the pain of residential school survivors. Many wished to bypass confession and move directly toward reconciliation without fully listening and taking responsibility for the sins of the church. Phipps addressed congregational reticence in the 1998 apology: "We know that many within our church will still not understand why each of us must bear the scar, the blame for this horrendous period in Canadian history. But the truth is, we are the bearers of many blessings from our ancestors, and therefore, we must also bear their burdens."[119] Phipps also acknowledged the fear of the First Nations that the apology would consist of words without action, and he prayed that they would witness the church's enactment of its apology.

Mending Creation

We participate in God's work of healing and mending creation.

—*A Song of Faith*

In light of the apologies and growing awareness of the harm caused by the UCC in its role with the residential schools, *A Song of Faith* brought a renewed emphasis on sin (both personal and corporate) and repentance. It echoed the recognition with the *Twenty Articles of Doctrine* of revelation in all of creation as well as the hope for a new creation. In *A Song of Faith*, the church is understood to help bring about that new creation through its ministry of healing and mending. Mission belongs to God, rather than to the church, indicating that God's mission includes but is not limited to the church. The church's purpose is to live out the Good News through "faith nurtured and hearts comforted, gifts shared for the good of all, resistance to the forces that exploit and marginalize, fierce love in the face of violence, human dignity defended, members of a community held and inspired by God, corrected and comforted, instrument of the loving Spirit of Christ, creation's mending."[120] The gospel is no longer shared for the purposes of conversion, but is lived with the purpose of working in partnership with others for the mending of creation.

To assist congregations in the difficult journey of truth telling, lamentation, repentance, and finally reconciliation, the Division of Mission in

Canada published resources and helped to organize workshops.[121] The UCC published *Circle and Cross* in 2008 as a dialogue planning tool for Aboriginal and non-Aboriginal people "seeking ways to live out the desire for healing and reconciliation expressed in the 1986 Apology." Additional funds were established to promote justice and reconciliation with Indigenous peoples. Since 2008, the UCC has worked closely with the Canadian government's Truth and Reconciliation Commission to support Indigenous individuals and communities at the residential school hearings. They have offered archival resources to assist with the documentation of abuses at the residential schools.

Given the depth and denial of racism and complicity in colonization, including cultural genocide, only in the mid-1990s and into the new millennium did the UCC begin to realize that it had much to learn from Indigenous cultures, values, and traditional teachings. Stan McKay helped to revise *A New Creed* in 1994 to include reference to the care of Creation. With respect for Indigenous ways of being and knowing, the wider UCC has begun to use sharing and learning circles, as practised in Indigenous ministry training centres. In 2012, the denomination changed its crest to reflect the four colours referring to the Indigenous teachings of the four directions and added the Mohawk words *Akwe Nia'Tetewá:neren* (all my relations) to indicate familial connection with all the races of the world and with all of God's creation. In this same year, it repudiated the Doctrine of Discovery.

Conclusion

The UCC has reflected the nation of Canada at its finest and at its worst. It has struggled to learn from social movements and marginalized peoples; it has acknowledged that it has been a harbinger not only of morality and justice within Canada and the world, but also of racism and colonization. At times, it has led the nation and the world in its work for justice and eventual recognition that the mission of God is larger than the church—indeed larger than Christianity. At other times, it has led the wider church in a confession of a multitude of sins including anti-Semitism, racism, sexism, heterosexism, environmental degradation, classism, ethnocentrism, and cultural genocide.

From its birth, the UCC has been at its most faithful when preaching and practising the whole gospel for the whole person for the whole world. Mission work, in its various manifestations, has remained at the centre of its life and identity. Where the UCC failed in its mission work was in the disparity that existed between home and overseas mission goals. While overseas missions sought, from the beginning, to indigenize the gospel and to help local churches become self-governing and self-sufficient, home missions originally sought to assimilate and integrate Indigenous people and immigrants into Anglo-Canadian culture while discouraging Indigenous elders from becoming church leaders. It was not until decades later that the breach between missionary work in Canada and overseas began to be crossed. As home missions began to listen to Indigenous people, the denomination started to assist them in their own leadership and goal setting, help train Indigenous clergy within their own cultural traditions, and support the establishment of Indigenous governance councils. The goal of self-sufficiency remains a more difficult one, after over a century of forcing Indigenous peoples into a culture of dependency. It was one of the most difficult goals for overseas mission but has proven to be crucial in the liberation of countries and local churches from colonization.

In spite of the UCC's role in colonization and cultural genocide of the First Nations, the Royal Commission on Aboriginal Peoples believes that the church still has a place at the table of reconciliation: "religious institutions have perhaps the greatest potential to foster awareness and understanding between Aboriginal and non-Aboriginal people."[122] The Royal Commission suggests that churches can also facilitate public discussions and engage in advocacy.[123] These tasks lead the church into a mission of partnership.

An approach to mission as partnership, rather than the imposition of norms or forced assimilation or integration, has and will continue to transform the UCC's work. Instead of congregations asking how they can "help" others, they need to explore how they might enter into relationship with others, and be open to being transformed themselves in the very act of partnership. This would help to remove paternalism from mission. Marilyn Legge argues that "God's mission for the sake of the beloved world includes healing ourselves with the solidarity of others" and that "justice-love is the single standard for diverse discourses of mission."[124]

The UCC has learned that mission work, both at home and overseas, must be conducted under the leadership of those most affected. By recognizing that God's mission includes the work of other faith traditions as well as secular organizations, evangelism focuses on living out the Good News for the mending of creation, rather than proclaiming the Good News for the conversion of non-Christians. Stan McKay suggests that we consider eliminating the very word "mission" because of its continuing attachment to colonial dependency, cultural genocide, and Christian supremacy: "We need to get rid of the helpers and bring in the relatives."[125] Rather than try-ing to change others, the church should acknowledge "all my relations" by seeking to live into right relations with all of creation.

NOTES

This chapter is adapted with permission from "From Colonization to Right Rela-tions: The Evolution of United Church of Canada Missions within Aboriginal Communities," *International Review of Mission* 103, no. 1 (April 2014): 153–71. I am grateful to Caryn Douglas, Cecile Fausak, Bob Haverluck, Kimiko Karpoff, Stan McKay, Nancy Pinnell, Arthur Walker-Jones, and students at the Sandy Saulteaux Spiritual Centre for their comments and reflections on this writing.

1 "Report of The Joint Committee on Church Union," issued for GC1 (1925), 56.
2 "Report of Home Missions," UCC, *Proceedings*, GC6 (1934), 340.
3 Phyllis Airhart, *A Church with the Soul of a Nation: Making and Remaking the United Church of Canada* (Montreal and Kingston: McGill-Queen's University Press, 2014), 77.
4 "Statement of Principles from the Report of Evangelism and Social Service," UCC, *Proceedings*, GC4 (1930), 86–87.
5 T. Albert Moore, "The Mission of the Church in Personal Evangelism and Redemption," *New Outlook*, June 10, 1925, 23.
6 John Webster Grant, "From Revelation to Revolution: Some Thoughts on the Background of the Social Gospel," *Toronto Journal of Theology* 12, no. 2 (Fall 1996): 159–68.
7 James Endicott, "Appraising Our Foreign Missions: Evangelism: The Supreme Task of Missions," *New Outlook*, March 1, 1933, 198.
8 "Report of the Commission on Christianizing the Social Order," UCC, *Pro-ceedings*, GC6 (1934), 235–48.
9 Ernest Thomas, "Creating a National Conscience: Great Achievements Demanded of the United Church," *New Outlook*, September 9, 1925, 5.
10 "Report of the Commission on Christianizing the Social Order," 235–48.
11 "Report of The Joint Committee on Church Union," 87.
12 Ibid., 74.
13 "Report of the Board of Evangelism and Social Service on Evangelism," UCC, *Proceedings*, GC6 (1934), 252.
14 Ibid., 63.
15 These reports stopped short of supporting civil disobedience for those seek-ing exemption from military service.

16 "The Call to the Church," UCC, *Proceedings*, GC3 (1928), 73–74.

17 "Killing Race Prejudice," *New Outlook*, January 6, 1926, 3–4.

18 Patricia Clarke, "The KKK: How the Klan Came to Canada," *United Church Observer*, December 15, 1965, 12–14.

19 "Report of Home Missions," UCC, *Proceedings*, GC4 (1930), 357.

20 "Arthur Barner, "Superintendents' Reports: Indian Missions," UCC, *Year Book* (1933), 137.

21 "Report of Home Missions," UCC, *Year Book* (1931), 166.

22 One example is the Winnipeg Jewish Mission, established in 1911 as the Presbyterian Mission to the Jews. See Fonds Ex-35, Jewish Mission Fonds, UCA, University of Winnipeg.

23 "Report of the Board of Evangelism and Social Service on Evangelism," UCC, *Proceedings*, GC6 (1934), 252.

24 Barner, "Superintendents' Reports: Indian Missions," 137.

25 "Report of the Woman's Missionary Society," UCC, *Proceedings*, GC8 (1938), 387.

26 "The Joint Committee on Church Union," 5, 6.

27 "Report of Home Missions," UCC, *Proceedings*, GC6 (1934), 363.

28 "Report of Home Missions," UCC, *Year Book* (1929), 145.

29 Thomas Buchanan Kilpatrick, *Our Common Faith: The United Church of Canada* (Toronto: Ryerson Press, 1928), 93–95.

30 Kilpatrick, *Our Common Faith*, 93–95.

31 Arthur Barner, "Superintendents' Reports: Indian Missions," UCC, *Year Book* (1933), 137.

32 "Report of Home Missions," UCC, *Proceedings*, GC7 (1936), 415.

33 Ibid., 414–16; "Report of Home Missions," UCC, *Year Book* (1937), 112.

34 "Report of Foreign Missions," UCC, *Proceedings*, GC6 (1934), 72.

35 Fred Ainsworth, "The Japan Mission Council, 1933," *New Outlook*, February 22, 1933, 182.

36 See Hyuk Cho's discussion of this in chapter 10 of this volume.

37 "Report of Home Missions," UCC, *Year Book* (1929), 129.

38 Winona Stevenson, "Calling Badger and the Symbols of the Spirit Language: The Cree Origins of the Syllabic System," *Oral History Forum* 19–20 (1999–2000): 19–24, www.oralhistoryforum.ca.

39 Arthur Barner, "Superintendents' Reports: Indian Missions," UCC, *Proceedings*, GC6 (1934), 339.

40 Harvey G. Forster, "All Peoples' Missions Show the Church Cares," *United Church Observer*, April 1, 1939, 18.

41 "Report of Home Missions," UCC, *Year Book* (1928), 310.

42 "Report of Home Missions," UCC, *Proceedings*, GC4 (1930), 313.

43 "Report of Home Missions," UCC, *Year Book* (1935), 174.

44 Stan McKay and Janet Silman, *The First Nations: A Canadian Experience of the Gospel-Culture Encounter*, Gospel and Cultures Pamphlet 2 (Geneva: WCC, 1995), 20.

45 "Report of Home Missions," UCC, *Proceedings*, GC6 (1934), 340.

46 McKay and Silman, *The First Nations*, 21.

47 "Report of Home Missions," UCC, *Year Book* (1931), 151.

48 "Report of Home Missions," UCC, *Year Book* (1931), 166; "Home Missions Report of the Former Methodist Church," UCC, *Year Book* (1926), 327.

49 "Report of Home Missions," UCC, *Year Book* (1937), 112.

50 Bob Weber, "Apology Sought over Nutritional Experiments," *Winnipeg Free Press*, July 19, 2013, A14.

51 Wayne Williams, comments during Learning Circle at Sandy Saulteaux Spiritual Centre, June 1–6, 2014.

52 "The Women's Missionary Society of The United Church of Canada," UCC, *Year Book* (1928), 331.

53 "Report of Home Missions," UCC, *Year Book* (1927), 110.

54 "Report of Home Missions," UCC, *Year Book* (1929), 151–52.

55 "Foreign Missions Policy," UCC, *Proceedings*, GC7 (1936), 263.

56 McKay and Silman, *The First Nations*, 16–17.

57 Bernice Saulteaux, "Nakota Massacre," in *Story after Story: Canadians Bend Bound Theology*, ed. Loraine MacKenzie Shepherd (Winnipeg: On Edge Publishing, 2003), 82.

58 Mrs. D.J. Scoates, "After Six Years with the Crees," *United Church Observer*, October 1, 1941, 6.

59 "Report of Home Missions," UCC, *Year Book* (1943), 130.

60 "Report of Home Missions," UCC, *Proceedings*, GC10 (1942), 89–90; "Minutes of the General Council Executive, April 29–30, 1941," UCC, *Proceedings*, GC10 (1942), 234.

61 "Report of the Woman's Missionary Society," UCC, *Year Book* (1943), 177.

62 W.H.H. Norman, "The Japanese in Canada," *United Church Observer*, June 1, 1944, 7, 23.

63 "Report of Home Missions," UCC, *Year Book* (1943), 21–22; "Minutes of the Executive, May 2–3, 1944," UCC, *Proceedings*, GC11 (1944), 191; Rev. R.J. McDonald, "Superintendent's Report for Southern Alberta," UCC, *Year Book* (1945), 166.

64 "Report of Home Missions," UCC, *Proceedings*, GC11 (1944), 309.

65 S.J., "The Racial Prejudice of Our Hymnary," *United Church Observer*, June 1, 1944, 13.

66 Blanche Hales Squires, "The War Has Made Me Over," *United Church Observer*, June 1, 1944, 22–23; Willard E. Brewing, "Racial Relationships after the War," *United Church Observer*, April 15, 1941, 15–25.

67 "Report of Home Missions," UCC, *Year Book* (1941), 119.

68 Norman, "The Japanese in Canada," 7.

69 "Report of Home Missions," UCC, *Proceedings*, GC11 (1944), 308–9.

70 Kahbaosa, "Have You Met the Indians?," *United Church Observer*, September 14, 1940, 21.

71 Ibid., 23.

72 "Report of Home Missions," UCC, *Year Book* (1943), 130; J.A.C., "Manitoba Indians and the War," *United Church Observer*, October 1, 1942, 3.

73 "Lo! The Poor Indian" *New Outlook* (between April 21, 1926, and May 26, 1926), 14; "Report of Home Missions," UCC, *Year Book* (1931), 150–51.

74 Jesse H. Arnup, Secretary of Overseas Missions, "Dr. J.G. Endicott and the Board of Overseas Missions," *United Church Observer*, March 15, 1948, 8, 28.

75 This quote was mentioned in the "Report of the Board of Evangelism and Social Service," UCC, *Proceedings*, GC17 (1956), 400.

76 David H. Gallagher, "Christianity Faces Other Faiths," *United Church Observer*, July 15, 1950, 13; A.C. Pound, "Undermine War," *United Church Observer*, January 1, 1952, 6.

77 L.J. Newcombe, "Christianity and World Leadership," *United Church Observer*, April 15, 1955, 11.

78 Editor, "New Look in Missions," *United Church Observer*, August 1957, 17.

79 "Take My Life and Let it Be; Consecrated, Lord, to Thee," *United Church Observer*, August 15, 1951, 1; C.H. Best, "Laymen Indispensable in Indian Work," *United Church Observer*, September 15, 1953, 5.

80 "Indians Help Themselves," *United Church Observer*, August 1, 1949, 4.

81 "Report of Home Missions," UCC, *Year Book* (1947), 168; McKay and Silman, *The First Nations*, 22.

82 "Report of the Board of Evangelism and Social Services," UCC, *Year Book* (1947), 122.

83 "Report of Home Missions," UCC, *Proceedings*, GC12 (1946), 73. This was a cause of embarrassment when the adviser to the Refugee Committee of the WCC told the Canadian Council of Churches in 1950 that Norway had accepted 500 blind, displaced persons. See Frank Chamberlain, "Canadian Council of Churches Acted on the Refugee Question," *United Church Observer*, December 15, 1950, 3.

84 C. de Mestral, "Disorders and Religious Persecution in Quebec," *United Church Observer*, June 15, 1950, 11.

85 UCC, *Proceedings*, GC14 (1950), 71, 76.

86 E.L. Homewood, "The Maritimes Colour Bar," *United Church Observer*, June 1, 1960, 20.

87 E.L. Homewood, "Race Discrimination," *United Church Observer*, February 1, 1956, 8.

88 E.L. Homewood, "Breaking the Race Barrier," *United Church Observer*, March 1, 1956, 26.

89 Lloyd B. Graham, "Those Japanese War Babies?," *United Church Observer*, December 1, 1956, 26–27; Homewood, "Breaking the Race Barrier," 10.

90 Claude de Mestral, "South Africa's Dilemma," *United Church Observer*, June 1, 1960, 11.

91 Isobel M. Loveys, "Conference Held on Indian Problems," *United Church Observer*, December 15, 1954, 12.

92 "Commission to Study Indian Work," UCC, *Proceedings*, GC17 (1956), 207–34.

93 E.L. Homewood, "Bus-Driving Missionary of Round Lake," *United Church Observer*, September 15, 1964, 19. In 1967, such preparation finally became obligatory in Manitoba for anyone going into First Nation communities. See "Report of Home Missions," UCC, *Year Book*, vol. 2 (1967), 148.

94 "Report of the Commission to Study the Indian Work of The United Church of Canada," UCC, *Proceedings*, GC17 (1956), 220.

95 "Indian Work," UCC, *Proceedings*, GC18 (1958), 185.

96 See the United Church's critique of an attempt to integrate Indigenous students into a town's public school: Dorothy Vipond, "Everything's Lily White in Dominion City," *United Church Observer*, November 15, 1966, 21, 40. See also the failed attempt at integration by Saskatchewan Conference's Good Samaritan Plan: Enos Montour, "A New Deal for Prairie Indians," *United Church Observer*, March 15, 1961, 8, 9, 20; Homewood, "Bus-Driving Missionary of Round Lake," 19.

97 Kenneth Bagnell, "Interview [with Gloria Webster]," *United Church Observer*, December 1, 1963, 21.

98 E.L. Homewood, "The Plight of Canada's Indians," *United Church Observer*, March 1, 1965, 14, 32.

99 E.L. Homewood, "The Indian and the Reserve," *United Church Observer*, March 15, 1965, 19–21, 45.

100 James A. Taylor, "You Have Three Years to Change Your Mind about Mike Thompson," *United Church Observer*, June 15, 1969, 12–13.

101 Bob Hunter, "There Is No Bounty on Indians Any More ... Or Is There?" *United Church Observer*, October 15, 1969, 25–26.

102 A.C. Forrest, "The Church within a Church," *United Church Observer*, November 1978, 29.

103 "Leadership from the Margins," United Church of Canada, http://www .united-church.ca/community-faith/being-community/leadership-margins.

104 General Council, "World Mission: Report of the Commission on World Mission" (November 1966): 137.

105 Editorial, "Radical Change in Mission," *United Church Observer*, October 15, 1966, 10.

106 The Board of World Mission became the Division of World Outreach in 1972.

107 Report of DWO, UCC, *Year Book* (1975), 162.

108 "Let's Forget about Converting the Jews," *United Church Observer*, April 1973, 34.

109 "The Lordship of Jesus," UCC, *Proceedings*, GC27 (1977), 419–47.

110 Phyllis Airhart, *A Church with the Soul of a Nation*, 223.

111 UCC, *Mending the World: An Ecumenical Vision for Healing and Reconciliation*, 1997.

112 "World Mission Beings at Home," *United Church Observer*, February 1971, 24.

113 General Council, "World Mission: Report of the Commission on World Mission (November 1966): 118.

114 Conversation with Stan McKay, November 18, 2015.

115 In 1973 the Indian Ministry Training Program began in Manitoba to prepare First Nations elders for ordination. This commitment led to the formation of three native ministry training centres in Ontario, the prairies, and British Columbia.

116 Rt. Rev. Bob Smith, General Council 1986, http://www.united-church.ca/ sites/default/files/resources/1986-1998-aboriginal-apologies.pdf.

117 Edith Memnook, All Native Circle Conference, responding to the apology, UCC, *Proceedings*, GC32 (1988), 79.

118 Rt. Rev. Bill Phipps, General Council Executive 1998, http://www.united -church.ca/sites/default/files/resources/1986-1998-aboriginal-apologies.pdf.

119 Ibid.

120 *A Song of Faith*, General Council Committee on Theology and Faith, 2006.

121 *Justice and Reconciliation: The Legacy of Indian Residential Schools and the Journey Toward Reconciliation* (Toronto: DMC, 2001); *Toward Justice and Right Relationship: A Beginning* (Toronto: UCC Justice, Global and Ecumenical Relations Unit, 2003).

122 *The Royal Commission on Aboriginal Peoples*, vol. 5 (Ottawa, 1996), 97.

123 Marilyn Legge, "Seeking 'Right Relations': How Should Churches Respond to Aboriginal Voices?," *Journal of the Society of Christian Ethics* 22 (Fall 2002): 27–48.

124 Marilyn Legge, "Negotiating Mission: A Canadian Stance," *International Review of Mission* 95, no. 368 (January 2004): 119–30.

125 Conversation with Stan McKay, November 18, 2015.

CHAPTER TWELVE

The End of the World as We Know It (Eschatology)

Michael Bourgeois

On January 26, 2017, the *Bulletin of the Atomic Scientists* advanced its Doomsday Clock by thirty seconds, announcing "it is two and a half minutes to midnight." When the *Bulletin* started the Doomsday Clock after the Second World War, it focused on the threat of nuclear weapons. Since then it has expanded its assessments to include other dangers to the health and safety of the earth and its inhabitants. As *Bulletin* Executive Director and Publisher Rachel Bronson noted in 2017:

> In 1947 there was one technology with the potential to destroy the planet, and that was nuclear power. Today, rising temperatures, resulting from the industrial-scale burning of fossil fuels, will change life on Earth as we know it, potentially destroying or displacing it from significant portions of the world, unless action is taken today, and in the immediate future. Future technological innovation in biology, artificial intelligence, and the cyber realm may pose similar global challenges. The knotty problems that innovations in these fields may present are not yet fully realized, but the *Bulletin*'s Science and Security Board tends to them with a watchful eye.[1]

In the early days of the Cold War, the *Bulletin* stressed "the urgency of the nuclear dangers" and set the 1947 Doomsday Clock at seven minutes to midnight. In subsequent years, the *Bulletin* has variously set the Doomsday Clock closer to or further from midnight. After the US tested its first thermonuclear weapon in October 1952, the *Bulletin* set the clock to two minutes to midnight—the closest to Doomsday the clock has ever been set. In the seventy years of its operation, the clock has been set as far as seventeen minutes from midnight, as in 1991 after the US and the Soviet Union agreed to the Strategic Arms Reduction Treaty. It has also been as close as three minutes to midnight, as in 1984, when relations between the US and the Soviet Union had badly deteriorated and the former was planning a space-based anti-ballistic missile system. In 2015, when the *Bulletin* noted that "unchecked climate change, global nuclear weapons modernizations, and outsized nuclear weapons arsenals pose extraordinary and undeniable threats to the continued existence of humanity, and world leaders have failed to act with the speed or on the scale required to protect citizens from potential catastrophe," it again set the clock at three minutes to midnight, where it remained for 2016.[2]

When the *Bulletin* advanced the Doomsday Clock another thirty seconds closer to midnight in January 2017, it based its assessment not only on military threats but also on the danger of global climate change and the limited success of efforts to address it. The *Bulletin* also argued that political risks such as "a rise in strident nationalism worldwide," "wavering public confidence in the democratic institutions required to deal with major world threats," and newly inaugurated US President Donald Trump's "intemperate statements, lack of openness to expert advice, and questionable cabinet nominations" have exacerbated the "already-threatening world situation." Compared to 2015 and 2016, the *Bulletin* concluded, "we find the danger to be even greater, the need for action more urgent. It is two and a half minutes to midnight, the Clock is ticking, global danger looms. Wise public officials should act immediately, guiding humanity away from the brink. If they do not, wise citizens must step forward and lead the way."[3]

When it created the Doomsday Clock, the *Bulletin* intentionally invoked "the imagery of apocalypse (midnight) and the contemporary idiom of nuclear explosion (countdown to zero) to convey threats to humanity and the planet."[4] The *Bulletin* intends the Doomsday Clock, however, not to induce despair but rather to inspire action to avert disaster. The Doomsday Clock is a striking example of how thoroughly the apocalyptic imagery of those traditions has permeated Euro-American cultures. Indeed, since the US detonated the first atomic bombs over Hiroshima and Nagasaki, Japan, in August 1945, the spectre of apocalypse has been prevalent in Western cultures. This spectre appears in the form of dangers, both real and imaginatively symbolic, such as nuclear war, global warming, asteroid impact, large-scale computer system malfunction, zombie outbreaks, domination by artificial intelligence, and post-apocalyptic dystopian societies. North American news and entertainment media have regularly employed apocalyptic imagery and narratives.[5] In many such examples, of course, apocalyptic scenarios function superficially to increase advertising revenues or ticket sales. In many others, such as the ways in which environmental activists employ apocalyptic narratives, the threat of the coming crisis functions, as it does with the Doomsday Clock, to motivate behavioural change in the hope of preventing or at least mitigating the otherwise likely catastrophe.[6] These narratives of possible futures thereby reflect key features of Jewish and Christian prophetic traditions: the reciprocal relationship between what we expect for the future and how we are to act in the present, and the hope that we can prevent a catastrophe then by our action now.

The area of Christian theology concerned with expectations for the future, or the "last things," is eschatology. Derived in part from the Greek word *eschaton* meaning "end" or "last," the term itself came into use in Christian theology only in the nineteenth century, but it encompasses concerns and themes that appear not only in early Christianity but also in other religious traditions such as Zoroastrianism, Judaism, and Islam. Eschatology includes personal, social, and cosmic dimensions, and is concerned with the ultimate end of individual persons and of all creation and how expectations of that end shape personal and social ethics. It is interwoven with understandings of creation, redemption, and discipleship, and can be cast in terms of either threat of catastrophic destruction or promise of marvellous renewal. Throughout the history of Christianity, specific social and historical contexts have shaped the eschatological beliefs of various Christian communities, including those of The United Church of Canada.

The prevalence of expectations of a bleak future in contemporary Euro-American culture differs sharply from the more optimistic expectations commonly held in the early twentieth century, the period during which the UCC took shape. Indeed, a more hopeful, socially oriented eschatology was a central theological motivation in the drive to form the UCC.[7] That more hopeful eschatology, rooted in late-nineteenth- and early-twentieth-century liberal evangelicalism and the broader Euro-American belief in progress, was however already being called into question by the time the UCC was established in June 1925. The changing fortunes of that more hopeful eschatology have marked the denomination's subsequent history. Understanding some of the main themes and diverse traditions in Christian eschatology and tracing how they have functioned in relation to the history of Christianity and of the UCC helps to illuminate prospects for eschatological reflection today, especially as that reflection relates to theologies of creation, redemption, and discipleship. The UCC began with a hopeful, socially oriented eschatology that was confident in the possibility of partially but significantly realizing the promised Reign of God in the present. That broadly hopeful eschatology seems untenable now, but an emerging eschatology that blends features of more hopeful and more realistic elements may help orient faith and practice today.

A Brief History of the End of the World

Most early Christians expected Jesus Christ to return soon, bringing about the general resurrection and the fulfillment of the Reign of God that he had preached and practised. In the early fourth century CE, many Christians interpreted the end of their persecution by the Roman Empire and official Roman adoption of Christianity as part of the coming of the Reign of God. The fall of Rome in the early fifth century CE, however, and the challenge it posed to beliefs about the religious significance of the Christianizing of the Roman Empire, led many Christians to look beyond history and this world for the fulfillment of the Reign of God. Augustine's *City of God*, written in the wake of the conquest and looting of Rome by Visigoths in 401 CE, characterized the City of God as an eternal, spiritual reality rather than a temporal, earthly one, and set the framework for eschatology in Catholic Christianity for the next eleven centuries.[8] During that time, some Christian groups continued to look for Christ's return in history (and were usually suppressed by church authorities), but it was only with the Protestant Reformation in Europe in the sixteenth century that more widespread hopes for Christ's imminent return were revived, hopes that included the realization of God's purposes not beyond but within history.[9] As John Webster Grant observed:

> By the seventeenth century there was widespread agreement with the Puritan Thomas Goodwin that history as the theatre of God's working must come to a satisfactory end. When religious revivals produced astonishing manifestations in eighteenth-century America, Jonathan Edwards wondered aloud whether they might not mark a significant advance toward this fulfilment. Gradually there emerged a tradition of expectation not only of religious renewal and missionary expansion but of a growth of general knowledge and prosperity, and millennial hopes inspired a rash of "benevolences" that ran the gamut from Sunday schools to temperance organizations to agitation against slavery.[10]

Various scholars of religion use somewhat different terms to describe the different types of eschatological expectation evident in the history of

Christianity. For the purposes of this discussion, I will use *millennialism* for the type that looks to a more or less imminent return of Jesus Christ within history and *amillennialism* for the type that envisions the fulfillment of the Reign of God as more of an eternal than historical reality. Amillennialism was the dominant type in Western Christianity between the fifth and sixteenth centuries, and Roman Catholic eschatology has continued to be primarily amillennial. Millennialism was the dominant type in Christianity's first four centuries, and since the Reformation in the sixteenth century most forms of Protestantism have been millennial in one way or another. The phrase "in one way or another" is important, however, because there are subtypes of millennialism with significant differences among them. Moreover, these differences are important for understanding eschatology in the UCC. The two main subtypes of millennialism are *post-millennialism* and *premillennialism*. In nineteenth-century Canada, Protestants tended to hold some version of these millennialisms without necessarily distinguishing sharply between them, but the differences grew more pronounced in the century's second half.

The primary difference between post-millennialism and premillennialism lies in their differing views of the timing of Christ's return in relation to the thousand-year reign of the saints (i.e., the "millennium") described in the Book of Revelation:

> Then I saw an angel coming down from heaven, holding in his hand the key to the bottomless pit and a great chain. He seized the dragon, that ancient serpent, who is the Devil and Satan, and bound him for a thousand years, and threw him into the pit, and locked and sealed it over him, so that he would deceive the nations no more, until the thousand years were ended. After that he must be let out for a little while. Then I saw thrones, and those seated on them were given authority to judge. I also saw the souls of those who had been beheaded for their testimony to Jesus and for the word of God. They had not worshiped the beast or its image and had not received its mark on their foreheads or their hands. They came to life and reigned with Christ a thousand years. (Revelation 20:1–4)[11]

Post-millennialism maintained that Christ would return at the *conclusion* of the millennium to bring it to its fulfillment, while premillennialism argued for Christ's return at the *start* of the millennium in order to initiate it. This difference was not, however, an arcane, inconsequential disagreement about when the Second Coming would occur. Rather, differences between post-millennialism and premillennialism on the timing of Christ's return are inextricably entwined with their different assessments of the worth and ultimate destiny of creation, the possibility of meaningfully realizing God's purposes in history, and the relative importance of divine action and human action in the realization of those purposes. Post-millennialism hopefully envisions "a gradual triumph of Christ's spirit within history," considers the possibility of a "new earth" as part of the fulfillment of God's purposes, and emphasizes the necessity of human co-operation with divine action. More pessimistically, premillennialism expects inevitable moral and spiritual decline until "a cataclysmic end of history ushered in by the physical return of Christ" initiates the final stages leading to the culmination of God's Reign. It sees no enduring value in creation, understanding it as ultimately dispensable, and regards human action as having little or no significance for the ultimate realization of God's purposes.[12] Table 12.1 summarizes these differing fundamental elements of post-millennialism and premillennialism, and their corresponding differences with amillennialism. As I will discuss below, while the relationships among these elements have characterized the main types of Christian millennial expectation into the twentieth century, the types themselves are not static. The twentieth and twenty-first centuries have made the post-millennialism that shaped the origins of the UCC difficult to maintain, but neither official church statements nor church members as a whole have embraced either amillennialism or premillennialism. Rather, as in other Protestant churches with similar histories, a type of millennialism that assembles the elements in a different way may be emerging in the UCC.

For Canadian evangelical Protestants in the mid-nineteenth century, premillennialism held sway for conservatives, but post-millennialism was the prevailing type. Indeed, "the expectation of gradual fulfilment within history was practically an axiom of Protestant thought."[13] Essential corollaries of this axiom included the conviction of the imminence of Christ's return and the urgent need for human effort to prepare themselves and the world for it. Even as liberal evangelicals embraced higher biblical criticism and adopted less literal understandings of the "Second Coming," post-millennialism remained a vital component of evangelical Protestant theology and fuelled the drive for the related aims of church union, social reform, and domestic and world mission. By the start of the twentieth century, Protestant evangelicalism in Canada and the US was fragmenting due to liberal-postmillennial and conservative-premillennial differences. Nevertheless, well into the second decade of the twentieth century, Protestant churches' perceived successes in mission, ecumenism, and social service—apparent

Table 12.1 Three main types of Christian eschatology

	Amillennialism	Post-millennialism	Premillennialism
Expectation of return of Jesus Christ	Jesus Christ will return someday to inaugurate reign of God, but reigns in spirits of believers now	Jesus Christ returns after reign of the righteous (perhaps not literal 1,000 years), bringing it to its completion	Jesus Christ will return to inaugurate the 1,000-year reign of the righteous
Assessment of history and historical events	Realistic: history may include both improvements and catastrophic events	Optimistic: gradual progress, improvement, and transformation in history	Pessimistic: spiritual decline and increasing catastrophic events in history
Value and end of creation	This creation will pass away, the "eternal state" a spiritual reality	This creation will be renewed and transformed into an ongoing new creation	This creation will be destroyed and a new creation will come to pass
Relation between divine action and human action	Fulfillment of Reign of God comes by divine power alone	Fulfillment of Reign of God initiated by divine power, but requires human co-operation	Fulfillment of Reign of God comes by divine power alone

signs of the gradual realization of the Reign of God in history—reinforced post-millennialism's influence.[14]

Of course, Canadian evangelical Protestants' conception of the Reign of God was just that—the conception primarily of the white, English-speaking, middle- and upper-class men who exercised leadership in the churches. As demonstrated, for example, by churches' participation in the residential school system in the nineteenth and twentieth centuries, what counted for Canadian evangelical Protestants as "success" in mission and social service, as signs of the coming of God's Reign on earth, could and did have devastating consequences for others.[15] Canadian Protestant churches have only recently begun to examine the ethnocentric and colonial assumptions underlying their theology and practice, including the ways in which the post-millennialism view of church mission and social service reinforced an insufficiently critical understanding of the relationship between civil government and the Reign of God.

Although not immediately apparent, the outbreak of the First World War in August 1914 marked the beginning of the end of post-millennialism as the dominant form of Protestant eschatological expectation. The war's devastating brutality, with the "Christian nations" engaged in what appeared to be interminable, pointless slaughter of their people, punctured early-twentieth-century Protestantism's hopeful vision of a gradual improvement in history. Douglas John Hall has well characterized the broad effect of the war on Euro-American culture, including Christianity:

> World War I was the shock that it was ... because the violence and viciousness that it revealed lying just beneath the urbane surface of the West's high culture had been so successfully repressed by that culture. If at the end of the war "disillusion" was "the one dominant result transcending all others," it was because so much of what had come to be by the end of the nineteenth century was sheer illusion: the illusion of unimpeded progress, of the moral neutrality of science and technology, of the essential goodness of the human spirit, of humanity's rightful mastery over nature, of the victory of rationality over ignorance and superstition, of the socially beneficial character of individual pursuit of wealth and power, and so on. So unconditionally positive were the expectations of the leading classes of European and North American societies that the experience of negation—and especially of a negation as bloody as "the Great War" proved to be—could only overwhelm.[16]

In the decades following the war, the hope for gradual improvement in history was further challenged by the global Great Depression, the rise of authoritarian communist and fascist governments in Europe, the outbreak of the Second World War, the dawn of the nuclear age, and the spread of the Cold War. As world events repeatedly and thoroughly disproved the belief in the ability of human efforts to effect gradual improvement in history, post-millennialism waned and premillennialism became the dominant type of millennialism among Protestants.

One manifestation of premillennialism's appeal today is the widespread popularity of the *Left Behind* book series, written by Tim LaHaye and Jerry B. Jenkins, with sixteen volumes published by Tyndale House from 1995 to 2007.[17] The series (which now includes four films and a video game) narrates how history will unfold according to dispensationalism, a form of premillennialism that arose in the mid-nineteenth century in the wake of failed predictions of the Second Coming on specific dates in the near future, such as the one by William Miller in 1844.[18] Historical premillennialism (as the approach by Miller and others came to be called) has abated, but it has not entirely disappeared. For example, as widely reported at the time, in 2010 a US-based evangelical radio broadcaster, Harold Camping, predicted that on 21 May 2011 Jesus Christ would return, the righteous would be raised to heaven, and the unrighteous remaining on earth would ultimately be killed by natural disasters and plagues, culminating in the total destruction of the world on 21 October 2011.[19]

The hope for possible, if not inevitable, improvement in history has not, however, been completely extinguished. Some Protestant churches' participation in the civil rights movement in the US in the 1950s and 1960s and in the anti-apartheid movement in South Africa from the 1970s to the 1990s provide important illustrations of the enduring power of post-millennially infused hope to inspire and empower progressive social change. The limited but significant successes of those struggles have also helped to nurture other struggles and the hope that sustains them. Martin Luther King Jr.'s "I Have a Dream" speech at the August 1963 March on Washington is perhaps the best and most influential twentieth-century example of the role of post-millennial thinking in churches' engagement with social justice. King's speech powerfully demonstrates appeals to the power of a hopeful vision of the future to shape moral action for justice making in the present, and to accelerate the arrival of the promised future:

> I have a dream that my four little children will one day live in a nation where they will not be judged by the color of their skin but by the content of their character.... I have a dream that one day every valley shall be exalted, and every hill and mountain shall be made low, the rough places will be made plains and the crooked places will be made straight, and the glory of the Lord shall be revealed and all flesh shall see it together. This is our hope. This is the faith with which I return to the South.... With this faith we will be able to work together, to pray together, to struggle together, to go to jail together, to stand up for freedom together, knowing that we will be free one day.... When we let freedom ring, when we let it ring from every village and every hamlet, from every state and every city, we will be able to speed up that day when all of God's children, black men and white men, Jews and Gentiles, Protestants and Catholics, will be able to join hands and sing in the words of the old Negro spiritual, "Free at last, free at last. Thank God Almighty, we are free at last."[20]

Eschatological Thinking in the UCC

Despite its decline since the early twentieth century, elements of post-millennialism have continued to guide the faith and practice of some Protestant churches and their members, including the UCC. Questions about the value and ultimate destiny of creation, the possibility of meaningfully realizing God's purposes in history, and the relative importance of divine action and human action in the realization of those purposes remain at least implicit in the church's theology and practice. Examining the shifts in eschatological thinking in the history of the UCC can help illuminate its shape today. Several UCC reports and related materials would be relevant for such a review.[21] For the purposes of this brief discussion, however, I will focus here on the following: the *Twenty Articles of Doctrine*; *A Statement of Faith*; the report by the Committee on Christian Faith, *Life and Death: A Study of the Christian Hope* (1959); *A New Creed*; and *A Song of Faith*.[22]

The *Twenty Articles of Doctrine* approved by the UCC's founding General Council in 1925 was very much a product of pre-war Protestant evangelicalism and its predominantly hopeful outlook.[23] The key parts for understanding the eschatology of the *Twenty Articles of Doctrine* are Article XIX, "Of the Resurrection, the Last Judgment and the Future Life," and Article XX, "Of Christian Service and The Final Triumph." In rather traditional terms, the former professes faith in the general resurrection leading to judgment, "the finally impenitent shall go away into eternal punishment and the righteous into life eternal." Article XX then begins by specifying, in effect, the criteria by which we must live to attain life eternal: "to further the extension of His Kingdom, to do good unto all men, to maintain the public and private worship of God, to hallow the Lord's Day, to preserve the inviolability of marriage and the sanctity of the family, to uphold the just authority of the State, and so to live in all honesty, purity and charity, that our lives shall testify of Christ." It also affirms that Jesus Christ bids "His people go into all the world and make disciples of all nations" and that by God's "power and grace all His enemies shall finally be overcome, and the kingdoms of this world be made the Kingdom of our God and of His Christ."[24] In *Our Common Faith*, the church's official commentary on the *Twenty Articles of Doctrine*, T.B. Kilpatrick commends the ancient and Reformation creeds' "wise restraint in speaking of these awful themes" of death and judgment, and exercises similar restraint in his discussion of Articles XIX and XX.[25] Addressing the connection between Christian service now and God's "final triumph," he maintains that "by such service at home and abroad, the kingdom of God is advanced, and His sovereignty established over the nations." Kilpatrick also cautions, however: "Such service, however, while indispensable and instrumental and our bounden duty, is not, of itself, the energy by which the Kingdom comes.... Thus, while we serve, we wait upon God for His grace, and we wait for God, that, in the fullness of time, He may vindicate His name, and accomplish the purpose of His love, and bring the whole world beneath the Sovereignty, once for all made victorious in Christ, crucified and risen."[26]

Despite the adoption of the *Twenty Articles of Doctrine*, many members of the churches involved in the union movement (including some supporting and some opposed to church union) were dissatisfied with it. Further, the effects of the broad cultural and theological reassessment prompted by the First World War began to be felt shortly after the UCC's formation. In 1936, then, only eleven years into the young church's life, the 7th General Council called for "a Statement of Faith that shall embody in concise and intelligible form what we in The United Church conceive to be the substance of Christian belief."[27] It also established a Commission on Christian Faith for that work, the result of which was presented to and approved by the 9th General Council in 1940.

Statement treats "Christian Life and Duty" and "The Consummation" in separate articles. This separation does not sever the connection between discipleship and eschatology seen in the last article of the *Twenty Articles of Doctrine*, but it does alter it. Article XI says in part: "We believe that they [Christians] are likewise called to live as those who are of the Kingdom of God, and to seek His righteousness both in individual and social life, serving their fellow-men in love for Christ's sake, and striving and waiting in prayer for an ordered common life where the will of God for the well-being and peace of men shall be done over all the earth." It also affirms that they "receive in this life a foretaste of the final redemption, assurance of the divine favour, peace and joy, and the confidence that He is able to keep them to the end." Article XII professes that Jesus Christ's resurrection "gives assurance that the long struggle between sin and grace will have an end, the Kingdom be revealed in its fullness, and God's eternal purpose accomplished" and that "we wait for the coming of the Kingdom which shall have no end."[28] *Statement*, then, affirms that the Reign of God will be fully realized and that it provides the framework for Christian life, but does not affirm that by "living as those who are of the Kingdom of God," humans help to accomplish its consummation. John Dow's discussion of these matters in *This Is Our Faith* illuminates this point:

> As the individual has set before him the imperative "Be ye perfect even as your
> Father in heaven is perfect" so the community is laid upon our conscience by
> the simple petition "Thy kingdom come, Thy will be done in *earth* as it is in
> heaven." It is not in human power to bring the Kingdom; but, having in our
> heart a picture of the heavenly realm, we cannot but strive to realize for men
> upon earth some foretaste of that perfect life to come.[29]

The vision of God's Reign remains that which inspires and empowers action in the present, but action in the present no longer serves to hasten the arrival of God's Reign.

In 1954, the UCC's 16th General Council instructed the Committee on Christian Faith to "prepare a statement regarding the Doctrine of Last Things, including the return of our Lord in glory; the Last Judgment and the 'Consummation of All Things' with special reference to Article XX of the Basis of Union, concerning the 'Final Triumph' of Christ, and Article XII of the Statement of Faith, entitled, 'The Consummation.'" The origin of this instruction is unclear.[30] Whatever the reason for the General Council's concern, the Committee on Christian Faith's 1959 report *Life and Death: A Study of the Christian Hope* remains the only extended discussion of eschatology generated by the UCC. In twenty-one short chapters and three appendices, it addresses standard questions in personal and cosmic eschatology, such as "Why Do We Believe in Life after Death?" and "Will Christ Come Again?" It also considers "What is the Kingdom of God?," "What Part Have Men in the Coming of the Kingdom?," "When Will the Kingdom Be Fully Realized?," and "Where Will the Kingdom of God Be Established?"

On these latter questions, *Life and Death* emphasizes God's role in the establishment of God's Reign, reflecting the twentieth century's sobered estimation of what human effort can accomplish:

> The first thing to note, then, is that the kingdom of God is the work of God
> Himself as He makes a final assault on the power of evil in the world and faces
> men with a decisive commitment to, or rejection of, His Kingship. The King-
> dom of God is not something men "bring in" or "build." It is not a Utopia nor a
> mustering of human forces for world betterment. It is God's active disclosure of
> Himself as King in which he confronts men in judgment and mercy and brings
> them to the point where they must accept or reject his rule.[31]

Acceptance of God's rule, however, does not entail inaction: "The Gospel of the Kingdom, then, is not only God's proclamation of His sovereign rule but also His summons to service. There should be no mistake about this. God calls us to work under His gracious rule for righteousness and peace on earth. And what we do in Christ's name and for his sake God uses, that His Kingdom may come."[32] On the question of *when* God's Reign will be accomplished, *Life and Death* reflects the twentieth century's tempering of post-millennialism's sense of imminence. It affirms that God already reigns—"He is now, and always has been, ruling over His creation"—but that "we do not know when the Kingdom of God will come in its fullness."[33] On the question of *where* it will be accomplished, however, it maintains post-millennialism's hope for the renewal and transformation of creation: "Only a new creation could be adequate to express the final purpose of God for man."[34]

As a brief creedal statement primarily intended for liturgical use, *A New Creed* does not address eschatology in as much detail as the *Twenty Articles of Doctrine* or *Statement*. At least implicitly, however, it connects discipleship and Christian service with eschatology through the sequence in which it first names tasks to which we are called, including "to seek justice and resist evil" and "to proclaim Jesus, our judge and our hope," and then professes: "In life, in death, in life beyond death, God is with us. We are not alone."[35] Its affirmation that humans are to "live with respect in creation" also suggests they are to emulate God's care for that which God has brought into being. The modesty of *A New Creed*'s eschatological claims well reflect the sobered expectations of many late-twentieth-century Christians in the global North. *Song* similarly affirms the eventual fulfillment of God's Reign, including the renewal of all creation, and addresses discipleship in the context of eschatology, but it does not suggest that people can hasten the arrival of God's reign by action today:

We place our hope in God.
We sing of a life beyond life
    and a future good beyond imagining:
    a new heaven and a new earth,
    the end of sorrow, pain, and tears,
    Christ's return and life with God,
        the making new of all things.
    We yearn for the coming of that future,
    even while participating in eternal life now.
Divine creation does not cease
    until all things have found wholeness, union, and integration
        with the common ground of all being.

As children of the Timeless One,
> our time-bound lives will find completion
> in the all-embracing Creator.
In the meantime, we embrace the present,
> embodying hope, loving our enemies,
> caring for the earth,
> choosing life.[36]

Conclusion: A Chastened Post-Millennialism?

The UCC began with a consistently post-millennial outlook, but its escha-tology has shifted in the context of one hundred years of historical events that have made belief in humanity's ability to effect gradual realization of the Reign of God on earth, even with divine assistance, difficult to sus-tain. This theological shift is analogous to the changes in Christian escha-tological thinking that followed, for example, the collapse of the Roman Empire in the fifth century and the Protestant Reformation in the sixteenth century. Like other Protestant churches with similar histories, however, the UCC and its members have not, as a whole, embraced premillennial-ism. On the contrary, they resist premillennialism's literal interpretations of the 'Second Coming,' its pessimistic outlook on the course of history, its negative assessment of the value of creation, and its dim view of the significance of human effort for accomplishing God's redemptive purposes. The prevalence of apocalyptic premillennial eschatology in contemporary Protestantism, however, as well as the loss of collective memory about post-millennialism's previous importance for the church, make it difficult for many UCC members to recognize that an alternative to premillennialism is both available and important for faith and practice.

An alternative eschatology may be emerging. Like traditional amillenni-alism, formal UCC statements and individual members seem largely uncon-cerned about the timing of the return of Jesus Christ and regard the course of history realistically, hoping and working for partial realizations of God's Reign but acknowledging that setbacks and failures are inevitable. At least implicitly but sometimes explicitly, however, formal UCC statements and individual members seem to retain two elements of post-millennialism: the enduring value of all creation, and the necessity of human co-operation with divine initiative, not primarily for the sake of personal salvation, but rather so that humans might share God's peace, justice, and love in ways that genuinely benefit all of God's creatures and offer witness to God's ultimate

Table 12.2 Chastened post-millennialism: UCC eschatology today?

	Amillennialism	Post-millennialism	Premillennialism
Expectation of return of Jesus Christ	Jesus Christ will return someday to inaugurate reign of God, but reigns in spirits of believers now	Jesus Christ returns after reign of the righteous (perhaps not literal 1,000 years), bringing it to its completion	Jesus Christ will return to inaugurate the 1,000-year reign of the righteous
Assessment of history and historical events	Realistic: history may include both improvements and catastrophic events	Optimistic: gradual progress, improvement, and transformation in history	Pessimistic: spiritual decline and increasing catastrophic events in history
Value and end of creation	This creation will pass away, the "eternal state" a spiritual reality	This creation will be renewed and transformed into an ongoing new creation	This creation will be destroyed and a new creation will come to pass
Relation between divine action and human action	Fulfillment of Reign of God comes by divine power alone	Fulfillment of Reign of God initiated by divine power, but requires human co-operation	Fulfillment of Reign of God comes by divine power alone

healing of all creation. Table 12.2 illustrates this blending of elements from the main types of Christian millennial expectation.

By employing elements of both amillennialism and post-millennialism, this alternative eschatology demonstrates not only that the leading types of Christian millennial expectation wax and wane in relation to historical events, but also that they can take new shape as their traditional forms are found wanting. "Types" are not static and eternal. "Types" such as the forms of Christian millennial expectation are tools crafted by observers to organize and explain faith practitioners' beliefs and behaviours in specific contexts. As faith practitioners' beliefs and behaviours change, observers must from time to time revise their tools. The form of eschatological thinking that may be emerging in the UCC and other similar denominations will coexist with the traditional amillennial, post-millennial, and premillennial types, and individual church members may embrace elements of these types in other hybrid versions. This "chastened post-millennialism," however, may offer a hopeful vision of God's redemptive purposes that can avoid some of traditional post-millennialism's shortcomings while still providing a compelling theological framework for working towards the healing of creation.[37]

NOTES

1   Rachel Bronson, "Statement of the Executive Director," in John Mecklin, ed., "It Is Two and a Half Minutes to Midnight: 2017 Doomsday Clock Statement," Science and Security Board, *Bulletin of the Atomic Scientists* (January 2017): 1. http://thebulletin.org/sites/default/files/Final%202017%20Clock%20 Statement.pdf.

2   "Timeline," *Bulletin of the Atomic Scientists*, http://thebulletin.org/timeline.

3   Mecklin, "It Is Two and a Half Minutes to Midnight," 2–8.

4   Ibid., 2.

5   See, for example, Tom Bissell, "A Comet's Tale: On the Science of Apocalypse," *Harper's Magazine*, February 2003, 33–47, and Gayle MacDonald, "Lights, Camera, Apocalypse!," *Globe and Mail*, July 19, 2003, http://www .theglobeandmail.com/arts/lights-camera-apocalypse/article4128894/.

6   John Allemang, "Lowering the Doom," *Globe and Mail*, December 5, 2009, F1; and Robin Globus Veldman, "Narrating the Environmental Apocalypse: How Imagining the End Facilitates Moral Reasoning among Environmental Activists," *Ethics and the Environment* 17, no. 1 (June 2012): 1–23.

7   John Webster Grant, "From Revelation to Revolution: Some Thoughts on the Background of the Social Gospel," *Toronto Journal of Theology* 12, no. 2 (Fall 1996): 159–68.

8   Augustine, *City of God*, ed. David Knowles, trans. Henry Bettenson (London: Penguin, 1972).

9   Grant, "From Revelation to Revolution," 160–61.

10   Ibid., 161.

11   All biblical citations are from the New Revised Standard Version.

12   Grant, "From Revelation to Revolution," 160–61; and Robert B. Bater, "Storm over the Kingdom of Peace: Conflicting Interpretations of the Kingdom of God," in *A Long and Faithful March: "Towards the Christian Revolution" 1930s/1980s*, ed. Harold Wells and Roger Hutchinson (Toronto: UCPH, 1989), 92–103.

13   Grant, "From Revelation to Revolution," 161.

14   Ibid., 161–67.

15   Loraine MacKenzie Shepherd, "Church of the Margins: A Call to Solidarity," in *Intersecting Voices: Critical Theologies in a Land of Diversity*, ed. Don Schweitzer and Derek Simoň (Ottawa: Novalis, 2004), 135–51; and Alf Dumont and Roger Hutchinson, "United Church Mission Goals and First Nations Peoples," in *A History of The United Church of Canada*, ed. Don Schweitzer (Waterloo, ON: Wilfrid Laurier University Press, 2012), 221–38.

16   Douglas John Hall, "'The Great War' and the Theologians," in *The Twentieth Century: A Theological Overview*, ed. Gregory Baum (Ottawa: Novalis, 1999), 6–7; Hall quotes Barbara Tuchman, *The Guns of August* (New York: Dell, 1962), 489.

17   See for example *Left Behind: A Novel of the Earth's Last Days* (Wheaton, IL: Tyndale House, 1995), the narrative of which provides a fictionalized account of events just before, during, and after "the Rapture."

18   Paul Boyer, "The Growth of Fundamentalist Apocalyptic in the United States," in *The Continuum History of Apocalypticism*, ed. Bernard McGinn, John Collins, and Stephen Stein (New York: Continuum, 2003), 516–44; and Barbara Rossing, "The Invention of The Rapture," *The Rapture Exposed: The Message of Hope in the Book of Revelation* (Boulder, CO: Westview Press, 2004), 19–46.

19   When May 21, 2011, passed without the predicted events, Camping initially responded that a "spiritual judgment" had occurred, and that the Second Coming of Christ and the other events leading to the destruction of the earth would happen simultaneously on 21 October 2011. Once again, however, events disproved Camping's prediction. Tom Bartlett, "A Year after the Non-Apocalypse," *Religion Dispatches*, 21 May 2012, http://religiondispatches.org/a-year-after-the-non-apocalypse-where-are-they-now/; Jennifer Leclair, "Harold Camping Admits Rapture Prediction was 'Sinful Statement,'" *Charisma News*, 7 March 2012, http://www.charismanews.com/us/32958-harold-camping-admits-rapture-prediction-was-sinful-statement.

20   Martin Luther King Jr., "I Have a Dream ...," 5–6, United States of America National Archives, https://www.archives.gov/files/press/exhibits/dream-speech.pdf.

21   Examples include, in chronological order: Commission on Christianizing the Social Order, "Report of the Commission on Christianizing the Social Order," UCC *Proceedings*, GC6, 1934, 235–48; R.B.Y. Scott and Gregory Vlastos, eds, *Towards the Christian Revolution* (Chicago: Willett Clark, 1936; reprint ed., Kingston: Ronald P. Frye, 1989); UCC, *Mending the World: An Ecumenical*

Vision for Healing and Reconciliation (Toronto: UCPH, 1997); Committee on Theology and Faith, "Reconciling and Making New," and DWO, "'To Seek Justice and Resist Evil': Towards a Global Economy for All God's People," UCC *Proceedings*, GC37, 2000, 383–405 and 784–857.

22 UCC, *The Manual, 2016*, 37th rev. ed. (Toronto: UCPH, 2013), 11–28; The Committee on the Christian Faith, *Life and Death: A Study of the Christian Hope*, ed. A.G. Reynolds (Toronto: BESS and Board of Christian Education, UCC, 1959).

23 John H. Young, "Sacred Cow or White Elephant: The Doctrine Section of the Basis of Union," *Touchstone* 16, no. 2 (May 1998): 30–41.

24 *The Manual*, 15.

25 Thomas Buchanan Kilpatrick, *Our Common Faith* (Toronto: Ryerson Press, 1928), 204–10.

26 Ibid., 209–10.

27 Young, "Sacred Cow or White Elephant," 39–40; UCC, *Proceedings*, GC7, 1936, 49.

28 *The Manual*, 18–19.

29 John Dow, *This Is Our Faith: An Exposition of the Statement of Faith of The United Church of Canada* (Toronto: BESS, 1943), 218.

30 UCC, *Proceedings*, GC17, 1956, 122; *Life and Death*, 2. The Committee on Christian Faith's report in UCC, GC17, 1956, 122, notes that this matter was one of two that the 16th General Council had referred to the Committee, but none of the memorials listed in the *Record of Proceedings of the Sixteenth General Council*, 55–62, reflect a concern about "the Doctrine of Last Things." A report to the 16th General Council from the Committee on the Church and International Affairs, 144–47, deals in part with "Disarmament, the Atomic Bomb and the Thermo-Nuclear Bomb," but makes no explicit reference to eschatology. Further, I have found no relevant reference in the minutes of the sessions of the 16th General Council, 14–54.

31 *Life and Death*, 85.

32 Ibid., 89.

33 Ibid., 93.

34 Ibid., 107.

35 *The Manual*, 20.

36 *The Manual*, 27–28.

37 I have not conducted scientific surveys to test my claim about the emergence among UCC members of the alternative eschatology I describe here, but I

have for several years tested it with groups of theological students in classes at Emmanuel College, Toronto, and with laypeople in various ucc contexts. While some people profess other hybrid forms, and a few affirm a consistent post-millennialism, by far most embrace the elements of what I call here "chastened post-millennialism."

CONCLUSION

... A Work in Progress

Don Schweitzer, Robert C. Fennell, and Michael Bourgeois

A hallmark of The United Church of Canada's theology as presented in the preceding chapters is that it remains a work in progress. The UCC's theology has a dynamic quality. Within its first hundred years, it has produced four different official statements of faith! Each was developed in a different era of the denomination's life, and yet in very recent years, all four have been affirmed as still authoritative and normative. Paradoxically, this dynamic quality is the result of faithfulness to what have been enduring sources and norms for its theology. Adherence to these has led to recurring, central theological themes being stated or understood differently throughout its history, as the UCC has continually sought to understand the meaning of the gospel in relation to changes in its context. What follows will conclude this book by examining the sources, norms, and approaches that give the UCC's theology this dynamic character.

Sources and Norms

Historically, the UCC's theology was rooted in the Reformed and Methodist theological traditions operative in the denominations that formed it. These traditions were foundational for the development of the doctrinal section of the denomination's *Basis of Union*.[1] However, the doctrinal section of the BOU also claimed an allegiance to affirmations of the early church councils.[2] Here and in subsequent materials, the UCC's official theology has typically been characterized by a loyalty to the theological heritage of the ecumenical church. That is, the broadly attested, historic, and globally shared theological convictions of the Christian movement as a whole have been normative for the UCC as well.

Scripture was acknowledged as the primary source for theology in the Reformed and Methodist theological traditions that the UCC inherited. Having Scripture as its primary theological source helped impart a dynamic quality to the UCC's theology, as the theological concepts and doctrinal formulations that it inherited have been understood to be open to ongoing, thoughtful review and reconsideration in light of the witness of Scripture. As changes in its context have led the UCC to read Scripture differently, its theology has changed. While Scripture has typically been affirmed as the primary source for its theology, the UCC has consistently affirmed Jesus Christ as the culmination of biblical revelation and therefore as the primary norm for its theology. While the denomination's understanding of the person and saving significance of Jesus Christ has changed, it has continued to confess that Jesus Christ is decisive for its understanding of God and salvation, and indeed for all aspects of theology, the church, and Christian life.

In the course of the UCC's history, a second norm for its approach to theology has emerged: Scripture must be read in relation to the church's present context. Douglas John Hall has insisted that "theology is by definition contextual."[3] The gospel must be understood in relation to the concrete realities, hopes, and fears of the time and place in which the church is situated. Hall's insistence on this reflects the way the UCC has typically done theology over the course of its history. In reading Scripture in relation to its context, the denomination has seen itself to be faithfully carrying on the Reformed and Methodist theological traditions that it inherited. These antecedent church traditions were keenly interested in and responsive to the world around them.

This second norm has meant that the UCC's theology has always also had a third source. Scripture has generally been the primary source for the denomination's theology. The theological traditions and concepts it inherited and received from the Reformed and Methodist traditions and those of the larger church, old and new, have been a second source, subordinate to the first. A third source is signalled at the beginning of the BOU in the declaration that church union was intended to create a church that in due time might come to be "fittingly described as national."[4] This indicated that the UCC was meant to be "vigorously engaged"[5] with its Canadian context. This has proven to be true. This kind of engagement on the part of the denominations entering union was a crucial source of the theological thinking that gave rise to the UCC. For instance, it helped promote a new understanding of John 17:21 ("that all may be one") as a mandate for organic union among unionists. As this example indicates, the denomination's engagement with its context has not been a source for its theology in the same sense as Scripture. But the two have generally been closely related. The UCC's understanding of the biblical message has shaped its engagement with its context. This engagement has in turn influenced its reading of Scripture. Involvement with issues and ideas in the Canadian context and overseas mission fields have especially impacted the denomination's thinking. As the UCC has read Scripture in light of its engagement with the issues and ideas present in its context, aspects of this context have entered into its understanding of the gospel. So also, the context has been understood and engaged in light of the church's interpretation and application of Scripture.

The UCC's engagement with its Canadian context has thus meant that its theology has been influenced for better or worse by ideas, attitudes, and modes of thought prevalent in Canada and the wider North Atlantic region. These ideas and attitudes have formed part of the background in relation to which the UCC interprets Scripture. Sometimes these ideas have been adopted as background theories[6] that helped determine the meaning of Scripture for the UCC. For instance, a shift in the socially prevalent understanding of homosexuality took place in Canada during the 1970s and '80s. The view that homosexuality was a form of deviance was losing ground to the view that it occurs naturally. For a variety of reasons, this latter understanding was adopted as a background theory regarding the nature of homosexual orientation in the 1984 *Report on Sexual Orientation and Eligibility for the Order of Ministry.*[7] This prompted a rereading of Scripture regarding the place of gay and lesbian persons in the UCC. This in turn helped lead to the General Council decision in 1988 that sexual orientation was not in itself a barrier to ordination. At other times, the UCC has challenged socially prevalent ideas and attitudes. In the 1960s and 1970s, an attitude of "self-sufficient finitude"[8] formed the horizon of thought for many Canadians, as exemplified in Pierre Berton's book *The Comfortable Pew.* That is, the modern person came to be seen as self-enclosed, self-defining, and completely autonomous, without any need for community in order to be a "whole self." While the UCC shared the sense of personal and social responsibility implied in this attitude, it rejected the notion that twentieth-century Westerners could and should be ultimately autonomous. Instead, it confessed Jesus Christ as its judge and hope,[9] and its Lord.[10] Through that Christological lens, human life is understood and meaningful only in relation to other lives, to creation, and indeed to the triune God.

UCC theology has always been developed in light of its engagement with its Canadian context. There is sometimes criticism of the denomination for tracking its thought too closely with cultural developments. But its relation to the surrounding social context has been determined not by mere imitation, but through thoughtful and prayerful discussions within the church and attempts to discern what the Spirit was leading it to say and do. These discussions do not always lead to consensus, so that sometimes roughly concurrent UCC statements or publications have expressed different views. On occasion, opposing views have appeared in the same UCC documents, sometimes as minority reports. But overshadowing such disagreement have been discernible shifts in the denomination's understanding of the faith. This is apparent through comparison of its four official faith statements or "subordinate standards." Because the UCC has been characteristically engaged with its Canadian context and beyond, as this context and its overseas mission fields have changed, so has its theology.

The failures and successes of the UCC's engagement with Canadian society and other societies and cultures through its overseas work have frequently been learning processes that helped shape its theology. Furthermore, the UCC's understandings of what it is called to do and to be have also been developed in relation to the possibilities for discipleship that its context and mission fields present. The hope expressed in the BOU that the UCC might one day be a determinative influence on the moral ethos of Canadian life is no longer viable. The nation is too pluralistic and diverse for any one religious tradition to exert that kind of normalizing power. Nor does the church any longer wish to exercise such dominance over others. But the UCC has always vigorously engaged its Canadian context and others, and this engagement has been an important contributing source to its theology.

The membership of the UCC, at the time of this book's writing, is predominantly middle class and anglophone. Partly as a result of this, the UCC's theology has often been experienced by Indigenous peoples in Canada and elsewhere as part of an oppressive imposition from which they seek liberation. Since the 1960s, the theology of the UCC has become that of a disestablished church (no longer claiming to be a definer of the whole nation's culture) and, since the 1980s, that of a church officially apologetic for its complicity in colonialism. Its theology has become increasingly accepting of cultural pluralism within the church; increasingly open to religious pluralism in its surrounding contexts; and increasingly dialogical in relation to other religions and minority populations, whether cultural, ethnic, racial, or sexual. The UCC now realizes more than it did in its first few decades that understanding the gospel contextually may at times require a confession of guilt and far-reaching repentance. One of the important features in ucc theological work in the last thirty-five years has been the increasing presence of voices and perspectives that are not Eurocentric. This is a welcome development, given the complexity of the ucc's and indeed of Canada's ethnic plurality and changing immigration patterns. Increasing awareness and valuing of First Nations' ways of doing theology, practising the faith, and living on the land continue to challenge and change the ucc. The 2006 General Council initiative to become an intercultural church is also crucial to the denomination's capacity to welcome and honour diverse voices. The dominant world views and assumptions of those of European descent are slowly—perhaps too slowly—giving way to an ever-greater multiplicity of theological perspectives and ways of doing theology. We see this reflected in this volume in the contributions of Adrian Jacobs, Hye-Ran Kim-Cragg, and Hyuk Cho. In future years, we can expect this diversity to continue to expand.

Approach

Equally important as the sources and norms of the ucc's theology are the ways in which these have been typically employed in formulating it. The formation of the denomination happened through a blending of Methodist, Congregationalist, and Presbyterian traditions. These were similar enough that they could be combined in a way acceptable to the majority of members in each denomination. This blending happened with a concern to state the truth, to lift up the gospel of Jesus Christ, to remain faithful to the denominational heritages of those entering church union, and to do so in a way that would enhance the engagement of Canadian Protestants with their context. The latter meant that while doctrinal precision was important in the formative theology of the ucc, so was the achievement of organic union. A lasting legacy of this concern—that theology would enable a more effective Christian witness and discipleship through the formation and maintenance of organic union—has been an openness within the ucc to a range of theological diversity. It has also shaped the recognition that theological statements like *A New Creed* or *A Song of Faith* should be written so that people within a spectrum of theological differences could see their views represented in them. This openness to a range of theological diversity is related to the ucc's emphasis on faith in action. Because the denomination emphasizes doing the truth as well as understanding it, it has sought to understand the Christian faith in ways that enable it to be communicated and enacted effectively and appropriately in its context.

A second characteristic of the UCC's approach to theology is the careful, critical, and appreciative reading of Scripture. While Scripture is generally affirmed as the primary source for its theology, the denomination has often interpreted it in light of contemporary biblical scholarship, and more recently with an explicit concern for how its interpretations function within the church and beyond. In the UCC's official theology, Scripture is understood to become the living Word of God through the inspiration of the Holy Spirit, which makes use of individuals' critical faculties to develop appropriate interpretations of Scripture. Furthermore, while Scripture speaks of more than Jesus Christ, the UCC has repeatedly affirmed that it was in Jesus that God's Word became incarnate in a uniquely definitive way. The Bible's particular capacity to witness to Jesus Christ, and to the presence and purposes of the triune God through time and across geography, has made it an incomparable resource for Christianity, including the UCC.

A third characteristic of the UCC's way of doing theology is the consultative approach it has employed in developing much of its theology. A standing committee addresses theological issues and questions, but much of the denomination's theology is found in reports from other committees or in resources that others in the church produce. In recent decades, the UCC has consulted congregations more deliberately in developing theological statements like *Song*. While professional theologians are often involved in the formation of its theology, and while in the denomination's early decades theological statements were often prepared by select committees, key statements and reports have always required final approval by the General Council or its executive, which represent the church as a whole. In this respect, theology in the UCC is a responsibility of the whole church. There is no one body or class of experts within it that develops or oversees its theology without consultation with representatives of the whole.

Fourth, the UCC typically understands itself as part of what God is doing through the larger church around the world. Its theology is often developed through dialogue and consultation with ecumenical partners and the theological heritage of the whole church and, more recently, in some cases with representatives of other religions. Its theology is sometimes decisively shaped by its ecumenical relations. To be sure, the denomination tends to favour Protestant expressions of the Christian faith. While the UCC's theology reflects its Canadian context and its Reformed and Methodist heritage, its ecumenical relationships, overseas missions, and commitment to the work of its global partners have helped to keep its theology from becoming narrow. Its theology is also often developed in dialogue with theological movements originating elsewhere. In the course of its history, Neo-Ortho-doxy, feminist theology, Latin American liberation theology, and other movements have all entered into the UCC's theology. As at its founding, the-ology in the UCC continues to be developed through a blending of theologi-cal traditions and movements.

Yet this characteristic is counterbalanced by a fifth. In the development of its theology, from its formation onward, the UCC has frequently demon-strated an evangelical freedom to go beyond inherited concepts, practices, and traditions. That is, the denomination embraces a gospel-based freedom to do or say something relatively new in church history on the basis of what God has done in Jesus Christ and in light of the witness of the Holy Spirit in the present. This freedom extends even to its own history. In various reports, in resources it has produced, in its apologies to Indigenous peoples, and in its later three subordinate standards, the denomination has shown itself willing to develop positions that go beyond or contradict aspects of what it has previously taught. For instance, the 1928 *Report of the Com-mittee on the Ordination of Women* argued that while Paul placed restric-tions on the participation of women in certain ministries, these were no longer binding on the UCC due to the "vastly altered conditions of modern society."[11] In another example, *A New Creed* and *Song* make no mention of "eternal punishment," which had been affirmed in the doctrinal section of the *BOU*.[12] In doing theology, the UCC is typically guided by its past, but not bound by it. This was evident in its formation and remains characteristic of how it does theology. The denomination's theological life has simultaneous commitments to freedom, flexibility, and faithfulness.

These observations lead to the conclusion that the UCC's approach to theology tends to be characterized by a triple loyalty: to the gospel, to the Canadian context, and to the global, ecumenical church. While the UCC has a few congregations outside of Canada, it is an inherently Canadian church, and its theology reflects this. Major changes in Canadian society frequently lead to changes in its theology. Thus, while there are recur-ring themes in its thought, these tend to be understood in different ways throughout its history. These three loyalties sometimes conflict with each other. For instance, when loyalty to the gospel and to the insights of femi-nism led the UCC to participate in a movement to develop baptismal formu-las that were not restricted to traditional male terms for God, this created tension with some of its ecumenical partners. These three loyalties are not always shared, or shared equally, by all its members or by unofficial theolo-gies expressed within the UCC. At times the denomination has chosen to exercise evangelical freedom in relation to and in contrast to the positions of its ecumenical partners, out of what it understood to be loyalty to Jesus Christ and the witness of the Holy Spirit. The welcoming of gay and lesbian persons into ministry is a good example of this: the UCC said "yes" when nearly all other Christian churches said "no." Still, this triple loyalty is characteristic of the UCC's official theology over the course of its history. In its typical approach to theology, tensions between these three loyalties tend to be treated as productive inducements to seek a theology that is contextually appropriate, faithful to Scripture, and in keeping with the consensus of the ecumenical church. This is a balancing act that is rarely easy to perform but is one to which the denomination is committed.

Themes

A first recurring theme in UCC theology is the centrality of Jesus Christ. The *BOU* described Jesus as the "chief cornerstone"[13] of its understanding of the Christian faith, and this has been reaffirmed throughout the denomination's history. Jesus Christ is both a central topic in UCC theology and frequently key to its understanding of God, creation, and redemption. Yet the centrality of Jesus Christ is balanced by openness to the Holy Spirit's work in the church and the world. While Christology is central to the UCC's theology, it has understood Jesus in various ways. Each of the subordinate standards affirms Jesus's saving significance, yet each understands this slightly differently. This openness to rethinking the church's understanding of the faith in light of cultural changes recognizes that as the face of evil changes from age to age,[14] so must the church's understanding of Jesus and his saving significance, if its theology is to be appropriate to its context.

A second related recurring theme is the trinitarian nature of God. The doctrine of the Trinity first developed as a result of the impact of Jesus Christ upon the early church's inherited understanding of divinity. Conversely, Jesus can be fully understood as the Christ only in trinitarian terms. As the person, work, and relationships of Jesus Christ remain recurring themes in UCC theology, so too does the Trinity.

The Holy Spirit has not been a recurring theme in UCC thought in the same way. While all four subordinate standards mention the Spirit, particularly *Song*, it has not been a featured topic in UCC theology to the same extent as Christology. However, the broad conviction that theology must be done with openness to what the Spirit is saying and doing in the present has been a recurring theme in the UCC's life and thought, so much so that this can be described as a defining characteristic of its approach to theology. The denomination's theological reservoirs would be deepened by further research and sustained reflection on the doctrine of the Holy Spirit.

The goodness of God and creation; the need for redemption and its availability through Christ and the Spirit; the possibility of sanctification; the calling of the church to give thanks to God and to participate in God's saving work—these have all been recurring themes in UCC theological thought. As an heir to Reformed and Methodist traditions of theology, the UCC looks for God's renewing work in all things. Individuals, families, the church, institutions, and society as a whole are to be made new in light of the eschatological hope given in Jesus Christ. But what this reconciliation and renewal should look like, and how Christians should work towards it, have been understood very differently in the course of the denomination's history. These differences continue to be features of the UCC's life and work.

Conclusion

As noted above, UCC theology tends to change. Is there a pattern to this change? The denomination has been accused of simply adapting its theology to the surrounding Canadian context and predominating trends. In one sense this is true. The UCC tries to express its theology in language and concepts that can communicate the gospel to its context. For this reason, the terminology it uses to articulate its theology tends to be adapted to changes in its context. But the content of its theology often challenges ideas and practices that are socially prevalent in Canada, even as aspects of these ideas enter into its theology. So in terms of content, it is not true that the UCC simply adapts its thinking to conform to the values and world view of its context. The witness of Scripture and the norming reality of Jesus Christ have been significant factors that lead to challenging (not acquiescing to) the broader culture, especially when the latter is perceived to be in error or treading closely to idols and distortions. Moreover, doctrine is largely stable, even if theological expressions vary from generation to generation.

Changes in the theology of the UCC do not necessarily follow a pattern of linear development. Linear or cumulative developments in thought often occur in order to resolve tensions or contradictions in it. But there are tensions in UCC theology, such as that between justification and sanctification, that are unresolvable, as these reflect tensions at the heart of the gospel. These tensions tend not to be resolved as UCC theology changes, but rather to be restated in new forms. Justification is about how one is reconciled to

God through what God has done in Jesus Christ. As one is justified by grace, one is accepted by God as one is. Sanctification is about how one is called and enabled to change by the transformative power of the Holy Spirit. Justification implies unconditional acceptance. Sanctification implies an expectation that one will change, in the sense of being made new in the image of Christ. Both express aspects of the gospel. The tension between the two is reflected in UCC practices. The denomination has sought to include people from many different backgrounds in its common life. Inclusion requires acceptance. Yet the UCC has also sought to form people into what it sees to be a more sanctified way of life, sometimes with beneficial and sometimes with disastrous consequences.

The tension between justification and sanctification makes it difficult for cumulative development in Christian theology, for this tension emanates from the encounter of God's love, which is at the heart of the gospel, with sin and evil. God's love both accepts the unrighteous and demands their sanctification. It is a simultaneous "yes" and "no" to one's current state. This tension will be overcome only in the eschaton, in the final fulfillment of God's purposes. In the meantime, the UCC, like other churches, lives within that tension. There are cumulative developments in some aspects of UCC theology.[15] But in many respects, the dynamism in its approach to theology runs not toward a resolution of this or other tensions, or toward a cumulative development, but toward a renewed statement in each era of basic, core aspects of the Christian message. As A Statement of Faith put in in 1940, "Christians of each new generation are called to state [the church's faith] afresh in terms of the thought of their own age and with the emphasis their age needs." This is typically the way in which UCC theology changes. And so the theology of The United Church of Canada remains a work in progress.

NOTES

1   See the Introduction to this volume for an account of the development of the Twenty Articles of Doctrine that were foundational for the UCC.

2   Twenty Articles of Doctrine, The Manual, 2016, 37th rev. ed. (Toronto: UCPH, 2013), 11.

3   Douglas John Hall, Thinking the Faith: Christian Theology in a North American Context (Minneapolis, MN: Augsburg Fortress, 1989), 85. Hall is a member of the United Church and served for a time on its Theology and Faith Committee.

4   *The Manual*, 3.

5   Sandra Beardsall, "Sin and Redemption in The United Church of Canada," chapter 4 in this volume.

6   Francis Schüssler Fiorenza, *Foundational Theology: Jesus and the Church* (New York: Crossroad, 1986), 310–11.

7   UCC, *Proceedings*, GC30, 1984, 198.

8   Paul Tillich, cited in Roger Shinn, "Tillich as Interpreter and Disturber of Contemporary Culture," *Bulletin of the American Academy of Arts and Sciences* 39, no. 4 (January 1986): 23.

9   *A New Creed, The Manual*, 20.

10 David Lochhead/The Committee on Christian Faith, *The Lordship of Jesus* (Toronto: DMC, UCC, 1978), 6–8.

11 UCC, *Proceedings*, GC3, 1928, 364.

12 *Twenty Articles of Doctrine*, 15.

13 *The Manual*, 11.

14 Gregory Baum, *Religion and Alienation* (New York: Paulist Press, 1975), 188.

15 On this, see chapter 3 in this volume.

The United Church of Canada's Four Subordinate Standards

Twenty Articles of Doctrine (1925)

We, the representatives of the Presbyterian, Methodist, and Congregational branches of the Church of Christ in Canada, do hereby set forth the substance of the Christian faith, as commonly held among us. In doing so, we build upon the foundation laid by the apostles and prophets, Jesus Christ Himself being the chief cornerstone. We affirm our belief in the Scriptures of the Old and New Testaments as the primary source and ultimate standard of Christian faith and life. We acknowledge the teaching of the great creeds of the ancient Church. We further maintain our allegiance to the evangelical doctrines of the Reformation, as set forth in common in the doctrinal standards adopted by The Presbyterian Church in Canada, by The Congregational Union of Ontario and Quebec, and by The Methodist Church. We present the accompanying statement as a brief summary of our common faith and commend it to the studious attention of the members and adherents of the negotiating Churches, as in substance agreeable to the teaching of the Holy Scriptures.

Article I. Of God. We believe in the one only living and true God, a Spirit, infinite, eternal, and unchangeable, in His being and perfections; the Lord Almighty, who is love, most just in all His ways, most glorious in holiness, unsearchable in wisdom, plenteous in mercy, full of compassion, and abundant in goodness and truth. We worship Him in the unity of the Godhead and the mystery of the Holy Trinity, the Father, the Son, and the Holy Spirit, three persons of the same substance, equal in power and glory.

Article II. Of Revelation. We believe that God has revealed Himself in nature, in history, and in the heart of man; that He has been graciously pleased to make clearer revelation of Himself to men of God who spoke as they were moved by the Holy Spirit; and that in the fullness of time He has perfectly revealed Himself in Jesus Christ, the Word made flesh, who is the brightness of the Father's glory and the express image of His person We receive the Holy Scriptures of the Old and New Testaments, given by inspiration of God, as containing the only infallible rule of faith and life, a faithful record of God's gracious revelations, and as the sure witness of Christ.

Article III. Of the Divine Purpose. We believe that the eternal, wise, holy, and loving purpose of God so embraces all events that, while the freedom of man is not taken away, nor is God the author of sin, yet in His providence He makes all things work together in the fulfilment of His sovereign design and the manifestation of His glory.

Article IV. Of Creation and Providence. We believe that God is the creator, upholder, and governor of all things; that He is above all His works and in them all; and that He made man in His own image, meet for fellowship with Him, free and able to choose between good and evil, and responsible to his Maker and Lord.

Article V. Of the Sin of Man. We believe that our first parents, being tempted, chose evil, and so fell away from God and came under the power of sin, the penalty of which is eternal death; and that, by reason of this disobedience, all men are born with a sinful nature, that we have broken God's law, and that no man can be saved but by His grace.

Article VI. Of the Grace of God. We believe that God, out of His great love for the world, has given His only begotten Son to be the Saviour of sinners, and in the Gospel freely offers His all-sufficient salvation to all men. We believe also that God, in His own good pleasure, gave to his son a people, an innumerable multitude, chosen in Christ unto holiness, service, and salvation.

Article VII. Of the Lord Jesus Christ. We believe in and confess the Lord Jesus Christ, the only Mediator between God and man, who, being the Eternal Son of God, for us men and for our salvation became truly man, being conceived of the Holy Spirit and born of the Virgin Mary, yet without sin. Unto us He has revealed the Father, by His word and Spirit, making known the perfect will of God. For our redemption, He fulfilled all righteousness, offered Himself a perfect sacrifice on the Cross, satisfied Divine justice, and made propitiation for the sins of the whole world. He rose from the dead and ascended into Heaven, where He ever intercedes for us. In the hearts of believers He abides forever as the indwelling Christ; above us and over us all He rules; wherefore, unto Him we render love, obedience, and adoration as our Prophet, Priest, and King.

Article VIII. Of the Holy Spirit. We believe in the Holy Spirit, the Lord and Giver of life, who proceeds from the Father and the Son, who moves upon the hearts of men to restrain them from evil and to incite them unto good, and whom the Father is ever willing to give unto all who ask Him. We believe that He has spoken by holy men of God in making known His truth to men for their salvation; that, through our exalted Saviour, He was sent forth in power to convict the world of sin, to enlighten men's minds in the knowledge of Christ, and to persuade and enable them to obey the call of the Gospel; and that He abides with the Church, dwelling in every believer as the spirit of truth, of power, of holiness, of comfort, and of love.

Article IX. Of Regeneration. We believe in the necessity of regeneration, whereby we are made new creatures in Christ Jesus by the Spirit of God, who imparts spiritual life by the gracious and mysterious operation of His power, using as the ordinary means the truths of His word and the ordinances of divine appointment in ways agreeable to the nature of man.

Article X. Of Faith and Repentance. We believe that faith in Christ is a saving grace whereby we receive Him, trust in Him, and rest upon Him alone for salvation as He is offered to us in the Gospel, and that this saving faith is always accompanied by repentance, wherein we confess and forsake our sins with full purpose of and endeavour after a new obedience to God.

Article XI. Of Justification and Sonship. We believe that God, on the sole ground of the perfect obedience and sacrifice of Christ, pardons those who by faith receive Him as their Saviour and Lord, accepts them as righteous, and bestows upon them the adoption of sons, with a right to all privileges therein implied, including a conscious assurance of their sonship.

Article XII. Of Sanctification. We believe that those who are regenerated and justified grow in the likeness of Christ through fellowship with Him, the indwelling of the Holy Spirit, and obedience to the truth; that a holy life is the fruit and evidence of saving faith; and that the believer's hope of continuance in such a life is in the preserving grace of God. And we believe that in this growth in grace Christians may attain that maturity and full assurance of faith whereby the love of God is made perfect in us.

Article XIII. Of Prayer. We believe that we are encouraged to draw near to God, our Heavenly Father, in the name of His Son, Jesus Christ, and on our own behalf and that of others to pour out our hearts humbly yet freely before Him, as becomes His beloved children, giving Him the honour and praise due His holy name, asking Him to glorify Himself on earth as in Heaven, confessing unto Him our sins, and seeking of Him every gift needful for this life and for our everlasting salvation. We believe also that, inasmuch as all true prayer is prompted by His Spirit, He will in response thereto grant us every blessing according to His unsearchable wisdom and the riches of His grace in Jesus Christ.

Article XIV. Of the Law of God. We believe that the moral law of God, summarized in the Ten Commandments, testified to by the prophets, and unfolded in the life and teachings of Jesus Christ, stands for ever in truth and equity, and is not made void by faith, but on the contrary is established thereby. We believe that God requires of every man to do justly, to love mercy, and to walk humbly with God; and that only through this harmony with the will of God shall be fulfilled that brotherhood of man wherein the Kingdom of God is to be made manifest.

Article XV. Of the Church. We acknowledge one Holy Catholic Church, the innumerable company of saints of every age and nation, who being united by the Holy Spirit to Christ their Head are one body in Him and have communion with their Lord and with one another. Further, we receive it as the will of Christ that His Church on earth should exist as a visible and sacred brotherhood, consisting of those who profess faith in Jesus Christ and obedience to Him, together with their children and other baptized children, and organized for the confession of His name, for the public worship of God, for the administration of the sacraments, for the upbuilding of the saints, and for the universal propagation of the Gospel; and we acknowledge as a part, more or less pure, of this universal brotherhood, every particular church throughout the world which professes this faith in

Jesus Christ and obedience to Him as divine Lord and Saviour.

Article XVI. Of the Sacraments. We acknowledge two sacraments, Baptism and the Lord's Supper, which were instituted by Christ, to be of perpetual obligation as signs and seals of the covenant ratified in His precious blood, as a means of grace, by which, working in us, He doth not only quicken but also strengthen and comfort our faith in Him, and as ordinances through the observance of which His Church is to confess her Lord and be visibly distinguished from the rest of the world. Baptism with water into the name of the Father and of the Son and of the Holy Spirit is the sacrament by which are signified and sealed our union to Christ and participation in the blessings of the new covenant. The proper subjects of baptism are believers and infants presented by their parents or guardians in the Christian faith. In the latter case the parents or guardians should train up their children in the nurture and admonition of the Lord and should expect that their children will, by the operation of the Holy Spirit, receive the benefits which the sacrament is designed and fitted to convey. The Church is under the most solemn obligation to provide for their Christian instruction. The Lord's Supper is the sacrament of communion with Christ and with His people, in which bread and wine are given and received in thankful remembrance of Him and His sacrifice on the Cross; and they who in faith receive the same do, after a spiritual manner, partake of the body and blood of the Lord Jesus Christ to their comfort, nourishment, and growth in grace. All may be admitted to the Lord's Supper who make a credible profession of their faith in the Lord Jesus and of obedience to His law.

Article XVII. Of the Ministry. We believe that Jesus Christ, as the Supreme Head of the Church, has appointed therein an ordained ministry of Word, Sacrament, and Pastoral Care and a diaconal ministry of Education, Service, and Pastoral Care, and calls men and women to these ministries; and that the Church, under the guidance of the Holy Spirit, recognizes and chooses those whom He calls, and should thereupon duly ordain or commission them to the work of the ministry.

Article XVIII. Of Church Order and Fellowship. We believe that the Supreme and only Head of the Church is the Lord Jesus Christ; that its worship, teaching, discipline, and government should be administered according to His will by persons chosen for their fitness and duly set apart to their office; and that although the visible Church may contain unworthy members and is liable to err, yet believers ought not lightly to separate themselves from its communion, but are to live in fellowship with their brethren, which fellowship is to be extended, as God gives opportunity, to all who in every place call upon the name of the Lord Jesus.

Article XIX. Of the Resurrection, the Last Judgement, and the Future Life. We believe that there shall be a resurrection of the dead, both of the just and of the unjust, through the power of the Son of God, who shall come to judge the living and the dead; that the finally impenitent shall go away into eternal punishment and the righteous into life eternal.

Article XX. Of Christian Service and the Final Triumph. We believe that it is our duty, as disciples and servants of Christ, to further the extension of His Kingdom, to do good unto all men, to maintain the public and private worship of God, to hallow the Lord's Day, to preserve the inviolability of marriage and the sanctity of the family, to uphold the just authority of the State, and so to live in all honesty, purity, and charity, that our lives shall testify of Christ. We joyfully receive the word of Christ, bidding His people go into all the world and make disciples of all nations, declaring unto them that God was in Christ reconciling the world unto Himself, and that He will have all men to be saved and come to the knowledge of the truth. We confidently believe that by His power and grace all His enemies shall finally be overcome, and the kingdoms of this world be made the Kingdom of our God and of His Christ.

A Statement of Faith (1940)

Preamble. It is the purpose of this Statement to set out briefly and simply the substance of the Church's faith. No attempt is made to answer all the questions which devout men may reasonably ask in regard to God and man and salvation. But we believe that we have included what is essential to the life of the Church. If our purpose were apologetic we should have to use more of the language of modern science and philosophy. Because our purpose is affirmative we have as far as possible adopted rather the language of Scripture, a language which matches the supreme facts it tells of, God's acts of judgment and of mercy. The Church's faith is the unchanging Gospel of God's holy, redeeming love revealed in Jesus Christ. It is declared in Scripture; it is witnessed to both in the creeds of the Universal Church and in the Confessions of the Reformed Churches; and it is formulated for a specific purpose in our Basis of Union. But Christians of each new generation are called to state it afresh in terms of the thought of their own age and with the emphasis their age needs. This we have attempted to do for the people of The United Church of Canada—seeking always to be faithful to Scripture and to the testimony of the Universal Church, and always aware that no statement of ours can express the whole truth of God.

I. God. We believe in God, the eternal personal Spirit, Creator and Upholder of all things. We believe that God, as sovereign Lord exalted above the world, orders and overrules all things in it to the accomplishment of His holy, wise, and good purposes. We believe that God made man to love and serve Him; that He cares for him as a righteous and compassionate Father; and that nothing can either quench His love or finally defeat His gracious purpose for man. So we acknowledge God as Creator, Upholder, and Sovereign Lord of all things, and the righteous and loving Father of men.

II. Jesus Christ. We believe in Jesus Christ, the Son of the Father, Who, for us men and our salvation became man and dwelt among us. We believe that He lived a perfect human life, wholly devoted to the will of God and the service of man. We believe that in Him God comes face to face with men; so that they learn that God loves them seeks their good, bears their sorrows and their sin, and claims their exclusive faith and perfect obedience. We believe that in Jesus Christ God acted to save man, taking, at measureless cost, man's sin upon Himself; that the Cross reveals at once God's abhorrence of sin and His saving love in its height and depth and power; and that the Cross is for all time the effectual means of reconciling the world unto God. We believe that Jesus was raised victorious over death and declared to be the Son of God with power; and that He is alive for evermore, our Savior and our Lord. So we acknowledge Jesus Christ as the Son of God Incarnate, the Savior of the world.

III. The Holy Spirit. We believe in the Holy Spirit by whom God is ever at work in the minds and hearts of men, inspiring every right desire and every effort after truth and beauty. We believe that the Spirit of God moves men to acknowledge their sins and accept the divine forgiveness and grace. We believe that the Spirit was present with power at the beginning of the Church, enabling the disciples to bear witness to what they had seen and heard, filling them with love of the brethren, and hope of the coming Kingdom, and sustaining them in the sense of Christ's continuing presence in their midst. We believe that by the same Spirit the Church is continually guided and empowered, and her members fortified against temptation, fear and doubt, and built up in faith and holiness unto salvation. So we acknowledge the Holy Spirit as the Lord and Giver of life, through whom the creative, redeeming love of God is ever at work among men.

IV. The Holy Trinity. Knowing God thus, as Creator and Father, as Redeemer in Christ, and as Holy Spirit working in us, we confess our faith in the Holy Trinity. So we acknowledge and worship one God, Father, Son, and Holy Spirit.

V. Man and Man's Sin. We believe that God gave to man, as He did not to the lower creatures, capacity to share His thought and purpose, and freedom to choose whether he would or would not love and serve Him. We believe that man has used his freedom of choice for low and selfish ends, thus estranging himself from God and his brother man, and bringing upon himself the judgment and wrath of God, so that he lives in a world of confusion and distress, and is unable of himself to fulfill God's high purpose for him. So we acknowledge man's sin, God's righteous judgment, and man's helplessness and need.

VI. Redemption. We believe that in the greatness of His love for man God has in Christ opened up a way of deliverance from the guilt and power of sin. We believe that Christ, by living our life without sin, by dying at the hands of sinful men with faith unshaken and unfaltering love, has done for man what man could not do for himself. On the Cross He bore the burden of sin, and He broke its power; and what He did there moves men to repentance, conveys forgiveness, undoes the estrangement, and binds them to Himself in a new loyalty. We believe that by His resurrection and exaltation Christ stands victorious over death and all evil, and that He fills those who commit themselves to Him with such grace and strength that in Him they, too, are conquerors. His redemption of man is at once an awful mystery and a glorious fact; it is the Lord's doing and marvelous in our eyes. So we acknowledge the unmerited love and the mercy of our God in giving His only-begotten Son that we might not perish but have everlasting life.

VII. The Church. We believe that the Church, the society of the redeemed, was brought into existence by God Himself through the work and risen power of Christ, Who in calling men into fellowship with Himself calls them by the same act into fellowship with one another in Him. We believe that the Church is the organ of Christ's mind and redemptive will, the body of which He is the Head. Under Him the Church is called to the proclamation of the everlasting Gospel with its offer of salvation, to the worship of God, Creator and Redeemer, to the loving service of mankind, and to the care and nurture of the flock. We believe that all members of the Church are one in Him, and that the life of the Church in every age is continuous with that of the first apostolic company. The groups commonly known as "churches" are called to share in the life of the whole Church, of all ages and of all lands, entering freely into the full heritage of thought, worship, and discipline, and living together in mutual confidence. We believe that for the fulfillment of her mission in the world God has given to the Church the Ministry, the Scriptures and the Sacraments. So we acknowledge one holy, catholic, apostolic Church, the Body of Christ, the household and family of God.

VIII. The Ministry. We believe that God has appointed a Ministry in His Church for the preaching of the Word, the administration of the Sacraments, and the pastoral care of the people. We believe that the Church has authority to ordain to the Ministry by prayer and the laying on of hands those whom she finds, after due trial, to be called of God thereto. We believe that, for the due ordering of her life as a society, God has appointed a government in His Church, to be exercised, under Christ the head, by Ministers and representatives of the people. So we acknowledge the Holy Ministry appointed by God for the spread of the Gospel and the edification of His Church.

IX. The Holy Scriptures. We believe that the great moments of God's revelation and communication of Himself to men are recorded and interpreted in the Scriptures of the Old and New Testament. We believe that, while God uttered His Word to man in many portions progressively, the whole is sufficient to declare His mind and will for our salvation. To Israel He made Himself known as a holy and righteous God and a Savior; the fullness of truth and grace came by Jesus Christ. The writings were collected and preserved by the Church. We believe that the theme of all Holy Scripture is the redemptive purpose and working of God, and that herein lies its unity. We believe that in Holy Scripture God claims the complete allegiance of our mind and heart; that the full persuasion of the truth and authority of the Word of God contained in the Scripture is the work of the Holy Spirit in our hearts; that, using Holy Scripture, the Spirit takes of the things of Christ and shows them unto us for our spiritual nourishment and growth in grace. So we acknowledge in Holy Scripture the true witness to God's Word and the sure guide to Christian faith and conduct.

X. The Sacraments. We believe that the Sacraments of Baptism and the Lord's Supper are effectual means through which, by common things and simple acts, the saving love of God is exhibited and communicated to His people, who receive them in faith. We believe that in Baptism men are made members of the Christian society. Washing with water in the name of the Father, the Son, and the Holy Spirit signifies God's cleansing from sin and an initial participation in the gifts and graces of the new life. The children of believing parents are baptized and nurtured in the family of God so that they may in due time take upon themselves the yoke of Christ. We believe that the Lord's Supper perpetuates the fellowship between Christ and His disciples sealed in the upper room, that at His table He is always present, and His people are nourished, confirmed, and renewed. The giving and receiving of bread and wine accompanied by His own words signifies the gracious self-giving of Christ as suffering and living Lord in such wise that His faithful people live in Him and He in them. So we acknowledge Baptism as God's appointed means of grace at initiation into the Christian fellowship; and the Lord's Supper as His appointed means of maintaining the fellowship in health and strength, and as the act of worship in which the whole soul of man goes out to God and God's grace comes freely to man.

XI. Christian Life and Duty. We believe that the Christian life is the life lived in fellowship with Christ and His Church. It begins with repentance and faith. In repentance men turn from sin to serve the holy and forgiving God with new and glad obedience. In faith they entrust themselves to Christ and rest upon Him alone for salvation. We believe that by the teaching and example of Jesus the Holy Spirit shows men the way and the end of the Christian life, what it means to love God with all the heart and soul and mind and strength, and to love their neighbour as themselves. We believe that Christian men are called to abide within the fellowship of the Church, to maintain its peace and unity, and to give diligent heed to prayer, to the reading of Scripture, to common worship and the sacraments. We believe that they are likewise called to live as those who are of the Kingdom of God, and to seek His righteousness both in individual and social life, serving their fellow-men in love for Christ's sake, and striving and waiting in prayer for an ordered common life where the will of God for the well-being and peace of men shall be done over all the earth. We believe that in denying themselves and in following Christ men are enabled by the Spirit of God more and more to die unto sin and live unto righteousness; that they are, under the hand of a faithful Father, in labour, love, and duty, in suffering, sorrow and defeat, renewed in the inner man after the image of the crucified and victorious Christ; and that they receive in this life a foretaste of the final redemption, assurance of the divine favour, peace and joy, and the confidence that He is able to keep them to the end. So we acknowledge the Christian life as the life lived within the family of God, with the graces and privileges, the duties and discipline, through which the Christian man grows up in all things into Christ.

XII. The Consummation We believe that the resurrection and exaltation of Christ, following on His crucifixion, gives assurance that the long struggle between sin and grace will have an end, the Kingdom be revealed in its fullness, and God's eternal purpose accomplished. We believe that God will judge all men by Jesus Christ, the Son of Man. We believe that, while salvation is offered to all, God does not take away or override the freedom with which He has endowed men. If they stubbornly refuse His mercy and prefer sinful ways they shut themselves out from the light and joy of salvation and fall under the righteous judgment of God. We believe that those who accept the offer of salvation and persevere in the Christian way do after death enter into the joy of their Lord, a blessedness beyond our power to conceive. They see God face to face, and in the communion of saints are partakers with the Church on earth of its labours and prayers. So we acknowledge the righteous and merciful judgment of God and we wait for the coming of the Kingdom which shall have no end.

"We know Whom we have believed, and are persuaded that He is able to keep that which we have committed to Him."

"To the only wise God our Savior be glory and majesty, dominion and power, both now and ever."

A New Creed (1968, revised 1980, 1995)

We are not alone,
we live in God's world.

We believe in God:
who has created and is creating,
who has come in Jesus,
the Word made flesh,
to reconcile and make new,
who works in us and others
by the Spirit.

We trust in God.

We are called to be the Church:
to celebrate God's presence,
to live with respect in Creation,
to love and serve others,
to seek justice and resist evil,
to proclaim Jesus, crucified and risen,
our judge and our hope.

In life, in death, in life beyond death,
God is with us.
We are not alone.

Thanks be to God.

A Song of Faith (2006)

Preamble:

This statement of faith seeks to provide a verbal picture of what The United Church of Canada understands its faith to be in its current historical, political, social, and theological context at the beginning of the 21st century. It is also a means of ongoing reflection and an invitation for the church to live out its convictions in relation to the world in which we live.

The church's faith is grounded in truths that are timeless. These truths, however, must be embraced anew by Christians of each generation and stated "in terms of the thoughts of their own age and with the emphasis their age needs" (Statement of Faith, 1940).

This is not the first time the United Church has formally expressed its collective faith. In the Basis of Union (1925), in the Statement of Faith (1940), and in A New Creed (1968), the United Church stated its faith in words appropriate to its time. This current statement of faith is offered within that tradition, and in response to the request of the 37th General Council (2000) for a "timely and contextual statement of faith" that especially engages "the church in conversation on the nature of the church (ecclesiology), ministry and the sacraments."

This statement of faith attempts to reflect the spirit of The United Church of Canada and to respond to various defining elements in our social, political, and historical context, including the place of the church in society, the cultural and intellectual setting in which we find ourselves, the meaning of "truth," the impact of the market economy on our daily lives, and the growing issue of the meaning of "security." These contextual elements are further explored in the appendices to this document.

This is not a statement for all time but for *our* time. In as much as the Spirit keeps faith with us, we can express our understanding of the Holy with confidence. And in as much as the Spirit is vast and wild, we recognize that our understanding of the Holy is always partial and limited. Nonetheless we have faith, and this statement collects the meaning of our song.

God is Holy Mystery,
beyond complete knowledge,
above perfect description.

Yet,
in love,
the one eternal God seeks relationship.

So God creates the universe
    and with it the possibility of being and relating.
God tends the universe,
    mending the broken and reconciling the estranged.
God enlivens the universe,
    guiding all things toward harmony with their Source.

Grateful for God's loving action,
We cannot keep from singing.

With the Church through the ages,
we speak of God as one and triune:
Father, Son, and Holy Spirit.
We also speak of God as
    Creator, Redeemer, and Sustainer
    God, Christ, and Spirit
    Mother, Friend, and Comforter
    Source of Life, Living Word, and Bond of Love,
    and in other ways that speak faithfully of
the One on whom our hearts rely,
the fully shared life at the heart of the universe.

We witness to Holy Mystery that is Wholly Love.

God is creative and self-giving,
    generously moving
    in all the near and distant corners of the universe.
Nothing exists that does not find its source in God.
Our first response to God's providence is gratitude.
We sing thanksgiving.

Finding ourselves in a world of beauty and mystery,
    of living things, diverse and interdependent,
    of complex patterns of growth and evolution,
    of subatomic particles and cosmic swirls,

we sing of God the Creator,
the Maker and Source of all that is.

Each part of creation reveals unique aspects of God the Creator,
    who is both in creation and beyond it.
All parts of creation, animate and inanimate, are related.
All creation is good.
We sing of the Creator,
    who made humans to live and move
    and have their being in God.
In and with God,
    we can direct our lives toward right relationship
    with each other and with God.
We can discover our place as one strand in the web of life.
We can grow in wisdom and compassion.
We can recognize all people as kin.
We can accept our mortality and finitude, not as a curse,
    but as a challenge to make our lives and choices matter.

Made in the image of God,
we yearn for the fulfillment that is life in God.
Yet we choose to turn away from God.
We surrender ourselves to sin,
    a disposition revealed in selfishness, cowardice, or apathy.
Becoming bound and complacent
    in a web of false desires and wrong choices,
    we bring harm to ourselves and others.
This brokenness in human life and community
    is an outcome of sin.
Sin is not only personal
    but accumulates
    to become habitual and systemic forms
    of injustice, violence, and hatred.

We are all touched by this brokenness:
    the rise of selfish individualism
    that erodes human solidarity;
    the concentration of wealth and power
    without regard for the needs of all;

the toxins of religious and ethnic bigotry;
the degradation of the blessedness of human bodies
and human passions through sexual exploitation;
the delusion of unchecked progress and limitless growth
that threatens our home, the earth;
the covert despair that lulls many into numb complicity
with empires and systems of domination.
We sing lament and repentance.

Yet evil does not—cannot—
undermine or overcome the love of God.
God forgives,
and calls all of us to confess our fears and failings
with honesty and humility.
God reconciles,
and calls us to repent the part we have played
in damaging our world, ourselves, and each other.
God transforms,
and calls us to protect the vulnerable,
to pray for deliverance from evil,
to work with God for the healing of the world,
that all might have abundant life.
We sing of grace.

The fullness of life includes
moments of unexpected inspiration and courage lived out,
experiences of beauty, truth, and goodness,
blessings of seeds and harvest,
friendship and family, intellect and sexuality,
the reconciliation of persons through justice
and communities living in righteousness,
and the articulation of meaning.
And so we sing of God the Spirit,
who from the beginning has swept over the face of creation,
animating all energy and matter
and moving in the human heart.

We sing of God the Spirit,
faithful and untameable,
who is creatively and redemptively active in the world.

The Spirit challenges us to celebrate the holy
    not only in what is familiar,
      but also in that which seems foreign.

We sing of the Spirit,
    who speaks our prayers of deepest longing
    and enfolds our concerns and confessions,
    transforming us and the world.

We offer worship
    as an outpouring of gratitude and awe
    and a practice of opening ourselves
    to God's still, small voice of comfort,
    to God's rushing whirlwind of challenge.
Through word, music, art, and sacrament,
    in community and in solitude,
    God changes our lives, our relationships, and our world.
We sing with trust.

Scripture is our song for the journey, the living word
    passed on from generation to generation
    to guide and inspire,
    that we might wrestle a holy revelation for our time and place
    from the human experiences
    and cultural assumptions of another era.
God calls us to be doers of the word and not hearers only.

The Spirit breathes revelatory power into scripture,
    bestowing upon it a unique and normative place
    in the life of the community.
The Spirit judges us critically when we abuse scripture
    by interpreting it narrow-mindedly,
    using it as a tool of oppression, exclusion, or hatred.

The wholeness of scripture testifies
    to the oneness and faithfulness of God.
The multiplicity of scripture testifies to its depth:
    two testaments, four gospels,
    contrasting points of view held in tension—
all a faithful witness to the One and Triune God,
the Holy Mystery that is Wholly Love.

We find God made known in Jesus of Nazareth,
and so we sing of God the Christ, the Holy One embodied.

We sing of Jesus,
    a Jew,
    born to a woman in poverty
    in a time of social upheaval
    and political oppression.
He knew human joy and sorrow.
So filled with the Holy Spirit was he
that in him people experienced the presence of God among them.
We sing praise to God incarnate.

Jesus announced the coming of God's reign—
    a commonwealth not of domination
    but of peace, justice, and reconciliation.
He healed the sick and fed the hungry.
He forgave sins and freed those held captive
    by all manner of demonic powers.
He crossed barriers of race, class, culture, and gender.
He preached and practised unconditional love—
    love of God, love of neighbour,
    love of friend, love of enemy—
and he commanded his followers to love one another
    as he had loved them.

Because his witness to love was threatening,
    those exercising power sought to silence Jesus.
He suffered abandonment and betrayal,
    state-sanctioned torture and execution.
He was crucified.

But death was not the last word.
God raised Jesus from death,
    turning sorrow into joy,
    despair into hope.
We sing of Jesus raised from the dead.
We sing hallelujah.

By becoming flesh in Jesus,
   God makes all things new.
In Jesus' life, teaching, and self-offering,
   God empowers us to live in love.
In Jesus' crucifixion,
   God bears the sin, grief, and suffering of the world.
In Jesus' resurrection,
   God overcomes death.
Nothing separates us from the love of God.

The Risen Christ lives today,
   present to us and the source of our hope.
In response to who Jesus was
   and to all he did and taught,
   to his life, death, and resurrection,
   and to his continuing presence with us through the Spirit,
we celebrate him as
   the Word made flesh,
   the one in whom God and humanity are perfectly joined,
   the transformation of our lives,
the Christ.

We sing of a church
   seeking to continue the story of Jesus
   by embodying Christ's presence in the world.
We are called together by Christ
   as a community of broken but hopeful believers,
   loving what he loved,
   living what he taught,
   striving to be faithful servants of God
   in our time and place.
Our ancestors in faith
   bequeath to us experiences of their faithful living;
   upon their lives our lives are built.
Our living of the gospel makes us a part of this communion of saints,
   experiencing the fulfillment of God's reign
   even as we actively anticipate a new heaven and a new earth.

The church has not always lived up to its vision.
It requires the Spirit to reorient it,
    helping it to live an emerging faith while honouring tradition,
    challenging it to live by grace rather than entitlement,
for we are called to be a blessing to the earth.

We sing of God's good news lived out,
a church with purpose:
    faith nurtured and hearts comforted,
    gifts shared for the good of all,
    resistance to the forces that exploit and marginalize,
    fierce love in the face of violence,
    human dignity defended,
    members of a community held and inspired by God,
    corrected and comforted,
    instrument of the loving Spirit of Christ,
    creation's mending.
We sing of God's mission.

We are each given particular gifts of the Spirit.
For the sake of the world,
    God calls all followers of Jesus to Christian ministry.
In the church,
    some are called to specific ministries of leadership,
    both lay and ordered;
    some witness to the good news;
    some uphold the art of worship;
    some comfort the grieving and guide the wandering;
    some build up the community of wisdom;
    some stand with the oppressed and work for justice.
To embody God's love in the world,
    the work of the church requires the ministry and discipleship
    of all believers.

In grateful response to God's abundant love,
    we bear in mind our integral connection
    to the earth and one another;
we participate in God's work of healing and mending creation.
To point to the presence of the holy in the world,

the church receives, consecrates, and shares
    visible signs of the grace of God.
In company with the churches
    of the Reformed and Methodist traditions,
we celebrate two sacraments as gifts of Christ:
baptism and holy communion.
In these sacraments the ordinary things of life
—water, bread, wine—
point beyond themselves to God and God's love,
    teaching us to be alert
    to the sacred in the midst of life.

Before conscious thought or action on our part,
    we are born into the brokenness of this world.
Before conscious thought or action on our part,
    we are surrounded by God's redeeming love.
Baptism by water in the name of the Holy Trinity
    is the means by which we are received, at any age,
    into the covenanted community of the church.
    It is the ritual that signifies our rebirth in faith
    and cleansing by the power of God.
Baptism signifies the nurturing, sustaining,
    and transforming power of God's love
    and our grateful response to that grace.

Carrying a vision of creation healed and restored,
    we welcome all in the name of Christ.
Invited to the table where none shall go hungry,
    we gather as Christ's guests and friends.
In holy communion
    we are commissioned to feed as we have been fed,
    forgive as we have been forgiven,
    love as we have been loved.
The open table speaks of the shining promise
    of barriers broken and creation healed.
In the communion meal, wine poured out and bread broken,
    we remember Jesus.
We remember not only the promise but also the price that he paid
    for who he was,

for what he did and said,
and for the world's brokenness.
We taste the mystery of God's great love for us,
and are renewed in faith and hope.

We place our hope in God.
We sing of a life beyond life
and a future good beyond imagining:
a new heaven and a new earth,
the end of sorrow, pain, and tears,
Christ's return and life with God,
the making new of all things.
We yearn for the coming of that future,
even while participating in eternal life now.

Divine creation does not cease
until all things have found wholeness, union, and integration
with the common ground of all being.
As children of the Timeless One,
our time-bound lives will find completion
in the all-embracing Creator.
In the meantime, we embrace the present,
embodying hope, loving our enemies,
caring for the earth,
choosing life.

Grateful for God's loving action,
we cannot keep from singing.
Creating and seeking relationship,
in awe and trust,
we witness to Holy Mystery who is Wholly Love.

Amen.

BIBLIOGRAPHY

Ainsworth, Fred. "The Japan Mission Council, 1933." *New Outlook*, February 22, 1933.

Airhart, Phyllis D. "Christianizing the Social Order and Founding Myths—Double Vision?" *Toronto Journal of Theology* 12, no. 2 (1996): 170–71.

———. *A Church with the Soul of a Nation: Making and Remaking the United Church of Canada*. Montreal and Kingston: McGill-Queen's University Press, 2014.

———. *Serving the Present Age: Revivalism, Progressivism, and the Methodist Tradition in Canada*. Montreal and Kingston: McGill-Queen's University Press, 1992.

Airhart, Phyllis, and Roger Hutchinson. "Introduction to Christianizing the Social Order: A Founding Vision of the United Church." *Toronto Journal of Theology* 12, no. 2 (1996): 156.

Allemang, John. "Lowering the Doom." *Globe and Mail*, December 5, 2009, F1.

Allen, Richard. *The Social Passion: Religion and Social Reform in Canada, 1914–28*. Toronto: University of Toronto Press, 1973.

Aquinas, St. Thomas. *Summa Theologiae*, vol. 8. London: Blackfriars, 1964.

Arnup, Jesse H. "Dr. J. G. Endicott and the Board of Overseas Missions." *United Church Observer*, March 15, 1948, 8, 28.

———. *A New Church Faces a New World*. Toronto: United Church Publishing House, 1937.

Augustine. *City of God*. Edited by David Knowles. Translated by Henry Bettenson. London: Penguin, 1972.

The Authority and Interpretation of Scripture. Toronto: United Church Publishing House, 1992.

Bagnell, Kenneth. "Interview [with Gloria Webster]." *United Church Observer*, December 1, 1963, 21.

Bailey, F.W. *A Modern Approach to Gambling*. Toronto: Board of Evangelism and Social Service, The United Church of Canada, 1949.

Baptism, Eucharist, and Ministry. Faith and Order Paper No. 111. Geneva: World Council of Churches, 1982.

Baptism and Renewal of Baptismal Faith: For Optional Use in The United Church of Canada. Toronto: The United Church of Canada, 1986.

Barth, Karl. *Church Dogmatics*, vol. 3, pt. 1. Translated and edited by T.F. Torrance and G.W. Bromiley. Edinburgh: T&T Clark, 1958.

———. *Church Dogmatics*, vol. 4, pt. 2. Translated and edited by T.F. Torrance and G.W. Bromiley. Edinburgh: T&T Clark, 1958.

———. *The Doctrine of the Word of God (Church Dogmatics* I/1). Translated by G.T. Thomson. Edinburgh: T&T Clark, 1936.

Bartlett, Ross. "1990–2003: The Church into the New Millennium." In *The United Church of Canada: A History*, edited by Don Schweitzer, 161–84. Waterloo, ON: Wilfrid Laurier University Press, 2012.

Bartlett, Thomas. "A Year after the Non-Apocalypse." *Religion Dispatches* (21 May 2012). http://religiondispatches.org/a-year-after-the-non-apocalypse-where -are-they-now/.

Baum, Gregory. "A New Creed." *Ecumenist* 6, no. 5 (July–August 1968): 166–67.

———. *Religion and Alienation.* New York: Paulist Press, 1975.

Beardsall, Sandra. "And Whether Pigs Have Wings: The United Church in the 1960s." In *The United Church of Canada: A History. The United Church of Canada: A History*, edited by Don Schweitzer, 97–118. Waterloo, ON: Wilfrid Laurier University Press, 2012.

Bearing Faithful Witness: United Church–Jewish Relations Today. Toronto: Committee on Inter-Church Inter-Faith Relations, United Church of Canada, 2003.

Behe, Michael J. *Darwin's Black Box: The Biochemical Challenge to Evolution.* New York: Free Press, 1996.

"Being Church: Women's Voices and Visions." *Making Waves* 2, no. 1 (Fall 2001): 12–24.

Berton, Pierre. *The Comfortable Pew: A Critical Look at Christianity and the Religious Establishment in the New Age.* Toronto: McClelland and Stewart, 1965.

———. "Out of This World." *Why the Sea Is Boiling Hot.* Toronto: United Church Publishing House, 1965.

Best, C.H. "Laymen Indispensable in Indian Work." *United Church Observer* (September 1953): 5.

Bissell, Tom. "A Comet's Tale: On the Science of Apocalypse." *Harper's Magazine*, February 2003, 33–47.

Bonhoeffer, Dietrich. *The Cost of Discipleship.* London: SCM, 1959.

—————. *Letters and Papers from Prison.* 3rd ed. Edited by Eberhard Bethge. London: SCM, 1967.

"'The Book of Common Order' in Our Readers' Forum." *New Outlook*, June 6, 1934, 430.

The Book of Common Order of the United Church of Canada. 2nd ed. Toronto: United Church Publishing House, 1950.

Borg, Marcus. *Meeting Jesus Again for the First Time.* New York: HarperCollins, 1995.

Bosch, David. *The Transforming Mission: Paradigm Shifts in Theology of Mission.* Maryknoll, NY: Orbis, 1991.

Bourgeois, Michael. "Awash in Theology: Issues in Theology in The United Church of Canada." In *The United Church of Canada: A History*, edited by Don Schweitzer, 259–78. Waterloo, ON: Wilfrid Laurier University Press, 2012.

—————. "Science and Religion: Evolution and Design." *Touchstone* 25, no. 3 (September 2007): 18–32.

Boyer, Paul. "The Growth of Fundamentalist Apocalyptic in the United States." In *The Continuum History of Apocalypticism*, edited by Bernard McGinn, John Collins, and Stephen Stein, 516–44. New York: Continuum, 2003.

Bradley-St.-Cyr, Ruth. "'The Substance of Things Hoped For': Peter Gordon White and the New Curriculum of The United Church of Canada." *Studies in Book Culture* 6, no. 2 (Spring 2015). https://www.erudit.org/fr/revues/memoires/2015-v6-n2-memoireso2039/1032711ar/.

Brewing, William E. "Racial Relationships after the War." *United Church Observer*, April 15, 1941, 15–25.

Bronson, Rachel. "Statement of the Executive Director" and "It Is Two and a Half Minutes to Midnight: 2017 Doomsday Clock Statement." Science and Security Board.

Brueggemann, Walter. *Israel's Praise: Doxology against Idolatry and Ideology.* Minneapolis, MN: Fortress Press, 1988.

Bulletin of the Atomic Scientists. Edited by John Mecklin (January 2017). http://thebulletin.org/sites/default/files/Final%202017%20Clock%20 Statement.pdf.

Burwash, Nathanael. *Manual of Christian Theology on the Inductive Method*, vol. 1. London: Horace Marshall and Son, 1900.

—————. *Wesley's Doctrinal Standards: The Sermons, with Introduction, Analysis and Notes.* Toronto: William Briggs, 1881.

Cahill, Lisa Sowle. *Global Justice, Christology and Christian Ethics.* New York: Cambridge University Press, 2013.

Calvin, John. *Institutes of the Christian Religion*. Edited by John Baillie. Translated by Ford Lewis Battles. *Library of Christian Classics*, vol. 20. Philadelphia: Westminster, 1960.

———. *Institutes of the Christian Religion*. Translated by Henry Beveridge. London: James Clarke, 1962.

Canada, Royal Commission on Aboriginal Peoples. *Report of the Royal Commission on Aboriginal Peoples.*, vol. 5: *Renewal, a Twenty-Year Commitment*. Ottawa: Indian and Northern Affairs Canada, 1996.

"Canadian Churches Have Their Own Racism." *United Church Observer*, September 1980, 17.

Canadian Council of Churches Commission on Faith and Witness. *Initiation into Christ*. Winfield, BC, and Ottawa: Wood Lake Books and Novalis, 1992.

Caron, Charlotte. *Eager for Worship: Theologies, Practices, and Perspectives on Worship in The United Church of Canada*. The McGeachy Papers, vol. 7. Toronto: Division of Ministry Personnel and Education of The United Church of Canada, 2001.

———. "A Look at Ministry: Diversity and Ambiguity." In *The United Church of Canada: A History*, edited by Don Schweitzer, 203–20. Waterloo, ON: Wilfrid Laurier University Press, 2012.

Celebrate God's Presence: A Book of Services for The United Church of Canada. Toronto: United Church Publishing House, 2000.

Chadwick, Henry. *The Early Church*. London: Penguin, 1993.

Chalmers, Randolph Carleton. *A Gospel to Proclaim*. Toronto: Ryerson Press, 1960.

———. *See the Christ Stand!* Toronto: Ryerson Press, 1945.

Chambers, Steven, ed. *This Is Your Church: A Guide to the Beliefs, Policies and Positions of The United Church of Canada*. Toronto: United Church Observer, 1982.

"Chapter XXVII. Of The Sacraments." *Westminster Confession of Faith* (1647). *Sacraments and Worship: The Sources of Christian Theology*. Edited by Maxwell E. Johnson. Louisville, KY: Westminster/John Knox, 2012.

Cho, Hyuk. "Partnership in Mission: William Scott's Ministry in Korea." *Touchstone* 31, no. 1 (February 2013): 57–66.

———. "Sharing Concern for Justice: Becoming an Intercultural Church as a Postcolonial Mission Practice in the Canadian Context of Integrative Multiculturalism." Th.D. dissertation, Toronto School of Theology, 2017.

Chown, Samuel Dwight. "Church Union." *Christian Guardian*, June 28, 1922, 13.

———. "That They May Be One" (January 1912). United Church of Canada Archives, Samuel Dwight Chown Papers, box 3, file 67.

Christ, Carol P., and Judith Plaskow, eds. *Womanspirit Rising: A Feminist Reader in Religion*. San Francisco, CA: Harper and Row, 1979.

Christianizing the Social Order: A Statement Prepared by a Commission Appointed by the Board of Evangelism and Social Service. Toronto: Board of Evangelism and Social Service, United Church of Canada, 1934.

Church Membership: Doctrine and Practice in The United Church of Canada. Toronto: Committee on Christian Faith, 1963.

Clark, Robert. "Christian Love and Daily Work." *Calling Canada to Christ*. Edited by W.G. Berry. Toronto: National Evangelistic Mission Committee, United Church of Canada, 1957.

Clarke, Patricia. "The KKK: How the Klan Came to Canada." *United Church Observer*, December 15, 1965, 12–14.

———. "Now What's Happening to Baptism?" *United Church Observer*, March 1980, 12.

Clifford, N. Keith. *The Resistance to Church Union in Canada, 1904–1939*. Vancouver: UBC Press, 1985.

Cline, Philip. "God Still Speaks through the Bible." In *Asking Questions, Exploring Faith: Sessions on Life Issues, Baptism, and Church Membership for Newcomers in the Congregation*, edited by Mary Anne MacFarlane, 33. Toronto: United Church of Canada, 1996.

Cobb, Jr., John B. *Transforming Christianity and the World*. Maryknoll, NY: Orbis, 1999.

Commission on World Mission. *World Mission: Report of the Commission on World Mission*. Toronto: United Church of Canada, 1966.

Committee on Christian Faith. *The Doctrine and Practice of Infant Baptism*. Toronto: United Church of Canada, 1954.

———. *Life and Death: A Study of the Christian Hope*. Edited by A.G. Reynolds. Toronto: Board of Evangelism and Social Service and Board of Christian Education, United Church of Canada, 1959.

———. *Catechism*. Toronto: Board of Evangelism and Social Service, United Church of Canada, 1944.

Committee on Church Ritual and Worship. *Forms of Service for the Offices of the Church*. Toronto: United Church Publishing House, 1926.

Committee on Inter-Church and Inter-Faith Relations. *Mending the World: An Ecumenical Vision for Healing and Reconciliation*. Toronto: United Church Publishing House, 1997.

———. *That We May Know Each Other: United Church–Muslim Relations Today*. Toronto: United Church of Canada, 2004.

———. *Toward a Renewed Understanding of Ecumenism*. Toronto: United Church of Canada, 1992.

Committee on Sexism. *Just Language: A Guide to Inclusive Language in The United*

Church of Canada. Etobicoke, ON: United Church of Canada, Division of Mission in Canada, 1997.

Committee on Theology and Faith. *The Authority and Interpretation of Scripture*. Toronto: United Church Publishing House, 1992.

Committee on Theology and Faith. *Reconciling and Making New: Who Is Jesus for the World Today?* Toronto: United Church of Canada, 1997.

Craig, Agnes Campbell, Margaret McLean, Robert K.N. McLean, and Olive D. Sparling. *The Kindergarten Teacher's Guide*. Toronto: United Church Publishing House, 1964.

Creeds: A Report of The Committee on Christian Faith. Toronto: Division of Mission in Canada, United Church of Canada,1969.

Crossan, John Dominic. *Jesus: A Revolutionary Biography*. New York: HarperCollins, 1995.

Daly, Mary. *Beyond God the Father: Toward a Philosophy of Women's Liberation*. Boston: Beacon Press, 1985[1973].

Darwin, Charles. *An Annotated Origin: A Facsimile of the First Edition of the Origin of Species*. Cambridge, MA: Harvard University Press, 2009.

Davidson, Richard H.N. *YOU and the Devil*. Toronto: Board of Evangelism and Social Service and the Board of Christian Education, United Church of Canada, 1958.

Dawkins, Richard. *The Blind Watchmaker*. London: Penguin, 1991.

de Mestral, Claude. "Disorders and Religious Persecution in Quebec." *United Church Observer*, June 15, 1950, 11.

———. "South Africa's Dilemma." *United Church Observer*, June 1, 1960, 11.

Division of Mission in Canada. *Future Directions for Christian Education in the United Church of Canada*. Toronto: United Church of Canada, 1987.

———. *In God's Image … Male and Female: A Study on Human Sexuality*. Toronto: United Church of Canada, 1980.

———. *Justice and Reconciliation: The Legacy of Indian Residential Schools and the Journey toward Reconciliation*. Toronto: United Church of Canada, 2001.

———. *The Planner for Lifelong Learning: Part of the Future Directions Project*. Toronto: United Church of Canada, 1991.

———. *Theological and Educational Convictions for the Learning of a Pilgrim People: Future Directions for Christian Education in The United Church of Canada*. Toronto: United Church of Canada, 1987.

Division of World Outreach. *Gender Justice and Partnership Guidelines*. Toronto: United Church of Canada, 1998.

———. *To Seek Justice and Resist Evil: Towards a Global Economy for All God's People*. Toronto: United Church of Canada, 2001.

Doepker, Jill. "St. Thomas-Wesley United Church: Importance of Church in the City." *Folklore* (Spring 2016): 14.

Dow, John. *This Is Our Faith: An Exposition of the Statement of Faith of The United Church of Canada*. Toronto: Board of Evangelism and Social Service, United Church of Canada, 1943.

Duck, Ruth C. *Gender and the Name of God: The Trinitarian Baptismal Formula*. New York: Pilgrim Press, 1991.

———. *Worship for the Whole People of God: Vital Worship for the 21st Century*. Louisville, KY: Westminster/John Knox, 2013.

Dumont, Alf, and Roger Hutchinson. "United Church Mission Goals and First Nations Peoples." In *The United Church of Canada: A History*, edited by Don Schweitzer, 221–38. Waterloo, ON: Wilfrid Laurier University Press.

Dyke, Doris Jean. *Crucified Woman*. Toronto: United Church Publishing House, 1991.

Endicott, James. "Appraising Our Foreign Missions: Evangelism: The Supreme Task of Missions." *New Outlook*, March 1, 1933, 198.

Endicott, Stephen. *James G. Endicott: Rebel Out of China*. Toronto: University of Toronto Press, 1980.

Ending Racial Harassment: Creating Healthy Congregations. Toronto: United Church of Canada, 2008.

Farris, Allan L. *The Tide of Time: Historical Essays by the Late Allan L. Farris*. Toronto: Knox College, 1978.

Fennell, Robert C. "How Does the United Church Interpret the Bible? Part 1: 1904–1940s: Tradition and Resistance." *Touchstone* 26, no. 2 (May 2008): 16–17.

———. "How Does the United Church Interpret the Bible? Part 3: A Song of Faith." *Touchstone* 29, no. 2 (May 2011).

Fennell, Robert C., and Ross Lockhart, eds. *Three Ways of Grace: Drawing Closer to the Trinity*. Toronto: United Church Publishing House, 2010.

Fennell, William O. *God's Intention for Man: Essays in Christian Anthropology*. Waterloo, ON: Wilfrid Laurier University Press, 1977.

The First Latin American Encounter of Christians for Socialism. Toronto: Latin American Working Group and the Student Christian Movement, 1972.

Flannery, Timothy. *Atmosphere of Hope*. Toronto: HarperCollins, 2015.

———. *Here on Earth: A Natural History of the Planet*. Toronto: HarperCollins, 2011.

Forms of Service for the Offices of the Church. Toronto: United Church Publishing House, 1926.

Forrest, A.C. "The Church within a Church." *United Church Observer*, November 1978, 29.

————. "What's Happened in the Church in the Last Ten Years?" *United Church Observer*, May 15, 1968, 16

Forster, Harvey G. "All Peoples' Missions Show the Church Cares." *United Church Observer*, April 1, 1939, 18.

Foster, Peter. "Nonsense on Tap over Bottled Water." *National Post*, November 24, 2006, FP15.

Fox, Matthew. *Original Blessing: A Primer in Creation Spirituality*. Santa Fe, NM: Bear and Company, 1983.

Fraser, Brian J. "Christianizing the Social Order: T.B. Kilpatrick's Theological Vision of the United Church of Canada." *Toronto Journal of Theology* 12, no. 2 (1996): 189–200.

Frye, Northrop. *The Double Vision: Language and Meaning in Religion*. Toronto: United Church Publishing House, 1991.

Future Directions for Christian Education. Toronto: Division of Ministry Personnel and Education, United Church of Canada, 1985.

Gallagher, David H. "Christianity Faces Other Faiths." *United Church Observer*, July 15, 1950, 13.

Geertz, Clifford. *The Interpretation of Cultures: Selected Essays*. New York: Basic Books, 2000.

Gonzalez, Justo L. *The Story of Christianity*, vol. 1: *The Early Church to the Dawn of the Reformation*. San Francisco: Harper, 1984.

Graham, Lloyd B. "Those Japanese War Babies?" *United Church Observer*, December 1, 1956, 26–27.

Grant, John Webster. *The Canadian Experience of Church Union*. Richmond, VA: John Knox Press, 1967.

————. *The Church in the Canadian Era*. Vancouver: Regent College Publishing House, 1972.

————. *The Churches and the Canadian Experience: A Faith and Order Study of the Christian Tradition*. Toronto: Ryerson Press, 1966.

————. *Moon of Wintertime: Missionaries and the Indians of Canada in Encounter since 1534*. Toronto: University of Toronto Press, 1984.

————. "From Revelation to Revolution: Some Thoughts on the Background of the Social Gospel." *Toronto Journal of Theology* 12, no. 2 (Fall 1996): 159–68.

Grethlein, Christian. *An Introduction to Practical Theology: History, Theory, and the Communication of the Gospel in the Present*. Translated by Uwe Rasch. Waco, TX: Baylor University Press, 2016.

Gutierrez, Gustavo. *The Truth Shall Make You Free: Confrontations*. Maryknoll, NY: Orbis, 1990.

Hall, Douglas John. *The Future of the Church: Where Are We Headed?* Toronto: United Church Publishing House, 1989.

———. "'The Great War' and the Theologians." In *The Twentieth Century: A Theological Overview*, edited by Gregory Baum, 3–13. Ottawa: Novalis, 1999.

———. *Imaging God: Dominion as Stewardship.* Grand Rapids, MI: Eerdmans, 1986.

———. *Professing the Faith: Christian Theology in a North American Context.* Minneapolis, MN: Fortress Press, 1993.

———. *Remembered Voices: Reclaiming the Legacy of "Neo-Orthodoxy."* Louisville, KY: John Knox Press, 1998.

———. *The Stewardship of Life in the Kingdom of Death.* New York: Friendship Press, 1985.

———. *Thinking the Faith: Christian Theology in a North American Context.* Minneapolis, MN: Augsburg Fortress, 1989.

———. *What Christianity Is Not: An Exercise in "Negative" Theology.* Eugene, OR: Cascade, 2013.

Hallett, Mary. "Lydia Gruchy—The First Woman Ordained in The United Church of Canada." *Touchstone* 4, no. 1 (January 1986): 18–23.

Halliday, Adele. "Introduction: A Transformative Vision." *Intercultural Visions: Called to Be the Church.* Edited by Rob Fennell. Toronto: United Church Publishing House, 2012.

Hamilton, Kenneth. *The System and the Gospel: A Critique of Paul Tillich.* Grand Rapids, MI: William B. Eerdmans, 1967.

Hansen, James. *Storms of My Grandchildren.* New York: Bloomsbury, 2009.

Harari, Yuval Noah. *Sapiens: A Brief History of Humankind.* Toronto: McClelland and Stewart, 2014.

Harding, Thomas Reginald, and Bruce Harding. *Patterns of Worship in The United Church of Canada, 1925–1987.* Toronto: Evensong, 1996.

Harris, Maria. *Fashion Me a People: Curriculum in the Church.* Louisville, KY: Westminster/John Knox, 1989.

Hartshorne, Charles. *The Divine Reality.* New Haven, CT: Yale University Press, 1948.

Haught, John F. *God after Darwin: A Theology of Evolution.* Boulder, CO: Westview Press, 2008.

Haughton, William. "A New Creed: Its Origins and Significance." *Touchstone* 29, no. 3 (September 2011): 20–29.

Herzog, Jonathan. "America's Spiritual–Industrial Complex and the Policy of Revival in the Early Cold War." *Journal of Policy History* 22, no. 3 (2010): 337–65.

Hiebert, Paul. "The Flaw of the Excluded Middle." *Missiology: An International Review* 10 (January 1982): 35–47.

———. "Lecture [Phenomenology and Folk Religion course]." Fuller Theological Seminary, Pasadena, CA, 1995.

Hockin, Katharine. "From 'Church to the World' to 'Church for the World.'" In *A New Beginning; An International Dialogue with the Chinese Church*, edited by Theresa Chu and Christopher Lind, 121–27. Montreal: Canada China Programme of the Canadian Council Churches, 1983.

———. "My Pilgrimage in Mission." *International Bulletin of Missionary Research* (January 1988): 30.

———. "Some Random Missiological Musings." *China Notes* (Winter 1983–1984): 281.

Homewood, E.L. "Breaking the Race Barrier," *United Church Observer*, March 1, 1956, 10, 26.

———. "Bus-Driving Missionary of Round Lake." *United Church Observer*, September 15, 1964, 19.

———. "The Indian and the Reserve." *United Church Observer*, March 15, 1965, 19–21, 45.

———. "The Maritimes Colour Bar." *United Church Observer,* June 1, 1960, 20.

———. "The Plight of Canada's Indians." *United Church Observer,* March 1, 1965, 14, 32.

———. "Race Discrimination." *United Church Observer*, February 1, 1956, 8.

Hord, Ray. "Where Is the Church in Canada Going?" *Canada and Its Future.* United Church of Canada, Board of Evangelism and Social Service, 42nd Annual Report, 1967.

Hunter, Robert. "There is No Bounty on Indians Any More … Or Is There?" *United Church Observer,* October 15, 1969, 25–26.

Hutchinson, Roger. "Christianizing the Social Order: A Three-Dimensional Task." *Toronto Journal of Theology* 12, no. 2 (1996): 227–36.

The Hymnary of The United Church of Canada. Toronto: United Church Publishing House, 1930.

"Indians Help Themselves." *United Church Observer*, August 1, 1949, 4.

International Missionary Council. *The World Mission of Christianity; Messages and Recommendations of the Enlarged Meeting of the International Missionary Council held at Jerusalem, March 24–April 8, 1928.* New York/London: IMC, 1928.

Isasi-Diaz, Ada-Maria. "Solidarity: Love of Neighbor in the 1980s." In *Lift Every Voice: Constructing Christian Theologies from the Underside*, edited by Susan Brooks Thistlethwaite and Mary Potter Engel, 31–40. San Francisco: Harper, 1990.

J.A.C., "Manitoba Indians and the War." *United Church Observer*, October 1, 1942, 3.

Jay, C. Douglas. *World Mission and World Civilization*. Toronto: Board of World Mission, United Church of Canada, 1967.

Johnson, Elizabeth A. *Ask the Beasts: Darwin and the God of Love*. London: Bloomsbury, 2014.

———. *Quest for the Living God: Mapping Frontiers in the Theology of God*. New York: Continuum, 2007.

———. *She Who Is: The Mystery of God in Feminist Theological Discourse*. New York: Crossroad Publishing, 2015 [1992].

Johnson, Maxwell E., ed. *Sacraments and Worship: The Sources of Christian Theology*. Louisville, KY: Westminster/John Knox Press, 2012.

Jones, Serene. *Feminist Theory and Christian Theology: Cartographies of Grace*. Minneapolis, MN: Augsburg, 2000.

Justice, Global and Ecumenical Relations Unit. *Toward Justice and Right Relationship: A Beginning: A Study Guide for Congregations and Church Groups as They Explore the Legacy of Indian Residential Schools and Forge New Relationships with First Nations*. Toronto: United Church of Canada, 2003.

Kahbaosa, "Have You Met the Indians?" *United Church Observer*, September 14, 1940, 21.

Kee, Kevin. *Revivalists: Marketing the Gospel in English Canada, 1884–1957*. Montreal and Kingston: McGill-Queen's University Press, 2006.

Kervin, William S. *The Language of Baptism: A Study of the Authorized Baptismal Liturgies of the United Church of Canada, 1925–1995*. Lanham, MD: Scarecrow, 2003.

———. *Ordered Liberty: Readings in the History of United Church Worship*. Toronto: United Church Publishing House, 2011.

———. "Worship on the Way: The Dialectic of United Church Worship." In *The United Church of Canada: A History*, edited by Don Schweitzer, 185–202. Waterloo, ON: Wilfrid Laurier University Press, 2012.

"Killing Race Prejudice." *New Outlook*, January 6, 1926, 3–4.

Kilpatrick, Thomas Buchanan. *Our Common Faith*. Toronto: Ryerson Press, 1928.

Kim-Cragg, HyeRan. "Baptism as Crossing beyond Belonging?" In *Liturgy in Postcolonial Perspectives: Only One Is Holy*, ed. Cláudio Carvalhaes, 201–11. New York: Palgrave Macmillan, 2015.

Kim-Cragg, HyeRan, and Joanne Doi. "Intercultural Threads of Hybridity and Threshold Spaces of Learning." *Religious Education* 107, no. 3 (2012): 262–75.

Kim-Cragg, HyeRan, and Don Schweitzer. *An Intercultural Adventure Part II: The Authority and Interpretation of Scripture in The United Church of Canada*. Daejeon, South Korea: Daejanggan, 2016.

King, Jr., Martin Luther. "I Have a Dream." United States of America National Archives. https://www.archives.gov/files/press/exhibits/dream-speech.pdf.

Langford, Norman. *Discovering Our Church:* Canadian Bible Lesson Series, October-November-December 1954 for the Intermediate Teacher Unit 2: "The Church's Faith." Toronto: United Church Publishing House, 1954.

Laverdure, Paul. *Sunday in Canada.* Yorkton: Gravelbooks, 2004.

Leclair, Jennifer. "Harold Camping Admits Rapture Prediction was 'Sinful Statement.'" *Charisma News,* 7 March 2012. http://www.charismanews.com/us/32958-harold-camping-admits-rapture-prediction-was-sinful-statement.

Lee, Sang Chul. "United in Faith." In *Voices and Visions: 65 Years of the United Church of Canada,* edited by John Webster Grant and Peter Gordon White, 153–61. Toronto: United Church Publishing House, 1990.

Legge, Marilyn L. *The Grace of Difference: A Canadian Feminist Theological Ethic.* Atlanta, GA: Scholars Press, 1992.

———. "Negotiating Mission: A Canadian Stance." *International Review of Mission* 95, no. 368 (January 2004): 119–30.

———. "Seeking 'Right Relations': How Should Churches Respond to Aboriginal Voices?" *Journal of the Society of Christian Ethics* 22 (Fall 2002): 27–48.

"Let's Forget about Converting the Jews." *United Church Observer,* April 1973, 34.

Lindbeck, George A. *The Nature of Doctrine: Religion and Theology in a Postliberal Age.* Louisville, KY: Westminster/John Knox, 2009.

Lochead, Arthur W. *A Companion to the Catechism.* Toronto: United Church Publishing House, 1945.

Lochhead, David. *The Lordship of Jesus.* Toronto: Division of Mission in Canada, United Church of Canada, 1978.

Lott, David B., ed. *Douglas John Hall: Collected Readings.* Minneapolis, MN: Fortress, 2013.

Loveys, Isobel M. "Conference Held on Indian Problems." *United Church Observer,* December 15, 1954, 12.

Lukey, Susan Ann. "Precious Jewels: A Study of the Baptismal and 'For Little Children' Hymns of *The Hymnary* (1930) of the United Church of Canada." Master of Theology thesis, Vancouver School of Theology, March 1995.

MacDonald, Gayle. "Lights, Camera, Apocalypse!" *Globe and Mail,* 19 July 2003). http://www.theglobeandmail.com/arts/lights-camera-apocalypse/article4128894/.

Macdonald, Stuart. "Death of Christian Canada? Do Canadian Church Statistics Support Callum Brown's Theory of Church Decline?" *Historical Papers: Canadian Society of Church History* (2006).

Mackintosh Shaw, John. *Christian Doctrine: A One-Volume Outline of Christian Belief.* Toronto: Ryerson Press, 1953.

MacLachlan, David. "Come to the Bible for Challenge Too." In *Asking Questions, Exploring Faith: Sessions on Life Issues, Baptism, and Church Membership for Newcomers in the Congregation*, edited by Mary Anne MacFarlane, 33–35. Toronto: United Church of Canada, 1996.

Mandate: The United Church of Canada's Mission Magazine, Special Edition, May 2005.

Manson, Ian McKay. "Religious Revival and Social Transformation: George Pidgeon and the United Church of Canada in the 1930s." *Toronto Journal of Theology* 12, no. 2 (Fall 1996): 213–22.

———. "The United Church and the Second World War." In *The United Church of Canada: A History*, edited by Don Schweitzer, 557–76. Waterloo, ON: Wilfrid Laurier University Press, 2012.

Marshall, David B. *Secularizing the Faith: Canadian Protestant Clergy and the Crisis of Belief, 1850–1940.* Toronto: University of Toronto Press, 1992.

Mathers, Donald M. *The Word and the Way.* Toronto: United Church Publishing House, 1962.

McFague, Sallie. *Life Abundant: Rethinking Theology and Economy for a Planet in Peril.* Minneapolis, MN: Fortress, 2001.

McIntire, C.T. "Unity among Many: The Formation of The United Church of Canada, 1899–1930." In *The United Church of Canada: A History*, edited by Don Schweitzer, 3–38. Waterloo, ON: Wilfrid Laurier University Press, 2012.

McIntyre, Tobi. "Visible Majorities: History of Canadian Immigration Policy." *Canadian Geographic*, January-February 2001. http://www.canadian geographic.ca/magazine/jfo1/culture_acts.asp.

McKay, Stan. "An Aboriginal Perspective on the Integrity of Creation." In *Ecotheology: Voices from the South and North*, edited by David G. Hallman, 213–24. Maryknoll, NY: Orbis, 1994.

———. "The Church Has Some History for Which It Must Repent." In *Stories of Survival: Conversations with Native North Americans*, edited by Kathleen and Remmelt Hummelen, 63–65. New York: Friendship Press, 1985.

———. *From Truth to Reconciliation.* Ottawa: Aboriginal Healing Foundation, 2008.

McKay, Stan, and Janet Silman. *The First Nations: Canadian Experience of the Gospel-Culture Encounter.* Geneva: WCC Publications, 1995.

McKim, Audrey. *God Is Always with Us.* Toronto: United Church Publishing House, 1964.

Meier, John. *A Marginal Jew: Rethinking the Historical Jesus*, vol. 2. New York: Doubleday, 1994.

Milton, Ralph. *This United Church of Ours*. 2nd ed. Winfield, BC: Wood Lake Books, 1991.

Moltmann, Jürgen. *God in Creation: An Ecological Doctrine of Creation*. Translated by M. Kohl. London: SCM, 1985.

Montour, Enos. "A New Deal for Prairie Indians." *United Church Observer*, March 15, 1961, 8–9, 20.

Moore, Arthur B.B. *Jesus Christ and the Christian Life*. Toronto: United Church Publishing House, 1965.

Moore, T. Albert. "The Mission of the Church in Personal Evangelism and Redemption." *New Outlook*, June 10, 1925, 23.

Morrow, E. Lloyd. *Church Union in Canada: Its History, Motives, Doctrine, and Government*. Toronto: Thomas Allen, 1923.

Morton, Arthur S. *The Way to Union, Being a Study of the Principles of the Foundation and of the Historic Development of the Christian Church as Bearing on the Proposed Union of the Presbyterian, Methodist and Congregational Churches in Canada*. Toronto: William Briggs, 1912.

Murphy, Fransesca Aran, and Philip Zeigler, eds. *The Providence of God*. London: T&T Clark, 2009.

Murray, Florence. *At the Foot of Dragon Hill*. New York: E.P. Dutton, 1975.

Naziansus, Gregory of. *On God and Christ: The Five Theological Orations and Two Letters to Cledonius*. Crestwood, NY: St. Vladimir's Seminary Press, 2002.

Newcombe, L.J. "Christianity and World Leadership." *United Church Observer*, April 15, 1955, 11.

"New Look in Missions." *United Church Observer*, August 1957, 17.

Newman, Paul. *A Spirit Christology: Recovering the Biblical Paradigm of Christian Faith*. Lanham, MD: University Press of America, 1987.

Ng, Greer Anne Wenh-In. "The United Church of Canada: A Church Fittingly National." In *Christianity and Ethnicity in Canada*, edited by Paul Bramadat and David Seljak, 204–46. Toronto: University of Toronto Press, 2008.

Niebuhr, Reinhold. "God's Design and the Present Disorder of Civilization." *The Church and the Disorder of Society: An Ecumenical Study Prepared under the Auspices of the World Council of Churches*. Volume 3 in *Man's Disorder and God's Design*. Edited by Willem Adolph Visser't Hooft. New York: Harper, 1948.

———. *Moral Man and Immoral Society*. New York: Charles Scribner's Sons, 1932.

———. *The Nature and Destiny of Man*. 2 vols. Louisville, KY: Westminster/John Knox Press, 1996.

Norman, W.H.H. "The Japanese in Canada." *United Church Observer,* June 1, 1944, 7, 23.

O'Leary, Denyse. *By Design or by Chance?* Kitchener, ON: Castle Quay Books, 2004.

Olson, Bruce E. *Bruchko.* Altamonte Springs, FL: Creation House/Strang Communications, 1973/1978.

"An Order for the Baptism of Children." *The Book of Common Order of The United Church of Canada.* Toronto: United Church Publishing House, 1932.

O'Toole, Garson. "Quote Investigator" (November 15, 2012). http://quote investigator.com/2012/11/15/arc-of-universe/.

Outler, Albert. "The Wesleyan Quadrilateral—in John Wesley." *Wesleyan Theological Journal* 20, no. 1 (1985): 7–18.

Pagels, Elaine H. "What Became of God the Mother? Conflicting Images of God in Early Christianity." *Signs, Chicago* 2, no. 2 (1976): 293–303.

Park, JungHee. "Mission as Companionship: Towards a Theology of Mission for the Diakonia of the United Church of Canada." *Toronto Journal of Theology* 25, no. 2 (2009): 257–74.

Peters, Ted, and Martinez Hewlett, *Theological and Scientific Commentary on Darwin's Origin of Species.* Nashville, TN: Abingdon Press, 2008.

Pidgeon, George C. "Foreword." In *Our Common Faith* by Thomas Buchanan Kilpatrick, v–vii. Toronto: Ryerson Press, 1928.

———. "The Message and Mission of the United Church of Canada." Layman's Conference, Massey Hall, October 7, 1928, 20–21. United Church of Canada Archives, 86.243C, box 52-2072.

———. *The United Church of Canada: The Story of the Union.* Toronto: Ryerson Press, 1950.

Polkinghorne, John. *The God of Hope and the End of the World.* New Haven, CT: Harvard University Press, 2002.

Pound, A.C. "Undermine War." *United Church Observer,* January 1, 1952, 6.

Presbyterian Church in Canada. *The Acts and Proceedings of the Forty-Ninth General Assembly of the Presbyterian Church in Canada.* Toronto: Presbyterian Church in Canada, 1923.

Procter-Smith, Marjorie. *In Her Own Rite: Constructing Feminist Liturgical Tradition.* Nashville, TN: Abingdon, 1990.

Pui-lan, Kwok. *Postcolonial Imagination and Feminist Theology.* Louisville, KY: Westminster/John Knox Press, 2005.

"The Racial Prejudice of Our Hymnary." *United Church Observer,* June 1, 1944, 13.

Rand, Thomas. *Waking the Frog: Solutions for our Climate Change Paralysis.* Toronto: ECW Press, 2014.

Rasmussen, Larry. "The Near Future of Socially Responsible Ministry." In *Theological Education for Social Ministry*, edited by Dieter Hessel, 14–33. New York: Pilgrim Press, 1988.

Reeve, Ted. *Claiming the Social Passion: The Role of the United Church of Canada in Creating a Culture of Social Well-Being in Canadian Society*. Toronto: United Church of Canada, 1999.

Reynolds, Arthur G. *The Means of Grace*. Toronto: United Church of Canada, 1952.

———. *What's the Difference? Protestant and Roman Catholic Beliefs Compared*. Toronto: Board of Evangelism and Social Service and the Board of Christian Education, United Church of Canada, 1962.

Richardson, David. *A Faith to Live By*. Toronto: United Church Publishing House, 1943.

Roberts, Richard. "The Oxford Group." *Christian Century*, February 1, 1933.

Robinson, John A.T. *Honest to God*. London: SCM Press, 1963.

Roman Catholic–United Church Dialogue Committtee. *In Whose Name? The Baptismal Formula in Contemporary Culture*. Toronto: United Church of Canada, 2001.

Ross, Sinclair. *As for Me and My House*. Toronto: McClelland & Stewart, 1989 [1941].

Rossing, Barbara. *The Rapture Exposed: The Message of Hope in the Book of Revelation*. Boulder, CO: Westview Press, 2004.

Ruether, Rosemary Radford. *Sexism and God-Talk: Toward a Feminist Theology*. Boston: Beacon Press, 1983.

Russell, Frank H. *New Days in Old India*. Toronto: Ryerson Press, 1926.

Russell, Letty M., and J. Shannon Clarkson, eds. *Dictionary of Feminist Theologies*. Louisville, KY: Westminster/John Knox Press, 1996.

Russell, Robert John. *Cosmology: From Alpha to Omega*. Minneapolis, MN: Fortress Press, 2008.

Sanguin, Bruce. *The Advance of Love: Reading the Bible with an Evolutionary Heart*. Vancouver: Evans and Sanguin, 2012.

———. *Darwin, Divinity and the Dance of the Cosmos*. Kelowna, BC: Woodlake/Copperhouse, 2007.

Saulteaux, Bernice. "Nakota Massacre." In *Story After Story: Canadians Bend Bound Theology*, edited by Loraine MacKenzie Shepherd, 82. Winnipeg: On Edge Publishing, 2003.

Schüssler Fiorenza, Francis. *Foundational Theology: Jesus and the Church*. New York: Crossroad, 1986.

Schweitzer, Don. "The Changing Social Imaginary of The United Church of Canada." In *The United Church of Canada: A History*, edited by Don Schweitzer, 279–98. Waterloo, ON: Wilfrid Laurier University Press, 2012.

———. "The Holy Spirit as Giver, Gift and Growing Edge of God." *Touchstone* 26, no. 2 (May 2008): 23–34.

———. *Jesus Christ for Contemporary Life: His Person, Work, and Relationships.* Eugene, OR: Cascade, 2012.

———. "Understanding Substitutionary Atonement in Spatial Terms." *Touchstone* 31, no. 2 (June 2013): 7–17.

———. "What Do Acts of Liberation Mean for God?" *Toronto Journal of Theology*, Supplement I (May 2008): 165–77.

Schweitzer, Don, and Derek Simon, eds. *Intersecting Voices: Critical Theologies in a Land of Diversity.* Ottawa: Novalis, 2004.

Scoates, D.J. "After Six Years with the Crees." *United Church Observer*, October 1, 1941, 6.

Scott, R.B.Y. and Gregory Vlastos, eds. *Towards the Christian Revolution.* Chicago: Willett Clark, 1936.

Scott, William. *Canadians in Korea: Brief Historical Sketch of Canadian Mission Work in Korea.* Toronto: Board of World Missions, United Church of Canada, 1975.

Shepherd, Loraine MacKenzie. "Church of the Margins: A Call to Solidarity." In *Intersecting Voices: Critical Theologies in a Land of Diversity*, edited by Don Schweitzer and Derek Simon, 135–53. Ottawa: Novalis, 2004.

———. *Feminist Theologies for a Postmodern Church.* New York: Peter Lang, 2002.

———. "From Colonization to Right Relations: The Evolution of United Church of Canada Missions within Aboriginal Communities." *International Review of Mission* 103, no. 1 (April 2014): 153–71.

———, ed. *Story after Story: Canadians Bend Bound Theology.* Winnipeg: On Edge Publishing, 2003.

Shinn, Roger. "Tillich as Interpreter and Disturber of Contemporary Culture." *Bulletin of the American Academy of Arts and Sciences* 39, no. 4 (January 1986): 23.

Silcox, Claris Edwin. *Church Union in Canada: Its Causes and Consequences.* New York: Institute of Social and Religious Research, 1933.

Sinclair, Donna. *Crossing Worlds: The Story of the Women's Missionary Society of the United Church of Canada.* Toronto: United Church of Canada, 1992.

Singh, Khushwant. *A History of the Sikhs*, vol. 2: *1839–1964.* Princeton: Princeton University Press, 1966.

Smillie, Ross L. *Practicing Reverence: An Ethic for Sustainable Earth Communities.* Kelowna, BC: Woodlake/Copperhouse, 2011.

Smith, Eveleigh. *Power to Become*. Toronto: United Church Publishing House, 1965.

Smith, W.C. *Patterns of Faith around the World*. Oxford: Oneworld, 1998.

Spong, John Shelby. *Jesus for the Non-Religious*. 2nd ed. New York: HarperCollins, 2008.

———. *A New Christianity for a New World*. San Francisco: HarperSanFrancisco, 2002.

Stebner, Eleanor. "The 1930s." In *The United Church of Canada: A History*, edited by Don Schweitzer, 39–56. Waterloo, ON: Wilfrid Laurier University Press, 2012.

Squire, Anne M. *Envisioning Ministry*. Toronto: Division of Ministry Personnel and Education, United Church of Canada, 1985.

Squires, Blanche Hales. "The War Has Made Me Over." *United Church Observer*, June 1, 1944, 22–23.

Stevenson, Winona. "Calling Badger and the Symbols of the Spirit Language: The Cree Origins of the Syllabic System." *Oral History Forum/Forum d'histoire orale* 19–20 (1999–2000): 19–24. www.oralhistoryforum.ca.

Stookey, Laurence Hull. *Baptism: Christ's Act in the Church*. Nashville, TN: Abingdon, 1982.

Swimme, Brian. *The Universe Story from the Primordial Flaring Forth to the Ecozoic Era*. San Francisco: HarperSanFrancisco, 1992.

"Take My Life and Let it Be; Consecrated, Lord, to Thee." *United Church Observer*, August 15, 1951, 1.

Taylor, Charles. *A Secular Age*. Cambridge, MA: Belknap Press of Harvard University Press, 2007.

Taylor, James A. "You Have Three Years to Change Your Mind about Mike Thompson." *United Church Observer*, June 15, 1969, 12–13.

Taylor, Jim, ed. *Fire and Grace: Stories of History and Vision*. Toronto: United Church Publishing House. 1999.

Taylor, Mark Lewis, ed. *Paul Tillich: Theologian of the Boundaries*. London: Collins, 1987.

Tertullian. *The Apology of Tertullian*. Translated by W.M. Reeve. London: Griffith Farran Okeden and Welsh, 1889.

Theology and Inter-Church Inter-Faith Committee. *Honouring the Divine in Each Other: United Church–Hindu Relations Today*. Toronto: United Church of Canada, 2014.

Thomas, Ernest. "Creating a National Conscience: Great Achievements Demanded of the United Church." *New Outlook*, September 9, 1925, 5.

Thomson, J.S. *God and His Purpose: The Meaning of Life*. Toronto: United Church Publishing House, 1964.

Tillich, Paul. *Systematic Theology*, vol. 2: *Existence and the Christ*. Chicago: University of Chicago Press, 1957.

Towards the Christian Revolution. Edited by R.B.Y. Scott and Gregory Vlastos. Kingston, ON: Ronald P. Frye, 1989.

Tracy, David. *On Naming the Present*. Maryknoll, NY: Orbis, 1994.

Trothen, Tracy J. *Linking Sexuality and Gender—Naming Violence against Women in The United Church of Canada*. Waterloo, ON: Wilfrid Laurier University Press, 2003.

———. "1980s: What Does It Mean to Be The United Church of Canada? Emergent Voices, Self-Critique, and Dissent." In *The United Church of Canada: A History*, edited by Don Schweitzer, 139–60. Waterloo, ON: Wilfrid Laurier University Press, 2012.

Truth and Reconciliation Commission of Canada. *Truth and Reconciliation Commission of Canada: Calls to Action*. Winnipeg: Truth and Reconciliation Commission of Canada, 2015. http://www.trc.ca/websites/trcinstitution/File/2015/Findings/Calls_to_Action_ English2.pdf/.

Tuchman, Barbara. *The Guns of August*. New York: Dell, 1962.

United Church of Canada. *Celebrate God's Presence: A Book of Services for The United Church of Canada*. Toronto: United Church Publishing House, 2000.

———. *The Manual of the United Church of Canada*. Toronto: United Church Publishing House, 1925–2016.

———. *Moving toward Full Inclusion: Sexual Orientation in The United Church of Canada*. Toronto: United Church of Canada, 2010.

———. *Our Words of Faith: Cherished, Honoured, and Living*. Toronto: United Church of Canada, 2010.

———. *Record of Proceedings of the General Councils of The United Church of Canada*. Toronto: United Church of Canada, 1925–2015.

———. "Reviewing Partnership in the Context of Empire." Toronto: United Church of Canada, 2009.

———. *Service Book for the Use of Ministers Conducting Public Worship*. Toronto: CANEC Publishing and Supply House, 1969.

———. "Statement on the United Nations Declaration on the Rights of Indigenous Peoples Rights as the Framework for Reconciliation," March 31, 2016. http://www.united-church.ca/sites/default/files/resources/undrip-united-church-statement.pdf.

———. "United Church of Canada." In *Churches Respond to BEM*, vol. 2, edited by Max Thurian, 276–86. Geneva: World Council of Churches, 1986.

———. *Voices United: The Hymn and Worship Book of The United Church of Canada*. Etobicoke: United Church Publishing House, 1996.

———. *Voices United: Services for Trial Use 1996–1997*. Etobicoke, ON: United Church Publishing House, 1996.

———. *Water: Life before Profit*. 2006. http://www.unitedchurch.ca/files/beliefs/policies/ 2006/pdf/w143.pdf.

———. *Year Book*. Toronto: United Church of Canada, 1926–2017.

Van Die, Marguerite. *An Evangelical Mind: Nathanael Burwash and the Methodist Tradition in Canada, 1839–1918*. Montreal and Kingston: McGill-Queen's University Press, 1989.

Veldman, Robin Globus. "Narrating the Environmental Apocalypse: How Imagining the End Facilitates Moral Reasoning among Environmental Activists." *Ethics and the Environment* 17, no. 1 (June 2012): 1–23.

Vipond, Dorothy. "Everything's Lily White in Dominion City." *United Church Observer*, November 15, 1966, 21, 40.

Walker-Jones, Arthur. *The Green Psalter: Resources for an Ecological Spirituality*. Minneapolis, MN: Fortress Press, 2009.

Watts, Mac. "A Suggestion for Trinity Sunday." *Touchstone* 25, no. 2. (May 2007): 5–6.

Weaver, Andrew. *Keeping our Cool: Canada in a Warming World*. Toronto: Penguin, 2010.

Weber, Robert. "Apology Sought over Nutritional Experiments." *Winnipeg Free Press,* July 19, 2013, A14.

Wells, Harold. *The Christic Center: Life-Giving and Liberating*. Maryknoll, NY: Orbis, 2004.

———. "Climate Holocaust, Mortal Planet and *Eschaton*." *Touchstone* 30, no. 3 (September 2012): 7–20.

———. "The Flesh of God: Christological Implications for an Ecological Vision of the World." *Toronto Journal of Theology* 15, no. 1 (Spring 1999): 51–68.

———. "The Making of the United Church Mind – No. II." *Touchstone* 8, no. 1 (January 1990): 26–27.

———. "The Resurrection of Jesus according to 'Progressive Christianity.'" *Touchstone* 30, no. 1 (January 2012): 35–43.

Wells, Harold, and Roger Hutchinson, eds. *A Long and Faithful March: 'Towards the Christian Revolution' 1930s/1980s*. Toronto: United Church Publishing House, 1989.

Wells, Harold, and Patricia Wells. *Jesus Means Life*. Toronto: Division of Communication, United Church of Canada, 1982.

Wells, Patricia. *Welcome to the United Church of Canada: A Newcomer's Introduction to A New Creed*. Toronto: United Church of Canada, 1986.

Wesley, John. *The Appeals to Men of Reason and Religion and Certain Related Open Letters.* In *The Works of John Wesley,* vol. 11. Edited by Gerald R. Cragg. Oxford: Clarendon Press, 1975.

———. "The Means of Grace." *The Wesley Centre Online.* http://wesley.nnu.edu/ john-wesley/the-sermons-of-john-wesley-1872-edition/sermon-16-the -means-of-grace/.

White, Christopher. "Question Box: The 'Splash and Split.'" *United Church Observer,* June 2016, 44.

White, James F. *Protestant Worship: Traditions in Transition.* Louisville, KY: Westminster/ John Knox Press, 1989.

———. *The Sacraments in Protestant Practice and Faith.* Nashville, TN: Abingdon, 1999.

White, Peter Gordon. "Introduction." *God and His Purpose: The Meaning of Life.* Toronto: United Church Publishing House, 1964.

———. "Introduction." *Voices and Visions: 65 Years of the United Church of Canada.* Toronto: United Church Publishing House, 1990.

Whitehead, A.N. *Process and Reality.* Edited by David Ray Griffin and Donald Shelburne. New York: Free Press, 1978.

Whitehead, Rhea M. "Gift and Challenge." Unpublished document, 1995.

Who Is Jesus for You Today? Toronto: Berkeley Studios, United Church of Canada.

Woman's Missionary Society. *Manual for Missionaries.* Toronto: United Church of Canada, 1950.

Woodsworth, J.S. *Strangers within Our Gates.* Toronto: Missionary Society of the Methodist Church, 1909.

Working Group on Worship and Liturgy, Division of Mission in Canada. *The Celebration of Marriage for Optional Use in The United Church of Canada.* Toronto: United Church of Canada, 1985.

———. *Pastoral Liturgies and Prayers for Special Occasions for Optional Use in The United Church of Canada.* Toronto: United Church of Canada, 1990.

———. *A Sunday Liturgy for Optional Use in The United Church of Canada.* Toronto: United Church of Canada, 1984.

———. *The Words We Sing: An Inclusive Language Guide to The Hymn Book.* Toronto: United Church of Canada, 1984.

"World Mission Begins at Home." *United Church Observer,* February 1971, 24.

Wright, Robert. *A World Mission: Canadian Protestantism and the Quest for a New International Order, 1918–1938.* Montreal and Kingston: McGill-Queen's University Press, 1991.

Young, John H. "A Golden Age: The United Church of Canada, 1946–1960." In

The United Church of Canada: A History, edited by Don Schweitzer, 77–96. Waterloo, ON: Wilfrid Laurier University Press, 2012.

———. "Sacred Cow or White Elephant? The Doctrine Section of the Basis of Union." *Touchstone* 16, no. 2 (May 1998): 29–46.

Young, Pamela Dickey. "Beyond Moral Influence to an Atoning Life." *Theology Today* 52, no. 3 (October 1, 1995): 344–55.

———. *Christ in a Post-Christian World*. Minneapolis, MN: Fortress Press, 1995.

———. *Re-Creating the Church: Communities of Eros*. Harrisburg, PA: Trinity Press International, 2000.

CONTRIBUTORS

GAIL ALLAN is Coordinator, Ecumenical, Interchurch and Interfaith Relations, at the General Council Office of The United Church of Canada. She holds a ThD in ethics from Emmanuel College, Toronto School of Theology, University of Toronto.

SANDRA BEARDSALL is an ordained United Church minister and Professor of Church History and Ecumenics at St. Andrew's College, Saskatoon, SK.

MICHAEL BOURGEOIS is Associate Professor of Theology at Emmanuel College, Toronto School of Theology, University of Toronto, and a lay member of The United Church of Canada. He served as Chair of the church's Committee on Theology and Faith 2000–2006, during which time it developed *A Song of Faith*.

HYUK CHO is an ordained United Church minister working with West Point Grey United Church in Vancouver, BC. He holds a ThD in systematic theology from Emmanuel College, Toronto School of Theology, University of Toronto.

ROBERT C. FENNELL is an ordained United Church minister and Associate Professor of Historical and Systematic Theology and Academic Dean at Atlantic School of Theology in Halifax, NS. He is author of *The Rule of Faith and Biblical Interpretation: Reform, Resistance, and Renewal* (Cascade, 2018).

ADRIAN JACOBS is Keeper of the Circle at Sandy-Saulteaux Spiritual Centre (SSSC), in Beausejour, MB, the national Indigenous ministry training school of the United Church of Canada. He is Ganosono of the Turtle Clan, Cayuga Nation of the Six Nations Haudenosaunee Community, Grand River Country in Southern Ontario. A lifelong carrier of Indigenous knowledge, he keeps the Red Buffalo Pipe for SSSC.

WILLIAM S. KERVIN is an ordained United Church minister and Associate Professor of Public Worship at Emmanuel College of Victoria University and the Toronto School of Theology in the University of Toronto.

HYERAN KIM-CRAGG is Lydia Gruchy Professor of Pastoral Studies at St. Andrew's College, Saskatoon. She is the author of many books, the most recent being *Interdependence: A Postcolonial Feminist Practical Theology* (2018).

MARILYN J. LEGGE taught at St. Andrew's College, Saskatoon, from 1988 to 1998 then at Emmanuel College of Victoria University as Associate Professor of Christian Ethics and member of the Toronto School of Theology Graduate Faculty.

LORAINE MACKENZIE SHEPHERD is an ordained United Church minister serving Westworth United Church in Winnipeg, MB. She has served on the Faith and Order Plenary Commission of the World Council Churches and teaches at various United Church theological schools, including Sandy Saulteaux Spiritual Centre in Manitoba and United Theological College in Montreal.

CATHERINE FAITH MACLEAN is Senior Minister at St. Paul's United Church in Edmonton, AB, and holds a DMin in preaching. With John H. Young, she is co-author of *Preaching the Big Questions: Doctrine Isn't Dusty*. She wishes to acknowledge grant support from the Louisville Institute.

DON SCHWEITZER is McDougald Professor of Theology at St. Andrew's College, Saskatoon, SK.

HAROLD WELLS is an ordained United Church minister. He served in three pastoral charges in Ontario, taught theology in Lesotho (southern Africa), and is professor emeritus of systematic theology, Emmanuel College, Toronto.

JOHN H. YOUNG is an ordained United Church minister who currently serves as the Executive Minister, Theological Leadership, in the General Council Office of The United Church of Canada. He holds a PhD in the History of Christianity, and he is the co-author, with Catherine F. MacLean, of *Preaching the Big Questions: Doctrine Isn't Dusty*.

INDEX

Aboriginal Ministries Circle, 192

Aboriginal Ministries Council, 192

Aboriginal spirituality. *See* Indigenous spirituality

abortion, 115

activism, 174

adult baptism, 27, 226, 227

adult study materials, 56–57, 65–66, 88, 110, 132–33

Advent, 118

advocacy, 174; as Christian responsibility, 176–78; and social justice, 190, 191, 280, 298

affirmations: of Jesus, 128–29, 130; Trinitarian affirmation of God, 144

Airhart, Phyllis, 175, 180–81, 272n22; fellowship, 218n12; on *The New Curriculum*, 33; on *A Statement of Faith*, 109

Alexandrian tradition, 128, 146–47n6

Allan, Gail, 173–202

All Native Circle Conference, 155, 184, 301

All Peoples' Missions, 279–80

alternative theologies, and Neo-Orthodoxy, 7–9

amillennialism, 317–21, 326

Anglican Church: *Articles of Religion*, 224; *Book of Common Prayer*, 106; union negotiations, 187, 188

Anglo-Saxon culture: assumed superiority of, 193, 286, 292; preferred immigrants, 283

Anselm of Canterbury, 8, 132

anti-apartheid movement, 321

Antiochean tradition, 128, 146–47n6

anti-Semitism, 141, 283, 284, 306n22

apocalypse, and apocalyptic imagery, 314–15

Apology to Native Congregations, 116, 155, 171n10, 184, 215

Apostles' Creed, 14, 22, 28, 34, 82, 90, 114, 127; objections to, 135–36

Aquinas, Thomas, 83–84, 88

Arianism, 32

Arnup, Jesse H., 273n32

Asian theologies, 7

Association of Local Union Churches, 175

Athanasian Creed, 22

atheism, as threat to Christian universalism, 255

atonement: substitutionary atonement, 104, 108, 129–30, 131, 146

Augustine, 37, 69, 146–47n6; *City of God*, 316; God, and love, 30, 32;